Achieving global sustainability: Policy recommendations

Edited by Takamitsu Sawa, Susumu Iai and Seiji Ikkatai

United Nations University Press
TOKYO · NEW YORK · PARIS

SYNERGY

Indian Edition, 2012

ISBN: 978-93-82059-03-5

First published in 2011 by the United Nations University Press,
The United Nations University, 53-70 Jingumae 5-chome,
Shibuya-ku, Tokyo 150-8925
For copyright reasons, this edition is for sale in South Asia only.

Indian Edition Published by:
Synergy Books India
(A Unit of M/s Bookwell Publications)
24/4800 Ansari Road, Darya Ganj,
New Delhi-110002
Phone: 011-23268786, 23257264
Fax: 011-23281315
Website: www.synergybooksindia.com
E-Mail: synergybooksindia@gmail.com
bookwell@vsnl.net

Printed at : DK FINE ART PRESS (P). LTD. Delhi-52

Contents

Figures

Tables

Plates

Equations

Contributors

Jiro Akahori is a professor of mathematics at the Department of Mathematical Sciences and a director of the Research Center for Finance at Ritsumeikan University. He is the editor-in-chief of *Asia-Pacific Financial Markets*, an associate editor of *JSIAM Letters* and has organized many international conferences on mathematical finance and stochastic calculus. He is a member of the Ritsumeikan Research Center for Sustainable Science.

Hans-Martin Füssel is project manager for climate change vulnerability and adaptation at the European Environment Agency and a guest scientist with the Potsdam Institute for Climate Impact Research (Germany). From 2007 to 2009 Dr Füssel was a professor by special invitation at the Ritsumeikan Research Center for Sustainability Science in Kyoto (Japan). He has advised the UNDP, UNFCCC, WHO, IPCC, the World Bank and the European Commission on climate change.

Haris Gunawan is director of the Center for Tropical Peat Swamp Restoration and Conservation, Riau University, Indonesia. He is currently a PhD candidate at the Graduate School of Asia and African Area Studies, Kyoto University.

Seiichiro Hasui is associate professor of international political science and peace studies, College of Humanities, Ibaraki University, Japan. His research focuses on climate security, environmental security, human security, and security and development studies.

Susumu Iai is professor in the Geo-hazard Division, Disaster Prevention Research Institute, Kyoto University, Japan. He also serves as director-general of the Kyoto Sustainability Initiative, Kyoto University, and promotes interdisciplinary research for global sustainability.

Seiji Ikkatai is a professor at the Institute of Economic Research, Kyoto University. After graduating from Tokyo University he joined the Environment Agency (Ministry of the Environment since 2001). He was appointed a professor at Kyoto University in 2005 and awarded a PhD in economics in 2008 for a study of climate change policies.

Satoshi Konishi is a professor at the Institute of Advanced Energy and the director-general of the Institute of Sustainable Science, Kyoto University. He is studying fusion technology and the socio-economics of energy systems from sustainability science aspects.

Kazuo Matsushita is professor of global environmental policy in the Graduate School of Global Environmental Studies, Kyoto University, Japan.

Kosuke Mizuno is a professor at the Center for Southeast Asian Studies, Kyoto University. He studies people's organizations and governance in democratizing Indonesia. His publications include *Populism in Asia* (NUS Press, 2009) and *Rural Industrialization in Indonesia: A Study on Community-based Weaving Industry in West Java* (IDE, 1996).

Akihisa Mori is an associate professor at the Graduate School of Global Environmental Studies, Kyoto University. In his research on development and environmental policies in East Asia, he has written and edited several books, including *Environmental Aid* (Yuhikaku, 2009) and *Environmental Policy in China* (Kyoto University Press, 2008).

Takashi Ohshima is a professor in the Department of Social Psychology, Toyo University, Japan. He is the head of the Social Research Group, Transdisciplinary Initiative for Eco-Philosophy, Toyo University.

Shiro Saka, a professor in the Graduate School of Energy Science, Kyoto University, has been a country representative of Japan for the International Energy Agency Task 39 (liquid biofuels), and was elected in 2008 as fellow of the International Academy of Wood Science. He has written 89 books in the field of biomass science.

Masayuki Sato is a project-specific associate professor at the Field Science Education and Research Center, Kyoto University. After receiving a PhD in economics from Kyoto University in 2006, he joined the Graduate School of Global Environmental Studies, Kyoto University, as an assistant professor in the Kyoto Sustainability Initiative Project.

Takamitsu Sawa is president of Shiga University, chairman of the Council of Transportation and member of the Central Environmental Council of the Japanese government. He was president of the Society of Environmental and Policy Studies in Japan from 1995 to 2006, and was awarded a Purple Ribbon Medal in 2007.

Yukari Takamura is professor in international law at Nagoya University. She has published extensively on international environmental law, recently focusing on issues related to the post-2012 climate regime. She is the co-author of *Will Global Warming Negotiations Lead? The Prospect of International Climate Change Regime Beyond 2012* (Daigaku tosho, 2005, in Japanese).

Kazuhiro Ueta is professor of environmental economics and public finance at the Graduate School of Economics and the Graduate School of Global Environmental Studies, Kyoto University.

Michinori Uwasu is an assistant professor at the Sustainability Design Center, Osaka University, Japan.

Abbreviations

ACES	American Clean Energy and Security Act
AOSIS	Alliance of Small Island States
APEC	Asia-Pacific Economic Cooperation
AR4	IPCC Fourth Assessment Report
ASEAN	Association of Southeast Asian Nations
AWG-KP	*ad hoc* working group on the Kyoto Protocol
AWG-LCA	*ad hoc* working group on long-term cooperative actions
CAP	Center for American Progress (USA)
CBI	Confederation of British Industry
CCAP	Center for Clean Air Policy (USA)
CCS	carbon capture and storage
CDM	clean development mechanism
CER	certified emission reduction
CIRF	climate impact response function
CNAS	Center for a New American Security
CO_2	carbon dioxide
COP	Conference of Parties
CVM	contingent valuation method
DSGE	dynamic stochastic general equilibrium
ECOSOC	UN Economic and Social Council
EF	ecological footprint
EPI	environmental policy integration
ETBE	ethyl tertiary butyl ether
ETS	EU Emissions Trading Scheme
EU	European Union
EV	electric vehicle

FAME	fatty acid methyl ester
FiT	feed-in tariff
GDP	gross domestic product
GEF	Global Environment Facility
GHG	greenhouse gas
GMT	global mean temperature
Gt	gigatonnes
HDI	Human Development Index
HPI	Happy Planet Index
IAM	integrated assessment model
IPCC	Intergovernmental Panel on Climate Change
IR3S	Integrated Research System for Sustainability Science
ISSP	International Social Survey Programme
kW	kilowatt
kWh	kilowatt-hour
N_2O	nitrous oxide
NAMA	nationally appropriate mitigation actions
NEDO	New Energy and Industrial Technology Development Organization (Japan)
NGO	non-governmental organization
NIE	newly industrializing economy
NOAA	National Oceanic and Atmospheric Administration (USA)
PHV	plug-in hybrid vehicle
ppm	parts per million
PV	photovoltaic
QOL	quality of life
THC	thermohaline ocean circulation
UN	United Nations
UNDP	UN Development Programme
UNEP	UN Environment Programme
UNFCCC	UN Framework Convention on Climate Change
WCED	World Commission on Environment and Development

Preface

This book forms part of a series on sustainability science. Sustainability science is a newly emerging academic field that seeks to understand the dynamic linkages between global, social and human systems, and to provide a holistic perspective on the concerns and issues between and within these systems. It is a problem-oriented discipline encompassing visions and methods for examining and repairing these systems and linkages.

The Integrated Research System for Sustainability Science (IR3S) was launched in 2005 at the University of Tokyo with the aim of serving as a global research and educational platform for sustainability scientists. In 2006 IR3S expanded, becoming a university network including Kyoto, Osaka, Hokkaido and Ibaraki Universities. In addition, the National Institute for Environmental Studies, Tohoku, Toyo, Chiba, Waseda and Ritsumeikan Universities and the United Nations University joined as associate members. Since the establishment of the IR3S network, member universities have launched sustainability science programmes at their institutions and collaborated on related research projects. The results of these projects have been published in prestigious research journals and presented at various academic, governmental and social meetings.

The sustainability science book series is based on the results of IR3S members' joint research activities over the past five years. The series provides directions on sustainability for society. These books are expected to be of interest to graduate students, educators teaching sustainability-related courses and those keen to start up similar programmes, active members of non-governmental organizations, government officials and people working in industry. We hope this series of books will provide readers with useful information on sustainability issues and present them with novel ways of thinking and solutions to the complex problems faced by people throughout the world.

Integrated Research System for Sustainability Science

1 Introduction

Takamitsu Sawa

1-1 The end of the era of CO_2 emissions

The twentieth century was an era in which economic development and growth were achieved by burning fossil fuels, or in other words by continually increasing carbon dioxide (CO_2) emissions. When delegations from 161 countries gathered in 1997 at the Kyoto International Conference Center and agreed to oblige industrialized nations to cut emissions of greenhouse gases (GHGs) – such as the CO_2 that was emblematic of the twentieth century – it was an epoch-making event that marked a historic turning point. At the same time, it signified a farewell to a twentieth-century model of industrial civilization that had been characterized by oil and automobiles. The Kyoto Protocol was viewed as standing in opposition to the morals and principles of market fundamentalism: its contents imposed "regulations" on industrialized nations in the sense that it set obligatory reduction amounts, and thus went against the basic principle of market fundamentalism, which believes that a free, competitive market economy is the optimal system.

At the same time, I do not think anybody believes that CO_2 emissions will be reduced through "market forces". If global warming and the accompanying climate changes are not alleviated, an unimaginable global tragedy awaits us in the second half of the twenty-first century. By creating the necessary economic measures (an environmental tax, emissions quota trading, an automobile tax that is proportional to fuel efficiency, etc.), governments can encourage energy conservation on the part of individuals and corporations and provide incentives for technological development that will contribute to a shift to low carbon usage. Supplementing these with regulatory measures to make up for the shortcomings is an appropriate strategy for mitigating global warming and climate change in a free market economy.

1-2 Green New Deal

As an economist who has worked on global environmental issues since 1990, I have continuously and vigorously disputed the view that "economic growth and environmental protection are incompatible". Both then and now I take the position that they are compatible. It is said that the twenty-first century is the "century of the environment", and I would summarize what is meant by this in two points. First, global environmental issues, and above all climate change, are becoming increasingly grave, and people are now showing an unprecedentedly high level of interest in them. Second, the objective of technological innovation will be to break through the limitations of the environment, and that kind of innovation will spur economic growth.

I have been espousing these points for a long time, and the fact that my explanation was not necessarily off the mark is demonstrated by President Obama's Green New Deal policy. This groundbreaking policy, started in the United States, tries to tailor the promotion of policies to mitigate climate change into a driving force for economic growth. Let us look at a few examples. Taking a cue from the Germans, it will produce employment through the promotion of renewable energy (green-collar workers), and provide large-scale government investment for an IT-based "smart grid" to stabilize the power distribution network system in preparation for an increase in renewable energy, which lacks stability in terms of the amount of power generated, voltage and frequency. In addition, through the development and distribution of eco-friendly goods, it will boost personal consumption expenditures. By adopting an emissions quota trading system, it will encourage companies to make their production and business processes green. Companies will also endeavour to develop eco-friendly goods and lower the prices of those goods in response to the demands of consumers.

1-3 The end of the era of automobiles and oil

The twentieth century was an "era of automobiles and oil". It was an era in which the diffusion of the automobile had an enormous inter-industry ripple effect, and that in turn provided traction for economic growth. Petrochemical products derived from ethylene became substitutes for natural rubber, leather, textiles, lumber and so on, while gasoline, diesel oil and jet fuel were used to fuel the engines for transportation vehicles. Until the sudden advent of the oil shock of 1973, oil-fired thermal power was inexpensive and it was easy to adjust the load, and thus it became the mainstream of electricity supply.

However, by the end of the twentieth century passenger vehicles had reached saturation point in all industrialized nations, closing the book on the era when the diffusion of automobiles propelled economic growth. Only if some kinds of durable goods become available and widely used does personal consumption, which represents 60 per cent of GDP, increase. In Japan's "take-off" period of rapid growth from July 1958 to October 1973, household electrical appliances such as black-and-white televisions and electric washing machines, refrigerators and vacuum cleaners flew off the shelves, allowing the Japanese economy to sustain a high real growth rate of nearly 10 per cent. Leaving aside the vacuum cleaner, the other three items just noted were referred to as the "three sacred treasures", and in 1970 their diffusion rate was more than 90 per cent. Next it was the 3Cs that drove economic growth, namely colour TVs, cars and coolers (i.e. air conditioners).

Taking Japan's household diffusion rate for automobiles as an example, in 1965 it was 10 per cent, in 1970 it was 22 per cent, in 1975 it was 40 per cent, in 1980 it was 57 per cent, in 1985 it was 67 per cent and in 1991 it was 80 per cent – nearly a straight-line ascent. In Japan, where the cost of car ownership is high, it appears unlikely that the household diffusion rate will exceed 90 per cent in the future. The average annual real economic growth rate from 1956 to 1973 was 9.1 per cent, and from 1974 to 1990 it averaged 3.8 per cent. The fact that Japan was able to maintain these high growth rates almost continuously, greatly exceeding those of the Western industrialized nations, was in large part due to the diffusion of passenger vehicles.

1-4 Automobiles and digital cameras

The electrical appliances that have become popular since the start of the Heisei recession in March 1991 are limited to digital products such as cell phones, personal computers, DVD recorders/players, digital cameras and so on. But no matter how widely diffused digital cameras, for instance, may become, they will produce no more than a tiny inter-industry ripple effect. Moreover, digital cameras took the place of film cameras, so for the camera industry there was a sense that it ended up as no difference.

Although it is plausible that the real economic growth rate remained at a low annual average of 1.1 per cent from 1991 to 2008 because of the lingering effects of the post-bubble recession, another cause was the low inter-industry ripple effect of digital products as compared to automobiles.

The cellular telephone offers an example that is easier to understand. A single cell phone that has multiple functions is similar to the digital camera in that it has a weak inter-industry ripple effect. The cell phone possesses functions that more or less "substitute" for books, cartoons, dictionaries, newspapers, TVs, train schedules, personal computers, clocks, cameras, GPS, personal organizers and so on. It makes one suspect that the long-term recession that has been going on since 1991 is perhaps the result of the diffusion of these little 100 g or so devices. In any case, if asked what the three major discoveries of the twentieth century are as measured by their impact on changing lifestyles, without hesitation I would say the automobile, TV and cell phone.

1-5 Measures to combat climate change will spur global economic growth

What will move the global economy forward is the resolute implementation of both global Keynesian measures to encourage the steady diffusion of durable goods in emerging and developing nations and the Green New Deal measures in industrialized nations. The clean development mechanism (CDM) set out in the Kyoto Protocol works as an incentive for global Keynesian measures. To that end, it is necessary to impose strict GHG emissions reduction obligations on industrialized nations. Reduction targets that are so high they are impossible to meet through domestic policies alone are required. Industrialized nations would then have to invest in emerging and developing nations (i.e. the CDM; however, if the emerging nation bears some obligation to cut or restrain emissions, it becomes a joint implementation project), and through such efforts the potential demand that exists in those countries can be developed. Through investment, industrialized nations can receive certified emission reductions (CERs), or in other words a carbon credit, and can thereby reduce the costs of achieving their emissions targets. Not only that, but they can expect a boomerang effect in the positive sense (i.e. increased exports from the industrialized nations).

In short, in the post-Kyoto era, imposing strict GHG emission reduction requirements on industrialized nations to alleviate climate change provides an incentive for global Keynesianism and the Green New Deal measures, and by extension brings about sustainable development in the global economy.

I have tried in the past to correct the fallacy that "climate change measures will slow economic growth", but that fallacy has remained resolutely intact. Recently, however, the world economic situation has completely changed. As a result of the global recession that struck the world in 2008, the curtains were drawn on the twentieth-century model of industrial civilization that took automobiles and oil as the driving forces of economic growth, and a new era of green capitalism has arrived. In order to prevent a recurrence of the global recession, and to spur domestic demand in industrialized nations, the greening of the capitalist economy is essential. Be that as it may, there are still university professors who deny the causal relationship between the increasing density of GHGs in the atmosphere and global warming/climate change, just as there are also university professors who refer to Prime Minister Yukio Hatoyama's call for 25 per cent emission cuts as utter nonsense. In mainstream economics, the claim that "GHG emission reductions will impede economic growth" is unyielding. The objective of this book is to correct the mistakes of those who profess that view, and to offer proactive proposals for restructuring the socio-economic system and implementing technological strategies to move us towards green capitalism.

2

Global sustainability

2-1

Global sustainability: Current issues and challenges

Michinori Uwasu

2-1-1 Sustainability issues in the twenty-first century

The twentieth century brought about enormous economic expansion and social changes in many nations: it was a century of growth and innovation. Technological and institutional innovation in one sector spurred innovation in other sectors, and also led to creation of new sectors. Moreover, expansion of trade across nations raised the productivity and competitiveness of many of the world's economies. Particularly in Asia, which experienced widespread economic stagnation during the 1950s, rapid economic growth occurred in the latter part of the twentieth century as trade systems spread across countries such as Japan, South Korea and China, and throughout Southeast Asia. The so-called "flying geese" pattern of development was instrumental in creating what we think of as the Asian economic miracle. Presently, this region comprises one of the largest economies in the world.

However, these incredible economic developments placed a substantial burden on the environment. Most developed countries experienced excessive pollution during rapid economic growth. For example, during the 1960s serious effects of pollution, such as illness and chronic disease, were observed in Japan. Many of these effects were combated using "end-of-pipe" technologies along with the introduction of environmental legislation and economic instruments for environmental management. Thus in developed countries pollution itself is not presently a serious environmental challenge, although patients and their families who continue to suffer from the effects of once-polluted areas still exist. In the twenty-first century, however, a number of pollution issues similar to those observed in Japan are now emerging in developing countries. Many of these issues are much more severe, with a larger scale of distribution compared to those previously observed in developed countries, and the complete picture is yet unclear.

Concerns about the global sustainability of economic growth and its consequent effects on the environment emerged in the late 1960s with Malthusian debates. Paul Ehrlich ([1968] 1995) argued in *The Population Bomb* that the current global consumption patterns and population levels were beyond the Earth's carrying capacity. Similarly, in *The Limits to Growth* the Club of Rome claimed that resource depletion, along with population growth, would limit our ability to grow (Meadows et al., 1972).

In the 1970s international environmental movements began to emerge. In 1972 the United Nations held the Human Environment Conference in Stockholm, the first international conference on environmental issues. This was followed by a series of international events and initiatives. The third UN Human Environment Conference – the Earth Summit, held in Rio de Janeiro in 1992 – spawned many international initiatives. The conference declared Agenda 21, which is still influential in the sustainability field as a touchstone for achieving balance between environmental conservation and socio-economic development. Participating countries also reached an agreement on adopting two important environmental treaties, the Convention on Biological Diversity and the UN Framework Convention on Climate Change (UNFCCC). In 1997 the third UNFCCC meeting in Kyoto produced the Kyoto Protocol, which was the first international treaty to create legally binding commitments for greenhouse gas (GHG) reductions.

International initiatives taken at the policy level for achieving global sustainability advanced in the late twentieth century, and research into and a greater understanding of sustainability conditions, including climate change and poverty, played an important role in the advancement of these initiatives. The Intergovernmental Panel on Climate Change (IPCC) was one of the most important agencies created as a result of that research. As for socio-economic development, international bodies such as the World Bank and the Consultative Group on International Agricultural Research accumulated scientific findings and produced the theoretical foundations for the direction and practice for challenging socio-economic development issues.

The global environmental issues in the twenty-first century are fundamentally different from the pollution issues the world faced in the twentieth century. At that time, local pollution issues were technically solvable by local initiatives, such as introduction of technologies and direct regulation. However, the current environmental issues – global warming, loss of biodiversity, resource depletion, water and food shortages, etc. – are rooted in socio-economic systems founded on mass production, consumption and disposal as their bases, all of which involve consumption of vast amounts of fossil fuels. Solving these issues thus requires a fundamental economic shift from reliance on manufacturing to service-sector-based economies that enhance people's quality of life (QOL) and are probably the main drivers for socio-economic development.

The renewal of urban infrastructure and transportation systems is critical in reducing the level of energy consumption. Moreover, the current agricultural practices, which use vast amounts of water, energy and fertilizer, are clearly unsustainable and result in environmental degradation in the form of soil erosion, increased salinity and deforestation. Our food supply is now struggling to meet the increasing demand created by population growth and economic development. Thus development of more sustainable agricultural systems is of particular importance.

Global environmental issues have thus been forged under the current socio-economic systems and are becoming global threats for sustainability. What exactly is the relationship between environmental issues and global sustainability? It is probably true that solving global environmental issues is necessary to achieve global sustainability. Having said this, however, it is essential to establish new socio-economic systems in the form of resource/energy-circulating societies in which services sectors enable achievement of global sustainability and enhance people's QOL through technological and institutional innovations. In this view, the role of policymakers and academics is to create long-term strategies that forge a path to sustainability through new types of development and environmental conservation.

The next section briefly reviews the current state of global sustainability for both environmental and socio-economic systems. It reveals an approach to achieve global sustainability with a framework in which challenges to this aim addressing the role of technologies and institutions are discussed.

2-1-2 The current state of global sustainability

Environmental sustainability

To what extent do human activities create an environmental burden on the planet? Many indicators and assessment systems, such as gross domestic product (GDP), energy and resource consumption, pollution emissions and deforestation levels, allow measurement of the environmental burden created by human activities and help understand their effects on ecosystems and society. Yet simply listing these indicators does not help us understand the current state of global sustainability. We focus instead on two key measures: the ecological footprint (EF), which is a measure of human consumption and activity; and climate change, because this is one of the largest threats to global sustainability.

The EF is an integrated indicator of the effect of human activity on Earth. It assesses the amount of consumption within a certain area in terms of the Earth's carrying capacity by calculating the land area necessary to produce needed goods and services and to absorb the pollutants emitted through that production by ecosystems (Wackernagel and Rees, 1996). According to the Global Footprint Network (2010), the land area necessary to supply the entire world's consumption needs has exceeded the global arable land since the 1980s. In other words, the world's consumption levels have been beyond the level of the Earth's carrying capacity for more than 20 years. Although it is not yet clear for how long this situation can last, it is clear that we are heading towards a crisis of sustainability.

For most countries, EFs are simply estimated, and there are large variations between countries. For example, the EF of a particular country can provide an estimate of arable land available on the Earth, provided the entire world's population follows a lifestyle similar to that of the particular country. In fact, all the developed countries need more than one Earth to sustain their current consumption levels (as of 2008, US consumption levels required seven Earths!), while many of the developing countries need less than one Earth. Clearly, lifestyles in developed countries are unsustainable in terms of the Earth's carrying capacity; although, using this measure, developing countries are clearly more environmentally sustainable, the results highlight the vast socio-economic gap between developed and developing countries.

Thus the EF is an intuitive and useful measure of environmental sustainability, but it does not measure the specific impacts of unsustainable lifestyles on the global environment and society. For that, we need to look at the IPCC reports. Although global warming arose as a threat in the 1980s when its effects were being widely recognized as substantial and irreversible, scant scientific evidence of these effects was available. In 1988 the IPCC was established within the UN bodies to provide scientific evidence about climate change. Specifically, the role of the IPCC, with the cooperation of thousands of researchers from various fields, is to summarize the current results of scientific research on global warming in order to deepen our understanding of the mechanisms of climate change, assess the impacts of global warming on ecosystems and human society, and propose countermeasures. Since 1989, the IPCC has published four synthesis reports.

Its Fourth Assessment Report (IPCC, 2007) was a cornerstone of international challenges to global warming. In the report, the IPCC concluded that rising temperatures throughout the twentieth century are very likely (more than 90 per cent probability) caused by GHGs emitted by human activities. This important conclusion became the rationale for taking more purposeful actions to combat climate change at both domestic and international levels. The report also gave recommendations for creation and implementation of countermeasures. For example, it noted that the Earth's average temperature increased by 0.74° Celsius between 1906 and 2005, and that this trend will continue if unaddressed, but that the temperature can be stabilized if GHG emissions are reduced.

In addition, the report examined various scenarios involving human activity and temperature increases, and concluded that temperatures will continue to increase by 2–4°C depending on the patterns of human activity. Although a temperature increase of 2–4°C seems inconsequential, it will have substantial impact on ecosystems, including the Earth's biodiversity, water, agriculture and human health. Furthermore, the degree of impact of climate change varies across regions and countries, and some areas are particularly vulnerable. For example, polar areas will face greater temperature fluctuations, leading to melting ice-caps and loss of animal species, and some African regions will experience severe stress on water supplies and a decrease in food production. The data and information summarized by this report have become fundamental in attaining a global consensus to limit global temperature increases to 2°C in the long term.

These observations imply that countermeasures to global warming must include both reduction of GHGs and adaptation of vulnerable regions against climate change. Technological innovation and diffusion of new technologies, as well as institutional arrangements such as carbon emission trading and changes in industrial infrastructure, are essential to achieve reduction of GHGs. As for adaptation of vulnerable regions, developing sustainable agricultural practices and the ability to deal with the effects of natural disasters, particularly in developing countries, is crucial. IPCC reports provide the scientific basis of climate change as well as its countermeasures. Through the work done by the IPCC, we now understand that not only is global sustainability facing crucial challenges, but also that implementation of devices to attain sustainability is becoming more technically and politically feasible.

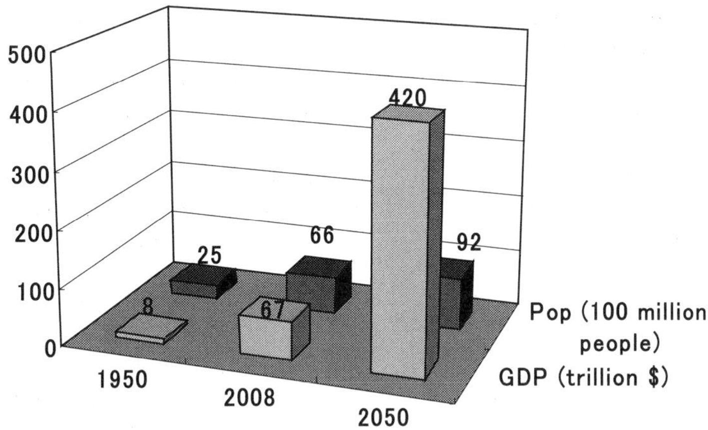

Figure 2.1.1 World population and gross domestic product, 1950, 2008 and 2050
Source: Constructed based on Sachs (2008) and UN World Population Prospects: The 2008 Revision database, http://esa.un.org/unpp/index.asp.

Global socio-economic realities

As discussed, rapid population growth and economic expansion occurred during the twentieth century. This trend will continue in this century, a crucial fact when thinking about environmental sustainability. Figure 2.1.1 summarizes this growth. The world's population was 2.5 billion in 1950 and 6.6 billion in 2008, and is projected to reach 9 billion by 2050 (UN Secretariat, 2006). Similarly, GDP also increased, from US$8 trillion to US$67 trillion in the same period, and is projected to reach US$420 trillion in 2050. This increase is particularly marked in Asia, which will account for 54 per cent of the world's GDP by 2050. On the other hand, developing countries have been and will stay behind the developed regions economically, but their negative impact on the environment through population explosion will rapidly increase. Many African countries, for example, will experience large population increases in the coming decades, but their economic stagnation will continue (Sachs, 2008).

The World Bank defines extreme poverty as a condition under which people cannot meet their basic needs such as shelter, water and education. Although robust economic growth has reduced the proportion of population in extreme poverty, 1.4 billion people are still living on less than $1.25 per day (United Nations, 2010). Importantly, although globalization led to expansion of economic systems worldwide, particularly in most developed countries and Asian countries in the late twentieth century,[1] income inequality has been increasing between and within countries. In developed countries, unemployment and low wages due to changes in the labour market structure and economic stagnation are critical issues, while in developing countries, in which millions of people have no access to safe water, sanitation and other social services, poverty and social discrimination are the enduring concerns.

The question thus becomes: "Is inequality bad for global sustainability?" The answer is yes, although various views on inequality exist, depending on the timeframe of our examination and our objectives. Severe inequality is also a by-product of discrimination between the sexes, ethnic groups and social classes, and such discrimination is present in many countries. As for income inequality, most people would agree that society is better off if income is more equally distributed for a given level of income. Studies have shown that vast inequalities in income negatively affect future development because they reduce motivation, thus stifling socio-economic development (Clarke, 1992).

It is important to note that social inequality and poverty are closely linked with environmental conditions (Homer-Dixon, 1999). Generally, people in developing countries rely more on the environment for their day-to-day needs. Poverty can thus be a cause of environmental degradation – deforestation due to fuelwood consumption is a well-known example.[2] Environmental degradation can also cause social conflict, which in turn aggravates poverty and inequality. The UN Security Council noted that non-military sources of instability in the environmental field become threats to human security (Najam, 2002). It is therefore particularly important to sever this link. Disparities in socio-economic development as well as environmental impacts between and within nations generate negative feedbacks among them in terms of sustainability. Thus these factors should be taken into account when assessing the realities of global sustainability. Finally, provided that the objective of global sustainability is not to increase consumption levels but rather to enhance QOL, looking into the relationship between QOL and economic achievement provides some insights into global sustainability.

Figure 2.1.2 plots indicators of QOL and economic achievements using data from 144 countries. The EF is used to indicate physical consumption levels per capita as a proxy for economic achievement. The Happy Planet Index (HPI) and the Human Development Index (HDI) are used as a proxy for QOL: the HPI measures people's life satisfaction through a survey that includes environmental considerations; and the HDI measures the degree of human development, including income, education and health.[3]

The inverted-U curves in both graphs in Figure 2.1.2 are plotted for two cases based on the regression estimates.[4] For the least-developed countries, economic attainments enhance QOL to a significant degree

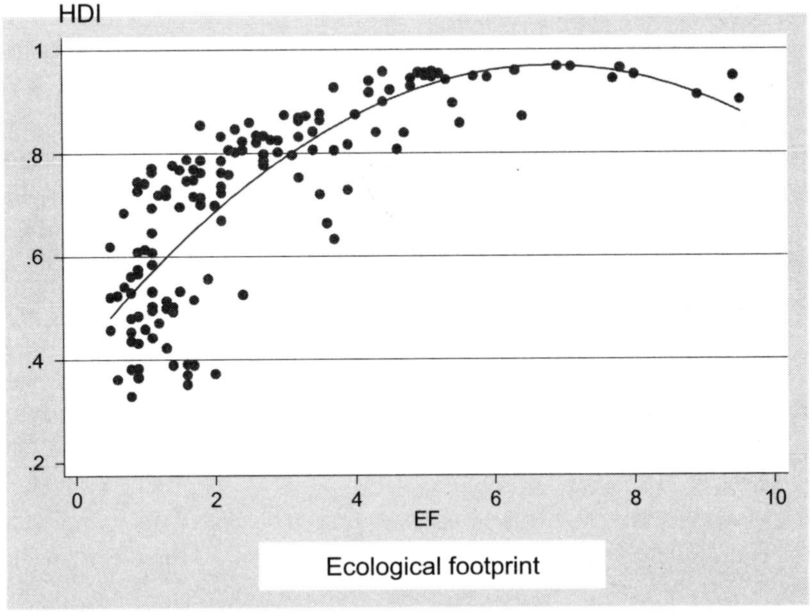

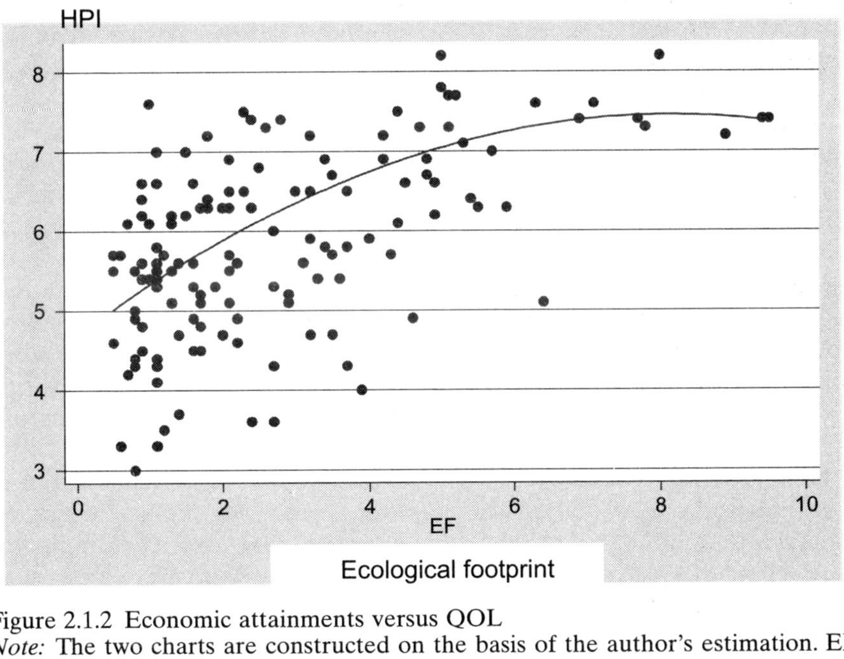

Figure 2.1.2 Economic attainments versus QOL
Note: The two charts are constructed on the basis of the author's estimation. EF is used as a proxy for economic attainments (consumption level), and HDI and HPI are used as a proxy for QOL.
Sources: 2008 EF was obtained from the Global Footprint Network, www.footprintnetwork.org. HDI and HPI were obtained from the UN Development Programme, http://hdr.undp.org/en, and the New Economic Foundation, www.happyplanetindex.org, respectively.

because basic human needs are much more likely to be provided to the poorest citizens. However, additional economic achievement increases QOL at a decreasing rate; the curves suggest that further consumption can have adverse effects on QOL.[5]

Our current economic system promotes increasing consumption, and thus increasing environmental burdens. The data suggest that shifting our social focus from economic growth to QOL could create a path to global sustainability. For example, redistribution of income between developed and developing countries increases QOL in developing countries but does not affect it in developed countries. This fact could be used as an important rationale for international environmental cooperation initiated by developed countries, with technological and financial support for developing countries.

2-1-3 Approaches to global sustainability

Before discussing the challenges for global sustainability, this section will attempt to clarify the numerous definitions of global sustainability. The Brundtland Report (World Commission on Environment and Development, 1987), for example, defined sustainable development as "development that meets the needs of the present without compromising the ability of future generations to meet their own needs", a notion which has been widely used in the debate around sustainability. This well-known definition is too vague, however, for practical applications and discussions.[6]

Issues related to global sustainability are vast, including global warming, loss of biodiversity, energy and resource depletion, poverty and water and food issues. Yet examining each issue alone probably neither provides a comprehensive understanding of sustainability nor suggests solutions needed to promote it. It is much more useful to provide a framework that gives us a solid approach to global sustainability in order to discuss its issues and challenges effectively.

Two major approaches to sustainability have been developed. The first is weak sustainability, in which man-made capital can be substituted for the environment to meet human needs; this allows for environmental destruction to some degree in the interests of development. The other approach is strong sustainability, which holds that the environment can never be replaced by man-made capital. Here, global sustainability is the state in which most people meet a certain level of QOL or social welfare and the level is not decreased in the long term, a view shared by the approach discussed below.

Figure 2.1.3 illustrates the hypothetical structure of global sustainability embraced by both approaches. As noted earlier, the goal of sustain-

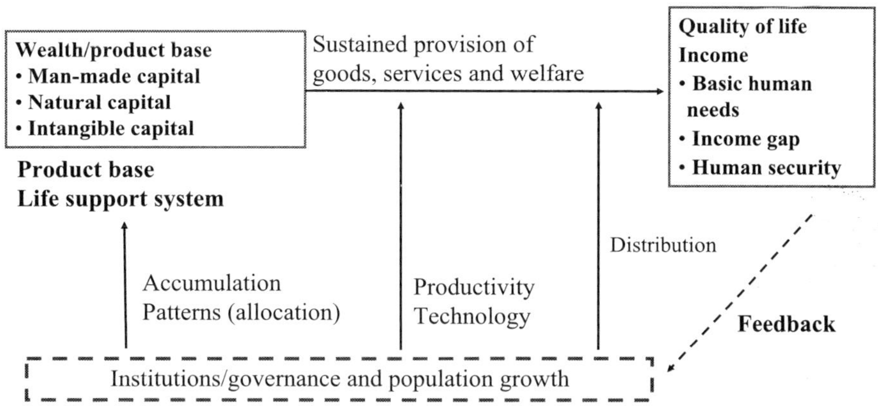

Figure 2.1.3 Approach to sustainable development
Source: Constructed based on Uwasu and Yabar (2008).

ability is to bring QOL/social welfare to a certain level and sustain the gradual improvement (or not allow a decrease) of QOL through provision of goods and services necessary to support people's lives. Several inputs of capital, including man-made (facilities, infrastructure, etc.), natural (ecosystems, resources, etc.) and intangible (knowledge, education, etc.), form the basis for the production of goods and services. Thus it is crucial that we do not deplete these resources in order to maintain and enhance QOL in both developing and developed countries.[7]

There are two important concerns when considering the second approach. First, traditional economic theory assumes that man-made capital is a unique product base. It is clear, however, that other types of capital, including natural and intangible, are essential for production; recent economic theory has begun to focus on these two factors. Second, this framework can contain both the abovementioned approaches because it states nothing about the substitutability between different capitals. Specifically, for those who do not obtain basic human needs, substitutability among different capitals should be allowed to achieve the minimum conditions for survival. In contrast, for those who can already meet the needs, the strong sustainability approach should apply.[8]

This framework also indicates that population, productivity and institutions/governance directly and indirectly influence QOL and welfare. Its argument about the effect of population levels follows the classical line: when population becomes larger, per capita natural capital available and goods and services produced become smaller, which has negative impacts on QOL. Institutions and governance also determine how goods and services are distributed, and rates of productivity likewise determine the production level of goods and services. These factors affect each other; bad institutions reduce incentives for economic stakeholders, thus lowering an economy's productivity. They also indirectly affect QOL through the capital stock (or wealth). High population growth, low-quality institutions/governance and low productivity tend to lead to lower levels of wealth (Uwasu and Yabar, 2008).

The framework thus provides a systemic basis for discussing the challenges for global sustainability. Given the fact that population control is generally a controversial topic, it is particularly important to examine the other two factors, including institutions/governance and technology, when discussing these challenges.

2-1-4 Challenges for global sustainability

Current socio-economic systems are characterized by mass production, mass consumption and mass disposal. For centuries the world economy has expanded through technological innovation. We now know that this expansion has threatened global sustainability, causing environmental and socio-economic problems. Our current socio-economic systems must therefore be reinvented in order to reduce the environmental burden and promote social development. It has been argued that sustained supplies of goods and services are needed in order to enhance QOL and social welfare, and not simply to contribute to economic growth. The framework has systematically shown that technology and high-quality governance/institutions are key to achieving global sustainability.

The role of technology and institutions

Better technology makes it possible to supply goods and services with less capital, including less energy and lower emissions. Indeed, development of elegant technologies can make breakthroughs in many sustainability fields, such as renewable energy, water and food, which can affect climate change.

Technological development alone is not, of course, sufficient: innovative technologies must be developed and used. Technology transfer and dissemination substantially contribute to development in poorer countries. Most technologies currently used in developing countries are much less efficient than those routinely used in developed countries. For example, in the cement industry, which accounts for 5 per cent of global GHG emissions, emission reductions would be substantial if the best available technologies were transferred to and employed in China, a country that produces half of the world's cement. Furthermore, even industrialized countries do not fully utilize the best available technologies; for example, in Japan, which is thought of as one of the most advanced countries in terms of environmental technology, additional GHG emission reductions of 70 per cent would be attainable if the most up-to-date technologies were employed in the industrial, transport and household sectors (Fujino et al., 2007).

What conditions, therefore, spur technological innovation and dissemination? Economists have argued that profit-making incentives are the key sources of innovation. One argument, the induced innovation theory, holds that a limitation of resource availability can spur technological development (and adoption), and thus save scarce resources. For example, it has been noted that Japan developed agricultural technologies to increase yields because arable land was scarce, while the United States developed labour-saving agricultural technologies in order to cut back on expensive labour (Hayami and Ruttan, 1985).

In this sense, if natural capital (including natural resources and the environment) is thought to be a basis of production, environmental degradation can also lead to the development and dissemination of environmental technologies. Of course, under market mechanisms, natural capital is not yet considered to be a basis of production. Investment in environmental technology involves a high degree of uncertainty, and this is a barrier to investment. Furthermore, scientific evidence has clearly shown that we need to act swiftly to avoid further environmental degradation, and thus the speed of technological development and dissemination is critical. The IPCC has already suggested reduction targets and paths, which should be immediately considered to avoid catastrophic global warming.

The implication of these observations is that institutional arrangements to create and implement environmental technologies are critical. Emissions trading markets and environmental taxes create a price on environmental pollutants. Subsidies for research and development, as well as dissemination of developed technology, decrease the uncertainty for technological investment. Finally, with the accumulation of scientific knowledge about the present environmental conditions and needed countermeasures, the provision of long-term strategies of technological development that are consistent with the goals and visions of a particular society is becoming feasible and increasingly important.

Challenges in developing countries

The challenges in implementation of innovative environmental technologies in developing countries are clearly enormous. We have seen that population and economic growth in developing countries will be enormous in future. Specifically, most of that growth will be concentrated in urban areas, in which major pollution issues and GHG emissions occur. Developed countries should take the lead in implementing such arrangements because they generally have good institutions/governance and stable politics. Moderate economic growth and stabilized population size in these countries will also benefit from tackling global environmental issues.

Developed countries have solved most urban environmental issues through the implementation of appropriate policy instruments and technologies during the process of economic growth. If developing countries follow suit by introducing advanced technologies, they could mitigate the peak of environmental degradation.[9] In actuality, however, many developing regions are facing even more severe environmental issues than the developed regions ever did. There are two main reasons for this. First, "megacities" with populations greater than 10 million are rapidly emerging in developing countries; only a few of these ultra-large urban centres exist in developed countries. With large populations and poor infrastructure, environmental management in these megacities is extremely difficult. Second, developing countries are experiencing much more rapid urbanization than developed countries, and this is becoming a major barrier to building the urban infrastructure needed for environmental management. Traffic congestion in cities with rapid economic growth, such as Bangkok, is a major issue, and even in cities such as Nairobi, where there are far fewer motorized vehicles, traffic congestion problems are emerging because of a lack of transportation infrastructure and a steadily increasing population. In fact, urban areas in developing countries have become a major source of GHG emissions: per capita GHG emissions in Beijing and Shanghai now exceed those in Seoul and Tokyo (Dhakal, 2005). Thus taking effective countermeasures in developing countries is an imperative for global sustainability.

Figure 2.1.4 plots the relationship between environmental degradation and economic growth over time in urban areas. Curve 1 depicts the developed countries' experience and Curve 2 shows the current situation of urban areas in developing countries; however, if appropriate technological transfer is made, they could have followed Curve 3, leading to fewer global environmental burdens. A shift from Curve 2 to Curve 3 requires capacity building and financial back-up, including the strengthening of operating and monitoring systems, in addition to technology transfer. Building a mechanism for implementing countermeasures to global warming in developing countries within the post-Kyoto framework is also important, especially the clean development mechanism,[10] in order to build a framework of financial and technological support.

Capacity building, including the creation of high-quality governance and institutions in developing countries, is crucial for international global sustainability initiatives. The experience of international economic devel-

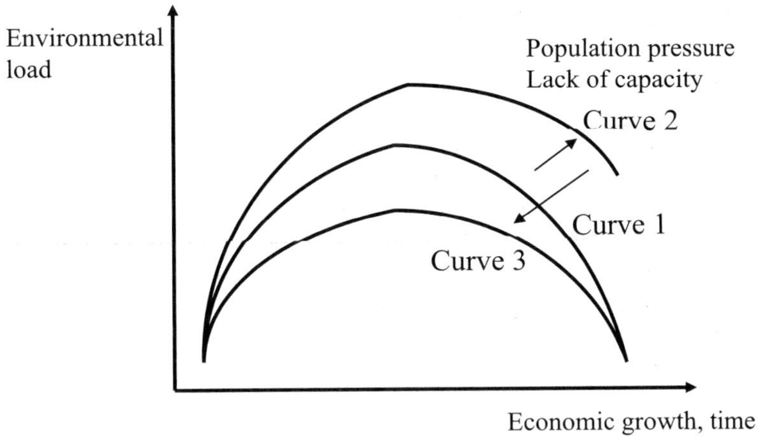

Figure 2.1.4 Environmental load and economic growth

opment aid is an important lesson in this regard; we know that simply providing capital and investment, which were thought to be necessary and sufficient for economic growth, has not contributed to economic development in most developing countries. It has been clearly demonstrated that poor-quality governance and institutions negated any investments in education, infrastructure and business (Pritchett, 1999; Hall and Jones, 1999). Moreover, it has become evident that most international aid cannot advance socio-economic development without high-quality institutions and governance (Easterly, 2002). And although micro-projects funded by international bodies and NGOs have played an important role in the improvement of QOL in developing countries, these project-based actions are not fundamental solutions for socio-economic development in these countries.

The international community needs to address capacity building and the improvement of institutions before addressing global sustainability. Of course, this kind of interference in domestic affairs has not been allowed historically. Nevertheless, decades of experience in the international aid arena has taught us that nothing is impossible, even in difficult cases such as Ghana, where the right incentives improved the quality of institutions during the 1980s and led to much better socio-economic outcomes (ibid.).

2-1-5 Conclusion

Rapid population growth and economic expansion have brought prosperity to much of the world. Average incomes dramatically increased during the twentieth century, and people became much healthier. The socio-economic systems that helped produce this increased prosperity are dominant in the twenty-first century as well. These systems were built upon mass production, mass consumption and mass disposal; and under these systems environmental degradation has become a major threat to global sustainability. It is clear that our current consumption levels are beyond the Earth's carrying capacity, resulting in global warming, resource depletion, extreme poverty and increasing inequality.

These threats will lead to catastrophic consequences unless we shift the current socio-economic systems to new models. Although this chapter did not touch upon specific recipes for these new models, it has discussed the importance of technology and institutions in creating a structural approach to global sustainability. In particular, developing countries will be the major sources of environmental loads as well as the most likely victims of global environmental threats. Thus the role of developed countries and international bodies is becoming more critical: they must begin providing financial foundations and technological innovation, as well as a platform for capacity building, including the improvement of institutions and governance. Fulfilling the role will, of course, entail enormous costs. Nevertheless, this is also an opportunity for developed countries to utilize their competitive advantage to create new business, employment and innovation, which will all lead to the enhancement of QOL and the welfare of the global society.

Notes

1. Assessment of globalization is beyond the scope of this chapter. While globalization leads to widening income gaps between and within countries, it has also increased productivity through the active mobilization of labour, capital and information. Changing the trend of globalization is not practically feasible. Rather, it is important to strengthen socio-economic systems, so that problems raised by globalization are mitigated (Stiglitz, 2006).
2. Of course, poverty is not the sole cause of this degradation. Poverty tends to be associated with high population pressure, poor access to energy sources and other social issues, all of which are causes of environmental degradation.
3. The former can therefore be thought of as a subjective indicator and the latter as an objective indicator of QOL.
4. Data from 144 countries were used to create the two estimations. In the two regression estimations, all the coefficients that can capture the U-inverted curve were statistically significant. The fitness of the regression equations was also statistically significant.
5. The idea behind this observation, although it should be examined further, is that too much focus on economic achievement produces stressors on the society – such as inequality and competition – that lower QOL.
6. In fact, this book attempts to establish a new concept of socio-economic development for this reason.

7. Country-level capital is estimated in monetary terms by the World Bank and used as a sustainability indicator. See Hamilton, Atkinson and Pearce (1997) and Dasgupta (2001) for theoretical background and applications.
8. Dasgupta (2007) made similar arguments – that there must be certain types of capital, which are not substitutable by other capitals, and there must be a critical level of them in order to constitute the basis of production.
9. This argument is based on Gerschenkron (1962), an English economic historian who found that less-developed countries generally show faster economic growth than developed countries by borrowing advanced technologies.
10. The clean development mechanism is a mechanism employed in the Kyoto Protocol that facilitates GHG mitigation in developing countries through technology introduction from developed countries.

REFERENCES

Clarke, George (1992) "More Evidence on Income Distribution and Growth", Policy Research Working Paper, World Bank, Washington, DC.

Dasgupta, Partha (2001) *Human Well-being and the Natural Environment*. New York: Oxford University Press.

——— (2007) "Measuring Sustainable Development: Theory and Application", *Asian Development Review* 24, pp. 1–10.

Dhakal, Shobhakar (2005) "Urban Energy Use and Greenhouse Gas Emission from Asian Mega-cities: Policies for a Sustainable Future", Institute for Global Environmental Strategies, Kanagawa.

Easterly, William (2002) *The Elusive Quest for Growth: Economists' Adventures and Misadventures in the Tropics*. Cambridge, MA: MIT Press.

Ehrlich, Paul R. ([1968] 1995) *The Population Bomb*. Cutchogue, NY: Buccaneer Books.

Fujino, J., T. Hibino, T. Enokihara, M. Matsuoka, T. Masui and M. Kainuma (2007) "Scenario for Low Carbon Society and Its Feasibility", *Earth Environment* 12, pp. 153–160 (in Japanese).

Gerschenkron, Alexander (1962) *Economic Backwardness in Historical Perspective*. Cambridge, MA: Harvard University Press.

Global Footprint Network (2010) "Ecological Footprint Atlas 2010"; available at www.footprintnetwork.org/images/uploads/Ecological%20Footprint%20Atlas%202010.pdf.

Hall, E. R. and I. C. Jones (1999) "Why Do Some Countries Produce So Much More Output per Worker than Others?", *Quarterly Journal of Economics* 114, pp. 83–117.

Hamilton, K., G. Atkinson and D. Pearce (1997) "Genuine Savings as an Indicator of Sustainability", CSERGE Working Paper GEC 97-03, Washington, DC.

Hayami, Y. and V. Ruttan (1985) *Agricultural Development*. Baltimore, MD: Johns Hopkins University Press.

Homer-Dixon, Thomas F. (1999) *Environment, Scarcity, and Violence*. Princeton, NJ: Princeton University Press.

IPCC (2007) "IPCC Fourth Assessment Report: Summary for Policy Makers"; available at www.ipcc.ch/pdf/assessment-report/ar4/wg1/ar4-wg1-spm.pdf.

Meadows, H. D., D. L. Meadows, J. Randers and W. W. Behrens (1972) *The Limits to Growth*. New York: Universe Books.

Najam, Adil (2002) "Environment and Security: Exploring the Links", in Adil Najam (ed.) *Environment and Security: Perspective from South Asia*. Lanham, MD: University Press of America.

Pritchett, Lant (1999) "Where Has All the Education Gone?", Policy Research Working Paper, World Bank, Washington, DC.

Sachs, Jeffrey (2008) *Common Wealth: Economics for a Crowded Planet*. Harmondsworth: Penguin.

Stiglitz, E. Joseph (2006) *Making Globalization Work*. New York: W. W. Norton.

UN Secretariat (2006) "World Population Prospects: The 2006 Revision and World Urbanization Prospects: The 2005 Revision"; available at http://esa.un.org/unpp.

United Nations (2010) "The Millennium Development Goals Report"; available at http://unstats.un.org/unsd/mdg/Resources/Static/Products/Progress2010/MDG_Report_2010_En_low%20res.pdf.

Uwasu, M. and H. Yabar (2008) "Sustainability Pathways and Indicators Based on the Capital Approach", paper presented at Eco-Balance 2008, Tokyo. Unpublished.

Wackernagel, M. and W. E. Rees (1996) *Our Ecological Footprint: Reducing Human Impact on the Earth*. Gabriola Island, PA: New Society Publishers.

World Commission on Environment and Development (1987) *Our Common Future*. New York: Oxford University Press.

2-2

Global sustainability: Globalization and sustainable development

Kazuhiro Ueta

2-2-1 Introduction

The Earth is often referred to as a piece of fabric without a seam. Indeed, the planet can be seen as one comprehensive ecological system where all the different species depend on each other. Boulding (1968) published an essay titled "The Economics of the Coming Spaceship Earth", arguing that it would amount to insanity and danger to believe in and seek infinite economic growth in the finite world of this Earth. Further, Boulding (ibid.) pointed out that "the closed earth of the future requires economic principles which are somewhat different from those of the open earth of the past". In spite of these warnings, however, the human race went on to experience pollution and an oil crisis. Again, in spite of all the warnings on the limits to growth, we have been slow in reshaping our economic system to suit the finite planet. On the global scale, the quantitative expansion in environmental load and resource consumption has never ceased. It is no surprise that global environmental issues have been aggravated.

If we look at the situation from the viewpoint of the relationship between environmental issues and the economic system, we see in the world today there are more, rather than fewer, factors complicating the mechanisms that create environmental issues; and it is even harder to solve them as the world economy becomes more globalized. This chapter first confirms what environmental changes the globalization of the world's economy is creating, and then considers how we can start and where we should go in our efforts to achieve global sustainability.

2-2-2 Today's patterns in global environmental changes

Globalization means that "mutual social interactions across the continents are not just expanding in scale and extent but also exercising stronger impacts". It also means that "people's organisations are connected to remote communities and spreading power relationships across the continents and regions of the world, with changes or transformations taking place in the degrees of such relationships" (Held and McGrew, 2002). While we can assume that global integration is in progress and mutual relationships are deepening, new hostilities and conflicts are arising at the same time. The issue here is how globalization has changed aspects of environmental issues.

The human race has experienced the phenomenon known as globalization several times in its history, but the globalization we are seeing today is characterized by changes in the global environment created by humans, as described below, which are bringing new problems in governance (Held et al., 1999).

First, while some environmental issues have existed since the birth of the human race on this planet, the environment aggravation we are facing today is more global than any similar problem experienced in any former age in human history. "Global environmental issues" has thus become a household term today, since people consider these issues to be one of the most serious risks and threats to the human race in its history. Moreover, these issues, as typified by climate changes, have several brand-new features. Especially notable is the problem that, in terms of time and space, the cause and effect of an environmental issue today are far apart from each other, with the issue requiring a very long-term viewpoint. Thus we often find that discharge waste (such as CO_2) today can cause damage several decades later, and that waste from Japan, for example, affects the environment of a certain island nation in the Pacific. This poses another very complicated problem; namely, we need to extend our decision-making process and policy systems so we can identify causes and effects of environmental issues.

Second, as the term suggests, global environmental issues consist of literally global problems, such as ozone-layer destruction and climate change, and these are interwoven in complex ways, with cross-border pollution and other regional problems as well as local issues. Some of these latter issues are local expressions of causes hidden in international economic relations, while others are purely local problems (Ueta, 1991; Teranishi, 1992). This complexity also complicates the relationships in international sharing of responsibilities and domestic political agendas related to the global environmental threat.

Third, while economic globalization has been the driving force of changes in the global environment, it has also been a result of the worldwide spread of the industrialization and economic growth patterns that originated in the Western world. This spread has expanded pollution geographically and increased the sum of resources consumed over the face of the Earth. Today, many people consider that the spread of these patterns does not guarantee environmentally sound development around the globe. This awareness is part of the background to the birth of the idea of "sustainable development".

In addition, Held, Barnett and Henderson (2005) point out that the World Bank and other international institutions have been providing capital, infrastructure and economic "advice" in order to facilitate industrialization which is environmentally unsustainable. For example, while Held and co-authors admit that the famines which have hit most of sub-Saharan Africa are partly ascribable to political errors made by the leaders of the affected nations, as well as to regional farming practices that invite ecological depletion, they condemn international economic restrictions for certainly playing some role in the creation of these famines.

2-2-3 Environment and economic globalization in East Asia

Mutual dependence between international specialization and environmental load

These problematic facts must be taken into account in considering "how can we and should we control globalisation" in terms of environmental issues (ibid.). The problems Held and colleagues pointed out are of special importance as we discuss the preconditions for building up an international environmental protection system and reshaping the international economic system. However, we need to note that influences from globalization do not emerge equally all over the world, but unevenly from one region to another. Thus it is reasonable to follow another methodology, in which we start off with evaluation of influences from globalization in a particular region and move on to consider how the international systems of economy and environmental protection should be shaped.

This chapter evaluates influences from globalization in East Asia and considers how to control them, introducing some recent studies on the region. One reason for choosing this particular region is that it has very high economic growth, now functioning as the world's factory, and is also expected to be a huge world market. What is more, the rapid economic expansion of East Asia cannot be explained by free-market ideology alone but is ascribable to the national governments' roles and effective governance as they deal with globalization and the world market. This is in line with the selective-openness policies adopted by many East Asian governments, one of the features of these nations pointed out by Stiglitz (2006) and others. One example is the Chinese government, which set an order of priorities as it tried to control globalization and let its economy enter the world market. The most important reason for choosing East Asia, however, is that it is where greenhouse gas (GHG) emissions are growing most rapidly among all the regions of the world. The region thus plays the key role in stabilization of the global climate, in both relative and absolute senses.

The Chinese phrase for globalization is *quan qiu hua*, which literally means "unification of the whole globe". This is easy to understand when we consider information and financial services today. The internet carries information all over the world in a moment. At least some of the international financial centres are open any time, and people can conduct transactions there. Truly, money and information are running around the world, and effects and influences of this appear in different ways in each region. When the subprime bubble burst in the United States and Lehman Brothers collapsed, the shock waves from Wall Street covered the entire world. It is still a fresh memory, and the shock affected more seriously those regions structurally dependent on external demand for income.

Turning to things directly related to environmental issues, globalization of the world economy expresses itself in the forms of repositioning of production facilities and global rearrangement of international specialization. The repositioning and rearrangement take shape by means of trade and direct investments. Generally, industrial firms try to place their production bases where they can minimize production cost. Even if they do not move existing plants, they will purchase cheaper parts and components produced abroad, if these are available. In short, many final goods are produced in one country, but the intermediate items employed in their production are made in another country. Such final goods are not exceptional today; rather, they are quite common.

This fact means that we should note a new issue as we consider responsibilities for carbon dioxide (CO_2) emission. In the UN Framework Convention on Climate Change, different nations of the world carry common yet differentiated responsibilities in their efforts to stabilize the world climate. Climate change is a global issue that can never be solved unless the nations of the world work together to overcome it. At the same time, however, on the specific issue of how to reduce GHGs, it is crucial to consider which nations should reduce emissions in which region. It is obvious that the developed nations have to cut down their GHG emissions dramatically to prove their leadership, abilities and responsibilities in this effort. Such reduction alone, however, is not sufficient to stop global warming. Those commonly called "emerging" nations should cut down their GHG emissions as well, as soon as possible. Also, developing nations must accomplish "low-carbon" development in the future. Yet another important fact is that developing nations, emerging nations and developed nations are isolated from one another. With globalization advancing further, they will become more closely involved with one another economically. How, then, should we allocate responsibilities for CO_2 emissions among the nations?

Currently, the Kyoto Protocol makes estimates when it mentions "CO_2 emissions from each nation". This might sound like a matter of course. As stated above, however, in today's globalized economy many of the production activities emitting CO_2 are not confined within a single country. It might be quite hard to find a CO_2-emitting production activity that employs only raw materials produced in that same country. In other words:

> Production of every kind of products requires natural resources including energy and intermediate products (materials). And if most of those intermediate products are made domestically, the environmental load created by production can be ascribed to that single nation alone. In today's globalised economy, however, it is a commonplace to use intermediate products imported from outside and many goods production processes extend across national borders. This also means that a product produced in one nation embodies environmental load created in multiple nations. (Shimoda et al., 2009)

This concept is known as "embodied environmental load". But how can we handle the issue of allocating CO_2 emission responsibilities among nations using this concept? One important point the idea of embodied environmental load sets out is that we cannot determine a priori that the responsibility for environmental load created by production activities in one country is to be borne by that country. This brings up two new questions. Is the environmental load from production to be attributed to the country of production, or to those of consumption? And what shares of this load are to be attributed to the entities involved in the complex chain of the production activities involved? In short, globalization of the world economy has clarified the problems inherent in the traditional method of sharing environmental responsibilities among nations of the world, which in this method are considered to be a group of nation-states. Though this traditional method is still important, globalization calls for some brand-new concepts to be used in attributing environmental load and allocating environmental responsibilities.

Shimoda et al. (ibid.) made estimates of embodied environmental load and its changes in the Asia-Pacific region, using the Asian international input-output tables for 1985 and 2000. In this paper, the Asia-Pacific region consists of 10 nations, namely Japan, the United States, China, the Asian NIEs (South Korea, Taiwan and Singapore) and the ASEAN 4 (the Philippines, Malaysia, Thailand and Indonesia). The results can be summarized as follows. In 1985 both Japan and the United States were exporters and importers of goods, sharing the load of CO_2 emission with the other nations of the Asia-Pacific region. In 2000, however, Japan and the United States were importers more than exporters, making other nations emit more CO_2 and consume more energy. In contrast, China grew into an exporter of goods rather than an importer, carrying the CO_2 emission load of other countries. Standing upon these analysis results, the study concludes that "in the Asia-Pacific Region, in the 15 years from 1985 to 2000, the two developed nations, namely the US and Japan, enhanced their tendency to push CO_2 emission load to other developing nations" (ibid.). In short, although we can ascribe a rapid increase of CO_2 emission in East Asia directly to the heated economic growth in the region, it also comes from a structural change in which two developed nations, namely the United States and Japan, have transferred their CO_2 emission load over to developing East Asian nations.

So far, we have seen the structural change in the international mutual dependence from the viewpoint of environmental load in East Asia. But how has the mutual interdependence changed to bring in such a structural change? This region has been showing high economic growth rates recently: what is it making of this high economic growth?

Watanabe, Shimoda and Fujikawa (2009) conducted a study to analyse changes in the East Asian structure of international specialization in terms of added value. With China included, the study analysed such changes in the Asia-Pacific region chronologically, using Asia-Pacific international input-output tables for 1985, 1990, 1995 and 2000 prepared by the Institute of Developing Economies, Japan. This study shows unexpected results.

When we look at the international trade aspect, we find a very interesting fact. Many East Asian nations have shifted the destinations of their export from the United States to East Asia. Thus we can say the economic ties within the region have grown closer. But this does not necessarily hold true when we look at incomes. The United States and Japan have high ratios of added value attributable to domestic production, which indicate that these two economies are close to self-containment. (The ratio of added value attributable to domestic production is equivalent to the coefficient of general added value in inter-industry analysis, and is also known as the "domestic production ratio". The reason for using this ratio is that, generally, those employed in the production process of a final end product can be roughly broken into three major categories: domestically produced intermediate products, imported intermediate products and added value. Yet production of such domestically produced intermediate products requires other domestically produced intermediate products, imported intermediate products and added value. Extending this classification into the three categories, therefore, we reach a conclusion that the value of a product consists of two sources: added value and import.) However, in East Asia the study found a trend of declining ratios of added value attributable to domestic production. Moreover, the portion of added value escaping from the East Asian nations into other regions has been expanding. This means that not much income remains inside East Asia. Given these findings, the study concludes that while the East Asian nations have been building closer ties with one another, a relatively small portion of added value remains within the region. Thus East Asia cannot be considered to have grown up into an independent economic bloc.

2-2-4 Sustainable development of Asia

Sustainable development of East Asia

Combining the results from the two studies described above, we consider what the strategy for sustainable development should be for East Asia. In order to discuss sustainable development, we need analyses in terms of specific aspects, such as environmental, economic, etc. However, we also need to combine all those aspects together.

We can summarize these two studies as follows. First, with respect to mutual dependence among East Asian nations in environmental issues, the rapid increase of CO_2 emissions from the region reflects not just its fast economic expansion but CO_2 emission load imposed on it by the United States, Japan and other developed nations as well. Second, as discussed above, even though mutual dependence within the region's economy has certainly been enhanced in terms of trade, it is not necessarily enhanced in added value. Moreover, although export-driven industrialization does create some added value, much of this value does not remain within East Asia but flows out into the United States and other regions, and this outward flow of added value has been growing stronger. Thus the rapid economic expansion of East Asia, brought in by export-driven industrialization, has been accompanied by structural changes in mutual dependence both within the region and with other regions, in terms of both environmental and economic issues.

To evaluate economic development of a region, whether East Asia or any other, we need to see the structural patterns of economic growth and the direction of structural changes, not just the growth rate. East Asia's pattern of economic growth has its weakness, as expressed by the phrase "impoverished growth" (Mori, 2009). This becomes obvious if we compare the region's economic structure with that of the European Union.

We need to analyse further the relationship between this structural weakness of the region's economy and the fact that the recent Lehman shock and subsequent financial crisis hit East Asia especially hard. Stopping global warming is a prerequisite to sustainable development. Efforts to stop it, then, should aim to overcome the weakness accompanying a rapid economic expansion brought in by export-driven industrialization. At the same time, this is necessary for the East Asian community as it builds up its economic foundation. Thus one task is to reshape international relationships in the economy and environmental protection, to change the pattern of economic development into a sustainable one.

Asia of growth and Asia with vulnerability

Achieving sustainable development in Asia is a prerequisite to achieving global sustainability. This is obvious when we look at the shares this particular region has in the world's population, market size, production, CO_2 emission and other indices, as well as its growth rates in all these indices. At the same time, Asia is culturally very diverse and contains many countries and regions of very different political systems and stages of economic development. In short, Asia summarizes the world. A coalition, for example, to stabilize the world's climate in this region would open up a way to global sustainability. In Asia today, many debates are in progress over different frameworks of regional economic collaboration, such as China-Japan-South Korea, ASEAN+3, APEC, etc. Japan's former Prime Minister Hatoyama proposed an East Asian community. It is crucial, then, to consider the issue of climate stabilization as part of such collaboration frameworks.

As people often say, however, the Earth is one but the world is not. No matter how hard you try to integrate the world into a single society and optimize it, in reality it is a collection of many different entities and countries with different intentions and behaviours. Similarly, Asia is a collection of many different entities. As we try to stabilize the climate in Asia, one thing we must carefully keep in mind is that Asia consists of both "Asia of growth" and "Asia with vulnerability".

One typical example of "Asia of growth" is China. Carrying on highly accelerated, export-driven industrialization, China has been working hard on environmental policies recently (Mori, Ueta and Yamamoto, 2008). Still, the nation has not changed its basic principle of development, partly because economic growth is considered to be the key to integrating its society. China is thus still increasing environmental load both domestically and internationally, creating friction in different places. Notably, however, inside China various environmental movements have arisen and become commonplace.

Chen (2009) reports that protests against pollution are arising in China, with many different forms of environmental conflicts seen within the nation. He categorizes these environmental movements into four types: those led by private individual activists, those led by NGOs, those led by social élites and those caused by crowds or collisions. Among these four types, protests led by NGOs and social élites have proven to be relatively more effective in solving conflicts and improving the environment. Still, Chen points out that these movements will face a huge roadblock unless the social and political infrastructure (i.e. local autonomy, democracy, etc.) is in place. This is very suggestive and helpful as we try to understand what can enable these environmental movements to develop fully and shift the balance between development and environment significantly towards the latter. Since people's awareness of environmental problems and activities to protect the environment is probably related to their economic standard of living, the relationship between social and political systems and environmental movements is not simple. Still, there are two sides to this: while social systems regulate and formulate people's behaviours, people's actions can create new systems. In China, the interactions over environmental issues and policies among politics, economy and society will probably develop differently than in Japan. The future development in China must be watched carefully.

The task discussed above is part of a greater task of how to incorporate environmental governance into an Asia of growth. Still, this "Asia of growth" is only one side of the region. We must not forget the other side of the coin, namely "Asia with vulnerability". For example, in Bangladesh some 30 million of its 130 million people live in coastal areas vulnerable to a rise in sea level. Moreover, a shocking 36 per cent of the whole population of that country lives on less than a dollar a day. If global warming raised the sea level by 1 metre, the outcome in Bangladesh would be desperately destructive and tragic. In Japan, one usually thinks of how to reduce GHG emission when hearing the term "climate change". In Bangladesh, however, people want prevention or alleviation of disastrous effects from climate change. Bangladesh alone cannot stop negative influences from climate change; to prevent irreversible and disastrous effects in the nation, the whole world needs to join hands in large-scale efforts that include diplomacy, projects, funds, etc. "Vulnerability" means not just that something is physically fragile due to negative influences from climate change, but also that there are insufficient means to prevent such influences. How should we prevent negative influences on vulnerable areas? This is a very common issue throughout Asia and the whole world.

When we try to build up a sustainable, low-carbon society in Asia, we must work on both "Asia of growth" and "Asia with vulnerability" (Kameyama et al., 2008). Here, we must reconsider the meaning of the word sustainable, as in the phrase "sustainable development". In general usage, the word refers to achieving more comprehensive sustainability, which covers ecological as well as social and economic sustainability. The problem "Asia with vulnerability" has revealed is one very basic fact: one of the minimum prerequisites to living humanly is freedom from risks and anxieties of irreversible, disastrous influences from climate change. And since this applies globally, it can be considered to be among the global minimum requirements.

To build a sustainable Asia, we must start with establishing a pattern of low-carbon development in Asia of growth, and at the same time let "Asia with vulnerability" gain abilities to get over its own crises. The first problem is how to build up Asia like that. Although we have many tasks to accomplish, what matters more than anything else is that, as a prerequisite to any economic cooperation, we need to make all the people of Asia aware of the problem of climate changes. To gain this awareness, they must know two things. One is what climate change have already brought to Asia and what they will bring in the future. The other is what Asia should do, what policies it should take. As in any other environmental problem, people should know what is happening, discuss the issues and thus share common recognition. Then they can come up with good, specific ideas for solutions. Asia is also in need of a mechanism that systematically produces core information for people to share as the common foundation from which they can strive for solutions.

2-2-5 Global sustainability and local initiatives

To achieve global sustainability, efforts are essential to overcome the current situation of "the earth is one, but the world is not" (Sachs, 2008). One example proposed is the creation of a global democratic institution (Stiglitz, 2006). Many proposals have been made that are related to other global issues, such as creation of a world environmental organization (Biermann and Bauer, 2005). Simultaneously with these efforts on the global level, we must work to change regional economies to become more in line with global sustainability.

We have to note, however, that global sustainability is not necessarily a collection of local sustainabilities. For example, very often indices to measure local sustainability include factors peculiar to that locality, and these outnumber those to measure global sustainability. "Think globally, act locally" is a principle to follow. Here we consider how local action should relate to global sustainability, using as examples some initiatives taken by local governments on the issue of climate change.

There are several background factors emphasizing the important role of local governments in stopping global warming. One very fundamental fact is that most sources of GHG emission are located in only some local areas, while climate change is a global issue. This means that cutting down GHG emission cannot be done on the global scale in a day. No global-level promise of such reduction can make sense unless all the relevant parties at the local level continue to reduce.

I heard an interesting example of a local government's effort at a farming village in China in early 2008. I will call that village simply "Village A". The village was working with a globally active environmental NGO to collect methane gas, a GHG with high global warming potential. In those days, China as a whole was in no way active in efforts to stop global warming; but this particular farming village, which was not wealthy, was already trying to reduce GHG emissions.

Mr Wang, chief of the energy section of Village A's office, visited farmers almost every day to discuss energy issues. To those farmers, energy issues meant securing a stable supply of energy and solving problems arising from use of energy. Village A was still underdeveloped, and most households used firewood and briquettes for fuel. This was accompanied by many problems, such as harmful gas arising while burning this fuel, soot painting people's faces black and so on. The village residents were thus searching for other sources of energy. Mr Wang noticed that many farmers were raising pigs or running hog farms. The village thus promoted a new energy supply system that let hogs' excrement ferment to produce methane gas, which was then delivered to households for cooking and heating. Since the new system required some investment in the methane fermentation equipment, etc., the village won support from the NGO, active worldwide, and spread this system.

As each household was obliged to bear part of the cost to install the new system, it seemed to be finding its way into wealthier families first. Nevertheless, methane gas which used to be simply released into the atmosphere was now collected. It was thus a good example of a project to stop global warming, and this is why the global NGO was supporting it. Yet the energy section chief did not launch the project for the sake of stopping global warming: Mr Wang was simply faithful to his responsibilities as the chief of the energy section, trying to improve the standard of living of his village people by providing them with a new, better source of energy. This resulted in a reduction of GHG emissions as well.

I visited Village A and talked to the chief and some farmers. I learned that efforts to stop global warming can be more successful if they are part of people's lives, and that local governments should play crucial roles in such efforts.

Looking back on how Japan overcame its pollution hazards, some local governments led the way. Japan's local initiative in environmental policies are known worldwide (Ueta, 1993). At the national government level, the first central administrative agency, the Environment Agency (the Ministry of the Environment today), was established in 1971. The agency was founded to enforce Japan's first national basic law for environmental protection, the Basic Act for Environmental Pollution Control, which was enacted in 1967. The Basic Act proved to be ineffective, however, thanks to its articles calling for a balance between economic growth and environmental protection. It was therefore drastically revised in the Diet Session on Pollution of 1970, and only after this major revision was the Environment Agency founded.

It is obvious, however, that Japan had pollution long before these laws and administrative agency were established. One well-known example is the air pollution caused by smoke from the Ashio copper mine (whose hazardous waste gas, including SO_x, polluted much of the neighbouring region from the late nineteenth century well into the twentieth). Another notorious incident of pollution, Minamata disease, was officially confirmed in 1956. In May that year a doctor at Chisso Corporation's hospital saw some patients with this disease, which at that time had no name, and reported to the Public Healthcare Centre of the city of Minamata that "in this area, patients with a central nerve disease whose cause has yet to be identified are emerging in a large number". At this point there was no established opinion on the cause of this disease. In addition, there were many cases of environmental pollution all over the nation – for instance, air pollution in the neighbourhoods of industrial complexes. As noted, the legal system and administrative mechanisms reacted only after these problems emerged. This lateness is part of the reason why, in some cases including Minamata, there still remain today problems to be settled with respect to relief for victims. In the case of Minamata, although a doctor first reported the disease as early as 1956, Japan's central government did not officially register it as a pollution-caused disease until 1968. During this long wait for registration, Chisso's Minamata plant kept releasing polluted water. The end result was a drastic hike in the number of Minamata patients: if the government had taken effective measures immediately in 1956, many of these patients would have been spared.

People often call Minamata disease a crime committed by a business, and this is true; at the same time, however, it was a crime committed by the government as well, and we all should be aware of this.

In Japan's history of environmental initiatives, some local governments took innovative, progressive measures before the central government built any effective system to promote environmental policies, and those local initiatives had powerful influences on the national government's policies, as well as those of some other nations. One typical example was the pollution control agreement signed by the city of Yokohama in 1964. At a time when no observance of the existing laws alone was able to prevent pollution, the city's government invented this agreement to stop pollution. More specifically, the city signed the agreement with the local power stations: it contained requirements much tougher than those of any national laws, drastically reducing emissions of pollutants. Today, Japan has more than 30,000 similar agreements in all. Also, inspired by this example, some European countries have signed agreements with industries to reduce GHG emissions. In addition, the municipal government of Tokyo in 1968 established its pollution prevention ordinance, whose spirit is believed to have greatly influenced the national Diet Session on Pollution of 1970.

These examples of local initiatives are from China and Japan, but progressive initiatives taken by local governments can create models that are actually universally acceptable around the world. Global warming is a global issue, and people often talk about environment taxation and emission trading schemes. Yet for such systems to have effects, we need much debate on how to let local communities initiate creative ideas and efforts. Decentralization is another issue that needs to be discussed further from this perspective (Terao and Otsuka, 2008). It would be no exaggeration to say that the key to achieving global sustainability lies in revitalizing local initiatives in environmental policies over the whole face of the planet.

2-2-6 Conclusion

Instead of considering the issue of global sustainability in itself, this chapter has discussed global sustainability in relationship to local sustainability initiatives in Asia. This author considers that global sustainability can be achieved only in interactions with regional and local sustainability. Global sustainability cannot stand apart from those regional and local efforts. This fact has much to do with the multilayered structure of environmental governance.

REFERENCES

Biermann, F. and S. Bauer (2005) *A World Environment Organization: Solution or Threat for Effective International Environmental Governance?*, Global Environmental Governance Series. Burlington, VT: Ashgate.

Boulding, K. E. (1968) "The Economics of the Coming Spaceship Earth", in K. E. Boulding (ed.) *Beyond Economics*. Ann Arbor, MI: University of Michigan Press, pp. 275–287.

Chen, Yun (2009) "Environmental Conservation and Local Autonomy in China", paper presented at Ninth Asia-Pacific NGO Environmental Conference, Kyoto, 20–21 November.

Held, D. and A. McGrew (2002) *Globalization/Anti-Globalization*. Cambridge: Polity Press.

Held, D., A. Barnett and C. Henderson (eds) (2005) *Debating Globalization*. Cambridge: Polity Press.

Held, D., A. McGrew, D. Goldblatt and J. Perraton (1999) *Global Transformations: Politics, Economics and Culture*. Cambridge: Polity Press.

Kameyama, Y., A. P. Sari, M. H. Soejachmoen and N. Kanie (eds) (2008) *Climate Change in Asia: Perspectives on the Future Climate Regime*. Tokyo: United Nations University Press.

Mori, A. (ed.) (2009) *Higashi Asia no Keizai Hatten to Kankyo Seisaku* (*Economic Development and Environmental Policies in East Asia*). Kyoto: Minerva Shobo.

Mori, A., K. Ueta and H. Yamamoto (eds) (2008) *Chugoku no Kankyo Seisaku – Genjo Bunseki, Teiryo Hyoka, no Tai-Chu Yen Shakkan* (*Chinese Environmental Policies – Analysis of Current Situation, Quantitative Evaluation, and Japan's Yen Loans to China*). Kyoto: Kyoto University Press.

Sachs, J. (2008) *Common Wealth: Economics for a Crowded Planet*. Harmondsworth: Penguin.

Shimoda, M., T. Watanabe, S. Kanoh and K. Fujikawa (2009) "Higashi Asia no Kankyo Fuka no Sogo Izon – CO_2 no Kizoku Haishutsu, Mizu to Tochi no Kansetsu Shiyoryo (Co-dependence of Environmental Load in East Asia – CO_2 Emission Attribution and Indirect Use of Water and Land)", in A. Mori (ed.) *Higashi Asia no Keizai Hatten to Kankyo Seisaku* (*Economic Development and Environmental Policies in East Asia*). Kyoto: Minerva Shobo, pp. 40–57.

Stiglitz, J. (2006) *Making Globalization Work*. New York: W. W. Norton.

Teranishi, S. (1992) *Chikyuukankyomondai no Seiji-Keizai-Gaku* (*Political Economy of Global Environmental Issues*). Tokyo: Toyo-Keizai Publishing.

Terao, T. and K. Otsuka (eds) (2008) *Asia ni okeru Bunkenka to Kankyo Seisaku* (*Decentralization and Environmental Policy in Asia*). Chiba: Institute of Developing Economies.

Ueta, K. (1991) "Jizokuteki Hatten to Kokusai Kankyo Seisaku (Sustainable Development and International Environmental Policy)", in K. Ueta, H.Ochiai, Y. Kitabatake and S. Teranishi (eds) *Kankyo Keizai Gaku* (*Environmental Economics*). Tokyo: Yuhikaku Publishing, pp. 233–249.

——— (1993) "The Lessons of Japan's Environmental Policy: An Economist's Viewpoint", *Japan Review of International Affairs* 7(1), pp. 30–49.

Watanabe, T., M. Shimoda and K. Fujikawa (2009) "Higashi Asia no Kokusai Bungyo Kozo no Henka – Fuka Kachi no Kyukyokuteki Bunpai (Changes in International Specialization Structure in East Asia – Ultimate Distribution of Added Value)", in A. Mori (ed.) *Higashi Asia no Keizai Hatten to Kankyo Seisaku* (*Economic Development and Environmental Policies in East Asia*). Kyoto: Minerva Shobo, pp. 21–39.

2-3

A new paradigm for economic growth

Takamitsu Sawa

2-3-1 Introduction

Lester Brown (1998), the renowned global environmental expert and activist, has described growth for growth's sake as no different from the growth strategy of a cancer cell. This comes as a wake-up call from the environmentalist community, warning against a growth ideology that has spread worldwide and flourished like an uncontrollable weed since the closing days of the twentieth century. Proliferating cancer cells eat away at the organs of their host and ultimately destroy the internal systems essential for its continued existence. Unbridled economic growth can be expected to destroy our global ecosystem in much the same way.

A review of economic history leaves no question that Japan's post-war growth strategy of catching up with and surpassing the advanced industrialized nations of the West did in fact fulfil the hopes and aspirations of a population strongly yearning for affluence. However, at some point this quest for economic growth morphed into an end unto itself, and in the process national economic policy appeared increasingly fixated on the single goal of boosting growth in real GDP. In the early 1990s environmental problems of global scale came into the limelight and alarms began to sound over the ideology of endless growth. But members of the business community banded together in a revolt against the green tax and other environmental protection initiatives that were brought out by the government (chiefly through the Ministry of the Environment). They did not question the logic of these initiatives, but simply adopted a reactionary stance, insisting that "growth for growth's sake", as depicted by Brown, was a must.

The ideological banner of the business community displayed the slogan "Economic growth, the essence of happiness". Assertions that GDP growth would suffer can be cited as the primary reason why the business community was against the proposed green tax. In reality, if the tax were implemented, higher production costs could, for example, be expected to hurt the steel industry's competitiveness in the international market because steel manufacturing processes are a major source of carbon dioxide (CO_2) emissions. It is obvious that the steel industry would be opposed to the green tax, given its perspective as a potential "victim". However, as an excuse for that opposition, trotting out the argument that the tax would be detrimental to growth in GDP seems questionable. Could it be that opponents of the green tax want to portray it as something that would be harmful to the nation as a whole?

Opposing the tax on grounds it would be detrimental to the entire national economy sounds like an assertion from a position with justice on its side. As a statement representing the position of business organizations and private firms, though, one cannot help but perceive of it as an attempt to shift the focus of debate. It is incumbent upon individuals and groups to pressure the government to do something about anything that causes them harm. In fact, the steel industry and other energy-intensive manufacturing sectors in Sweden have been exempted from the green (carbon) tax now applied there to the consumption of raw coal and fuel oil.

Let me return to Lester Brown (ibid.). He stated that he is calling not for zero growth, but for a review of the content or nature of growth. In some fields even more growth is still needed: for example, renewable energies, the recycling industry, energy-efficient vehicles and power-saving consumer appliances, to name a few. On the other side of the coin, we have resource-wasteful industries and other sectors that need to be downsized. (For example, following the oil shocks of recent decades, aluminium production – a heavy consumer of electric power – virtually disappeared from Japan, where the price of electricity is high, and shifted to countries like Ireland and Canada, where electricity generation is based on renewable sources and prices are accordingly lower.)

Sustainable economic growth incorporates the untraditional idea of meeting the needs of the current generation while devoting consideration to meeting the needs of future generations as well. In effect, we are faced with the task of achieving a paradigm shift in economic growth that abandons the traditional ideology of growth for growth's sake.

In this chapter, I hope to demonstrate that building a new economic system centred on the primary goal of global environmental protection will provide the biggest investment opportunity of our time. Indeed, measures to protect the global environment and, above all, help us alleviate and adapt to climate change are not only reconcilable with the goal of economic growth, but without investments in these areas (including household consumption in durable goods) the twenty-first century may go down in history as a "lost century" with no economic growth whatsoever. Japan has gained global distinction as a leader in the field of energy conservation technology. Assuming this to be the case, it would allow the conclusion that Japanese technological prowess will provide a crucial springboard for economic growth through the current century. Indeed, the companies that win out in the competition to develop new power-saving technologies will be best positioned to form a new industrial engine of growth in this century for Japan's economy and the global economy at large.

2-3-2 The twentieth century as the century of CO_2

It has been a while since the twenty-first century earned the title "century of the environment". However, it should be noted this designation has two meanings. In one sense, it implies that the global environment will likely display serious levels of pollution and degradation, with increasingly severe climate change in particular, coupled with an unprecedented increase in levels of public concern directed towards environmental problems. In a second sense, the label underlines hopes that progress made in overcoming environmental hurdles will help set the stage for fresh economic growth and development in this century.

Perhaps this second point deserves further elaboration. Usually, innovations in technology emerge in response to some sort of shortage (limitation) or constraint, and eventually spur further economic advancement and growth. The twentieth century was an age abundant with innovation. To give but a few tangible examples, we witnessed a significant acceleration in flows of human resources, capital, material and information, vastly improved convenience in daily life thanks to modern consumer appliances, the debut of petrochemical-based substitutes for natural rubber, textiles and leather, the eradication of numerous diseases, gains in farm productivity, the installation of new power transmission grids and telecommunications networks, advances in the speed and mobility of digital communications and the construction of modern high-rise buildings. In every case, such innovations demonstrated enormous effectiveness in overcoming a variety of human shortcomings (limits) and removing constraints.

These innovations led to the debut of an array of new products, the majority of which ran on the fossil fuels or electric power that humanity had harnessed by the end of the nineteenth century. In that context, the twentieth century may be termed the "century of electric power and oil", but the other side of that banner would have to bear the title "century of CO_2". The point is that we acquired our enormous levels of wealth and affluence through the continued and increasing release of CO_2 emissions into our atmosphere.

With the end of the twentieth century drawing near, in December 1997 the Kyoto Protocol was adopted after extensive debate and with country-specific differentials included. This agreement mandated that over a 12-year span beginning in 2008, all of the advanced industrialized nations achieve a minimum 5 per cent reduction – compared to 1990 levels – in the five-year moving average (an amount combining the converted CO_2 equivalents of an assortment of greenhouse gases – GHGs) of their GHG emissions, which of course included CO_2, the component arguably most emblematic of the century. Personally, I viewed the adoption of the Kyoto Protocol as signalling the end of the twentieth-century variety of industrial civilization. However, that view was in the minority, at least in Japan. The majority view was, to summarize, that the Kyoto Protocol seemed equivalent to the so-called unequal treaties of Japan's Ansei era, in that it unfairly obligates Japan to achieve further emissions cuts despite the progress it has already made in the arena of energy conservation.

2-3-3 The basis for President Bush's withdrawal announcement

On 24 March 2001 President George W. Bush startled the international community with his bombshell announcement that the United States would withdraw from the Kyoto Protocol. In retrospect today, this decision would prove to be nothing less than a precedent for the unilateralist policies the Bush administration embraced. President Bush cited two reasons for the decision: the Kyoto Protocol was imperfect in that it did not mandate any GHG emission curbs by China or other developing countries; and it could be expected to do serious harm to the US economy. Given that these were two of the arguments opponents of the Kyoto Protocol had voiced years earlier, Bush's action left many wondering, with suspicion, "What is he trying to do now?"

Furthermore, Bush's announcement constituted nothing less than a declaration of the – in my opinion mistaken – view that reductions in CO_2 emissions would inevitably sacrifice economic growth. However, I have reached the following conclusions based on what I think Bush was trying to say.

As an agreement mandating that the advanced industrialized nations achieve short-term reduction targets, the Kyoto Protocol could encumber the process of developing major technologies that are seriously effective in reducing emissions of CO_2. Consequently, over the medium and longer term, the protocol could do harm without providing any lasting benefit. In this context, major technologies would include those for space photovoltaics; high-temperature gas reactors; next-generation light-water reactors; carbon capture and storage technologies that capture the CO_2 in emissions from coal-fired power stations and similar facilities and store it underground; fuel cells; and methods for the large-scale and economical production of hydrogen.

To justify the reasoning that I have read into Bush's statements, the following propositions would have to be true. Climate change will not have an impact on the survival of humankind until concentrations of CO_2 in the atmosphere reach 550 ppm (the danger zone). Over the next 30 years, atmospheric CO_2 will not rise more than 2 ppm per year even if we continue to increase the volume of emissions at our current pace. Hence the concentration level will not exceed 440 ppm, giving us plenty of time before we reach the danger zone. In the next 30 years, it is practically assured that we will succeed in developing an assortment of major new technologies effective in curbing CO_2 emissions.

2-3-4 Adaptation to climate change

However, a series of subsequent events in climate change were more than enough to shake the rationale underpinning President Bush's withdrawal declaration. I cite a few examples below.

- Seventeen of the last 18 years have been among the hottest on record since 1850.
- Over 35,000 people died in the heatwave that struck Europe in 2003.
- Over 2,000 people died in torrential rains that flooded parts of India and Bangladesh in 2004.
- Over 1,700 people died when Hurricane Katrina hit the United States in 2005.
- Russia has experienced an epidemic of forest fires caused by the leakage of methane gas into the atmosphere from melting tundra fields.
- China has been dealt a double blow: flooding in the Yangtze River basin and drought in the Yellow River basin.
- Rising ocean levels attributable to melting mountain glaciers are contributing to the salinization of drinking water in island countries.
- In 2006 drought conditions reduced wheat crop yields in Australia by 60 per cent.
- In 2008 over 100,000 people lost their lives in cyclones that struck Myanmar.

Actually, it appears there may be no scientific basis for the generally accepted value of 550 ppm as the lower threshold of the danger zone for CO_2 concentrations in the atmosphere. I would venture it is nothing more than a rough estimate based on the 280 ppm concentration that was measured prior to the Industrial Revolution. Professional meteorologists I have consulted have not dispelled this doubt. Currently, Earth's atmospheric CO_2 concentration is around 380–390 ppm. The manifestations of climate change listed above are indisputable facts. Although my opinions are those of a layman without professional training in the field of meteorology, I believe it more accurate to view the cited 550 ppm threshold concentration not as a value that determines whether we will experience climate change or not, but as the value at which the frequency and intensity of climatic anomalies can be expected to increase as atmospheric GHG concentrations rise. Assuming that to be the case, we must not fail to act to the best of our ability to mitigate climate change.

Not all countries around the globe will necessarily experience rising sea levels, damage from storms and flooding, food shortages and other adverse effects of climate change on an equal scale. Many developing countries are at risk of being impacted more severely. Let me paraphrase Rajendra Pachauri, chair of the Intergovernmental Panel on Climate Change (IPCC), as follows. Precisely because it was an economic power, the Netherlands succeeded in protecting its lands from water submersion by building dikes along its coastline. However, as a poor country, Bangladesh cannot do the same thing. In other words, the principal victims of climate change will be the poor nations of the world, and in particular the relatively impoverished classes of citizens residing in those countries.

It was on this understanding that the international Adaptation Fund was established to assist developing countries impacted by the adverse effects of climate change. Advanced industrial nations are obligated to finance this fund with 2 per cent of their certified emission reductions (CERs) through the clean development mechanism. For now, funds obtained through the trade and exchange of issued CERs on the EU's emissions credit market are to be utilized as aid financing for climate adaptation projects in developing countries.

2-3-5 Franklin D. Roosevelt and Barack Obama

In 2007, the tenth anniversary of the adoption of the Kyoto Protocol, the IPCC published its Fourth Assessment Report and concluded it "very likely", with an accuracy of 90 per cent or more, that rising levels of GHGs in the atmosphere are causally correlated with climate change. Additionally, in his book *An Inconvenient Truth* and the documentary by the same name, former US vice-president Al Gore (2006) brought to light the threats posed by climate change. The Nobel Peace Prize was awarded to both Mr Gore and the IPCC in 2007.

During the 2008 US presidential race, climate change became one of the issues for debate. On the campaign trail, Democratic Party candidate Barack Obama declared that by the year 2050 the United States would cut its GHG emissions by 80 per cent. By contrast, his Republican opponent, John McCain, declared an emissions reduction target of 60 per cent. In declaring their support for such sweeping reductions, both candidates pledged to distance themselves from the course taken by President Bush and demonstrated their credentials as members of the anyone-but-Bush camp on this issue.

Nonetheless, the two candidates were far apart in the means they would use to achieve these reductions. Whereas Obama voiced his support for the development of renewable energy technologies and fuel-efficient vehicles, McCain assigned nuclear power the central role in his strategy for the reduction of GHGs. Following his landslide victory in the November 2008 election, President Obama assumed his new post amidst an international financial meltdown and global recession that together have been dubbed the worst economic crisis in a hundred years, and in doing so drew comparisons to President Franklin D. Roosevelt, who assumed office in March 1933 at the height of the Great Depression.

Under his "New Deal" package of economic programs, President Roosevelt implemented sweeping revisions to the free-market style of economic management that had been followed to that point in time, and boldly moved forward with a set of arguably socialist-oriented initiatives backed by the modality of active federal government intervention in the marketplace. Several specific examples may be cited: the Emergency Banking Relief Act; public works projects comprising mainly the construction of 32 multipurpose dams under the supervision of the Tennessee Valley Authority; enactment of the National Industrial Recovery Act, which was designed to protect companies with anti-trust legislation and guarantee the labour unions collective bargaining rights; and expansion of the social security system.

Despite widespread misunderstanding, the programmes of the New Deal were by no means an implementation of the fiscal-stimulus-based recovery strategies that British economist John Maynard Keynes had advocated. Keynes published his *General Theory of Employment, Interest and Money* in 1936. The Roosevelt-Keynes connection boiled down to the after-the-fact support that Keynes offered in making the case for the effectiveness of Roosevelt's New Deal policies and programmes.

Be that as it may, opinions have been mixed as to the actual effectiveness of the New Deal. Keynes himself even criticized it for the supposedly half-hearted scale of its efforts at fiscal stimulus. Perhaps it had demonstrated that it would be difficult, if not impossible, to build a democratic state based on the "presuppositions of Harvey Road", namely the notion that the policies of the British government would continue to be influenced by a small group of highly knowledgeable élites exercising their powers of persuasion. (The "Harvey Road" designation comes from the address of Keynes's birthplace on Harvey Road, a neighbourhood of élites.) Although the US president has veto power over legislative bills passed by Congress, he cannot implement policies and programmes without having them deliberated by Congress.

It is readily understandable that many Americans felt uncomfortable with the New Deal programmes, given the strongly socialist orientation on which some were based. Both then and now, many economists who espouse free-market principles, namely the notion that free and open market competition always leads to the best solutions, have been critical of the New Deal (i.e. asserting it was ineffective). On the other hand, Keynes and other economists who considered the markets to be imperfect were essentially supportive of the New Deal and its programmes.

In the final analysis, while the New Deal succeeded in bringing the unemployment rate down to a mid-teens percentage from a peak of almost 25 per cent, that was the limit of its effectiveness. The free-market economists accordingly asserted that the New Deal was of questionable benefit overall, and that a full-fledged economic recovery would have to wait until the Second World War. The Keynesians, however, argued that a pronounced improvement in the unemployment rate was not forthcoming because the New Deal programmes (packages of domestic stimulus harnessing fiscal and monetary policies) simply did not go far enough.

2-3-6 Keynesian economics reborn

In October 2008 the US House of Representatives voted down the proposed Emergency Economic Stabilization Act. Although it later approved a revised version, one had to respect the policy coherence shown by the free marketers in the conservative ranks of Congress. The amended version of the Financial Stabilization Act may be summarized as follows. From a total budget of $700 billion in public funding, it earmarks $250 billion to be injected into the banking sector for acquisitions of preferred stock, etc. In short, the government plans to buy up non-performing loan assets now burdening the banks. This will expand the supply of liquidity to the financial marketplace. Further, the government will guarantee the liabilities from interbank transactions. It will assist fundraising through the issuance of money market funds and buy corporate commercial paper. It will strengthen its facilities for depositor protection and inject public funds into insurance companies (AIG in particular). Additionally, it plans to guarantee mortgage loans in an effort to slow the pace of home foreclosures.

Not only that, but in December 2008 the Automotive Industry Relief Act failed to pass in the Senate and was abandoned, with only the essential relief measures integrated into the Financial Stabilization Act instead. In effect, the federal government was to use taxpayer funds to bail out companies that had failed in a free and competitive marketplace. This was fundamentally unacceptable to conservative members of Congress who put their faith in the free-market system. I want to express my heartfelt respect for the tenacious consistency of these conservatives in sticking to their principles and ideals in the face of both a US-triggered international financial crisis and a global recession.

Following the September 2008 Lehman shock (the business bankruptcy of the investment bank Lehman Brothers), the repercussions of the international financial crisis spread to the real economy, confronting not only Japan, the United States and Europe but also the emerging economies and developing nations with a sharp contraction in domestic demand. It would not be overstating the case to describe this as the arrival of a global-scale recession. Surprisingly, the national economy hit hardest by this development has been Japan, a country that had suffered comparatively insignificant damage from the meltdown in subprime mortgage loan-backed securities. In the October–December quarter of 2008 and the January–March quarter of 2009, Japan's real economic growth rate (based on preliminary estimates) literally nosedived, measuring a negative 12.1 per cent and negative 15.2 per cent, respectively, in annualized terms. This can only be interpreted as a stark reminder of the Japanese economy's heavy dependence on foreign demand. In fact, the January 2009 reading for the current account balance (the balance of trade in goods and services plus net factor income and net unilateral transfers from abroad) posted its first deficit in 13 years. On 9 March the Nikkei stock index closed at 7,086.03 points, its lowest level in over 26 years. Prices on the New York Stock Exchange later rebounded, and the Tokyo Stock Exchange followed suit as it usually does, with prices eventually turning around and shifting into an upward trend. In May 2009 the unemployment rate reached 5.2 per cent, but left the impression it would eventually surpass the 5.5 per cent reading set in 2003.

Practically all the economists in government, the financial community and academia who had been champions of free-market capitalism up to early autumn 2008 are now crossing over *en masse* to the camp of the Keynesians, who posit that monetary loosening and fiscal stimulus are the only ways to offset a shortfall in domestic demand. In stating that he will not refrain from issuing deficit-financing bonds as a measure to resolve the crisis, even Kaoru Yosano, a proponent of fiscal discipline and minister of finance and minister of state for financial services and economic and fiscal policy, has signalled that he has converted to the Keynesian ideology. The situation is that serious.

2-3-7 The Green New Deal declaration

Before allowing the discussion to go off on a tangent, let me return to President Obama. In his inaugural address, Obama demonstrated his commitment to a Green New Deal with the following comments (paraphrased). America will run its automobiles and factories with energy sources derived from solar, wind and geothermal power. This is within the realm of possibility and something America must do. Furthermore, over the next three years we will take action to double the production of renewable energy sources so that America can start building a clean-energy economy. At least 75 per cent of all federal government buildings will be rebuilt. We will improve the energy efficiency of 2 million American households and cut the cost of fuel for consumers and taxpayers by several billion dollars. In the process, we will bring in sufficient revenues and put our citizens to work in long-term jobs: for example, jobs installing solar panels and wind turbines, and jobs building fuel-efficient cars and energy-efficient structures. Specifically, we will generate more employment and develop new energy technologies that put us on the path to a more energy-efficient, cleaner and safer world.

In short, President Obama pledged to move forward with innovations in technology for the utilization of renewable energies and to implement countermeasures against climate change. In his internet address on 24 January 2009, Obama detailed proposals for a public works project-based strategy against climate change, specifically pledging to double the production of wind, solar, biofuel and other renewable energy resources in only three years and lay a combined 4,800 km of new power transmission line infrastructure. He further stated that his administration would invest \$2 billion over the next 10 years to create jobs for 5 million new green-collar workers. The federal government is in the process of providing tens of millions of dollars in emergency relief funding to the troubled automakers GM and Chrysler on the condition they accelerate their efforts to implement technological innovations in the development and production of environmentally friendly automobiles. The steep drop in auto sales is emblematic of the current US recession. Auto sales volume for the month of February 2009 was down 40 per cent from its comparable level a year earlier. Consider that the weight of a single car alone exceeds a metric tonne. The slump in car sales has also severely impacted industries in a wide range of materials-related sectors, from steel and non-ferrous metals to glass, chemical products and rubber. In America, the automobile is an essential commodity; it is also considered to be a durable product. That is why auto sales volume in general can be expected to drop abruptly if the average replacement purchase cycle is extended by several years.

The US research firm JD Power & Associates projected 2009 vehicle sales volume in the United States would shrink 13 per cent from the year before, to around 11.4 million units (the lowest level since 1982). Worldwide, vehicle sales volume is expected to fall 8.2 per cent year on year (12.3 per cent in North America, 14.9 per cent in Europe, 3.9 per cent in South America and 2.6 per cent in Asia). However, for 2010 and 2011 JD Power projects sales will recover to around 13.4 million units and 14.7 million units, respectively, on the assumption that consumers have been putting off new purchases as a consequence of the extended replacement cycle.

Nonetheless, these projections could be too optimistic if one takes into account the reality that consumer credit checks for auto loans have become much tougher, the unemployment rate is higher, personal incomes are unlikely to grow and cars equipped with electronic components have a longer service life. Additionally, more consumers are buying used instead of new cars, another factor that suggests the increase in sales of new vehicles will be below forecasts, and the trend towards smaller cars is expected to gain momentum.

What is more, if a green (carbon) tax is enacted as one of the measures under the Green New Deal, it could conceivably spur increased replacement demand for fuel-efficient vehicles, in turn boosting market share for Toyota, Honda and other Japanese automakers and thus spelling deeper trouble for America's Big Three automakers.

2-3-8 Penetration of consumer durables to drive future growth

In retrospect, the twentieth century was the century of the automobile and oil. The current global recession bears historic significance because it heralds both the end to the twentieth century's industrial civilization and the dawn of a new civilization for the twenty-first century. As noted earlier, the spread of the automobile had a ripple effect on practically every industry in the materials sector. On top of that, it enabled industries in oil, non-life insurance and mass retailing to thrive and created huge numbers of gasoline station jobs. Fully aware of the automotive industry's value as a locomotive force for economic growth, many developing countries have devoted themselves to increasing domestic production of their own "national car".

Figure 2.3.1 shows that during the first half of Japan's economic boom era (July 1958 to November 1973), sharply rising penetration rates for refrigerators, washing machines, vacuum cleaners, black-and-white TVs and other electric appliances provided much of the locomotive fuel for economic growth. By 1970 the household penetration rate for most of these goods (other than vacuum cleaners) had surpassed 90 per cent and began to level off. Penetration by the "three Cs" – colour TVs, cars and coolers (air conditioners) – served as the next engine of growth. The oil shock of 1973 marked the end of the boom phase for Japan, and from that point the economy transitioned into an era of slowing growth (Figure 2.3.2). Annual economic growth (real GDP growth) averaged 9.4 per cent during the boom phase. Although it dropped by more than half, to 4.1 per cent, during the slowdown, that still amounted to a more than adequately rapid pace of growth compared to the average 2 per cent registered by the advanced industrial countries of Europe and North America at the time. During this period the Japanese economy began to assume a heightened presence in international trade. At the same time, exports of Japanese-made merchandise rose sharply and trade tensions with the United States flared.

Let us examine the trend in the penetration of automobiles. Although it measured no more than 40 per cent in 1975, by 1991 it had doubled to 80 per cent, but by 2008 was still hovering around the 80 per cent level. The reality is that it is rather expensive to own a car in Japan. Indeed, because the expenses associated with ownership – property taxes, garage space leasing fees, car inspection fees, car insurance, etc. – are so high, it seems unlikely that the penetration rate will ever top 90 per cent. By comparison, most European countries have acted to lower the cost of ownership but have increased the cost associated with driving (gasoline taxes). In terms of reducing CO_2 emissions, Europe's regulatory approach is better: even if a relatively high cost of ownership keeps the household penetration rate below 90 per cent, there is less incentive to reduce the distance driven per car (i.e. curb unnecessary driving) if gasoline is inexpensive. Conversely, if you raise the price of fuel, the incentive to reduce distance driven is much stronger. In fact, by some estimates, the total volume of gasoline consumed can be cut by a margin of 10 per cent or more using this approach, even in an economy with a hypothetical 100 per cent car ownership rate.

Looking at Figure 2.3.1 again, note that the penetration rate for air conditioners, cars, VCRs and certain other items reached the saturation point around the year 2000. Cell phones, personal computers, digital cameras and DVD players and recorders are the key consumer durables that

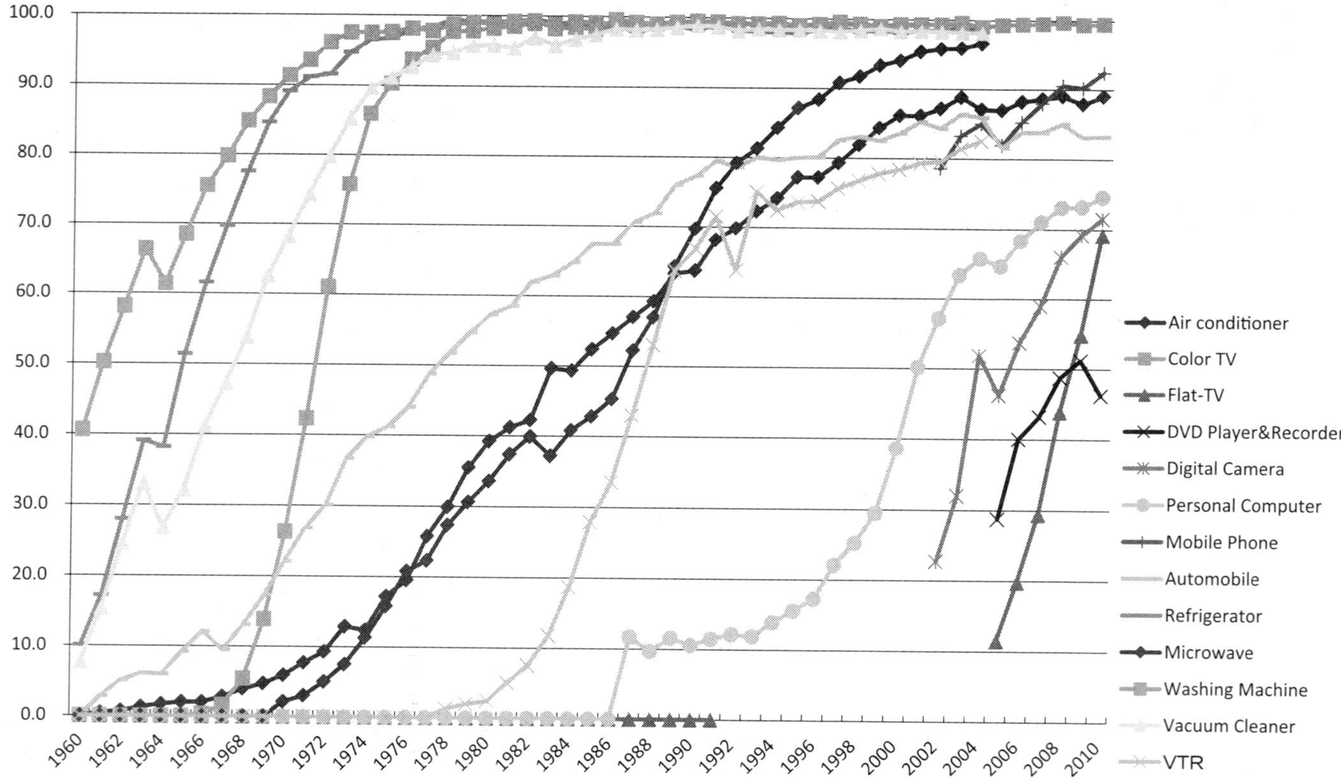

Figure 2.3.1 Trend in the household penetration rate for key consumer durables
Source: Cabinet Office, Government of Japan.

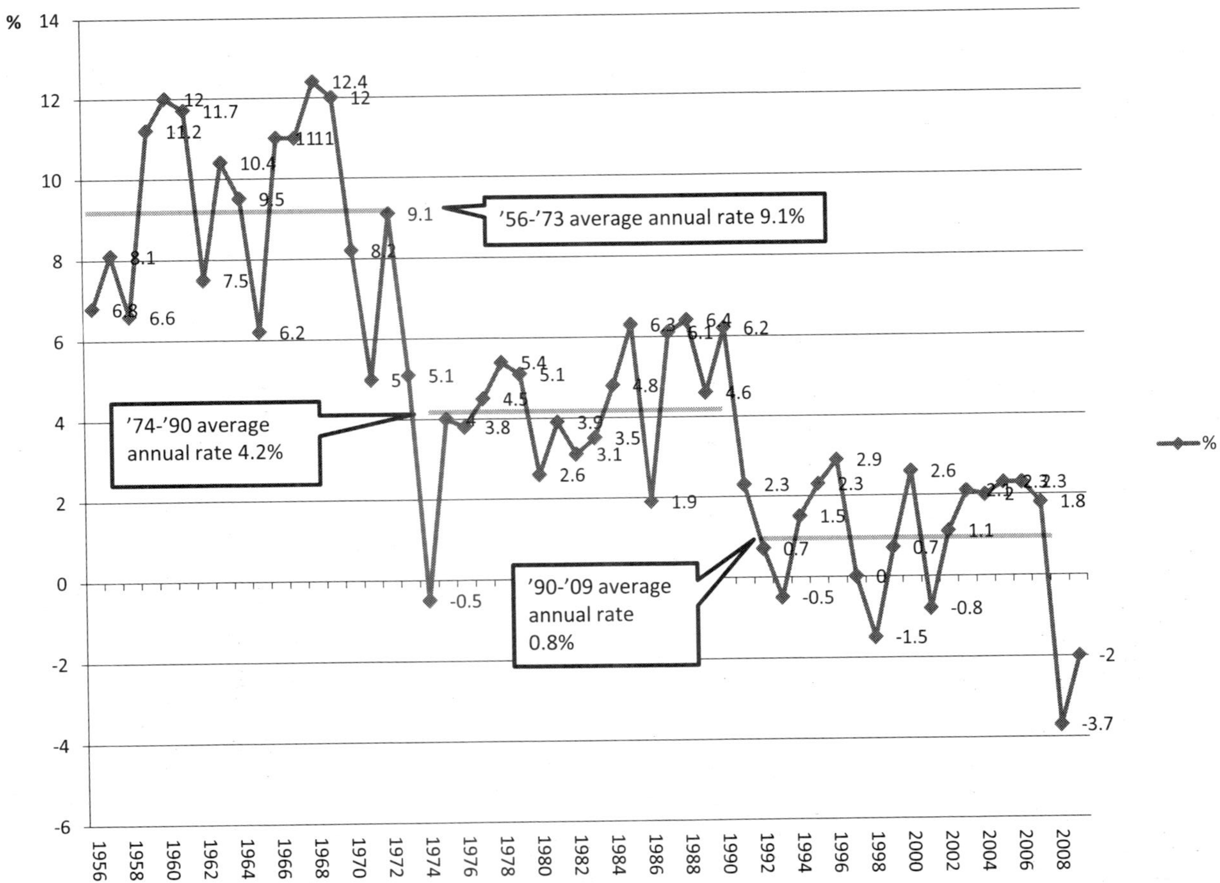

Figure 2.3.2 Trend in the real economic growth rate
Source: Cabinet Office, Government of Japan.

have shown strong penetration in more recent years. Now compare the trends for cars and digital cameras. As mentioned, cars have an enormous ripple effect on other industries, but what about the ripple effect from digital cameras? Manufacturers of electronic components are about the only industry that has benefited from the household penetration of digital cameras. From 2000 to 2007 real economic growth averaged only 1.3 per cent a year in Japan, effectively highlighting the poor ripple effect that digital merchandise has had on related industrial sectors.

Such comparisons help to bring the implications and significance of the Green New Deal into better focus. What new consumer durables will be the next wave to follow on the penetration of digital goods? My best guess is they will be none other than energy and environmentally related products.

2-3-9 What needs to be done to facilitate the penetration of solar panels?

Let us explore the situation with solar photovoltaic panels. Currently, the household penetration rate for solar panels in Japan stands at less than 1 per cent. The reason for this low rate is clear. The solar panels that are installed on the roof of a standard-size Japanese home generate no more than 3.0–3.5 kW of power, on average. However, the cost of installing a set of solar panels on the roof of an existing home is around ¥2.3 million. Thanks to incentives in the form of programmes that enabled solar-panel-equipped households to sell their surplus daytime electricity to power companies at a price equivalent to the market price for electricity, not to mention government subsidies up to 2005 for households that installed solar panels, Japan ranked number one worldwide in terms of total solar-generated power (in kW). However, with the termination of subsidies in 2006, the pace of solar panel penetration in Japan slowed sharply.

The Fukuda Vision unveiled prior to the 2008 Toyako summit incorporated a set of ambitious targets for national solar-generated power: a 10-fold increase by 2020 and a 40-fold increase by 2030. This prompted the Ministry of Economy, Trade and Industry to include funding in its 2009 budget request for the purpose of reinstating the former subsidy programme. However, with subsidies set to range around ¥210,000–250,000 per household, it is questionable whether this new programme will actually provide any useful incentive.

Germany and other European countries have demonstrated startling gains with the household penetration rate for solar panels under a "feed-in tariff" (FiT) framework they inaugurated to require power utilities to buy electricity generated with renewable energy sources (such as solar photovoltaics, wind power, biomass, etc.). For example, Germany revised its renewable energy laws in 2004, mandating that power utilities buy electricity generated with renewable energy sources at a fixed price (equivalent to triple the market price for electricity) for a period of 20 years following generating facility installation. This has had the effect of spurring a sharp increase in the household penetration rate for solar panels.

As of 2007, a total of 46 states or districts in 18 of the 25 EU countries had adopted FiT frameworks. At a press conference given following a cabinet meeting on 24 February 2009, Toshihiro Nikai, the minister of economy, trade and industry, announced that an agreement had been reached with Japan's Federation of Electric Power Companies on the adoption of a FiT framework in Japan, mandating that power utilities buy the surplus power generated by household solar panel installations at double the market price for electricity. The proposed framework emulates the German version, in that the cost of purchasing surplus electricity will be borne by the power industry (and offset through electricity rate hikes). Nonetheless, it deserves commendation as a bold step forward. In years past, I recommended that Japan adopt a FiT framework of its own. However, the idea of building a consensus for consumer sharing of the related costs through price hikes was viewed with pessimism. One of the strengths of the FiT approach is that it entails no administrative costs because the billing software applications that power companies provide for the preparation of invoices need only slight modification. By contrast, the provision of government subsidies entails significant administrative costs.

2-3-10 Stationary fuel cells and electric cars

Stationary fuel cells hit the market on 1 May 2009. Right now, their penetration rate is essentially zero. They generate heat and electricity by chemically combining atmospheric oxygen with hydrogen derived from natural gas, leaving water as a by-product (water electrolysis in reverse). Fuel cells are designed for cogeneration applications that supply hot water and electricity. On-site power generation is possible, and utility fee burdens can be effectively reduced if hospitals and hotels with extensive demand for heat install large fuel-cell systems while homes install smaller systems. Fuel-cell systems for home use are priced at about ¥3.46 million and would generate annual cost savings of around ¥50,000–60,000 in utility fees per household (according to estimates posted on Tokyo Gas Company's website). Although subsidies of up to ¥1.4 million are available, at this price point such systems currently are not even close to being economically worthwhile. Still, there is no question that the cost benefits of mass production will emerge as these systems come into more widespread use in the years ahead. In any event, supportive measures by the government will be essential from the outset.

Mitsubishi Motors began selling an electric vehicle (EV) in 2009, while Nissan Motors plans to bring a version of its own to market in 2010. Toyota has announced that it will introduce a new plug-in hybrid vehicle (PHV) in 2010. Mitsubishi's car, the i-MiEV, has the following performance characteristics. If charged overnight for seven hours from a 200 V power source, it will store 16 kWh of electricity in its on-board lithium-ion battery system. One kilowatt-hour is enough to drive the car for about 10 km. In other words, the car may be driven up to 160 km on a single charge. Furthermore, it has a rated top speed of around 130 kph (according to data on Mitsubishi Motors' website). Its rated driving range and top speed are certainly adequate for everyday use. And considering that the night-time electricity rate runs around ¥7 per kWh, the driving cost associated with electric cars is far less than that for their gasoline-powered counterparts. Even so, the EV will be priced significantly higher than a comparable gasoline-powered vehicle in the same size class. Hence, in the absence of government incentives aimed at promoting their popularization, the risk is that such cars will remain a luxury item out of reach for the majority of households. A comparison of CO_2 emissions reveals that electric cars emit about 420 grams of CO_2 for every 10 km travelled (emissions per kWh), whereas gasoline-powered cars emit 2,300 grams. Accordingly, an electric car that is driven 10,000 km per year will give an annual reduction of 1,880 tonnes in CO_2 emissions.

Two initiatives should be effective in encouraging the popularization of EVs and PHVs. First, pro rata excise tax and property tax rates for automobiles should be introduced on the basis of fuel efficiency (with drastically lower taxes for fuel-efficient cars and higher taxes for cars with poor fuel efficiency). Second, the government should enact a green tax and raise gasoline prices. In both cases, the goal will be to lower the life-cycle cost of electric cars while boosting the incentive to purchase them.

One point, though, must be acknowledged. Increased sales of EVs and PHVs in Japan will have the effect of eroding sales volume for gasoline-powered cars. As such, the trend in total unit vehicle sales will likely be unchanged. Nonetheless, if Japanese automakers gain a head start in the international race to develop these cars, exports of EVs and PHVs can be expected to provide a foundation for renewed economic prosperity in Japan.

Additionally, initiatives to promote the improved energy efficiency of buildings and homes will be effective in terms of both mitigating climate change and spurring economic growth. The greenscaping of building rooftops and walls, changing from incandescent to fluorescent and eventually LED lighting, the installation of double-glazed windows and similar measures will contribute to reductions in electricity consumption and reduced CO_2 emissions in turn, and in the short term will be a godsend to the ailing and increasingly ossified construction industry. Although we need measures to adapt to climate change, including civil engineering projects to reinforce infrastructure against increasingly common torrential rains, the benefits as measured in domestic demand will be huge.

2-3-11 Closing remarks

Because the refrigerators, TVs, cars, air conditioners and other consumer durables that fuelled Japan through its economic boom years provided convenience and comfort that virtually anyone would perceive and enjoy, there were always consumers ready to spend good money to acquire these goods. These products possessed what sociologist-economist Thorstein Veblen referred to as the "demonstration effect". This was why, as illustrated in Figure 2.3.1, the household penetration rates for products of this nature shot up so sharply until they had reached their saturation point.

That being said, renewable energy sources and new environmentally related products do not always engender significant benefits or comforts. Using electricity generated by rooftop solar panels to watch TV is hardly any different from using electricity purchased from a power company to do the same thing. The only benefit gained from the former is the sense of satisfaction: you are "doing something good for the planet". Furthermore, in general terms one cannot expect these high-priced durables to achieve high penetration rates if left to market forces alone. Granting incentives for the purchase of solar panels or eco-cars will be a role for the government.

In recent years the voices of the free-market capitalists have faded into distant cursing noises, while a tone of heightened assertiveness seems to colour the voices of the Keynesians who support increased fiscal outlays. If Keynes were alive today and someone asked him to give his prescription for the current global recession, his response might be as follows: "Fiscal stimulus packages are a good idea but we must not err in the way we put them to work. Use the money for investments in the future, including education, healthcare, the environment and energy. I do not recall ever declaring that we need big government. Big and smart government is what we need now!"

"Green New Deal" is a phrase that has been gaining fashion even in Japan of late. To ensure that it does not end up yet another empty slogan, I urge that our smart government take swift action to prime our markets with clever new incentives backed by preferential tax rates and other measures.

REFERENCES

Brown, Lester (1998) *State of the World 1998*. New York: W. W. Norton.
Gore, Al (2006) *An Inconvenient Truth: The Planetary Emergency of Global Warming and What We Can Do About It*. Emmaus, PA: Rodale Press.
IPCC (2007) *Fourth Assessment Report*. New York: Cambridge University Press.
Keynes, John Maynard (1936) *General Theory of Employment, Interest and Money*. New York: Harcourt, Brace.

3

Paradigm shift of socio-economic development

3-1

Sustainable development and social common capital

Kazuhiro Ueta

3-1-1 Introduction

Many people are sincerely attracted to the concept of sustainable development, although it is known to have many different definitions. The definition most often cited, and which has brought this concept to the attention of the world, is that provided by the UN World Commission on Environment and Development, commonly known as the Brundtland Commission, which states that "sustainable development is development that meets the needs of the present without compromising the ability of future generations to meet their own needs" (World Commission on Environment and Development, 1987).

The Brundtland Commission was originally proposed by Japan: rather than being just a collection of economists' views, its report (ibid.), which extols sustainable development, also includes plenty of analysis and opinions from non-economic perspectives, such as international politics. In other words, although there are keywords describing what sustainable development is, there are no passages that give economic definitions or explain systems in economic terms. This makes it possible for a variety of different views on sustainable development to be presented (Ueta, 2010).

For the principles of sustainable development to be specifically and practically utilized, there must be a variety of practical approaches and a further deepening of the theory. This chapter focuses on social common capital as the key concept in mediating between the theory and practice of sustainable development. As is well known, the concept of social common capital has been pioneered and promoted by Hirofumi Uzawa (2005). In addition to attempting to interpret and formulate sustainable development using the concept of social common capital, this chapter will also evaluate the issues surrounding global warming based on this perspective.

3-1-2 Economic models of sustainable development

Since the release of the World Commission on Environment and Development (1987) report, sustainable development has extended in many directions. As theoretical and empirical research on the subject has progressed, more practical measures have also spread. Specific details have begun to take shape: sustainable cities, sustainable transportation, sustainable farming, sustainable architecture ... the list is endless. Another practical measure has been the treatment of sustainable development as a concept within laws and treaties.

Raising the issue of sustainable development brings with it the expectation of system reform and practical policies, but one of the key ways in which to turn the concept into a practical reality is by making it a social norm. In the real world of international and local communities, through treaties and declarations, specific norms and frameworks are increasingly being implemented in city planning measures. Beginning with the 1992 Rio Declaration on Environment and Development, Agenda 21 and the UN Framework Convention on Climate Change, the concept of sustainable development has been adopted in many treaties and declarations. Each of these may have slight differences, but they are virtually unanimous in indicating that sustainable development includes three elements (Otsuka, 2006: 48–49).

Firstly, any use of the natural environment must be sustainable, and that use must preserve ecosystems and be kept within the carrying capacity of the natural environment. The consideration of the environment and resources (ecological prudence) should be regarded as a legitimate part of all decision-making processes, and on this basis should be fully integrated with the consideration of economic factors. In order for this to occur, we must identify the reasons why the environment and resources have not been considered in economic activities in the past, and review the development processes and evaluation criteria that individual economic actors use in making decisions, so that these decisions can be based on environmentally sound and sustainable standards.

The second element is intergenerational equity. Principle 3 of the Rio Declaration states that "the right to development must be fulfilled so as to equitably meet the developmental and environmental needs of present and future generations". Exercising the right to develop in the present greatly impacts the environment and the development potential of not only the present but future generations as well, and the exercise of these rights must take into account generational equality. For example, the impact on climate change of present-day greenhouse gas emissions is still decades away, and in some cases these effects may take on a very large scale in more than a century, making this a keen point in intergenerational equity.

The third element is the realization of a fair international society with equity between North and South, including the eradication of poverty. Principle 5 of the Rio Declaration states that "All states and all people shall cooperate in the essential task of eradicating poverty as an indispensable requirement for sustainable development, in order to decrease the disparities in standards of living and better meet the needs of the majority of the people of the world." This issue cannot be discussed without some method for eradicating poverty and achieving equality in standards of living. Based on the fact that inequality of income has increased, the theory that the efficient distribution of resources by the market economic system would result in a trickle-down effect to eradicate poverty can be seen to be bankrupt. It is likely that the role of international organizations will expand in response to global issues such as environmental problems and poverty, but the important issue will be how well these organizations can facilitate the flow of funds so that they have the greatest redistributive effect. Evaluation of current official development assistance programmes will be an important part of this discussion.

There is no question that these three elements are all included in the concept of sustainable development, but at the same time they conflict in certain ways. While the sustainable development concept should be able to integrate these elements into a common theory, the way in which to achieve this is not yet clear.

In the first place, these elements alone are insufficient to ensure sustainable development. In particular, from an economic perspective it is important to add the issue of social efficiency. Of course, the sustainability of nature and society has been depleted by the kind of shortsighted and selfish pursuit of efficiencies seen in the past, so it is important that specific policy aims in the future include a consideration of the environment and resources, as well as a concept of social efficiency which focuses on the long term for future generations. The outputs of the economy and society should place more importance on non-monetary factors and not be limited to the decisions of the market economy (Stiglitz, Sen and Fitoussi, 2010). The evaluation of these outputs should also be based on their contribution to the "quality of life", and the degree to which people have been able to achieve their potential (Sen, 1985).

Combining all these elements is no easy task, but several attempts have been made. Here I introduce a typical example of these theories, the Dasgupta model. Dasgupta (2001) understands the Brundtland Commission definition of sustainable development as follows:

> The idea is that, relative to their respective demographic bases, each generation should bequeath to its successor at least as large a productive base as it inherited from its predecessor. If it were to do so, the economic possibilities facing the successor would be no worse than those it faced when inheriting productive assets from its predecessor.

Here, the productive base is defined as those goods that determine quality of life. Dasgupta argues that there are two methods for measuring the quality of life: to study its constituents, and to assign values to the individual determinants of the quality of life. The constituents include health, happiness, freedom to live and act, and, more broadly, fundamental human freedom.

Dasgupta places more importance on assigning value to the determinants of quality of life, as opposed to the individual elements that make it up. The determinant of quality of life is defined as the productive base that creates the goods and services that contribute to the quality of life. In other words, sustainable development is the same as the continuous improvement of per capita quality of life, but this does not measure quality of life *per se*, but rather changes in the production base that underlies the quality of life, in order to determine the sustainability of any given economy or society.

According to Dasgupta, the productive base of any given economy or society is equivalent to the combination of its capital assets and its infrastructure. So in order to determine the sustainability of a particular economy or society, it is necessary to determine whether the productive base that has created the society's quality of life is being left to future generations. However, in this respect GDP and the HDI (Human Development Index) can be misleading. This is because GDP ignores the depreciation of capital assets, which means that even if a country's GDP is increasing, it is possible that its productive base is being depleted. The same issue exists with the HDI (Dasgupta, 2007).

Capital assets are made up of human capital, man-made capital and knowledge, as well as natural capital. However, the productive base includes not only capital assets but also institutions. Here, institutions refer to the overall mechanism for allocating resources, including markets, communities, enterprises, households and governments. If capital assets are not combined with an appropriate institution, this will result in a reduction in the value of the productive base. Further, even if there is a temporary quantitative improvement in capital assets, it does not follow that this will equate to sustainable development unless there is an institution that can make use of it.

3-1-3 Productive base and social common capital

Dasgupta (ibid.) proposed a model which, based on a comparable population, estimates changes to the productive base of an economy for a given period, to determine whether or not a certain level of economic development is sustainable, and completed a simple empirical study based on this model. However, the policy implications of the model, for example in terms of using it to derive optimal investment for the future, and the relationship between capital assets and institutions still need to be investigated further. In doing so, the work of Hirofumi Uzawa on social common capital will be useful.

> Social common capital can be divided into the three main components of natural environment, social infrastructure, and institutional capital. The air, forests, rivers, and land of the natural environment; the roads, transportation infrastructure, water supply and sewerage, and gas and electricity etc of the social infrastructure; and the education, medical care and judicial and economic systems that make up the institutional capital all go to constitute important elements of social common capital. Both cities and rural areas are made up of a variety of social common capital. (Uzawa, 2000)

As opposed to Dasgupta's productive base, where the capital assets fundamentally expand the elements of production, Uzawa's social common capital model points to the systems and facilities that form the common base for both production activities and consumption activities. If we divide the scarce resources that constrain production, distribution and consumption into either social common capital or private capital, under Dasgupta's framework these are both considered together as simply capital assets. Thus any distinctions between the management and operation of private assets by individual economic actors from a private perspective and the management and operation of social common capital by society as a whole, for the benefit of the entire society, are simply made within the system. Of course, it could also be said that since it is difficult to separate capital assets from institutions, and since each individual capital asset operates in relation to a certain institution, it is not possible to remove them from the system for the purpose of discussing the capital assets in isolation.

Bringing Uzawa's concept of social common capital into Dasgupta's formulation could lead to the deepening of the content of institutions under the framework, as well as a deepening of the relationship between institutions and capital assets.

According to Uzawa (ibid.), social common capital is a social apparatus which makes it possible for the people of a particular country or region to have an abundant economic life, expand their culture and develop an attractive, stable and sustainable society. Based on what specific elements go to make up the social common capital, how it is managed and administered and what standards govern its use, as well as whether or not services are distributed, the social or economic structure of a particular country or region can be characterized.

Even if this social common capital is made up of scarce resources that are allowed to be managed privately, it is still the property of the society as a whole, and as such is managed and administered according to social criteria. In this way, social common capital contrasts scarce resources with the pure definition of private capital, but the specific composition is not determined in advance on theoretical grounds; rather it is determined by means of the political process, taking into account a variety of natural, historical, cultural, social, economic and technical elements.

In other words, social common capital can be said to provide the institutional conditions for the smooth function of the market system and the stable and practical distribution of income. According to Uzawa (ibid.), this capital should not be managed by bureaucrats under the organs of state, and must not be allowed to be affected by market conditions or the pursuit of profit. Each element must be managed and maintained by experts, based on established expertise and in accordance with professional norms.

Social common capital can be discussed on the basis of dividing it into the three elements of the natural environment, social infrastructure and institutional capital, but it can also be discussed as a single principle and a single concept. It should not be forgotten that it is also governed by various established principles (Mamiya, 2002). For example, the natural environment is regulated by biological and ecological factors such as reproductive processes, and therefore the time required to restock natural capital depends on the effects of biological, ecological and weather conditions. Due to its complexity, the rate of change over time of natural capital is fundamentally different to the way in which "capital" is depleted in the industrial sector.

Social common capital and its related services play an important role in fulfilling the basic rights of citizens, and are therefore "vital" to society. Scarce resources are themselves social common capital, and when these resources or their related services are vital to the fundamental rights of citizens as members of a national economy they should not be allowed to be privately controlled.

The fundamental rights of citizens are not necessarily straightforward to define. For different kinds of national economies they would naturally be different, and even for similar economies and societies the historical processes would differ. The process of social development, in a sense, can be said to be the process of diversity, or the enrichment of the basic rights of citizens.

For some specific scarce resources, it is fundamental to consider them social common capital and not private capital, depending on social or institutional conditions, and it is not necessary to view them only from economic or technical viewpoints. It is not always easy to determine which scarce resources should be regarded as private capital to be traded in the market and subjected to the profit motive, but which should be considered social common capital, to be constructed or managed by society.

Services that are generated from social common capital have two features. First, they can be enjoyed by individual economic actors, and the amount of these services that can be utilized can be chosen freely by individual actors. The second feature is the resulting congestion. The services that are generated from social common capital are considered public goods in an economic sense, but the Samuelson concept of the "collective consumption good" does not include these two features.

Another point on which the concept of public goods and social common capital differs is that while public goods are goods with the technical features of non-rivalness and non-excludability, the Uzawa social common capital is determined by political processes based on the conditions of different regions.

3-1-4 Social common capital and climate change

Social common capital is basically that property that is most crucial to individuals and society, and cannot be replaced with money. Therefore, sustainable development must enhance this common property in such a way that the enhanced society can be sustained. By considering sustainable development based on the principles of social common capital, a society must be developed that has an enhanced common base, not only in terms of the environment, but in terms of other common infrastructure such as education, healthcare, etc. In the same way, the financial system must perform a role as social common capital. To put it boldly, in order to achieve sustainable development, it is essential that social common capital is enhanced.

Social infrastructure such as roads and bridges, institutional capital such as education, medical care and financial system, and natural capital together make up social common capital. Of the three, natural capital forms the foundation for the very survival and development of human life.

As has already been mentioned, the climate is social common capital. It is easy to see that ours is an agricultural society. Just as we used to speak of the "O-Tentosama" that watched over us all, the climate existed outside of human society, as something that could not be changed. However, climate change now threatens to destroy the very foundations of current human activities and society. When thought of in this sense, sustainable development can be said to be an issue of the maintenance and management of social common capital. It becomes a question of who will manage this capital, on what basis, so that it can be handed down to the next generation.

Consider climate change as an example of the meaning and significance of the concept of social common capital. The climate is a typical form of such capital. The common foundations of society must be managed by society, according to social standards. An international community is required which can accomplish just that. It can be argued that a global government should take on this management, but this would result in the creation of a bureaucracy, which can lead to inefficiencies and unfairness. The market mechanism also has its defects.

In short, the prevention of global warming comes up against the problem of whether or not a system can truly be implemented that treats the climate as social common capital to be managed for the "common wealth" of the planet (Sachs, 2008). It is clear that we hold in common the capacity of the environment and the ecological base, but with the responsibility for managing them unclear this is a fundamental reason why there has been such excessive use of environmental capacity and ecological infrastructure on a global scale. There have been proposals such as implementing an emission trading scheme to manage markets, or as Stiglitz (2006) suggested, the establishment of a global democratic institution for the control of global issues, including finances. These both have their merits, but it should not be forgotten why the Nobel Prize for Economics was given to Elinor Ostrom in 2009.

The primary work for which she was given the award was *Governing the Commons* (Ostrom, 1990), which, as can be seen in the title, was based on Ostrom's field research carried out around the world where she explored the role of communal governance in the management of common-pool resources instead of government and/or market control.

Ostrom has carried out a great deal of field research, but in particular she analysed success factors and management of communal forests. In forest management, it is often stated by policy analysts that when government is involved this can lead to severe damage to forests owned by the government, and economists also tout the effectiveness of private management. Ostrom has said, based on a great deal of empirical studies, that it is not such a simple matter and we should not rush to conclusions. And since the provisions related to ownership and usage, and the role of conservation in the use of forests, are so complex and diverse for different regions, it is important to create an effective regime of usage and ownership which makes use of the local ecology and social structure.

When Ostrom's ideas are applied to the issues of managing the global commons, it becomes necessary to reform the international community in order to create communities that can manage them. To make this possible, the international community first needs to establish common principles such as norms, trust and networks.

The problem here is that a community is originally intended to be in a local form, and the governance and management of common resources are different for each community. Therefore, the trust, norms and networks that have been created in local communities also differ. As has been stated many times before, the use of the global commons of environmental capacity is governed by local entities, and it is inconceivable that they would be removed from local governance.

The negotiations of governments and the environmental NGOs are currently taking place under an international framework to prevent global warming, and it is possible to view these activities as forming a base of global governance for climate stabilization, but this conflicts with the principles of local governance, which means that the formation of a network is a step-by-step process.

3-1-5 Conclusion

When discussing the issue of sustainable development, the actors and units are problematic. This is not only the case in terms of the fundamental units of nations – it is also an important international issue to consider how to preserve the individual cultures and rights of indigenous peoples. At the same time, as the globalization of the economy continues to advance, local areas continue to gain identity and importance. Initially, sustainable development is about making use of the traditional cultures, historical backgrounds and resources of local societies to establish a basis for endogenous development (Miyamoto, 2007). Further, creating sound environmental governance by encouraging citizen participation in decisions relating to the environment and through the reform of local government and management (Matsushita, 2007) must be considered vital to the realization of sustainable development.

REFERENCES

Dasgupta, P. (2001) *Human Well-Being and the Natural Environment*. Oxford: Oxford University Press,

——— (2007) *Economics: A Very Short Introduction*. Oxford: Oxford University Press.

Mamiya, Y. (2002) "Commons in Resource and Environmental Issues", in T. Sawa and K. Ueta (eds) *Environmental Economic Theory*. Tokyo: Iwanami Shoten, pp. 181–208.

Matsushita, K. (ed.) (2007) *Environmental Governance*. Kyoto: Kyoto University Press (in Japanese).

Miyamoto, K. (2007) *Environmental Economics*. Tokyo: Iwanami Shoten (in Japanese).

Ostrom. E. (1990) *Governing the Commons: The Evolution of Institutions for Collective Action*. Cambridge: Cambridge University Press.

Otsuka, T. (2006) *Environmental Law*, 2nd edn. Tokyo: Yuhikaku Publishing (in Japanese).

Sachs, J. (2008) *Common Wealth: Economics for a Crowded Planet*. Harmondsworth: Penguin.

Sen, A. (1985) *Commodities and Capabilities*. Amsterdam: North-Holland.

Stiglitz, J. (2006) *Making Globalization Work*. New York: W. W. Norton.

Stiglitz, J., A. Sen and J.-P. Fitoussi (2010) *Mismeasuring Our Lives: Why GDP Doesn't Add Up. The Report by the Commission on the Measurement of Economic Performance and Social Progress.* New York: New Press.

Ueta, K. (2010) "On the Economic Model of Sustainable Development", *Review of Environmental Economics and Policy Studies* 3(1), pp. 1–6 (in Japanese).

Uzawa, H. (2000) *Social Common Capital*. Tokyo: Iwanami Shoten (in Japanese).

——— (2005) *Economic Analysis of Social Common Capital*. Cambridge: Cambridge University Press.

World Commission on Environment and Development (1987) *Our Common Future*. Oxford: Oxford University Press.

3-2

Social norms and people's values in light of sustainability

Takashi Ohshima

3-2-1 Introduction

According to the Fourth Assessment Report of the Intergovernmental Panel on Climate Change (IPCC, 2007), there is a high possibility that most of the global average temperature increases observed since the mid-twentieth century have been caused by an increase of greenhouse gases from human activities. Global warming significantly damages ecological systems and causes sea-level rises, and it is predicted that it will present serious threats to the sustainability of human society. Therefore, we are at a critical juncture: we have to reduce the emission of greenhouse gases sometime soon. When we look at our daily life, we can find that large volumes of greenhouse gases are emitted by, for example, energy consumption, the use of automobiles and the incineration of home and workplace garbage. So it is important for every individual to take a good look at life again and try to save energy, refrain from using automobiles and reduce their amount of garbage.

However, reality is not so simple, because such reduction efforts contradict every activity leading to a comfortable and easy life. In other words, in order to reduce emissions of greenhouse gases, each person must pay the cost in sacrificing the comforts and conveniences of modern life. One may ask, "Why do I have to pay such a cost?" The reason lies in the sustainability of human society. But one may suspect that even if one makes such efforts, the contributions of a single person are negligible. However, if no one makes such efforts, there is no improvement in the situation and the sustainability of human society will be threatened. This structure is generally called a "social dilemma". In this chapter, based on concepts in social psychology such as social norms and values, I discuss the necessary conditions for individuals to behave in a way corresponding to sacrificing comforts and conveniences, and then look at social survey data to identify problems characteristic of present-day Japanese society.

3-2-2 Sustainability and social dilemma

Social dilemmas

According to Dawes (1980), social dilemmas are defined as situations when an individual can choose between socially cooperative or defecting choices: each individual receives a higher payoff for a socially defecting choice than for a cooperative choice, no matter what the other individuals do, but all individuals receive a lower payoff if all defect than if all cooperate.

A well-known example of a social dilemma is the "tragedy of the commons" introduced by Hardin (1968). A hypothetical group of herders share a common parcel of land (the commons), where every herder in the neighbourhood can bring their cows to graze. Each herder is free to put as many cows as he wishes on to the land. The total amount of grass on the land is limited, therefore the number of cows that can feed on the grass in the commons is also limited. In this situation, a herder receives all of the benefits by adding cows, while the loss caused by overgrazing the commons is shared by the entire group. If all herders make the individually rational decision to add cows, the commons is destroyed and all herders suffer because they cannot keep cows any more and thus lose their bread and butter.

In this story, a herder not adding cows is cooperative behaviour, while adding cows is defecting behaviour. Applying this hypothetical example to the environmental problems mentioned above, leading a comfortable and convenient life is beneficial for individuals but everyone living on the Earth will eventually suffer from climate change caused by the increased greenhouse gases emitted into the atmosphere. Although it is inconvenient, behaving in a pro-environmental way corresponds to cooperative behaviour, while continuing a comfortable life is defecting.

Studies of social dilemma have discussed the conditions in which the dilemma is solved – that is, in what conditions individuals behave cooperatively. Dawes (1980) discussed the possibility that changing the payoff structure might provide the simplest solution. An example is the establishment of a government which offers a reward for cooperative behaviour while imposing a punishment on defecting behaviour. However, implementing such a management system is costly, and even if everyone chooses cooperative behaviour, the payoff becomes lower than the payoff gained by choosing cooperative behaviour without the system. For example, in the case of the "tragedy of the commons", deciding on the number of cows each herder can keep is one solution. Since it is impossible to secure financial resources outside the group to reward herders who follow the rule, a system to punish those who do not follow the rule is necessary. However, monitoring whether the herders follow the rule for the number of cows or not is costly (such as in wages to be paid to wardens), and such costs must be shared by the entire group. In that case, there will be a "secondary dilemma" to go along with the defecting choice of not sharing the cost. As a result, a management system with strong binding power is required. Thus changing the payoff structure simply by giving rewards or imposing punishments is not an effective solution. In particular, to solve a social dilemma in environmental problems, which is part of a large-scale social system, implementing a management system with strong binding power is not easy. Currently, although some manipulative payoff structures are found in the policies of some nations and local governments, strictly implementing the policies is not easy since there is so much conflict of interest. This is even more the case with global issues.

Importance of communication

Acceleration of communication is one possibility for introducing cooperative behaviour in a social dilemma situation. For example, consider the "prisoner's dilemma" game. The story involves two prisoners who are separately given the choice between testifying against the other and keeping silent. When one prisoner keeps silent while the other testifies, the latter receives a lighter sentence than when both prisoners remain silent, as such behaviour is considered a mitigating factor. At the same time, the one who keeps silent receives a heavier sentence than when both testify, as the sentence is increased. Considering the situation rationally, whether one prisoner keeps silent or testifies, the other is better off by testifying, and if they both pursue this rational strategy, both prisoners end up testifying against each other. However, both are better off by keeping silent. Applying this theory to the definition of a social dilemma, keeping silent is a cooperative behaviour while testifying is a defecting behaviour. In this case, it is apparent that a large driving factor to testify is the lack of communication: these two prisoners cannot discuss committing to silence with each other. (Of course, a discussion does not necessarily provide an assurance of silence, and there is still a possibility of a betrayal by one testifying to receive a lighter sentence than the other.)

Axelrod (1984) found in his simulation of a iterated prisoner's dilemma game that the most effective way to obtain high scores was a "tit-for-tat" strategy which is history dependent, i.e. choosing cooperation for the first round, then from the second round on using the past game history to make the decision that was made by the opponent in the previous round. In this case, even though direct communication is not available, when the opponent chooses a defecting behaviour, the player can take revenge by choosing a defecting behaviour, while if the opponent chooses a cooperative behaviour, the player can follow suit. It can be assumed that communication between the two prisoners exists in this case. However, in the case of *n*-person prisoner's dilemma, or in general social dilemma situations, an individual's decision has very little effect on the decisions made by the others. Dawes (1980) introduced three items as differences between the iterated two-person prisoner's dilemma and general social dilemma situations.

- In the two-person prisoner's dilemma, the player's decision to defect is directly reflected in the loss of the opponent; however, in general social dilemma situations, a loss caused by one person's defection spreads among many people and is diluted.
- In the two-person prisoner's dilemma, the behaviour chosen by the opponent is clearly known to the player; however, in general social dilemma situations, defecting behaviour is anonymous.
- In the two-person prisoner's dilemma, it is possible to control the behaviour of the opponent to a certain extent by demonstrating defection or cooperation, while in general social dilemmas one person's behaviour seldom has a direct effect on the behaviours of others.

Since behaviour does not perform communicative functions in general social dilemma situations, a need for direct communication among participating members arises. In his experiment with *n*-person dilemma games, Dawes (ibid.) demonstrated that cooperative behaviours were not accelerated by superficial face-to-face communication in which participants were only casual acquaintances, while having deeper communication that involved discussions to solve problems dramatically increased cooperative behaviours. By sharing knowledge of the social dilemma situation, the participants can expect the others to behave in a cooperative manner. Kollock (1998) suggested that as an effect of communication, a moral sense is stimulated because the "behaviour to be taken" is discussed and a group identity is reinforced. The same can be applied to the case of the "tragedy of the commons". When the herders communicate with each other and share the understanding that if everyone keeps adding cows, the grass on the commons will disappear, selfishly adding cows is an immoral act; and when a sense of group identity is enhanced, it is not difficult to imagine that there is a higher possibility of solving the dilemma. However, as Dawes (1980) pointed out, while others' behaviours are predictable through discussion, the behaviour of an individual depends on the situation. For example, when it is expected that many people will take a cooperative stance, an individual may conform to them and follow the same behaviour. On the other hand, it is known in advance that even if an individual defects, the loss imposed on the entire group is relatively small while the payoff the individual can obtain is large. That would induce defecting behaviour. Therefore, in order to maintain cooperative behaviour, not only the expectation of cooperation from others but trust in others are necessary assumptions. It appears that mutual trust among group members plays an important role in inducing mutual cooperative behaviour.

Efficacy for cooperation

In social dilemma situations, a feeling of efficacy possessed by individuals is an important factor in encouraging cooperative behaviour (Kollock, 1998). Generally, when many people are involved in the situation, since an individual's decision on cooperating affects the others very little, only a small feeling of efficacy is generated in using cooperative behaviour. However, there might be a situation in which an individual has a strong influence over other members; this person takes a leading role in taking a cooperative behaviour, and the behaviour of this person encourages other members. As a result, the cooperative behaviours in the entire group will increase. For example, in the "commons" dilemma suppose that one herder is anxious about the seriousness of the situation, and proposes implementing a management system and pays all costs from his own pocket – that is, the emergence of a volunteer. When this volunteer takes the leading role and acts in the cause of justice, there is a possibility that the other herders will follow him and use cooperative behaviour. Fujii (2003) points out that the concept of "justice", discussed in the long history of philosophy dating from Socrates, has significant meaning in whether such behaviour would bring success or not. He also suggests the importance of studying how people react towards such a "righteous" volunteer, as well as the social structure fostering such a volunteer.

Inherent features of environmental problems

As stated, environmental problems have a social dilemma structure, and in the example of climate change caused by increased greenhouse gases, an individual's pursuit of a comfortable and convenient life corresponds to a defecting behaviour that brings losses to human society. In addition, it is considered that there are inherent features in actual environmental problems on top of the characteristic features of general social dilemmas.

The first inherent feature is that in environmental problems, scales to measure an individual's gains from defecting behaviours are different from those to measure social losses; in a general social dilemma situation, gains and losses are measured on the same scale. For example, in the prisoner's dilemma games, whether points are high or low shows the degree of gains. As a result of one player's effort to increase his score, all prisoners lose points, which creates a dilemma. In the "commons" dilemma the amount of grass cows can graze is a scale for gains. On the other hand, increasing greenhouse gases and setting air conditioners to low temperatures in summer cannot be measured by the same scale for individuals. The reason for not using plastic bags in supermarkets out of consideration for the environment is not because we will run out of plastic bags when everyone uses them. That is, in order to understand social dilemma situations in environmental problems and behave in a cooperative manner, knowledge characteristic to environmental problems is necessary to judge what is beneficial and what causes losses.

Secondly, with environmental problems there is a significant time lag between an individual's defecting behaviour and losses caused by such behaviour imposed on society. A dilemma situation in which the behaviour of an individual increases short-term individual profit and decreases long-term social profit is called a "social trap" (Platt, 1973). Environmental problems can be viewed as social trap examples; moreover, the time involved is very long and losses caused as a result of an individual's pursuit of profit might actually fall upon future generations. It is highly likely that the individuals receiving the profit would not suffer from the losses. When the parties receiving profits and losses are different, it is not a social dilemma but a conflict of interest. In addition, since the future generations do not exist here at the present time, when viewing environmental problems as social dilemmas it is necessary to regard the Earth as "the commons" with limited resources, and own a transgenerational viewpoint of a "group of human beings". These are premises for discussing "sustainability".

3-2-3 Morality and social norms

Psychological factors in the social dilemma

As discussed, communication is essential for solving a social dilemma. Dawes (1980) pointed out that psychological factors of knowledge, morality and trust are also important for enhancing cooperation in social dilemma situations. After investigating strategies to solve social dilemmas from a multifaceted viewpoint, Fujii (2003: 156) stressed a need for inspiring a moral sense that "in social dilemma situations, people should behave in a cooperative manner". He concluded that "according to the basic structure of social dilemmas, only the moral sense as a 'consideration for social and public payoff' can motivate people who routinely act in an defecting manner to take the trouble to act in a cooperative manner". However, it is not easy to inspire a moral sense in all people. In a society consisting of a variety of humans, there are people of high morality and low morality. Also, within one person a moral sense is sometimes inspired, while other times it remains dormant. In a social dilemma situation it is known that defection becomes dominant once such behaviour emerges, no matter how small the number of defectors may be, due to what is called the "rotten-apple effect" where people tend to follow defecting behaviours. That is, it takes only one rotten apple to ruin the barrel. Fujii (ibid.) also introduced "Darwin's dilemma", an argument based on an evolutionary viewpoint.

For example, with the "tragedy of the commons" there is a structure that cannot sustain cooperative behaviour. If one herder understands the social dilemma and willingly limits his number of cows, while the other herders add cows and receive higher payoffs for defecting behaviour, there will be a wealth gap between the cooperative herder and the defectors. As the defecting herders can afford to create an advantageous environment with higher payoffs to keep cows, the wealth gap between the herders expands and the herder who used cooperative behaviour has no choice but to terminate his business. As a result, only defecting herders remain and ruin is the destination: all herders continue to add cows, each pursuing his own best interest.

Therefore, in order to make people keep behaving in a cooperative manner, it is necessary to set "rules" to encourage morality. However, the psychological meanings of these "rules" should be taken into consideration. For example, you can give people who behave in a cooperative manner a reward of some sort to praise them as "people of high morality". Or it might be possible to impose punishment on people with defecting behaviours for being "immoral". In that case, there are two possibilities where the significance of behaving in a cooperative manner transforms into something else. One possibility is that people might recognize the situation as a "transactional issue" rather than a "moral issue", and thus the degree of the reward and punishment starts to define the behaviour. If people come to recognize that the payoff from defecting behaviour is greater than the punishment, they will not use cooperative behaviour any more. The other possibility is that, regardless of whose behaviour it is, their understanding of the cause of a cooperative behaviour (attribution of the behaviour) may change from moral motivation to obtaining a reward or avoiding a punishment. Strategies to arouse a moral sense in people should be always considered from psychological viewpoints.

Social norms for cooperation

We can consider "norms" as the psychological rules. Norms are standards that encourage or inhibit behaviours within a society or organization. There are cases where norms are classified into two: "personal norms" that are internalized within individuals, and "social norms" that are based on the requirements of a society. However, in relation to social dilemmas, a widely discussed problem of "social norms", regardless of whether internalized within individuals or not, is the function of encouraging socially preferable cooperative behaviour and inhibiting socially unwanted defecting behaviour. Social norms do not have one-sided binding power like laws, but they are "rules" for members in a group of some sort, and these people have a shared understanding that it is preferable to follow them. It is expected that failure to follow the norms results in punishment of some sort from the group, while at the same time one's inner self would suffer from a "guilty conscience" or "guilty feeling". Therefore, the motivation to follow social norms comes from one's morality.

In a social dilemma situation where behaving in a cooperative manner is established as a social norm, some conditions are required to maintain the norm. Firstly, a sense of fairness is necessary when an individual follows the norm. For example, if one behaves in a cooperative manner by paying some sort of cost, and others do not behave in a cooperative manner but are benefited without cost, the situation is not fair. A situation in which one who is paying no cost benefits by taking advantage of another's costs is called "free riding", and in many cases this can be a big obstacle in finding a solution for a social dilemma. It has also been pointed out that free riding tends to spread easily in a group by the rotten-apple effect. Secondly, in order to maintain social norms in a group, it is considered preferable to have a sense of reciprocity among members. A reciprocal relationship is mutually beneficial through mutual cooperation. However, in order to establish a reciprocal relationship in a group, a long-term interaction among members is necessary. Though establishing a reciprocal relationship in a small community is possible, it is quite difficult in a large society with an anonymous nature.

Two types of social norms

Cialdini, Reno and Kallgren (1990) identify two types of social norms: "injunctive norms" and "descriptive norms". Injunctive norms are based on what many people approve, while descriptive norms are based on what many people actually do. With field experiments, they demonstrated that in a realistic situation the role of descriptive norms was more important. The experiment was performed in a parking garage adjacent to a hospital, and participants were hospital visitors. When they got out of the elevator on the floor where their cars were parked, the participants came across an experimental confederate who looked like a college student. Two situations were prepared: half of the participants saw this confederate walking while reading a handbill, and then dropping the paper on the floor; the other half saw the confederate just walking past them without carrying a handbill. Other conditions were pre-arranged: the floor of the garage was heavily littered with trash or it was spotlessly cleaned. When visitors arrived at their cars, each found a large handbill stuck under the windshield wiper. The aim was to see whether the visitors littered the handbill or not. From the results, where more people drop handbills in a littered garage than in the clean environment, it is understood that a situation in which other people littered in the parking garage (descriptive norms) triggered the behaviour to drop wastepaper. In particular, when the confederate dropped the paper in front of the visitors, this difference was greater. (In the clean situation, fewer people littered, while in the littered situation more people dropped wastepaper.) In these results, the behaviour of the confederate had a role in emphasizing the descriptive norm.

The results of these experiments indicate that cooperative and defecting behaviours appear in harmony with the behaviours of others. In the littered garage situation, dropping wastepaper was accelerated, indicating the existence of a rotten-apple effect which increased defecting behaviour. On the other hand, attention must be paid to the fact that cooperative behaviour in accordance with the injunctive norm of "not littering" was accelerated by a situation where others followed it. It is thought that even in a group with an anonymous nature, a sense of fairness or reciprocity as conditions to follow social norms was provoked by situational factors. In another result from a similar experiment (Reno, Cialdini and Kallgren, 1993), when visitors saw an experimental confederate picking up a piece of litter, littering behaviour was inhibited. As mentioned, it is thought that by meeting a "righteous" volunteer, attention was attracted to an injunctive norm which accelerated cooperative behaviour.

3-2-4 Keys to solving social dilemmas in the local community

Community and social capital

Many studies suggest that one's identity as a member of a group (group identity) accelerates cooperative behaviours within the group. In particular, this effect is enhanced when there is a competitive relationship with other groups. Important conditions to establish a group identity are interdependent relationships, the existence of reciprocity, the recognition that such relationships last long into the future and information about how the member has behaved in the past (Kollock, 1998). That is, in a group consisting of relatively fixed members who know each other and have strong interaction, social dilemmas are likely to be solved. In the "tragedy of the commons", there was a premise that the commons can be used by anyone and there were no definite rules for this use. However, in reality there are many cases in which there is a closed community in the commons and members share knowledge and rules of using the land (Ostrom, 1990).

Putnam (2000) defined activity consisting of trust, norms and a network possessed by a community as "social capital". He insists that in a community with rich social capital, voluntary solutions are likely to be found for the "tragedy of the commons" or social dilemmas. He suggests that members' positive attitudes towards contributions to community activities, the degree of relationship between members and the trust in others form an index of social capital. Based on this index, he shows that people living in areas with rich social capital have a higher quality of life. There are two types of social capital: inner-directed "bonding social capital" that unites people within a group, and outer-directed "bridging social capital" that unites different groups and disparate people. Of these two types, bonding social capital stays within a small but highly homogeneous group. While it creates a strong group identity, it often has negative aspects of exclusiveness and inwardness; in some cases it produces a new subgroup inside the group and causes conflicts. Therefore, fostering bridging social capital is usually desirable to form a stable community.

Generally, a system that prevents creating free riders is necessary in order to maintain a cooperative relationship in a group. That will be an environment in which free riding without cooperating is not always beneficial. In a community with bonding social capital, it is highly likely that free riding is promptly detected and, in return, the free rider is excluded from the group. So what about a community with bridging social capital? Yamagishi and Kiyonari (2008) discussed the reason why cooperative relationships are generated in a group. They suggested that in order to maintain a generalized exchange system, which is characteristic of human society, there must be a kind of cognitive bias in people's understandings of group status. It is considered that the members of a group follow behavioural principles (group heuristic); that is, members expect implicit reciprocity to exist within the group and try to avoid being detected and excluded when taking a free ride. Also, groups consisting of people with such tendencies actually come to devise a system to detect and exclude the free riders. On the other hand, in groups in which members are free to come and go with a highly anonymous nature and obscure borders, free riding is not likely to be detected. In those groups any disadvantage involved in exclusion from the group is not especially serious, so free riding becomes an advantageous behaviour. It is suggested that the key to solve a social dilemma is the regulation by which group members themselves construct the group and operate it.

Local governance

In recent years there have been increasing numbers of attempts to solve various problems in local communities by procedures involving citizens. In particular, it has been difficult to reach a consensus in relation to environmental problems because there are different views among government, companies, residents and specialists. It thus becomes necessary to collect an array of opinions from as many people as possible in open discussions to determine policies. Hirose (2008) suggests the importance of procedural fairness as a condition under which decisions made through open discussion involving citizens are to be accepted by the entire society. He lists four requirements of fairness: representativeness of the participants in the discussion; disclosure of information; opportunities to express arguments and opinions; and appropriateness of the decisions. Also, in local communities there is no coercive system led by an authoritative body, as exemplified by the government, but rather we see examples of residents or concerned people establishing rules and managing and operating communities by themselves. Such a joint control system by diverse people is called "governance", and those realized in local communities are "local governance". Examining the process and results of the "anti-studded-tyre movement", especially in Sendai city, Yamamoto (2008) explores the possibility that local governance functions effectively in solving social dilemmas. This shows a possibility for solving a dilemma using not a coercive system, as Hardin (1968) suggested in his commons tragedy, but rather a system in which herders and people trading cows voluntarily decide the methods to use and manage the "commons" through discussion. To realize a sustainable society, establishing cooperative relationships and stimulating community activities are considered necessary.

3-2-5 Surveys on people's values in four Asian countries

As mentioned, pursuing solutions for social dilemmas is one direction to realize sustainability. The keys to solving social dilemmas exist in local communities. It is suggested that mutual trust, communication networks and moral values complying with social norms in communities play important roles. In this section, based on surveys (Ohshima, 2007, 2008, 2009), I examine the problems of current Asian societies, and above all problems in Japan today.

From 2007 to 2008 Toyo University's Transdisciplinary Initiative for Eco-Philosophy carried out surveys on people's values with respect to environmental issues, targeting inhabitants of four Asian countries. Subject areas, survey periods and sample sizes are as follows.

- Singapore: January/February 2007; nationwide; 1,037 samples.
- Japan: May 2007; Fukuoka city; 400 samples.
- China: June 2007; Shanghai, Hangzhou and Suzhou; 1,000 samples.
- Viet Nam: December 2008; 19 urban areas; 1,021 samples.

Each survey was carried out by home-visit interviews with adults aged 20 or over. The samples were chosen randomly from the strata of residential areas. Referring to previous surveys carried out in various areas, 45 questions were devised that included recognition of environmental issues and views on nature, science and life. Eight demographic questions about age, gender, occupation, income, etc. were added. Four languages were used for the Singapore survey (English, Mandarin Chinese, Malay and Tamil), Japanese in the Japan survey, Mandarin Chinese in the China survey and Vietnamese in the Viet Nam survey. The questionnaires were prepared by translating from an English questionnaire. Before conducting the surveys, each translated questionnaire was back-checked by people who understood both the subject language and Japanese. I show some of the data from the survey results and discuss sustainability in Asia based on this framework.

Efficacy with cooperation

First, let us look at the characteristic problem in social dilemmas. When a group has a large number of members, an individual's cooperative behaviours have a very little effect on the entire group. Thus people may gain very little feeling of efficacy through choosing cooperative behaviours. To investigate consciousness of this problem, we asked how much a person agrees or disagrees with the statement "There is no point in doing what I can for the environment unless others do the same" (Table 3.2.1). Not surprisingly, the ratios combining the answers "strongly agree" and "agree" are fairly high, with 64.1 per cent in Singapore, 77.4 per cent in China, 72.3 per cent in Viet Nam and 70.6 per cent in Japan. As expected, the results show that the feeling of efficacy with cooperative behaviour for the environment is very low.

It should be noted that the same question was included in the survey carried out by the International Social Survey Programme (ISSP) in 2000.

Table 3.2.1 Percentage of agreement/disagreement with the statement: "There is no point in doing what I can for the environment unless others do the same."

Countries	Strongly agree (%)	Agree (%)	Neutral (%)	Disagree (%)	Strongly disagree (%)
Singapore	21.3	42.8	11.7	20.8	3.4
China	25.5	51.9	9.4	12.3	0.9
Viet Nam	39.0	33.3	8.7	15.0	4.0
Japan	48.0	22.6	8.8	10.8	9.8

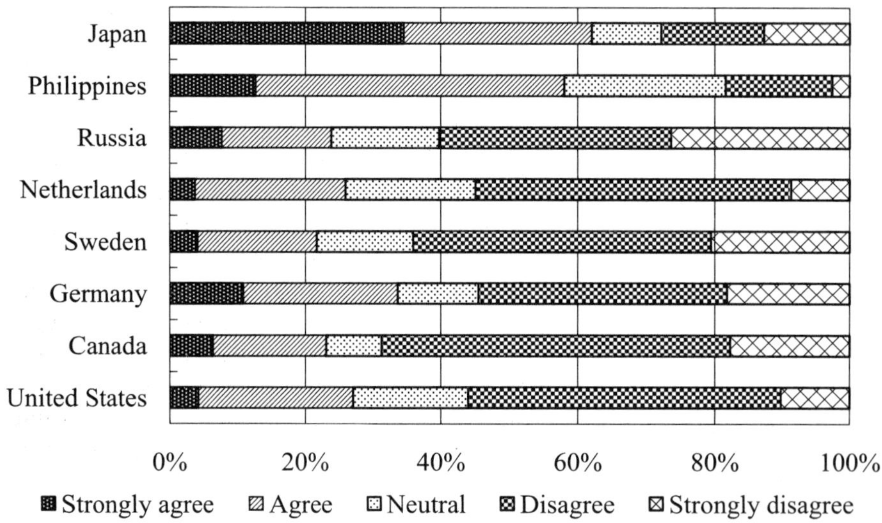

Figure 3.2.1 Rates of agreement/disagreement with the statement: "There is no point in doing what I can for the environment unless others do the same."

ISSP surveys are carried out every year, targeting mostly Western nations, and a specific theme is established each year. In the 2000 survey on environment, Japan and the Philippines were included as Asian nations. To compare the results of our survey with ISSP's survey, the results of ISSP's survey from eight countries including Japan are shown in Figure 3.2.1. From these results, the combined ratio of "strongly agree" and "agree" is 62.1 per cent in Japan; although this result is slightly lower than the result of our survey, it exceeds 60 per cent. The result for the Philippines is 58.0 per cent. On the other hand, the combined answer ratios in Western countries are 27.1 per cent in the United States, 23.1 per cent in Canada, 33.7 per cent in Germany, 21.8 per cent in Sweden, 26.0 per cent in the Netherlands and 23.9 per cent in Russia. Each result is around 20–30 per cent, considerably lower than those of Asian countries. As mentioned, a feeling of efficacy relates to volunteer consciousness.

Table 3.2.2 Percentage of agreement/disagreement with the statement: "If I am in trouble, my neighbors will help me."

Countries	Gender	Strongly agree (%)	Somewhat agree (%)	Somewhat disagree (%)	Strongly disagree (%)	Average score
Singapore	Male	28.8	53.6	12.2	5.3	1.12
	Female	33.4	50.6	12.5	3.6	1.28
	Total	31.2	52.1	12.3	4.4	1.20
China	Male	32.6	58.2	7.7	1.5	1.44
	Female	39.6	51.7	8.1	0.6	1.60
	Total	36.1	54.9	7.9	1.0	1.52
Viet Nam	Male	62.2	23.7	9.7	4.4	1.88
	Female	66.3	19.4	9.1	5.2	1.94
	Total	64.5	21.3	9.3	4.9	1.91
Japan	Male	9.9	49.5	28.0	12.6	0.13
	Female	23.0	49.0	20.5	7.5	0.75
	Total	16.8	49.2	24.1	9.9	0.46

Although the attitude of "I undertake cooperative behaviour regardless of the behaviours of others" is a key to solving social dilemmas, this result appears to reveal that in Asian nations such consciousness is lower than in Western nations. It is possible, however, that this result is not only caused by efficacy but by differences of cultural backgrounds between West and East. Generally, in Western culture the value of "independent self" is dominant, while in Eastern culture the value of "interdependent self" dominates (Markus and Kitayama, 1991). It is considered that in Asian nations, in relation to efforts to tackle environmental problems, people are aware of the "norm for cooperativeness", i.e. people think that "everyone should be cooperative and participate in the activity".

Trust in local community

As mentioned, although solving a social dilemma in a large-scale society under the premise of anonymity is difficult, local community activities could be a key to a solution. Let us look at the answers to the statement regarding mutual trust in the community: "If I am in trouble, my neighbors will help me" (Table 3.2.2). The combined answers of "strongly agree" and "somewhat agree" are 83.3 per cent in Singapore, 91.0 per cent in China, 85.8 per cent in Viet Nam and 66.0 per cent in Japan. From this result, we can see that Japan's ratio is quite low. The table shows the average scores, calculated to show the degree of mutual trust by numbers: "strongly agree" is given 3, "somewhat agree" is given 1, "somewhat disagree" is given –1 and "strongly disagree" is given –3. From this, we can

Table 3.2.3 Percentage of agreement/disagreement with the statement: "If I am in trouble, my neighbors will help me."

Countries	Gender	Strongly agree (%)	Somewhat agree (%)	Somewhat disagree (%)	Strongly disagree (%)	Average score
Japan	Male	20.5	50.3	20.3	8.9	0.65
	Female	23.1	55.8	16.1	5.1	0.94
	Total	22.0	53.4	17.9	6.7	0.81
United States	Male	45.9	32.9	11.7	9.5	1.30
	Female	56.9	28.6	7.3	7.3	1.70
	Total	51.4	30.8	9.5	8.4	1.50

Source: Ohshima, Katayama and Yashiro (2006)

see that Japan's scores are extremely low. Moreover, in Japan it is apparent that male scores are notably lower than female scores, though there are no large gender differences in the answers of other countries. Since this survey was carried out in urban areas, it could be that this is a characteristic tendency in urban Japan. However, Singapore is a city-state, and in China and Viet Nam the survey was also carried out in urban areas. It is thus considered that at least this tendency points out a decline of community consciousness in Japanese urban areas.

This question was also used in a survey comparing Japan-US community consciousness undertaken by Toyo University's 21st Century Human Interaction Research Center in March 2004 (Ohshima, Katayama and Yashiro, 2006). The survey was carried out on a nationwide basis in both Japan and the United States. The method applied in Japan was home-visit interviews, while in the United States telephone survey through random-digit dialling was adopted. The result is shown in Table 3.2.3. The combined answers of "strongly agree" and "somewhat agree" in Japan total 75.4 per cent, while the total in the United States is 82.2 per cent. Answers obtained in Japan are higher than those shown in Table 3.2.2; nevertheless, the results in Japan are lower than those in the other Asian nations (Table 3.2.2), as well as in the United States (Table 3.2.3). Also, the average scores of Japan calculated by the method explained above are considerably lower. If these results indicate a decline of mutual trust in Japanese local communities, it is not a welcome situation in view of seeking possibilities for solving environmental problems in local communities.

Transgenerational identity

As mentioned, in order to solve environmental problems it is necessary to have transgenerational group identity. Let us look at the answers to

Table 3.2.4 Percentage of agreement/disagreement with the statement: "I want to be respected by my descendants."

Countries	Strongly agree (%)	Somewhat agree (%)	Somewhat disagree (%)	Strongly disagree (%)
Singapore	65.0	32.5	2.0	0.6
China	53.0	43.6	3.1	0.3
Viet Nam	95.5	4.3	0.1	0.1
Japan	23.5	51.0	21.7	3.8

the statement "I want to be respected by my descendants" (Table 3.2.4). The combined answers for "strongly agree" and "somewhat agree" are 97.5 per cent in Singapore, 96.6 per cent in China, 99.8 per cent in Viet Nam and 74.5 per cent in Japan. From these results, we can see that Japan's ratio is considerably lower compared with the other three countries. This does not necessarily indicate a lack of caring for one's descendants in Japan. However, assuming that consciousness of reciprocity with one's descendants would foster transgenerational group identity, these data make us feel slightly uncomfortable when it comes to realizing a sustainable society.

REFERENCES

Axelrod, Robert (1984) *The Evolution of Cooperation*. New York: Basic Books.

Cialdini, Robert B., Raymond R. Reno and Carl A. Kallgren (1990) "A Focus Theory of Normative Conduct: Recycling the Concept of Norms to Reduce Littering in Public Places", *Journal of Personality and Social Psychology* 58, pp. 1015–1026.

Dawes, Robyn M. (1980) "Social Dilemmas", *Annual Review of Psychology* 31, pp. 169–193.

Fujii, Satoshi (2003) *Prescription of Social Dilemmas*. Kyoto: Nakanishiya Shuppan (in Japanese).

Hardin, Garrett (1968) "The Tragedy of the Commons", *Science* 162, pp. 1243–1248.

Hirose, Yukio (2008) "Why Citizens' Participation in Environmental Planning is Necessary", in Yukio Hirose (ed.) *Social Psychology of Environmental Activities*. Kyoto: Kitaoji Shobo, pp. 104–113 (in Japanese).

International Social Survey Programme (2000) "Environment II"; available at www.issp.org/.

Kollock, Peter (1998) "Social Dilemmas: The Anatomy of Cooperation", *Annual Review of Sociology* 24, pp. 183–214.

Markus, Hazel R. and Shinobu Kitayama (1991) "Culture and the Self: Implications for Cognition, Emotion, and Motivation", *Psychological Review* 98, pp. 224–253.

Ohshima, Takashi (2007) "A Survey of Values in Singapore", *Eco-Philosophy* 1, pp. 55–104 (in Japanese).

——— (2008) "Environmental Consciousness and Views on Life and Nature: From Surveys Conducted in Three Asian Countries", *Eco-Philosophy* 2, pp. 71–106 (in Japanese).

——— (2009) "Environmental Issues and a Sense of Community in Viet Nam", *Eco-Philosophy* 3, pp. 39–65 (in Japanese).

Ohshima, Takashi, Miyuki Katayama and Kaoru Yashiro (2006) "Restoration from Disaster and Social Capital (2): Japan-US Community Consciousness Comparison", Annual Research Report of Toyo University 21st Century Human Interaction Research Center, 3, pp. 89–96 (in Japanese).

Ostrom, Elinor (1990) *Governing the Commons: The Evolution of Institutions for Collective Action*. Cambridge: Cambridge University Press.

Putnam, Robert D. (2000) *Bowling Alone: The Collapse and Revival of American Community*. New York: Simon & Schuster.

Platt, John (1973) "Social Traps", *American Psychologist* 28, pp. 641–651.

Reno, Raymond R., Robert B. Cialdini and Carl A. Kallgren (1993) "The Trans-situational Influence of Social Norms", *Journal of Personality and Social Psychology* 64, pp. 104–112.

Yamagishi, Toshio and Toko Kiyonari (2008) "Cooperation and Trust in the Group – Social Dilemma and Generalized Exchange System", in Doba Gaku and Shinoki Mikiko (eds) *Conflict of Individuals and Society: Possibility of Social Dilemma Approach*. Kyoto: Minerva Shobo, pp. 125–156 (in Japanese).

Yamamoto, Hidehiro (2008) "Solving Problems by Local Governance: Social Dilemma and Local Communities", in Doba Gaku and Shinoki Mikiko (eds) *Conflict of Individuals and Society: Possibility of Social Dilemma Approach*. Kyoto: Minerva Shobo, pp. 201–220 (in Japanese).

3-3

Measuring sustainability and economic valuation of the environment

Masayuki Sato

3-3-1 Economic development and sustainability

Sustainable development is associated with a wide range of concepts: environment, economics, society and more. To define it is so difficult that the resulting phrase is tinged with ambiguity. But, at present, the most frequently quoted definition is: "Development that meets the needs of the present without compromising the ability of future generations to meet their own needs" (World Commission on Environment and Development, 1987).

Here, "meets the needs" is mentioned, but needs cannot be met without using anything. Materials used to meet needs can be broadly classified into manufactured capital, human capital, natural capital, knowledge, etc., which are collectively referred to as inclusive wealth (Dasgupta, 2007). This definition requires that the total wealth given to this generation should be passed on to the next generation without being diminished.

One of the controversial points here is how to measure "total wealth", and in particular determining the degree to which one capital could be substituted for another gives rise to sharp conflicts. Examples are "weak" versus "strong" sustainability, "shallow ecology" versus "deep ecology", "anthropocentric" versus "ecocentric" and more. "Weak sustainability" holds that even if one capital (natural capital, for example) were to decrease, if another capital (manufactured capital, for example) increases sufficiently, "total wealth" does not decrease. This, however, is not an acceptable substitute for "strong sustainability".

Many in the field of economics assume the former.[1] Although there are many possible criticisms from the viewpoint of economics, in this chapter I give a general survey of the economic theories developed so far from a global stance in order to come up with a comprehensive environmental economic analysis.

Firstly, the relationship between the basic concepts underlying the economics of sustainability – "well-being", "wealth" that determines well-being, "accounting prices" that measure wealth – will be laid out, followed by the role of methods of environmental valuation used to measure associated accounting prices during the assessment in practice.

3-3-2 Well-being, wealth and accounting prices

For purposes of economic analysis, it is necessary that the definition of sustainable development should be reformulated in economic terms. Substituting "well-being" for the term "needs" in the Brundtland Report definition (World Commission on Environment and Development, 1987), sustainable development can be reformulated in economic terms as "without diminishing well-being in the future".[2]

The term "well-being" used in this reformulation is a broader concept that includes elements that cannot be incorporated in the concepts of "utility" or "welfare" used traditionally in economics – that is, non-welfare constituents such as freedom, fairness, rights, personal conditions, etc. – and aims to express "quality of life". A problem with utilitarianism as viewed until now and singled out by Sen (1985) is "informational parsimony"; that is, putting emphasis only on utility to the person concerned and neglecting "non-utilitarian information" such as the degree of freedom and rights attained. The broader concept of well-being addresses this criticism and, as a classic non-welfare element, incorporates political as well as civil freedom, political as well as individual rights and individual social conditions. In keeping with this concept, Partha Dasgupta (2004) redefined welfare standards as a function of traditional welfare elements (consumption of goods and services) and non-welfare elements (degree of freedom, fairness and rights, personal conditions, etc.).

Measurement of these elements is quite difficult. Many of the associated concepts, such as Gini coefficients, for one, cannot be quantified using proxy variables at present. For example, Taylor and Jodice (1983) measured degree of political freedom in terms of the extent of people's contribution to political decisions (lowering the numerical values for despotic countries) and degree of personal freedom in terms of freedom to disseminate information publicly, freedom of the mass media, independence of the judiciary[3] and so on.

Here, an inspection of the major points shows that consumption standards which maximize "utility" and those that maximize "well-being" are, in general, different.[4] Assuming that sustainability should dwell more on well-being rather than on welfare, it is clear that utilitarianistic optimization cannot satisfy sustainability requirements. Hence, for the purposes of economic analysis, it is necessary that the existing economic framework is expanded.

In reality, measuring well-being is quite difficult. Likewise, it is difficult to identify targets of measurements that will serve as clues for assessments.[5] As a material basis for measurement, the concept of "wealth" helps to some extent. Wealth, as presented earlier, is defined as the weighted sum of capital stock that brings about the well-being of individuals.[6] Although there are problems involved in the measurement of capital, capital is easier to grasp than very abstract concepts such as well-being because it contains physical aspects such as manufactured capital and natural capital. The biggest problem here is how much weight must be assigned to it in the computation. Weights used for purposes of observing changes in well-being should be expressed in terms of social values per unit of capital. This social value, using the term introduced by Tinbergen (1954), is called "accounting price".[7]

In so doing, it is clear that two processes of measuring the amount of existing capital stock and estimating accounting prices are needed in measuring wealth. It is necessary to examine the relationship between well-being and the different forms of capital and their accounting prices prior to evaluating methods of measuring wealth. In general, the value of changes in capital is referred to as "net investment" during a given period. When this is evaluated as social values, it is called "genuine investment".[8] Since the different capitals are sources of well-being, if the resource allocation mechanism is sound then an increase in various capitals means an increase in well-being. In other words, it is clear that the social value of the increase in various capitals is a genuine investment – a relationship indicating that well-being increases.

In summary, sustainable development requires that well-being does not diminish or, expressed differently, positive genuine investment should be made at all times in the future. This means that since enhancement or diminution of well-being can be evaluated by looking at whether genuine investment is positive or negative, then measurement of sustainability can be made from that evaluation.

Thus, problems can be summarized into two: how to measure the (change in the) amount of the various capital stocks, and how to estimate their accounting prices.[9] Although a wide array of difficulties arise in the estimation of accounting prices based on well-being, insight into the possibility and various problems can be obtained from clues gained from environmental valuation methods developed for the purposes of estimating shadow prices of natural capital.

3-3-3 Estimation of accounting prices

From the discussion above, enhancement or diminution of well-being can be measured by looking at signals from properly measured genuine investments. If the abundance of capital is measured separately, the most important point of verification of the signs of genuine investment (judging whether sustainability conditions are satisfied or not) is an estimation of the accounting price of capital without passing through the market.

Attempts to evaluate contributions to human welfare without going through market mechanisms are called "non-market valuation". Specifically, the research field regarding estimation of accounting prices for the environment is "environmental economic valuation". This section summarizes the results and problems of environmental valuation techniques in sustainability assessment.

Significance and role of economic valuation of the environment

Generally speaking, the significance of valuing the environment in terms of economic units (i.e. monetary terms) is that it provides information useful in decision-making. In typical usage, it serves as social cost-benefit analysis. Social cost benefit is intimately related to the concept of accounting prices. Here, "social" includes not only private value but also external market value. The accounting price reflects social value, and could be different from the market price. Sustainability concerns not private cost benefit but social cost benefit.

Making a valid social cost-benefit analysis requires that all social benefits and social costs are computed. However, since (most) environmental services are "things of value without price" (Ueta, 1996) that contribute to human welfare without going through the market, information about cost (or benefit) will tend to be disregarded or treated lightly. Hence, this measurement of cost and benefit of the environment, which tends to be disregarded, becomes the role of environmental valuation methods. In this regard, based on the previous discussion, social cost benefit should be measured in terms of "well-being". And information regarding this well-being cannot be obtained without a conscious survey being done as project evaluation.

By placing the economic foundation of benefit evaluation on individual well-being, changes caused by whatever policy project can be measured through the enhancement or diminution of well-being. "Compensating surplus" is a concept of valuation propounded from this idea.[10] Compensating surplus is the change in monetary value that just negates the changes in well-being brought about by changes in the quality of the environment. Over the past 40 years, techniques in estimation of the accounting prices of environmental capital have been developed in environmental valuation theory. What follows is a simple summary of these techniques.

Revealed preference method

For the purpose of estimating the value of the environment, a series of techniques were developed to estimate marginal willingness to pay for environmental change, and the accounting prices of the environment were developed. The pioneering research that propelled the development of this field was done by Mäler (1971, 1974) and Rosen (1974). The environmental valuation technique that Mäler developed is nowadays called the travel cost method, while the technique developed by Rosen is called the hedonic pricing method.

Although the idea of the travel cost method is said to be the brainchild of Hotelling (1949), it was Mäler (1971, 1974) who established it as a valuation method by providing the economic base (weak complementarity approach). The technique adopts environmental value from the relationship of travel cost and travel demand (frequency of visits), and was developed mainly as a recreation evaluation method. It provides demand curves under the initial quality of the environment. When environmental qualities are improved, the demand curves may shift to the right. The travel cost method assigns the computed consumer surplus at this point as the value of improving environmental quality.[11] The area $ABp_c^1p_c^0$ in Figure 3.3.1 indicates the consumer surplus for the environmental change. This figure suggests why it is used in recreation evaluation. The conditions at which this evaluation is valid are those when there is an existing choke price – that is, the prices p_c^0 and p_c^1 where demand becomes zero. Since this requires that the target be non-essential, possible targets for evaluation are limited. Further, there are several problems in what items should be computed as travel cost (Randall, 1994), so data gathering during experimental demonstration is fraught with difficulty.

The hedonic method established by Rosen (1974) looks at the influence of environmental variables, focusing on market price or labour wages. Here, considering a very simplified concrete example, the focus is on the relationship between land price and the many variables that determine land price. What is decisively important in estimating the value of environmental capital is the assumption that land price reflects the environment (capitalization hypothesis). For example, noise and atmospheric

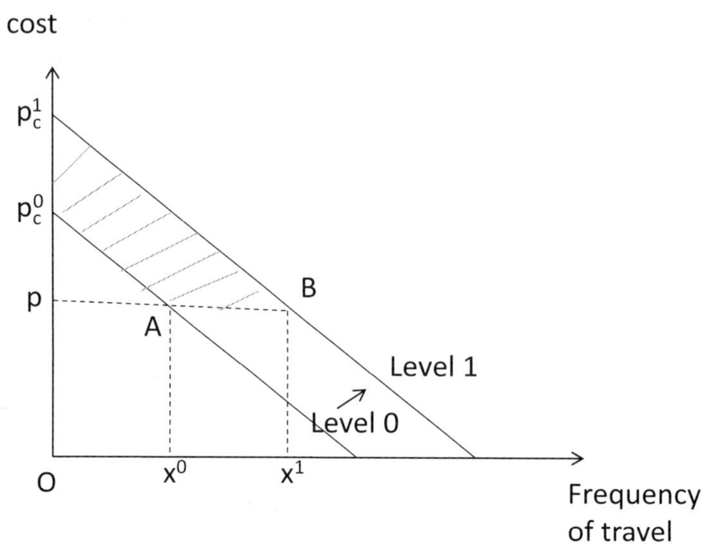

Figure 3.3.1 Measuring consumer surplus using the travel cost method

pollution levels come to mind. Assuming other conditions are the same, land price decreases as noise or atmospheric pollution levels worsen. In this case, the change in value that brings about marginal change in natural capital as determined by regression analysis or other methods reflects the value of the capital.

Assumption of weak complementarity is necessary in the travel cost method, while the hedonic method requires the assumption of capitalization. Both are strong assumptions. Further, as the two methods are "revealed preference methods" that allocate environmental values indirectly by observing the market more than the inevitable use of market data, this makes it possible to measure use value. However, non-use value is almost disregarded in these methods.[12] In that case, the targets for measurement by the revealed preference method in environmental valuation are limited and caution is always needed with regard to which part of environmental value was measured.

Stated preference method

The contingent valuation method (CVM) was developed in response to the requirement for an estimate of non-use value. CVM seeks the value of environmental benefits directly through the use of questionnaires; hence it is called a "direct method". Based on this method, determining surplus in the Hicks sense is easy and, depending on the design of the questionnaire, there is no need to worry about the existence or multicolinearity of data. However, since the questionnaire is a method suspected of being easily prone to bias, the design process and the validity and reliability of results are gravely questioned.

CVM has a relatively long history. The concept was first proposed by Ciriacy-Wantrup (1947), and demonstrated by Davis (1963). However, in its highly polished form it dates back approximately 20 years.[13] The impetus was provided by the *Exxon Valdez* incident and an Ohio trial of 1989.

In the *Exxon Valdez* incident a very large quantity of crude oil (some 42 million litres) was discharged off the shores of Alaska from a tanker belonging to Exxon Corp., causing serious marine pollution and great damage to coastal recreation, fishing resources, marine ecosystems and beaches, killed around 250,000 auks, 2,800 sea otters, 300 harbour seals, 22 orcas and so on. The estimation of the legal damages caused a large controversy over whether non-use value should be included or not. The government of Alaska estimated the damage using CVM and came up with a figure for damage to the ecosystem (non-use value) of approximately $2.8 billion (Carson et al., 2003). After receiving this estimate, Exxon entered into negotiation that resulted to a settlement whereby Exxon paid around $1 billion on top of clean-up costs and damage to the fishing industry, but private lawsuits are still ongoing. During the first trial, $5 billion was assessed for exemplary damages, $287 million for damages to the fishing industry and $3.5 million for damages to the populace, regional government and agencies and industries in the region.

The Ohio trial pits the Ohio state government and environmental protection organizations against the industrial world concerning the Department of the Interior ruling with regard to procedures in the valuation of damages under the Comprehensive Environmental Response, Compensation and Liability Act. The decision of the court expanded the range of the coverage of valuation to include non-use value, and affirmed the validity of the appropriateness of CVM.

Even after the settlement was reached in the *Exxon Valdez* case, criticisms from industry of non-use value and its estimation techniques and results increased: a symposium was held on the effectiveness of non-use value and estimation techniques;[14] and the debate concerning non-use value and the stated preference method is still not finished.[15] Despite this, the NOAA (National Oceanic and Atmospheric Administration of the US Department of Commerce) decided to recognize the validity of CVM in 1993.[16] Agreement on non-use value continued to grow, and the stated preference method as a technique to estimate non-use value developed to a large extent from 1989 through this series of incidents.

After the NOAA guidelines were established, experimental research using CVM to estimate non-use value produced many results. The greatest flaw of CVM is that many biases can seep in,[17] and one of the main problems is how to minimize bias. For that purpose, strong emphasis is given in research to the preparation of questionnaires and devising methods of answering them.

Issues on environmental valuation in sustainability studies

Present methods of estimating environmental value are basically founded on classic utilitarianism ideas. Hence it is also true that useful information can be obtained by focusing only on efficiency. Conducting economic valuation of the environment based on efficiency standards must surely enable diagnosis of social welfare. That being the case, if correcting the flaws of efficiency standards and non-welfare constituents such as standards of fairness is adopted unreasonably, valuation may no longer discharge the role (i.e. checking efficiency) that it has played to date. Basing efficiency standards on economic valuation and entrusting other valuation standards (fairness, justice, rights and so on) to political and policy processes might just possibly be a modest role for economic valuation of the environment.

However, the goodness of social conditions should be measured based on well-being and not on welfare, and if welfare and well-being are sometimes estranged, the significance of social measures aimed at increasing welfare is called into question. This is because as long as social policies are designed to make society better, enhancing well-being should be sought. In this case, the importance of social diagnosis based on welfare is de-emphasized. What is sought is an evaluation that diagnoses whether society has become better or not – that is, an evaluation based on standards of well-being. From this point of view, environmental valuation expansion and enlargement could be obtained from the expansion and extension of welfare standards. Research on sustainability is not aimed at economic efficiency only, but at analysing the development process by observing the increase in well-being and considering the broad range of society, economics and environment. Assuming that techniques of environmental valuation play a fixed role in sustainability research, expansion of the current framework is sought.

In connection with this, Amartya Sen (1995) casts doubt on the approach, be it a market analysis technique (revealed preference method) or a quasi-market analysis (stated preference method), applied to evaluation fitted to the market mechanism analogically when used to value the environment. Sen points out that conducting a valuation of the environment, whether in real or virtual goods, is restricted to buying and selling activities only; he wants an alternative evaluation from the standpoint of the individuals who constitute the main body of valuation as citizens, using a social view that considers the well-being of these individuals. This requires that placing the standards of valuation on well-being and not on utility should be reflected in the estimation of accounting prices.

Today, in environmental valuation techniques, investigations to clarify individuals' choices reflect the results of psychology and experimental economics. Psychological mechanisms and backgrounds to the choice situation, which should affect individuals' choices, are introduced into economic analysis. Perhaps the impact of important factors such as social justice, freedom, etc. on individual evaluation and selection will also be addressed.

3-3-4 Benefit transfer and sustainability assessment

The earlier discussion has verified that an accounting price of capital is necessary for sustainability assessment; in particular, an accounting price of natural capital is information that methods of environmental valuation are expected to provide. Generally speaking, however, accounting prices change with changes in location or prevailing conditions, even with the same natural capital. Since methods of environmental valuations are site-specific applications, accounting prices must be estimated for each country in order to check their sustainability. In principle, although it is good to perform a method of environmental valuation appropriate to that region in the world and estimate the accounting prices for each country, this costs time and money and is realistically impractical. Hence, consideration is given to the applicability of the method called benefits transfer.

Much experimental research on environmental valuation has accumulated over the past decade, and a number of databases on environmental valuation have been systematically organized. Benefits transfer from actual examples of environmental valuations is a method focusing on the value of currently targeted environments.[18] There have been cost-benefit analyses to evaluate policy implementation; however, such analysis requires much time and expense. In the United States, for example, guidelines on whether a benefits assessment estimate should be done for existing evaluative research have been prepared (Desvousges, Johnson and Banzhaf, 1998). Research on benefits transfer proceeded under these kinds of policy background.

Benefits transfer presupposes the existence of convergence validity as a standard for estimated environment values (Mitchell and Carson, 1989). This is the difference in the estimated environmental value for similar values taken at different places and different times: it should be explainable statistically, and requires that evaluated amounts should not be

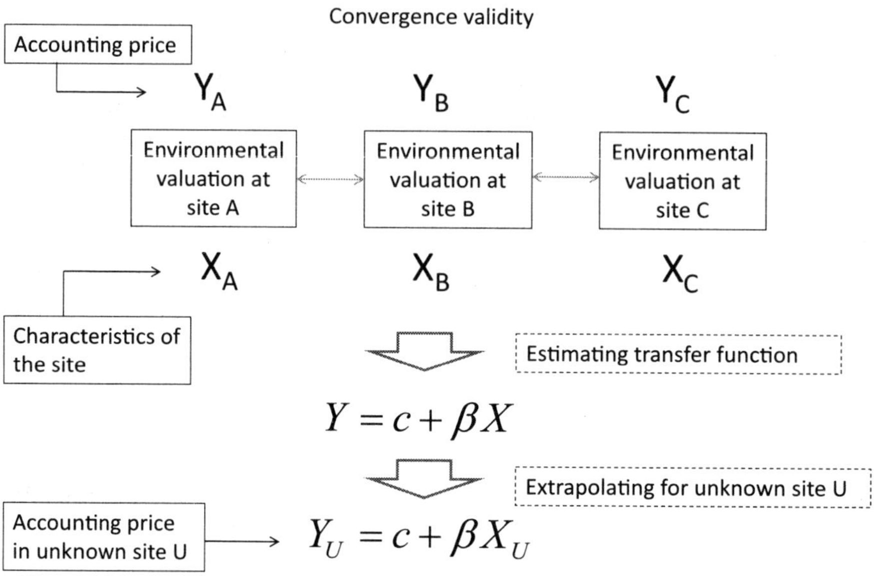

Figure 3.3.2 Benefits transfer

different without basis. Odoko, Kokubo and Takeuchi (2007) pointed out three causes of these differences.

- Causes related to the main body of evaluation: errors caused by differences in the attributes of the main body of evaluation.
- Causes related to targets of evaluation: errors arising from the properties of evaluation targets, such as project content, type and scale of environmental goods, weather conditions, vegetation, etc.
- Causes related to time: errors arising from causes such as time of survey, project start time, time and frequency of payment, etc.

Although methods of benefits transfer include unit requirement, meta-analysis and benefits function transfer, the one most suitable to assess sustainability by inclusive wealth is meta-analysis. Meta-analysis gathers a number of actual existing valuations, assigns explained variables to estimate values and computes meta-function using explanatory variables for the causes of errors mentioned above (Figure 3.3.2). Here it is necessary to introduce the diversity of causes that regulate sustainability, mentioned earlier.

3-3-5 Assessing sustainability through genuine investment

In this chapter sustainability has been expressed as an economic formula and a methodical measure that has been performed. A further step is to evaluate the World Bank's precious World Development Indicators database, which contains indices appropriate to the genuine investment introduced earlier.[19] However, changes in manufactured capital are measured from net savings of the populace, changes in human capital from educational expenditure and changes in natural capital from reduction in energy and mineral resources and forests and damage from carbon dioxide emissions. Needless to say, this list is not perfect. Firstly, many capitals that cannot be disregarded are not accounted for. Secondly, market prices are used for the respective accounting prices and are not ideally computed. Nevertheless, the fact that genuine investment as a concept is actually measured is valued highly as a first step in assessing sustainability.

From these data, the development path that each country has taken up to the present can be checked in parts from the point of view of sustainability. Based on that, sustainable development is not pursued in many developing countries, particularly in sub-Saharan Africa. Further, the accounting prices of natural capital dealt with here use figures that are fairly conservative, such as $20 per tonne of carbon dioxide. Being judged as non-sustainable rings an alarm regarding the way development is being pursued.

More detailed research on these kinds of data analysis is going on. For example, Arrow et al. (2004) conducted analysis considering the productivities of all elements. Hamilton, Clemens and Atkinson started an analysis that included the major causes of population growth; much of their research is collected in Hamilton and Atkinson (2006). Dasgupta (2007) analyses the relationship with the HDI and other indices. Sato, Samreth and Yamada (2009) analysed the future apprehension over judgement on sustainability, focusing on index volatility.

Enrichment of databases drives sustainability studies onward, and thus may bring about improvements and new theories. When discussing sustainability, it is very important to understand fully whether development is sustainable at present, and up to what extent it would be sustainable. That is why there are high expectations regarding developments in these fields.

3-3-6 Summary

This chapter dealt with the points at issue connected to assessing sustainable development as an economic formula and the associated techniques in estimating the accounting prices of natural capital. Whether as genuine investment or environmental valuation techniques, the methods can be seen as continuously indicative to some extent. However, there also remain many and varied problems to resolve and many desperately difficult points regarding their resolution, such as how to evaluate accurately the price of natural capital based on the concept of well-being. However, efforts are proceeding, and progress is steadily being made. There is very little room to relax, though, because the manner by which society pursues development should be corrected before it falls irreversibly into a condition of non-sustainability. Assessment of sustainability is an urgent task that greatly needs more research.

Notes

1. However, many in the field of ecology economics adopt the latter viewpoint. The difference in the viewpoints of environment economics and ecology economics becomes a topic of dispute every now and then.
2. Arrow, Dasgupta and Mäler (2003) expressed well-being at time t as U_t, $V_t = \int_t^{\infty} U_\tau e^{-\delta(\tau-t)}\, d\tau$ and required that for all t, $dV_t/dt \geq 0$ be a condition for sustainability. Here, δ stands for discount rate.
3. The more the judiciary is independent from the relevant governmental unit, the more freedom of speech (especially political speech).
4. Sen (1970) called this the "impossibility of a Paretian liberal".
5. Related to this point, Stiglitz, Sen and Fitoussi (2009) refer to social capital, happiness, health and mental well-being.
6. Here, wealth is broadly broken down into the components investment to manufactured capital, M, human capital H, natural capital, N, and knowledge, Z.
   In so doing, the wealth for generation t is expressed as $W_t = \sum_i p_{it}M_{it} + \sum_j h_{jt}H_{jt} + \sum_k r_{kt}N_{kt} + \sum_m q_{mt}Z_{mt}$ with p, h, r *and* q as weights. The sum requires when adding different capital that the unit is converted, for example into an economic unit (money). And sustainability requires "non-declining wealth in the future".
7. Also called "shadow price". For a capital, for example, the accounting price of the ith manufactured capital M_i, from the definition, is the increase in the social well-being when that capital increased marginally by one unit, written as $p_{it} = \partial V/\partial M_{it}$. The other capitals H, N, Z are the same.
8. Represented as I, genuine investment is expressed as $I = \sum_i p_{it}\frac{dM_{it}}{dt} + \sum_j h_{ji}\frac{dH_{jt}}{dt} + \sum_k r_{kt}\frac{dN_{kt}}{dt} + \sum_m q_{mt}\frac{dZ_{mt}}{dt}$. Although also called genuine saving, adjusted net saving, comprehensive investment, etc., all refer to the change in wealth as the source of well-being.
9. The former problem is the subject of different academic fields. For example, measurement of natural capital (current resource capital, ecosystem environmental amount, etc.) is researched in physical resources and biology (Wackernagel and Rees, 1996). The measurement of human capital is social research (Putnam, 1993). Measurement of anthropogenic capital is done in the economics field.
10. By assigning 0 to pre-change and 1 to post-change, the value of CS that satisfies $V(C, Q^0, Y) = V(C, Q^1, Y - CS)$ is the valuation. C is the consumption vector; Q^0 is the environmental services/function prior to project implementation; Q^1 is the environmental services/function after project implementation; Y is income.
11. Strictly, this is a form of the travel cost method called a single-site model. Seen from the quality of usable data, this technique is based on Marshall demand curves, and needs calculation in order to derive the compensating surplus.
12. With regard to the practice of environmental evaluation, cases where non-utilitarian is greater than utilitarian value are seen (Hausman, 1993).

13. Coupled with econometric development, progress during this period is rapid – see Bateman and Willis (1999), Louviere, Hensher and Swait (2000), Bateman et al. (2002) and Haab and McConnell (2002).
14. This content is summarized by Hausman (1993).
15. For the dispute over CVM see Hausman (1993) and *Journal of Economic Perspectives* 8(4) (1994). McFadden (1994) gives three disputable points regarding CVM: psychological soundness; validity of statistical methods; and rationality of the respondent. Further, criticisms from the field of psychology were raised by Kahneman and Knetsch (1992), indicating the failure of rationality and effects of consideration. However, Sen (1995) pointed out that in determining what is non-rational, detailed observations of how selectors look at the problem of selection and how they attempt solutions are required.
16. The NOAA panel concluded that CVM offers sufficient reliability as the launching point for the trial process on damage evaluation. Within that, the lost passive use value is included (Arrow, Dasgupta and Mäler, 1993). For details on the NOAA panel see Mitchell and Carson (1989) and Takeuchi (1999).
17. Mitchell and Carson (1989) and Kuriyama (1998) have summarized the various biases.
18. Research on benefits transfer is popular all over the world. For example, *Ecological Economics* 60 (2006) is a special edition on benefits transfer.
19. Named "adjusted net saving" in the database.

REFERENCES

Arrow, K. J., P. Dasgupta and K.-G. Mäler (2003) "Evaluating Projects and Assessing Sustainable Development in Imperfect Economies", *Environmental and Resource Economics* 26, pp. 647–685.

Arrow, K. J., R. Solow, P. R. Portney, E. E. Leamer, R. Radner and H. Schuman (1993) "Report of the NOAA Panel on Contingent Valuation", *Federal Register* 58(10), pp. 4601–4614.

Arrow, K. J., P. Dasgupta, L. Goulder, G. Daily, P. Ehrlich, G. Heal, S. Levin, K.-G. Mäler, S. Schneider, D. Starrett and B. Walker (2004) "Are We Consuming Too Much?", *Journal of Economic Perspectives* 18(3), pp. 147–172.

Bateman, I. J. and K. G. Willis (1999) *Valuing Environmental Preferences*. Oxford: Oxford University Press.

Bateman, I. J., R. T. Carson, B. Day, M. Hanemann, N. Hanley, T. Hett, M. Jones-Lee, G. Loomes, S. Mourato, E. Özdemiroĝlu, D. W. Pearce, R. Sugden and J. Swanson (2002) *Economic Valuation with Stated Preference Techniques*. Cheltenham: Edward Elgar.

Carson, R. T., R. C. Mitchell, W. M. Hanemann, R. J. Kopp, S. Presser and P. A. Ruud (1992) "Contingent Valuation and Lost Passive Use: Damages from the *Exxon Valdez* Oil Spill", *Environmental and Resource Economics* 25, pp. 257–286.

Ciriacy-Wantrup, S. V. (1947) "Capital Returns from Soil-conservation Practices", *Journal of Farm Economics* 29, pp. 1181–1196.

Dasgupta, P. (2004) *Human Well-Being and the Natural Environment*. Oxford: Oxford University Press.

——— (2007) *Economics*. Oxford: Oxford University Press.

Davis, R. K. (1963) "The Value of Outdoor Recreation: An Economic Study of Maine Woods", PhD dissertation, Harvard University.

Desvousges, W. H., F. R. Johnson and H. S. Banzhaf (1998) *Environmental Policy Analysis with Limited Information*. Cheltenham: Edward Elgar.

Haab, T. C. and K. E. McConnell (2002) *Valuing Environmental and Natural Resources: The Econometrics of Non-Market Valuation*. Cheltenham: Edward Elgar.

Hamilton, K. and G. Atkinson (2006) *Wealth, Welfare and Sustainability*. Cheltenham: Edward Elgar.

Hausman, J. A. (1993) *Contingent Valuation: A Critical Assessment*. Amsterdam: North-Holland.

Hotelling, H. (1949) *An Economic Study of the Monetary Valuation of Recreation in the National Parks*. Washington, DC: US Department of the Interior.

Kahneman, D. and J. L. Knetsch (1992) "Valuing Public Goods: The Purchase of Moral Satisfaction", *Journal of Environmental Economics and Management* 22, pp. 57–70.

Kuriyama, K. (1998) *Kankyo no Kachi To Hyoukasyuhou* (*Environmental Value and Valuation Methods*). Sapporo: Hokkaido University Press.

Louviere, J. J., D. A. Hensher and J. D. Swait (2000) *Stated Choice Methods: Analysis and Application*. Cambridge: Cambridge University Press.

Mäler, K.-G. (1971) "A Method of Estimating Social Benefits from Pollution Control", *Swedish Journal of Economics* 73, pp. 121–133.

——— (1974) *Environmental Economics: A Theoretical Inquiry*. Baltimore, MD: Johns Hopkins University Press.

McFadden, D. (1994) "Contingent Valuation and Social Choice", *American Journal of Agricultural Economics* 76, pp. 689–708.

Mitchell, R. C. and R. T. Carson (1989) *Using Surveys to Value Public Goods: The Contingent Valuation Method*. Washington, DC: Resources for the Future.

Odoko, T., K. Kokubo and K. Takeuchi (2007) "The Benefit Transfer of Air Pollution Control Measures and Environmental Accounting", *Environmental Science* 20(1), pp. 7–20.

Putnam, R. (1993) *Making Democracy Work*. Princeton, NJ: Princeton University Press.

Randall, A. (1994) "A Difficulty with the Travel Cost Method", *Land Economics* 70, pp. 88–96.

Rosen, S. (1974) "Hedonic Prices and Implicit Markets: Product Differentiation in Pure Competition", *Journal of Political Economy* 82, pp. 34–55.

Sato, M., S. Samreth and K. Yamada (2009) "A Simple Numerical Study on Sustainable Development with Genuine Saving", ISER Discussion Papers No. 728, Osaka University.

Sen, A. (1970) "The Impossibility of a Paretian Liberal", *Journal of Political Economy* 78, pp. 152–157.

——— (1985) "Well-being, Agency and Freedom", *Journal of Philosophy* 82, pp. 169–221.

——— (1995) "Environmental Evaluation and Social Choice: Contingent Valuation and the Market Analogy", *Japanese Economic Review* 46(1), pp. 23–37.

Stiglitz, J. E., A. Sen and J.-P. Fitoussi (2009) "Report by the Commission on the Measurement of Economic Performance and Social Progress", Commission on the Measurement of Economic Performance and Social Progress, Paris.

Takeuchi, K. (1999) *Kankyo Hyouka No Seisaku Riyou* (*Contingent Valuation Method and Travel Cost Method*). Tokyo: Keiso Shobo.

Taylor, C. L. and D. A. Jodice (eds) (1983) *The World Handbook of Political and Social Indicators*, 3rd edn. New Haven, CT: Yale University Press.

Tinbergen, J. (1954) *Centralization and Decentralization in Economic Policy*. Amsterdam: North-Holland.

Ueta, K. (1996) *Kankyo Keizaigaku* (*Environmental Economics*). Tokyo: Iwanami Shoten Publishers.

Wackernagel, M. and W. Rees (1996) *Our Ecological Footprint*. Gabriola Island, BC: New Society Publishers.

World Commission on Environment and Development (1987) *Our Common Future*. Oxford: Oxford University Press.

4

Strategies for sustainable society

4-1

Basic mitigation strategy for climate change

Seiji Ikkatai

4-1-1 Trends in global emission of greenhouse gases and carbon dioxide concentration

Measures for mitigating climate change are designed to reduce the emission of greenhouse gases that cause global warming, arrest the progress of global warming and stabilize the concentration of greenhouse gases in the atmosphere. These measures are aimed at solving the very roots of the problem by reducing anthropogenic greenhouse gas emissions and increasing absorption of these by plants. By virtue of the extent of their contribution to climate change, these most basic measures should be implemented immediately.

The international community, having awakened to the gravity of the global warming problem and the importance of taking measures to mitigate it, seized the opportunity during the Earth Summit (UN Conference on Environment and Development) of 1992 to adopt the UN Framework Convention on Climate Change and launch the campaign to get the signature of all countries. The treaty took effect in 1995. In order to strengthen it further, the Kyoto Protocol, aimed at reducing the emission of greenhouse gases from developed countries by an average of 5 per cent against 1990 levels for the period 2008–2012, was adopted in 1997. Ratification by each country met many difficulties during the negotiations over details, however, so the protocol only took effect in 2005.

During this period the United States, the country with greatest greenhouse gas emissions, withdrew from the protocol for fear of the severe

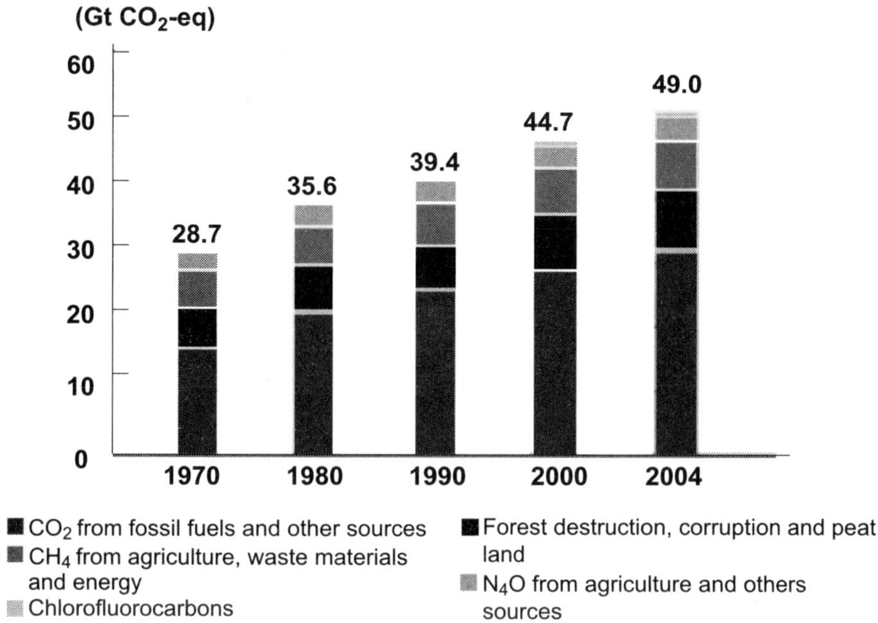

Figure 4.1.1 Trends in global emission of greenhouse gases
Source: IPCC (2007).

impact of emission reduction measures on its economy, imparting a severe blow to the main pillar supporting the effectiveness of the Kyoto Protocol. The trend from 2000 to 2004 shows a marked rise in the rate of increase of greenhouse gases (Figure 4.1.1). The main reason behind this trend is that the reduction in greenhouse gas emissions did not proceed as thought.

Developed countries, beginning with China, failed to discharge their epoch-making accountability and impartiality *vis-à-vis* the Kyoto Protocol to reduce emissions, so that gas emission accompanying high economic growth continued to increase. In fact, how to realize the agreed reduction targets for the developed countries was left to the judgement of each country, hence countries that were not able to set up effective ways to realize the targets were unable to achieve the intended reduction.

As a result, the concentration of carbon dioxide in the global atmosphere increased at a steady rate of approximately 1.9 ppm each year. One cannot help but conclude that the UN Framework Convention on Climate Change did not improve the effectiveness of climate change mitigation despite the efforts of the parties concerned after the adoption of the treaty. This is a very serious situation.

4-1-2 Recommendations for reduction of greenhouse gas emissions in the IPCC Fourth Assessment Report

This situation causes serious alarm from the standpoint of natural science. The IPCC Fourth Assessment Report (IPCC, 2007) showed that, without a doubt, global warming of the climate system is accelerating: the temperature has risen during the past 100 years, and global changes in the climate have affected many natural ecosystems. More, the impact of the predicted climate changes if temperature rise exceeds the average increase from 1980 to 1999 of 1.5–2.5°C is that 20–30 per cent of the living things evaluated so far face the high likelihood of increased risk of total extinction. If the temperature rise exceeds 2°C, the number of persons who will suffer from coastal flooding will increase by several hundred thousand each year. If the temperature rise exceeds 3°C, all cereal production at lower latitudes will decrease while a part of cereal production will decrease in the higher latitudes.

To obviate this serious damage in the future, assuming an average increase in global air temperature since the Industrial Revolution of 2.0–2.4°C, the amount of carbon dioxide emission in 2050 should be reduced by 50–85 per cent from the emissions in year 2000. However, at this juncture realizing this level is difficult in practice because the target temperature increase should be set to the range 2.4–2.8°C. Even so, the amount of carbon dioxide emission in 2050 should be reduced by 30–60 per cent. Under these conditions, it has been strongly argued, mainly in Europe, that global greenhouse gas emissions should be reduced by half by the year 2050. Japan is basically of the same viewpoint.

In order to realize this goal of reducing global emissions of greenhouse gases to the atmosphere by half, taking into account the economic growth of developed countries in the future, it is necessary that developed countries reduce emissions by −50 to −80 per cent from the current levels by the year 2050, which is clearly a daunting figure. How a nation will balance its economic growth with the measures to mitigate climate change that will be needed to realize this goal will become a grave political issue for each country.

4-1-3 Trends in measures to mitigate climate changes in Europe

Although members of the European Union started to adopt carbon taxes in the 1990s, the adoption of a common carbon tax within the region was evaluated and abandoned as each country took its own measures to mitigate climate change. The EU secretariat adopted a common system stipulating caps on the amount of emissions for large-scale combustion facilities in 2005. More, prior to agreeing on international reduction targets, the European Union as a whole has already established a greenhouse gas emission reduction target of –20 per cent by the year 2020 (or –30 per cent, should there be a high degree of international consensus). Thus at this point the European Union is a step ahead of the rest of the world in the pursuit of this endeavour. Further, the United States, which up to now has been dragging its feet in taking measures to mitigate climate change because of their grave impact on the economy, made a big turnaround following the inauguration of the Democratic Obama administration with regard to the aggressive measures to mitigate climate change that form the presuppositions of the post-Kyoto international framework, as indicated by its acceleration of congressional discussions on the adoption of an EU-type emissions management system.

The idea of EU measures to mitigate climate change is similar to the view expressed in the Stern Review (Stern, 2007): "the benefits that result from taking bold and immediate measures to address climate change exceed the cost", and rest upon the fundamental recognition that "although the shift to low carbon economy may be criticized severely from the point of view of competitiveness, it also provides opportunities for economic growth". The European Union, regardless of other international agreements, has already resolved to reduce greenhouse gases by the year 2020 by up to –20 per cent of the 1990 levels and increase the ratio of renewable energy to up to 20 per cent of all energy production. Moreover, caps on emission rates will continue beyond the year 2013 and a shift will be made from the current free allocation system to an auction-regulated system of emission rights. This indicates a decision to strengthen methods that give emphasis to exploiting market mechanisms. The European Union crafted three strategic objectives to express this desire: coping with the problem of climate change; strengthening guarantees of energy security for the European Union; and strengthening the international competitiveness of the EU economy.

The European Union is planning to secure medium-term international competitiveness while also giving international leadership in resolving problems attendant to climate change, by exerting pressure on industrial companies to limit emissions using the market mechanism, and by hastening the transition to a low-carbon social economy through technological innovations and the creation of new business models. However, industry has strong apprehensions regarding non-industrial emissions, so the European Union will conduct an investigation of the impact of the problems mainly on large energy-consuming industries and, if necessary, propose adjustments to the free allocation framework or countermeasures to importers of the affected commodities.

4-1-4 Trends in measures to mitigate climate change in Japan

As a measure to mitigate climate change in Japan, a voluntary reduction plan addressing global warming established by the former Nippon Keidanren (Japan Business Federation) in 1997 for different industrial sectors shoulders much of the load of reducing greenhouse gases. Obviously, although there are laws on energy conservation, on improving the efficiency of energy utilization and on adoption of renewable energy, these cannot be regarded as comprising strong policies and procedures for the control of absolute values of emission reduction. Moreover, in measures for residential and office sectors, although there is some guidance on energy saving, the basic approach consists of derivative energy conservation measures using citizen initiatives such as information dissemination and conservation campaigns. Earnest economic measures that exploit market mechanisms have not been adopted. The background to this is that Japan has already engaged in energy conservation activities, so there is a deep-seated and strong opposition in economic circles against measures such as setting carbon taxes and emission caps that would only burden Japan's economy. As a result, the trend in Japan against the base year shows repeated rises and falls in greenhouse gas emissions, but with the overall trend increasing (Figure 4.1.2).

In particular, the situation indicated by data gathered for the three-year period from 2005 to 2007 shows that emissions increased again after dropping down in 2006. There are three reasons that can be attributed to this trend. First, 2006 had a record-breaking warm winter, so large savings on domestic and office heating energy resulted in reduction in the emission of carbon dioxide, which in turn cancelled the marginal increase that the industrial sector was producing. Second, economic conditions in Japan from 2005 to 2007 were such that there was relatively smooth transition and the emission of greenhouse gases from the industrial sector continued to increase. Third is the operational condition of nuclear power plants: in 2007 additional thermal power plant operations became necessary when the Kashiwazaki Kariwa nuclear power station stopped as a result of the earthquake that hit the Chuetsu region, thus causing an overall increase in greenhouse gas emission.

Greenhouse gas emission in Japan is greatly affected by these three factors. Although it was predicted that emissions from 2008 will decline because of economic slowdown, the possibility that emissions will rise is very high should economic recovery occur. The reasons why these conditions prevail in Japan can be attributed largely to a delay in defining post–Kyoto Protocol medium-term objectives and, at the same time, the failure to establish basic policies on reducing greenhouse gases as a measure to mitigate climate change.

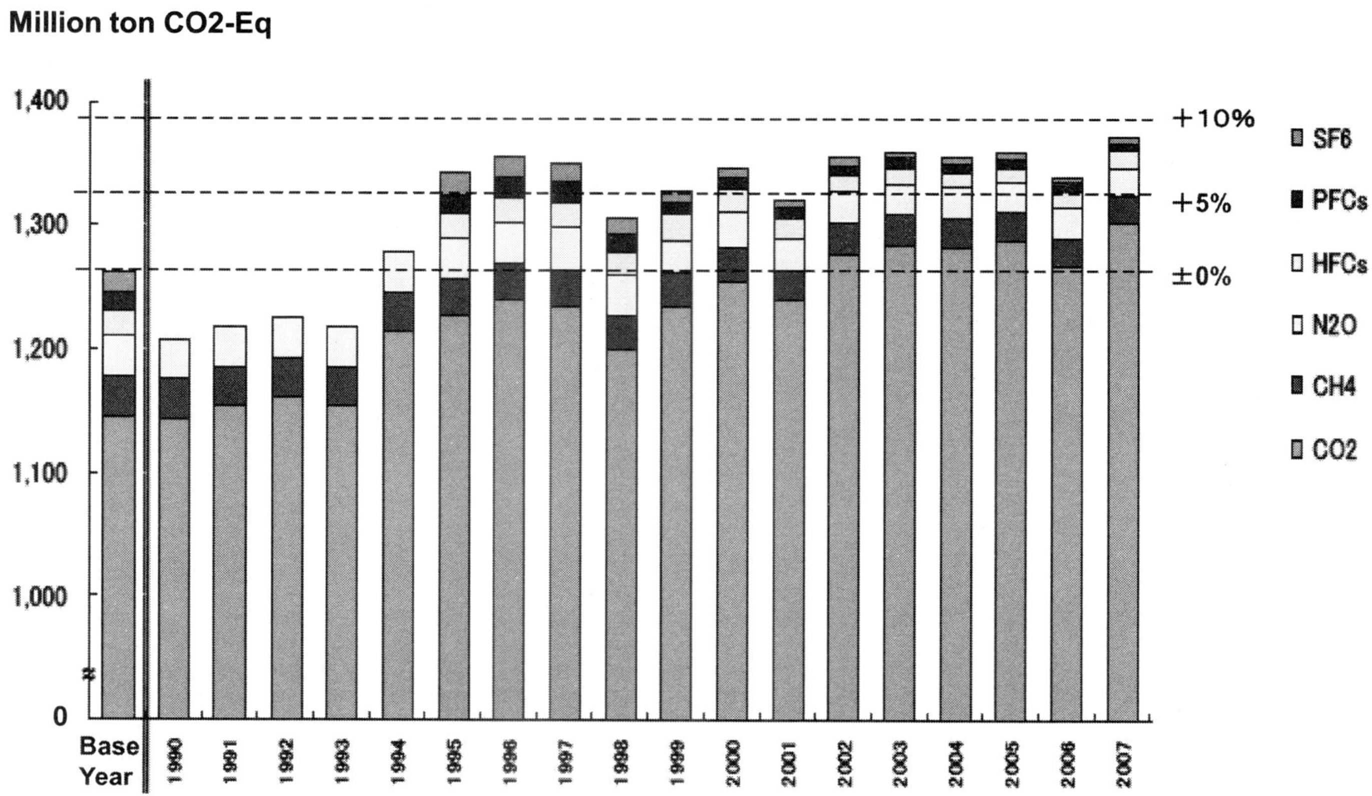

Figure 4.1.2 Trend of GHG emissions in Japan, 1990–2007
Source: Ministry of the Environment.

Under these circumstances, the government initiated trial implementation of emissions trading in the domestic integrated market from 2008, targeting industries. However, participation in this trial was based on voluntary judgement, and therefore goal setting was autonomous in principle. Further, penal rules were not defined. Hence there is much doubt regarding the effectiveness of the scheme compared with the EU system. Furthermore, the Japanese government belatedly announced the medium-term emission objectives for June 2009 of –15 compared to the year 2005 (–8 per cent compared to 1990). The setting up of these objectives was fraught with difficulties stemming from the clash of opinions among economic circles that are against large reduction objectives because of their adverse impact on the economy, environmental NGOs (non-governmental organizations) that campaign on problems brought about by climate change and are therefore compelled to lead global advocacy of large emission reduction objectives, and researchers who emphasize the positive economic impact of technological innovations and creation of new industries brought about by large-scale reduction objectives.

In the Japanese general election of 2009, the Democratic Party took power and new Prime Minister Yukio Hatoyama declared a new greenhouse gas reduction target of –25 per cent compared to the 1990 base by 2020. He expressed his political will to introduce ambitious climate change policies such as carbon tax and a cap-and-trade scheme. It is expected that Japanese climate change policy will be enhanced from now on. In contrast, President Obama stated a US greenhouse gas reduction target of –17 per cent compared to the 2005 base by 2020 at COP15 in December 2009.

4-1-5 Fundamental directions for measures to mitigate climate change

With the conditions surrounding the issues on climate change described above, what directions should measures to mitigate global climate change take? Thinking of the gravity and urgency of problems as well as the deep connection to the economic development of a country, I think that, regardless of whether a country is developed or still developing, the three directions described below must be important to all countries and regions.

Establishing the framework for long-term policies considering their impact on investment decisions

Current investments, particularly in public infrastructure such as power, transportation and facilities, determine what the future Japan will look like several decades from now. Forecasting what the economic environment will be in the future, within which long-term recovery of these investments must be made, is critically important to industries. This perspective requires policies that provide the proper influence based on signals from the market regarding every type of industrial and personal investment decision. In other words, when signals from the market on long-term costs incurred in the emission of greenhouse gas are clear, then investments in production facilities, manufacturing and consumption that involve large gas emissions can be avoided and incentives for lower-emission production and consumption behaviour would have more effect. For that reason, establishing a framework for policies that would provide such incentives is a priority, including long-term policies, mid-term goals, such as the reduction targets for greenhouse gases up to the year 2050 and interim targets, and the adoption of definite procedural measures to realize these objectives.

Also, what this framework brings about is not mere maintenance of the current situation of the social economy, but the need for building a common consciousness that comes with changing the industrial and consumption structure as well as lifestyles and sense of values: that is, reduction of global emission of greenhouse gases by half by the year 2050, with reduction from developed countries by 60–80 per cent, and measures for these reductions that require the expenditure of cost. Strictly speaking, there is a need for a fundamental consensus to shift across the market from industries and goods that produce relatively more greenhouse gases to industries and goods that produce relatively less emissions. However, even with the establishment of the framework for long-term policies, it is natural that developed and developing countries will differ in their objectives and steps to realize them in the light of their current situation. Viewed from this perspective, the policy framework of Japan should be sectoral in nature.

Adoption of effective measures driven by market mechanisms

The voluntary built-up approach to the reduction of emission among the industrial sectors practised in Japan to date has come to the point that it can no longer cope with the large-scale reductions that will be needed. In the current industrial situation, industries that are concerned with environmental problems and can afford the cost do come up with countermeasures to reduce emissions, but industries exposed to intense competition will find it hard to do so because of the cost incurred, and will need strong signals from the market.

On one hand, when market-driven measures that have already been adopted in Europe, such as capped emission trading, are put in place, if an industry fails to reduce emission of carbon dioxide to the predetermined cap, it must purchase emission rights from the market. The industry should bear the cost of purchasing these emission credits. If an industry exceeds emission reduction beyond the cap through technological innovation or other methods, it can sell that excess to the market. It is expected that this will act as a strong and continuing incentive for technological development and energy conservation. More, by linking this to the global carbon market, the cost of emission reduction could be lowered further than by limiting the system to one country only. In that sense, measures driven by market mechanisms such as trading of greenhouse gas emission rights could gain greater importance in mitigating climate change in the future. However, as can be gleaned from the example of the European Union, covering the behaviour of all major players by emissions trading is not practical from the point of view of a cost-benefit analysis that includes governmental expenses. Hence, with regards to sources of small-scale emission that cannot be covered by emissions trading, there is a need to design a comprehensive system that combines market-driven measures such as carbon tax and other measures to strike a balance in pursuit of a low-carbon social economy.

Further, although crafting measures on a national or regional basis is admittedly difficult at this point in time, it is possible to link these measures. A system to cover the entire globe, developed from the point of view of international fairness and economic rationality among developed and developing countries, was proposed by Tokyo University's Hirofumi Uzawa (2003). It involves a system of carbon tax that is proportional to per capita income of the populace and an international fund for atmospheric stabilization. This proposal is expected to become an effective alternative when the crisis consciousness of the people of the world is greatly heightened and a global consensus to resolve the crisis becomes possible.

Establishing new environmental and economic policies that integrate the environment with the economy

Beyond establishing measures to mitigate climate change, in particular measures to reduce greenhouse gases, it is important that the policies to reduce emissions should build a socio-economic system that does not contradict the directions of economic development. That is, society is not forced to choose between reduction in greenhouse gases and economic development, but links emission reduction more intimately with economic development in a proactive manner. Without this kind of system, the fruitless dispute over whether priority is given to the economy or to the environment will continue and, as a result, it is highly possible that measures to mitigate climate change will be taken too late.

The key to building such a socio-economic system is, first, to dissociate greenhouse gas emission from economic development as much as possible by improving energy efficiency drastically, reducing use of energy, replacing fossil-fuel energy with renewable energy and shifting to low-carbon production systems and consumption behaviour, including shifting from purchase of goods to purchase of services. It is also effective to adopt measures that proactively link reduction of greenhouse gases with employment generation, such as in the example where revenues from the German fuel (carbon) tax are used to alleviate the social security cost burden of company employees.

In particular, it is natural from the perspective of fairness for developing countries to aim at sustainable development premised on increased per capita energy consumption and increased income that is comparable to developed countries. In that regard, just as with developed countries, it is important that emission of greenhouse gases be dissociated from economic development as much as possible and that developed countries provide support towards that end.

4-1-6 Fundamental elements of measures to mitigate climate change and their driving forces

The IPCC Fourth Assessment Report (IPCC, 2007) cites the major techniques in mitigating climate change and how these can be implemented to be commercially viable in the fields of energy supply, transportation, buildings, industry, agriculture, forestry, waste, etc.; it also describes their visible environmental benefits and major constraints or opportunities in implementation. Concrete techniques include regulations and standards, taxes and duties, emissions trading systems, funding incentives, voluntary agreements, information techniques, research and development/dissemination and more. This information is useful in giving a glimpse of the overall picture of measures to mitigate climate change. However, I would like to consider these problems from the slightly different perspectives of fundamental elements of mitigation measures and the driving forces behind them.

Fundamental elements

In the preparation of measures to mitigate climate change, I propose four fundamental elements that form the axis of development, viewed from the three points essential to the survival of the human race, namely "ecological (climatic) stability", "economic (employment) stability" and "social equality". These four elements were discussed in *Natural Capitalism* (Hawken, Lovins and Lovins, 2001), which contains many suggestions to think about when reflecting over the directions that measures to mitigate climate change might take.

Radical improvement in resource efficiency

Since the dawn of history, man has lived and shaped civilization using energy and resources at the same time. Broadly dividing the process, the period up to the Industrial Revolution can be described as a time when man basically led life and consumed resources in accord with nature. In Japan, the Edo era was highly cultured and developed a socio-economic system that was very efficient from the point of view of resources; however, the use of fossil fuel started with coal, and that energy eventually led to the Industrial Revolution. Man developed production and consumption behaviour using large amounts of energy and resources to produce goods and services, something not experienced previously, and built a new social economy with poor standards of resource efficiency. On the one hand, that brought great wealth that satisfied many people and was handed down to the present-day civilization. On the other hand, this system produced goods and services at a speed that is much faster than the workings of nature, and bringing these back to be in accord in a short time is difficult.

However, the use of large amounts of fossil fuel led to serious climate change problems, and it is not farfetched to say that it brought about the rebirth of a consciousness of the importance of producing goods and services using less energy and resources. Looking back to the beginning of industrial history, boilers using coal were initially very inefficient in terms of energy use. Later developments in technology introduced automobile engines, electric motors and others with vastly improved efficiencies which were closely linked to economic benefits. More, with the recent development of new systems like biotechnology and nanotechnology, room for improving resource efficiency has broadened further. Thinking of how to resolve problems associated with climate change in the future shows how gravely important it is to grope for ways to improve resource efficiency drastically, and there are excellent possibilities for this.

For instance, if we look at cars, 80 per cent of the energy consumed from fuel is lost through heat escaping from the engine and exhaust gases, while at most 20 per cent is transmitted to driving the wheels' rotation. Of that, 95 per cent is used up in moving the car itself and 5 per cent is used in driving the driver. In other words, the energy used to drive the driver is just 1 per cent of all the energy used for the car. Thinking of energy and resources as a means to drive the car, the possibility of producing transportation with drastically low energy/resource consumption through a lot of creativity and new systems of car usage is quite high.

Biomimicry

In the human world, the production of goods is accomplished using much energy and resources at high temperatures and high pressures accompanied by a lot of discharged waste. However, in natural systems – photosynthesis for example, powered by the sun – the production of carbon dioxide in the atmosphere, sugars (carbohydrates) in the soil and oxygen does not need high temperatures and high pressures and does not produce waste. Moreover, natural systems do not produce noise and bad odours either. If natural systems were considered as manufacturers producing air and carbohydrates, they are incredibly excellent high-technology factories.

The problem is, in using those technologies in the natural world as they are, it does not necessarily follow that they can be linked with fast large-scale production; under the present socio-economic system, profit is largest in the economic sense using technologies invented by humans. However, from the moment that biotechnologies first came close to the high technologies of the ecosystem, the movement to apply ecosystem biotechnologies in human production systems widened.

From the beginning, modern civilization was in a sense created from clearly inefficient and wasteful production and consumption behaviour. Studying high technology within extremely efficient, waste-free ecosystems and harnessing these in modern-day production and consumption systems based on the sustainability of biotechnologies that have stood the tests of time are clearly important elements when considering the directions of technological development in the future.

From purchasing goods to purchasing services

This element models the paradigm behind natural ecosystems: that is, "nothing in the natural world can be disposed of after its lifetime". In other words, in the natural world, over the years, only those things that are recycled completely and reproduced continuously without interruption are left as raw material for production and as production systems. Let us try to introduce these in human society. In societies where such a system has been established, the fundamental is not that manufacturers produce and sell goods, but that services offer those goods and sell them to consumers. Hence, manufacturers produce goods that perform better and are more durable. What is important to society is that the management of goods from production to recycling becomes simple, shifting to a basically lease system from the purchase-and-disposal system practised up to this time. In other words, it is expected that manufacturers will conduct production with buyback in mind, and, in order to control cost, will build a system where recycling of the manufactured goods becomes easier. Moreover, by purchasing services and not goods, it is expected that excess production of goods will be controlled and thereby contribute to improving resource efficiency. To ensure that this kind of a system succeeds from the beginning, simply shifting from the prevailing system of selling goods to leasing goods will not do. It is necessary that both producers and consumers create a new business model that is more profitable. However, since the basics of that new model must, of course, be a rational exclusion of waste seen from the perspective of the ecosystem, there is much room for creativeness in the future.

Reinvesting in natural capital

The last fundamental element is deeply associated with the absorption of greenhouse gases that forms a pillar of measures to mitigate climate change. Needless to say, man's daily life rests on nature: the natural environment consisting of the Earth's atmosphere, water, soil and forests formed over the years as stock, and all renewable natural agricultural, forest and aquatic resources as flow. Bearing in mind that these natural resources are indispensable to the continued survival of man makes us understand that the current problems of climate change stem from the fact that, starting with developed countries, there has not been enough investment made by the entire human race to maintain natural capital, and the world should exert all efforts to create a global system that will manage the maintenance of such capital.

However, the problem is directly connected to the monetary problem of who will shoulder how much of the maintenance management cost – a system whose establishment, in the absence of a world government, is fraught with difficulties because it has to be adjusted between all countries.

From the viewpoint of measures to mitigate climate change, it is necessary to stop reducing forests that serve as absorption sinks of greenhouse gases and build a global mechanism to expand these forests to the maximum possible. In that regard, a reference could be made to the cap-and-trade philosophy. One can imagine that by assigning caps on forest area and adjusting the excess through trading, the expense burden could be adjusted between countries. Further, as discussed earlier, the systems of proportional carbon tax and an international atmospheric stabilization fund are candidates for effective mechanisms. At any rate, this problem is a grave issue that human society will face in the future.

Driving forces

In order to propel these four fundamental elements of measures to mitigate climate change, it is necessary to consider the synergy of three driving forces.

(1) Change in people's perception and sense of values towards environmental problems.
(2) Emergence of innovative technologies and business models/lifestyles.
(3) Reforming socio-economic systems.

For example, adopting capped emissions trading in order to attain greenhouse gas reduction objectives in developed countries involves (3), reforming socio-economic systems. In this case, if we assume no changes in people's perception and sense of values in (1) and no emergence of innovative technologies in (2), this strongly implies that, to mitigate climate change, people's greed has to be suppressed. However, if the reformation of the socio-economic system is accompanied by the birth of innovative technologies and changes in people's perception and sense of values, it is possible that such implications will change considerably.

These kinds of changes do not necessarily happen in the direction of (3) → (2) → (1), but may also happen in the directions (1) → (2) → (3) and (2) → (1) → (3). For example, if we experience a great change in people's sense of value about cars with the appearance of hybrid cars, one of today's innovative technologies, and more lavish cars have the opposite effect of being perceived badly, then it is possible that consumer taste in cars would change, bringing a rapid change in the trend of car sales. Additionally, it is possible that this kind of change in perception will heighten the acceptability of measures to introduce a socio-economic system characterized by capped emissions trading, carbon tax and similar measures.

From the start these three driving forces, rather than being autonomous, have developed synergistically and changed society and the economy along the way. Further, although those who advocate these driving forces overlap, a closer look indicates that advocacy of "change in sense of values and perception" should fall on the private sector, such as environmental NGOs, consumer groups and, depending on the situation, industrial groups as well. Although the government and consumers are deeply involved in the implementation and realization of "development and dissemination of innovative technologies", it is an issue that should be the responsibility of industry. "Reforming the socio-economic system", by its nature, should be the responsibility of the state and governmental agencies, with the support of the electorate and politicians. Examining how to combine these driving forces strategically in concrete terms to bring about changes in the social economy is an issue that researchers will find significant.

4-1-7 Historic paradigm shift regarding measures to mitigate climate change

Looking at the EU package of measures on climate change and energy in recent years and the Green New Deal of the Obama administration, it can be seen that the paradigm governing these measures has changed gradually during the past 10 years. Measures aimed at mitigating and stabilizing climate change are now deemed indispensable to the human race, and, based on this, what should be proactively addressed is not what would adversely affect the economy of a country, but what has a high possibility of positive impact. Conversely, avoiding mitigation measures that only aim to secure gains for the near future is indicative of the growing understanding of the possibility that not only risks associated with climate change but also risk to the economy could increase from the viewpoint of international competition. For example, although the subprime lending problem pulled the trigger of the predicament facing the car industry in the United States at present, the background is that because of securing short-term gains, measures by the US car industry to mitigate climate change such as improving car fuel efficiency were very much half-hearted.

In connecting mitigation measures as a positive influence to the economy from the start, sustained creativity and efforts are needed in the future. How to establish ambitious mitigation measures and connect these to sustainable development of a country whose climate change is stabilized demands the wisdom of the human race.

REFERENCES

Hawken, Paul, Amory B. Lovins and Hunter Lovins (2001) *Natural Capitalism*, Japanese version, trans. Ryukou Sawa and Sugiko Obata. Tokyo: Nihonkeizeishinbunsha.

IPCC (2007) *Summary for Policymakers, Fourth Assessment Report, Climate Change 2007: Synthesis Report*. Cambridge: Cambridge University Press.

Stern, Nicholas (2007) *The Economics of Climate Change*. Cambridge: Cambridge University Press.

Uzawa, Hirofumi (2003) *Keizai gaku to Ningen no Kokoro* (*Economics and the Heart of Man*). Tokyo: Toyo Keizai.

4-2

Technology development strategy towards global sustainability

Satoshi Konishi

4-2-1 Introduction

This chapter discusses the roles and strategy of scientific and technological research and development within the context of a socio-economic strategy geared towards achieving global sustainability.

Science and technology are neutral with regard to sustainability. They could work for or against it, depending on whether research and development, as well as subsequent application in society, are intentionally undertaken towards a specific goal. From the Industrial Revolution until the recent onset of the so-called "business-as-usual" society, science and technology have been the driving force behind global economic growth, the increasing consumption of energy and resources, population growth and production activities. At the same time, they have been the main cause of jeopardizing sustainability, as typified by global environment problems. Nonetheless, only science and technology allow us to reorganize our human society into a sustainable society. In this chapter, I analyse "extended externality", or the impact exerted by energy technology on human beings through society and the environment, as one perspective on appraising the sustainability of science and technology, particularly energy technology. As one example of extended externality, I discuss ideal energy systems in a sustainable society.

In the first place, all the biological species on the Earth always consume a roughly constant amount of resources from their ecosystems and nature itself, and discharge the same amount of substances in order to survive while maintaining a good balance with their surrounding environments. In this sense, "modern human beings" (since the beginning of recorded history) as a whole have seen ever-increasing population and have yet to reach a steady state, and thus should be regarded as a species that has not established a stable existence for an extended period in biological time on the Earth. Unless the population becomes stable over a considerable number of generations, humans cannot be expected to achieve a steady state with the environment and other species. Of course, the "development of humankind" almost inevitably increases the production and consumption of energy, as well as the consumption of materials even if they are circulated. Therefore, as seen in current developed countries, the consumption of resources and environmental impact continue to increase despite nearly steady populations. This means that ongoing development cannot achieve a steady state or sustainability. In fact, the term "sustainable development" itself embraces such an essential contradiction.

In addition to the population, we must stabilize the concentration of carbon dioxide in the atmosphere – a typical global environment issue – and hopefully reduce it to a level where we can avoid the risk of the climate change known as global warming. At the least, the currently observed increase caused by the huge consumption of fossil materials cannot continue over a period of generations. It is apparent that only zero emissions of carbon dioxide in aggregate (e.g. total collection of carbon dioxide, increase of carbon sinks) can achieve this goal because the concentration would otherwise only increase. Basically, sustainable resources can only be realized through recycling or if ultimate reserves prove sufficient for consumption during the survival period of humankind.

The purpose of this chapter is to consider a technology strategy for establishing a sustainable society by revising a socio-economic strategy to counter the increasing loads of human activities imposed on the global environment. It focuses on energy technology.

4-2-2 Technology strategy and investment effect

From the Industrial Revolution until the twentieth century, technological innovations have taken place successively, and the technology pertaining to the generation, conversion and use of energy is no exception. Ample energy sources that have been supplied at an increasing pace have driven human activities to expand by responding and trying to satisfy the energy demands of a growing economy.

Technological innovation has usually been made possible as the consequence of research and development resources devoted to social demand or in view of constraints. Such innovation is just one of the various aspects of a growing economy, so setting targets for technological innovation is not always normative. In the rapidly growing economy of the past, constraints placed on resources and their supply were thought to be a major cause of lower growth and possible lost shares in expanding markets. In response, research and development investments were made to meet the social demand for technological solutions to such constraints. Even in academic science, which is pursued primarily for the sake of serendipity, investments must be made in the research and development of practical technologies for implementation in society at a stage where the products are actually used.

Development efforts made with social investments expand productivity to recoup those investments when such efforts prove successful. When applied to achieve more effective production, technological innovation has stimulated economic growth. Once a developed economy makes investments in ongoing development to meet greater demand, a fast-growing economy will continue to expand through a self-amplifying mechanism.

As global environmental issues have been manifested, environmental conservation and economic growth are considered to conflict. For global environmental issues, some even claim that technology itself, which consumes a large amount of resources to cope with expanding consumption, is to blame. In some respects this is actually true. However, technological innovation does not have any independent norm or standard of value. Now that people are considering the environment, instead of resources, as a major constraint on the survival and development of humankind, it should be possible to produce further economic growth using technology developed through appropriate investments made to remove the environmental constraints.

Until now, however, we have not fully understood the effects of research and development investments in advance, or received expected social changes through such investments. It can hardly be said that the cost-benefit performance of research and development investments has been properly evaluated, especially in cases of public funding. One major reason for this is that priority has been placed on governmental policy needs. Moreover, few people have assessed, from the standpoint of sustainability, effects other than the direct return on the investments, particularly off-market investment effects (externality) on the environment and society.

This chapter first analyses the effects of research and development in terms of impact, and the expanded concept of externality, and then considers the innovations made in energy technology from the perspective of a sustainable society and permanent human survival. The basic assumption here is that there is no answer for achieving sustainability in the paradigm of research and development in the past, which has been driving technological innovation as part of the mechanism of a high-growth society. I will consider a new concept of research and development by analysing and examining its impact, as well as a technology strategy as one of the means to realize a sustainable society. Decision-making by society as a whole is another issue, and what will be presented here is just a scenario. The purpose of this discussion is to provide possible reasonable choices for stakeholders who can make rational decisions by assessing the effects and appropriateness of decision-making by society. Such a consideration is expected to suggest possible criteria to guide the technology development to promote low-carbon society and global sustainability under a reforming market regulation.

4-2-3 Energy research and development, and a growing economy

This section discusses the issues of technology strategy and a sustainable society, using the research and development of energy technology as a main example.

Since the Industrial Revolution, energy technology has been the driving force behind the drastic expansion and growth of human economic activities; it has also been regarded as a major cause of the mass consumption of resources and environmental destruction. In fact, society up to the seventeenth century, which was dependent on classical biomass energy, can be viewed as one that determined the rate of growth of the whole society based on solar energy (i.e. the source of such biomass) and the growth rate of forests, which rely on solar energy – the constraint of energy resources. What should be noted is that solar energy and biomass, both of which are renewable and inexhaustible, suffer from resource constraints in terms of supply. The Industrial Revolution removed these constraints on growth with the new energy of coal, which launched explosive economic development through a self-amplified mechanism supported by technological innovation. In other words, coal simply replaced forest resources, which had almost disappeared in Western Europe.

Since then, this paradigm of a growing society typically evaluated with GDP (gross domestic product) as a measure has been expanding based on a persistent craving for energy. Up to modern times, energy sources such as electricity, oil, gas and nuclear power have been desperately desired and promising, irrespective of the methods of generation. If the constraints of energy resources limit economic growth, the development of new energy must bring us economic growth.

In today's society, however, environmental as well as resource constraints are recognized as threats not only to our growth but also to our survival. The sustainable development of human beings on a global basis is thus the most important issue. In this respect, energy technology is merely one element, despite its major impact, in the overall picture of sound and permanent development of the global environment, economy and human society. In fact, solar energy, wind power and other forms of renewables are being developed as potential new sources of energy due to their inexhaustibility. Conversely, some deprecate fossil fuel and nuclear power simply because of their environmental constraints. These views are one-sided, and all energy technologies must be evaluated based on their positive and negative effects on the environment and society in the context of human survival.

Because proper evaluation has not always been implemented in the past, energy technology (even if technically feasible and "Earth-friendly") is subject to the possibility of failing to make major contributions to our future society or have any meaning for development in our present society. This evaluation, including the choice of markets, is not determined only by costs and market mechanisms, but also by off-market costs such as so-called "externality" (external economy). In addition, the evaluation involves constraints and preferences because energy technology is not always converted into costs. These constraints are not limited to capacitive ones such as resource reserves and environmental constraints, but include logistics, which could be a decisive factor in some cases.

4-2-4 Sustainability of energy technology

Our research on "sustainability science" involves a comprehensive evaluation of future energy technologies from the viewpoint of their environmental and social impacts. From this view, we can extract a certain framework for the ultra-long-term roles of energy technology and technological innovation. Even if a technology is developed for the far future, development itself requires a current viewpoint, because resources are spent in the current framework.

In developed countries, energy markets are nearly oversaturated and stable. Conversely, developing countries still need a considerably high economic growth rate and a corresponding increase in energy consumption, at least until increases in population stabilize, to ensure healthy and cultured lives for their people. A completely different technological system that removes various constraints as currently seen is necessary to establish energy systems for meeting such increased energy demand and

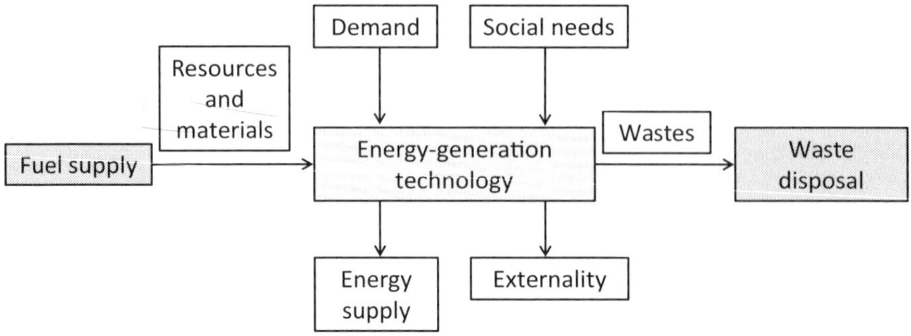

Figure 4.2.1 General structure of energy technology

creating human societies that are both stable and sustainable on a long-term basis.

For the analysis of energy supply, economic methods are applicable for the near future, until 2050 at the latest. Conversely, when we consider sustainability for the period up to 2100 and beyond, we can no longer use economic model calculations, and must rely on scenarios. This is because analyses using quantitative models are not effective in the distant future, where the composition of energy will be greatly affected by external factors and off-market constraints, and are subject to change by assumptions. Instead, we must analyse such externality factors qualitatively: qualitative analyses can determine whether the energy scenario has a sustainable mechanism from these externality aspects. Figure 4.2.1 shows the general structure of energy technology.

Energy, an important element of a sustainable society, is relatively inexpensive in terms of unit cost and, like food and water, large in quantity. As a result, transport, storage and distribution have much greater importance in both cost and supply constraints. This should be kept in mind as an issue related to the finite nature of energy resources.

Unlike certain mineral resources, energy resources rarely face the problem of scarcity of absolute abundance in fact. Resource constraints can be deemed a dynamic phenomenon that occurs when a large amount of resources is acquired at a necessary time and speed and then transported to the places that require those resources, rather than limited abundance. This feature of energy technology – where logistics have a large impact – often constrains and controls supply. It is also necessary to understand that these energy resource constraints are not only an issue of transport, but mainly an issue of the entire supply chain, including disposal and transfer of by-products and wastes, and process coordination of all materials and products.

As shown in Figure 4.2.1 as a typical case, all energy generation technologies (e.g. power generation) transform a given input into output (energy) while generating wastes and imposing environmental loads. Since energy never disappears, according to the conservation law of energy, all energy technologies actually convert energy to meet the social demand for supply. In this process, the flow of inbound energy must equal the flow of outbound energy. Moreover, an entire energy system must secure upstream sources and downstream users, and correspond with the flows. In case of any mismatches and fluctuations, a sufficient stock of energy must also be secured on the way.

Let us use the generation of hydropower as an example. Power is generated corresponding to the demand of the grid. At this point, the reservoir must retain the necessary amount of water while the areas downstream of the dam must be ready for the release of water. However, this requirement is not always satisfied in actual power generation systems. Since the lower reaches cannot always expect timely rainfall throughout the year, these areas may suffer from water shortage during periods of high power demand. Furthermore, reserved water must sometimes be used for agriculture, or reduced or released in preparation for heavy rains. In addition to the presence or absence of resources, the requirement for discharging water must also be satisfied. In other words, all inexhaustible resources still have constraints on supply. It is the same in the case of solar energy and wind power. It is meaningless to focus only on resources that are sources of energy. For the generation of photovoltaic power, sunny locations where it is easy to install and maintain solar panels are much rarer "resources" than places that simply capture sunlight. In this sense, the roofs of houses are suitable places. However, if we seek a new place and manufacture a support structure for a PV panel/module for that location, it may be impossible to record a surplus in the energy budget due to the excessive cost. For this reason, the supply curve of photovoltaic power generation could show a steep slope.

We must be aware that fossil and nuclear energy could face extremely large and strict constraints when we view such energy not only from the perspective of resources but also from that of supply chains. Aside from resource constraints in the original sense, fossil energy actually has logistics problems, such as remote locations and weather conditions that may make mining difficult. Although fossil resources are known to exist, we must keep in mind that waste disposal capacity restrains energy supply, given such carbon dioxide emission control approaches as CCS (carbon capture and storage).

In addition to location, nuclear electricity is subject to various constraints such as capacity of uranium isotope separation plants and the interim spent fuel storage, reprocessing and ultimate disposal of wastes.

Japan is one of the few countries boasting almost all fuel-cycle technologies, but its generation capacity cannot yet meet its domestic power demand. What is more, the expected future capacity is inconsistent with plans for generating nuclear power. In particular, there is a crucial shortage in the capacity for reprocessing spent fuel and combusting the resulting plutonium.

These supply-chain constraints not only restrict supply at a certain point of time in the energy system, but will also influence long-term marketability and growth potential. Even with abundant resources, energy technology cannot grow and increase its market share if there are logistics constraints. Even if the individual elements (e.g. a power plant) of an energy technology seem to work well, the technology must be consistent with all systems connecting to these elements (such as supply-chain management) in order to be marketable. Energy markets themselves are global, as seen in the oil markets, but also have many local aspects when viewed from the supply-chain level. Electric power is directly linked to national security in most of the countries which find it difficult to connect their grids to those of other countries, with the exception of European countries and some geographically isolated nations like Japan. Waste cannot be imported or exported, with some exceptions such as carbon dioxide emission rights. Regarding nuclear power, the issue of nuclear proliferation must be addressed. Many energy supply chains function as social infrastructure, and the (lack of) development of such infrastructure has often hampered economic growth in developing countries. The growth of energy markets in these countries is greatly affected by energy logistics and the pace of infrastructural development for such logistics. It should be noted that the analysis of future energy markets often underestimates these constraints, and deems that supply capacity is guaranteed simply by reserves and cost of resources. In order to introduce renewable electricity, particularly solar and wind power, it is essential to ensure grid stability. Local characteristics must be considered, because the scale, composition and technological maturity of the grid system itself have a significant influence.

The mechanism of how the energy composition of an energy market is determined greatly differs between rapid-growth and stable periods. Important factors in the market expansion period, when a dynamic mechanism has great impact, are construction speed and the readiness for responding to demand, prospective supply of long-term resources, prices and fundraising. International public capital investments, particularly environmentally conscious energy investments, are essential in transforming the energy systems of developing countries into futuristic systems oriented towards zero emissions. Moreover, such investments are inseparable from the development of energy infrastructure. Even if it is apparently disadvantageous from a short-term cost perspective, the development of energy infrastructure should be beneficial to both developing countries and the cooperating developed countries, in considering the global sum of long-term energy and environmental costs.

Developed countries that have already entered a mature market period and enjoy well-developed infrastructure and equipment, however, cannot expect a significant increase in energy demand because slow economic growth is offset by a decrease in the carbon dioxide emission rate that requires energy consumption reduction. Conversion of energy sources will progress slowly in line with the demand for replacing ageing facilities and be sensitive to choices made based on short-tem costs, since there are relatively many energy options. In these circumstances, introducing a technology that requires replacement of old infrastructures with new is possibly socially, not technically, more difficulty than in developing countries.

4-2-5 Conversion of energy technology

As mentioned, other than resources and costs there are restricting factors that greatly affect conversion to energy composition suited for a sustainable society in both developing and developed countries, and these factors must be considered. However, the conversion of energy technology driven by technological innovation has occurred before and will occur in the future, so there should be a generally applicable conversion pattern.

Figure 4.2.2 illustrates such a pattern. Energy technology is classified as being either resource-dependent or technology-dependent. One typical

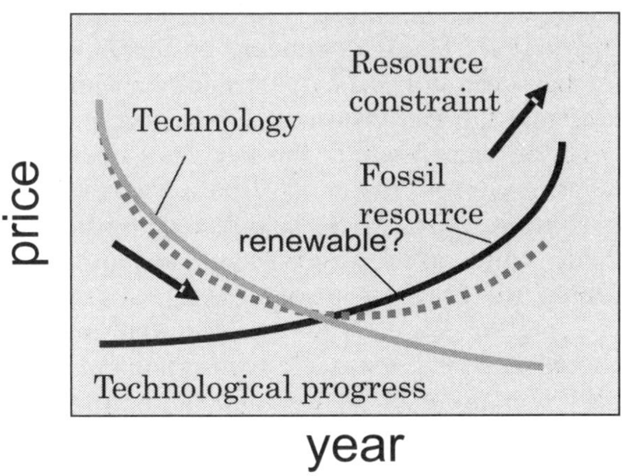

Figure 4.2.2 Power generation technology and changes in long-term costs

resource-dependent technology is thermal power generation. This type of technology tends to be more costly and less efficient due to soaring prices and deteriorating quality of resources over time, because resources account for a large portion of cost and supply. In contrast, energy highly dependent on technology, as typified by nuclear power, tends to be less costly and more efficient because the technology progresses with the increase in accumulative energy production.

The general tendency shown in Figure 4.2.2 is that fossil resource energy will ultimately be replaced by technology-dependent energy because people always prefer less expensive power. In other words, technological progress inevitably produces a less expensive option than one more costly in terms of resources, and the less expensive technology will replace the more costly technology based on social preference. Given the fact that research and development investments typically result in new and more advanced technologies, society generally selects less expensive energy technology that can supply more energy and stimulate economic growth. However, the timing of when to switch between different technologies, and which technology will win in view of increases and decreases in the cost factor, remain unpredictable. Since multiple technologies are constantly being developed, the technology of choice will be decided by supply-chain constraints according to social circumstances and investment activities for technological development based on social preference. In any event, the energy ultimately supplied will prove less expensive for society.

The conceptual mechanism shown in Figure 4.2.2 helps explain previous technological innovation and energy source conversion. All sources of energy, including fossil fuel highly dependent on resources, are somewhat dependent on technology, and as such technology progresses, society has selected less expensive and more readily available energy. Regarding sources of energy that are highly dependent on technology, the preferred energy differs as the value created by technology assumes greater importance. This means that the mechanism in Figure 4.2.2 – showing that the price of energy is determined where the two lines intersect – has gradually reduced the price per unit of energy. This is a generally observed fact, while escalating fossil resource prices as indicated on the right of the figure are hypothetical and rarely observed in the real world in the long run. In other words, the prices of resources do not actually soar due to their scarcity or depletion. We can thus conclude that technology replaces resources before they become scarce or very expensive. The fact that virtually all primary commodities have dropped in price worldwide with long-term increases in production supports this conclusion.

We need to keep in mind here that renewable energy (basically considered technology-dependent energy) remains highly dependent on resources as long as it is natural energy. For this reason, assuming that technological progress continues to lower costs, supply-chain constraints will be viewed as a scarcity of "resources" restricted by nature or surrounding conditions. For instance, the renewable resources of sunshine and wind are both inexhaustible, but costs could increase due to the increased use of such energy because places with abundant and favourable sun or wind conditions are limited. The use of solar cells and wind turbines initially spreads from locations close to an energy use system and subject to abundant sunshine or favourable wind conditions. As the dissemination rate of solar power rises, available locations will be limited to areas with less sunshine or wind and where the installation is inconvenient, thereby possibly reducing the technological cost but increasing the total cost.

This tendency can also be seen in the area of nuclear power. The installed capacity of facilities used for uranium enrichment, reprocessing and waste disposal is increasing very slowly on a global scale, falling far behind the rate at which nuclear power plants increase. In terms of high-level radioactive waste disposal sites, only one construction plan has been formulated worldwide until now, and such a site has yet to be constructed.

As mentioned, energy – an essential element of a sustainable society – remains relatively inexpensive in unit cost and large in volume, much like the food and water that are necessary for human survival. Consequently, the costs of transport, storage and distribution and supply-chain constraints have more influence over the supply of energy. Although energy is obviously a valuable product, its stocks are much smaller than its flow. In particular, there is no practical means of storing electric power; therefore, all storage by discharging and charging (excluding pumping-up power generation) remains surprisingly costly as compared to electricity generation.

4-2-6 Externality of energy technology

Energy technology has both positive and negative effects on the environment and society via off-market routes, called "externality"; but this concept must be expanded from that used in the monetary conversion of environmental loads to include broader effects, covering impacts including social effects and elements not convertible into monetary value. The expanded concept of externality shown in Figure 4.2.3 is closely related to the issue of human sustainability through human survival risks and social issues that remain difficult to quantify. The supply-chain constraints discussed using Figure 4.2.1 and the sudden cost increases due to such constraints examined using Figure 4.2.2 are not always reflected as costs

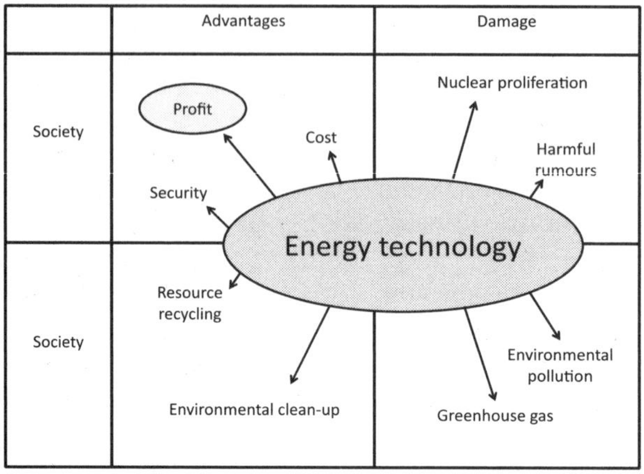

Figure 4.2.3 Expanded concept of energy externality

in the market economy, or are often difficult to convert into external cost or monetary value. It is thus necessary to evaluate both positive and negative effects of energy technology quantitatively from the standpoint of its conformity to society and the environment by expanding the concept of externality. It should be noted that many such effects are recognized as hypothetical risks or effects before they actually occur. Figure 4.2.3 illustrates various routes through which energy technology affects the environment and society (Konishi et al., 2005).

Most issues that can be considered as externality relate to recovery from actual damage, mitigation of it or compensation, but in many cases relate to risks. For example, we assess the damage by air pollution and radiation hazards based not on the environmental discharge of pollutants or radioactivity, but on the increased risks of health damage resulting from such discharge. This is also true for harmful rumours about nuclear proliferation and nuclear energy, which are not actually damaging society with nuclear weapons or the environment by radioactive pollution. Their impact is widely recognized not when nuclear weapons or pollution actually cause damage, but when the costs for prevention, response or recovery arise, or the prices of other products increase or decrease. So-called backstop effects and energy security effects are similar; since when a certain amount of energy resources exist domestically, even if costly and unmarketable, energy technology is sometimes beneficial to society by functioning as an upper limit against the soaring prices of other types of energy. Likewise, crops-originated biofuel has a great impact not only on the supply of energy technology and energy prices, but also on food prices before it actually affects the supply of food. Many of these effects can be evaluated on an economic basis but are very difficult to internalize.

Among these externalities of energy technology, global environment issues are very important; above all, the impact of carbon prices has now become the priority. In the development of energy technology, most global environment issues can be considered internalized through conversion into carbon dioxide emissions, especially in developed countries. "Global warming" was already a reality, existing worldwide and a central issue for politics, economy and society, before being scientifically projected or observed as facts. Global warming holds monetary values in hypothetical future climate change risks because it has been given such values. Irrespective of actual damage, these monetary values have helped to give credits and promote renewable energy.

This incorporation of external effects into the economic system can be a viable method of evaluating the sustainability effects of a technology strategy and implementing that strategy in society. Although such evaluation has not actually been conducted, or reflected in the development of energy technology or an introductory strategy, we can easily clarify the effectiveness of individual technologies and the effects of introducing those technologies to society by considering the constraints and effects based on the routes shown in Figure 4.2.1. However, it is essential but not easy to build a social consensus based on normative considerations in order to introduce technologies to society from the standpoint of sustainability. In fact, there have been few cases of successful institutionalization. For instance, if conducting such transactions as nuclear power CDM (clean development mechanism) became possible, profits would be obtained in the form of energy security or emission rights, which might not be negligible even when compared with the sales of electric power.

4-2-7 Effects of technological innovation and investment and intergenerational issues

Future returns are expected from the development of energy technology by making investments in candidate energy resources for the future. Should such candidate energy technology be successfully developed, those resources must be able to achieve a certain level of sales in the energy market. However, when comparing the value to be obtained in the distant future with the present value, we find that the upper limits on such investments deemed to be reasonable are not that high. This is because a discount rate applied to the distant future significantly reduces the present value in terms of investment. As stated above, the effects of an energy technology, in the context of potential and significance in the future, are evaluated as the degree of contribution to society in the sustainable development of humankind, such as measures to address global environment issues, zero emissions of energy systems and social decarbonization, rather than the energy product's market value. Since these effects will extend over many generations, how we evaluate the value of energy technology properly is often simplified to a single question: what discount rate should be reasonable for profits or so-called "negative legacies" for future generations, given the time preference and normative sense of value?

The discount rate issue has yet to be resolved in this respect, since a discount rate for the long-term development of technology could significantly differ from the interest rates in real society. However, the discount rate can at least be an effective indicator for evaluating the sustainability of energy technology development, especially the long-term effects over generations. A common value must therefore be used when a universal scale is needed for the evaluation of climate change risks in the future and the social/environmental externality effects of various future-oriented technologies.

As discussed, energy technology is not necessarily related to sustainability, and the technology itself can be expanded on an autocatalytic basis to support and promote a rapid-growing economy, regardless of supply-chain constraints. Conversely, when we consider sustainable and gradual economic growth, the discount rate should be sufficiently low to be consistent with market interest rates. Of course, a reasonable discount rate will differ corresponding to different timescales. If we try to evaluate the effects of advanced technologies by treating economies with different growth rates equally within the same generation and over many generations, we must use different discount rates in correlation with different growth rates and timescales.

The effects of future energy technologies such as advanced nuclear power and renewables must be equally evaluated using the same methodology and indicators. Such effects will be analysed based on the impacts of energy to be exerted on the environment and society through off-market routes, particularly the effects on human survival risks. A strategy for the development of energy technology must not simplistically seek to develop large-scale energy sources that can meet the demand for consumption and depletion of resources, or a technology that does not emit carbon dioxide for curtailing global warming. Although it may be far more difficult to plan, a technology strategy for sustainable development and methodology and indicators for evaluating the effectiveness of such a strategy from the standpoint of sustainability have almost been clarified, as already described.

However, many of the current projects for developing energy technology are still based on the previous paradigm of a high-growth society after the Industrial Revolution, whereby energy supply needs only to meet energy demand. Such a simple strategy may be adopted even when renewable energy is introduced, despite a full awareness of global environment issues. When reminded of the self-contradicting mechanism where energy demand has always been stimulated by energy supply, we should recognize that simply supplying energy is not necessarily beneficial. The sustainability of an energy technology can be analysed with constraints that appear in the interaction of energy technology with society and the environment in the energy supply chain. Therefore, the effectiveness of a technology strategy must be evaluated from this standpoint.

REFERENCE

Konishi, S., K. Okano, Y. Ogawa, S. Nagumo, K. Tokimatsu and K. Tokita (2005) "Evaluation of Fusion Study from Socio-economic Aspect", *Fusion Engineering and Design* 1151, pp. 75–79.

4-3

Technological strategy for renewable bioenergy

Shiro Saka

4-3-1 Introduction

Since the Industrial Revolution, our civilization has developed with the support of fossil fuels like petroleum. However, the use of fossil fuels releases greenhouse gases such as carbon dioxide (CO_2) that result in global warming; recent indications point to the danger linked to weather anomalies, changes in the ecosystem and other radical transformations of the global environment. Moreover, there have been apprehensions since the middle of the twentieth century regarding depletion of fossil resources due to massive consumption, thus making it difficult for civilization to survive.

Under such circumstances, in recent years "biofuels" such as bioethanol and biodiesel, developed from biomass raw materials, have captured the world's attention as clean energy alternatives to petroleum. In Japan biofuels are regarded as one of the renewable "new energy" petroleum alternatives, with the Kyoto Protocol demand for liquid biofuels to account for 500 million litres (crude-oil basis) of liquid fuels used for transport by the year 2010. As a part of this total, gasoline blended with bio-ETBE (ethyl tertiary butyl ether) is being trialled, and the effective usage of biomass resources is being advanced nationwide.

Hence, this chapter considers the future trends and horizons of biomass use, focusing on bioethanol and biodiesel.

4-3-2 Biomass resources in Japan

According to our research in recent years (Minami and Saka, 2001, 2002), approximately 370 million tonnes of biomass resources are produced annually in Japan. Of these, approximately 77 million tonnes are disposed of without effective utilization, and converted to CO_2 dispersed into the atmosphere. By weight, this amounts to approximately 127 million tonnes of CO_2, and accounted for some 11 per cent of Japan's CO_2 release in 1990. Consequently, the use of these biomass resources as biofuels and chemicals is not only helpful in achieving Japan's Kyoto Protocol target of reducing greenhouse gas emission but also a key issue of the post-Kyoto framework.

4-3-3 Bioethanol

Government bioethanol policies

In June 2003 the government of Japan lifted the ban on the use of gasoline mixed with 3 per cent of bioethanol (E3). At this low concentration there are no problems regarding engine corrosion, and today's automobiles are able to use E3 unaltered. On Miyakojima Island, the use of E3 gasoline was scheduled to begin in 2008 across the island as part of a national collaborative government agency project, but coordination with the Petroleum Association of Japan has been delayed. Moreover, the government plans to study an envisioned future expansion to E10, but for this to be effective, 6 billion litres of the approximately 60 billion litres of gasoline that Japan consumes would have to be substituted with ethanol. There is a challenge in securing this kind of volume.

To meet this challenge, various regional projects on bioethanol production are now ongoing (Figure 4.3.1). Sugar and starch resources and lignocellulosics are suitable for ethanol production. For the former, at present sugarcane molasses on Miyakojima Island and substandard wheat in Hokkaido are coming into use. However, due to concerns regarding food problems, lignocellulosics from construction debris in Sakai, Osaka, and mill-ends from lumber mills in Maniwa, Okayama, are studied for practical use.

However, there are several problems encountered in the mixing of ethanol with gasoline. One is that the vapour pressure of mixed gasoline increases due to an azeotropic phenomenon with ethanol, with an increase in evaporative emissions. Furthermore, addition of ethanol, which absorbs water readily, contaminates the mixed gasoline with moisture, leading to

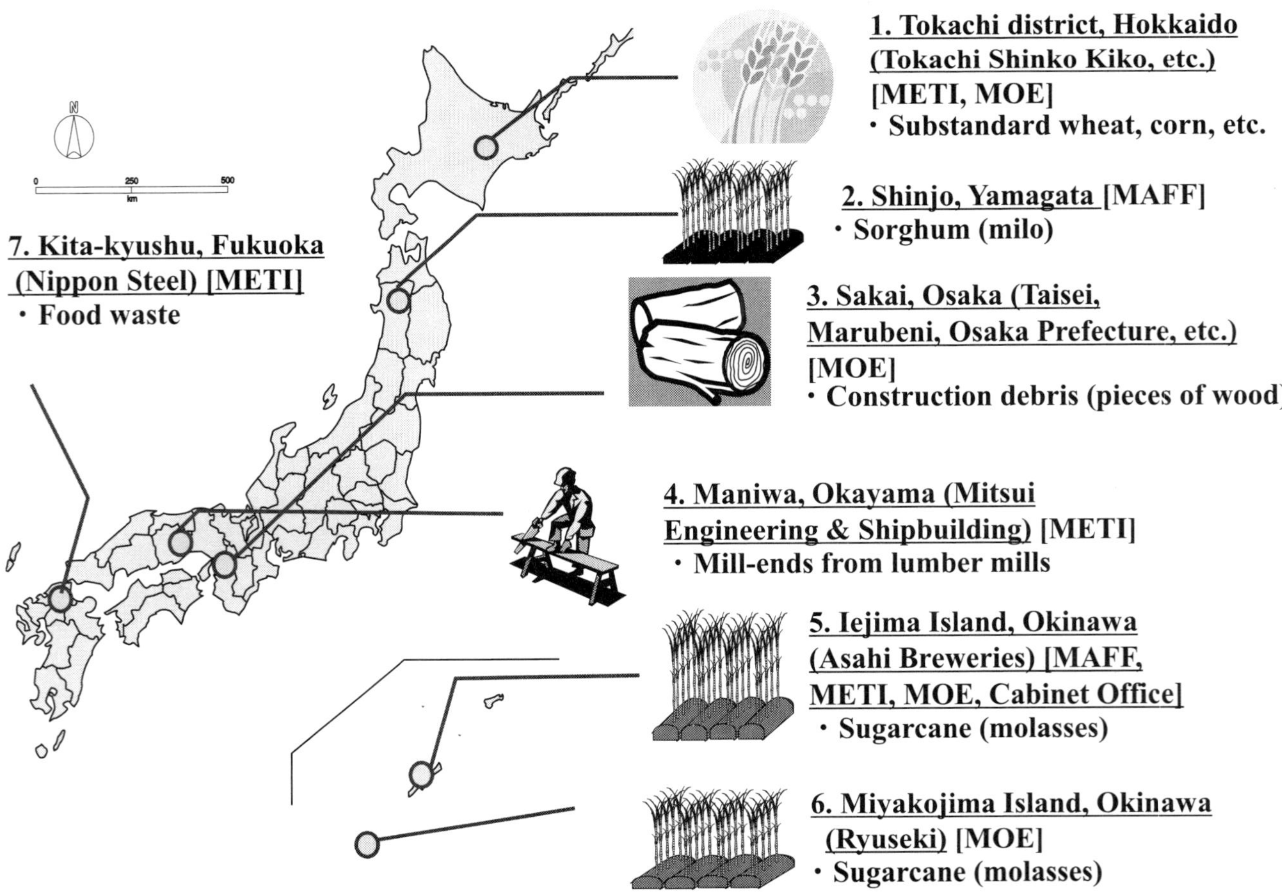

Figure 4.3.1 Regional projects on bioethanol production
Source: Courtesy of METI and MAFF, Japan.

phase separation and resulting in deterioration of fuel quality, which is problematic. Keeping these points in mind, the addition of ETBE to gasoline was studied, and "biogasoline", or gasoline to which 7 per cent ETBE (the equivalent of 3 per cent ethanol) has been added, went on sale at 50 gas stations in the Greater Tokyo metropolitan area from 27 April 2007. It is predicted that this will spread nationwide by 2010, with a usage of 840 million litres (equivalent to 360 million litres as ethanol; 210 million litres as crude oil) (Petroleum Association of Japan, 2008: 36).

It is believed that bioethanol will garner more and more attention. In particular, the establishment of technologies for converting ethanol from lignocellulosics is extremely important in the generation of "Japan-produced energy", and is a big challenge facing a nation that prides itself on being formed on the basis of scientific and technological innovation.

Japan, however, lacks a sufficient volume of resources, such as rice and wheat straw, to provide raw materials for a wide variety of biofuels. Timber is the only resource in sufficient abundance, and it is desirable that cedar trees planted after the Second World War are used. These trees were planted by the government at the end of the war as a useful future resource; however, the plan was futile and now they cause allergic reactions in humans. The mountains harbour forests, which cover 67 per cent of the surface of Japan, but not all mountains are steep – trees can be used effectively from easily accessible forest land. The time has come for serious investigation regarding the effective use of mill-ends, etc., in conjunction with lumber as raw materials for the production of ethanol. There is a need for effective use of cedar trees in a manner which will be convincing to the public.

Fermentative ethanol

Among ethanols, bioethanol is derived from biomass and has a role in controlling global warming; synthetic ethanol is derived from ethylene, a fossil resource. Bioethanols are divided into fermentative ethanol, synthetic ethanol made from biogas and bioethanol via acetic acid fermentation.

Fermentative ethanol uses raw materials such as molasses from sugarcane, starch from rice and wheat, and lignocellulosics from wood, rice straw and wheat straw. In each case, fermentation is to D-glucose ethanol, D-glucose being a constituent of sugar. Molasses and starch resources have mainly been used thus far, but because of the relationship with food problems, attention has been given to lignocellulosics in recent years.

As one example of the established bioethanol process for lignocellulosics, a concentrated sulphuric acid process developed by Arkenol in the United States was imported to Japan for further development by JGC Corporation (Figure 4.3.2) under the NEDO (New Energy and Industrial

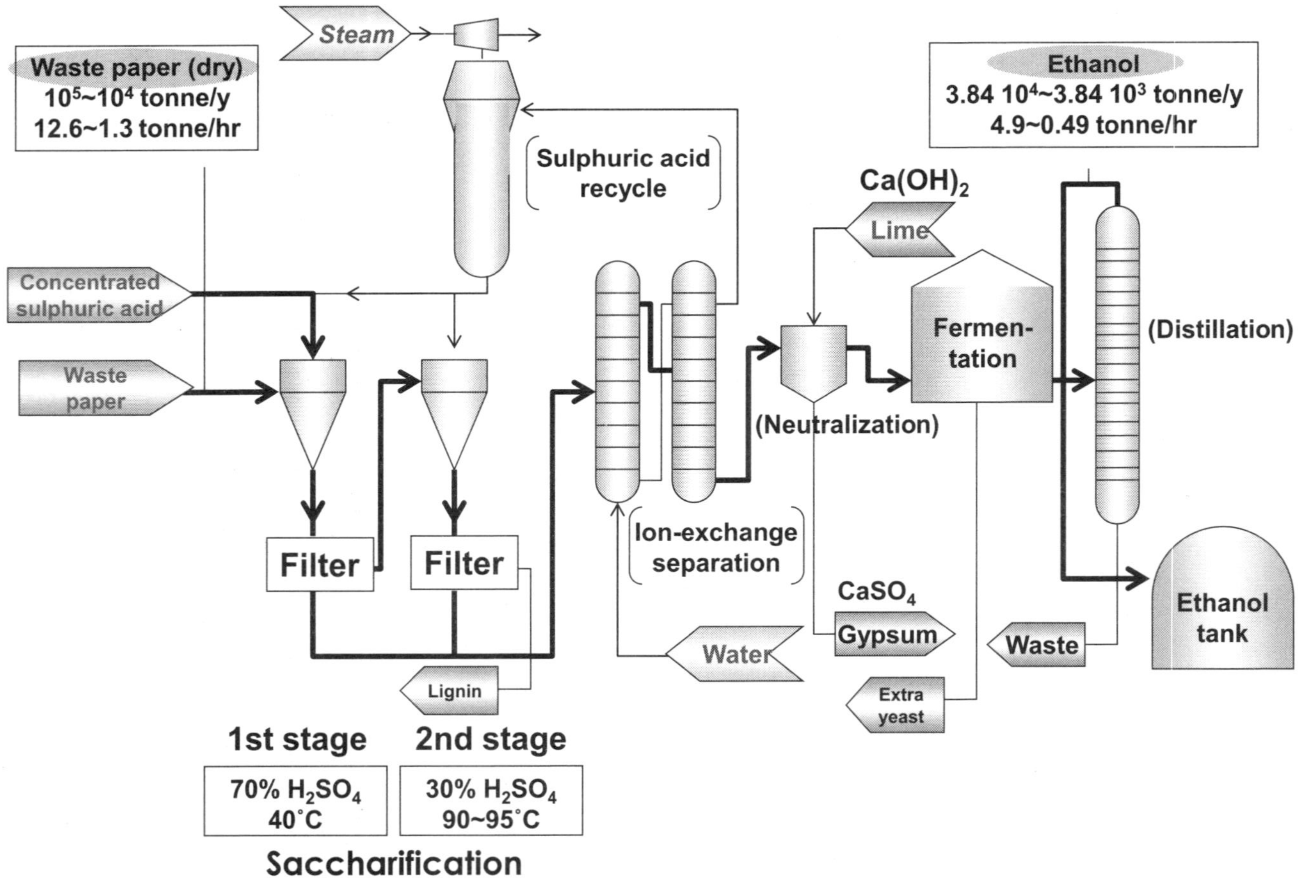

Figure 4.3.2 Concentrated sulphuric acid process (Arkenol-JGC) for lignocellulosics
Source: Saka (2006).

Technology Development Organization) High Efficiency Bioenergy Conversion project (2001–2005) (NEDO, 2005: 12–13). This process involves two treatments, first with 70–75 per cent sulphuric acid at 30–40°C to hydrolyse hemicelluloses and decrystallize cellulose; subsequently it is diluted with hot water to 30–40 per cent sulphuric acid, raising the temperature to 90–95°C to hydrolyse decrystallized cellulose. The hydrolysates from these two stages are separated through an ion-exchange column, and separated sulphuric acid is recycled. The obtained saccharides are then fermented by genetically modified micro-organisms such as yeast under anaerobic conditions to get ethanol. Commercial application of this Arkenol-JGC process is now under way in the United States.

More recently, for a big step towards the generation of "Japan-produced energy", the Biofuels Technology Innovation Council has been investigating innovative technologies for the manufacture of bioethanol from lignocellulosics. Towards this end, the council has proposed ethanol production costing ¥40/litre by the year 2015 using plantations of high-yield plants such as *Erianthus* spp. and *Miscanthus sinensis*, whose yield can be more than 50 dry tonnes/ha/year; thus in a field of 6.5 km diameter, sufficient raw materials can be harvested for annual production of 100–200 million litres of ethanol (Biofuels Technology Innovation Council, 2008: 14). As another candidate, fast-growing woods such as poplar and willow give a yield of more than 17 dry tonnes/ha/year. Innovative technologies in fermentative ethanol production will be soon developed for these raw materials.

However, as shown in Figure 4.3.3, lignocellulosics do not saccharize into simple sugars as easily as starch or molasses, and must be pre-treated. In addition, 1 mole of glucose is converted to 2 moles of ethanol and CO_2 by micro-organisms such as yeast under anaerobic conditions (Equation 4.3.1), thus indicating low utilization efficiency of carbon to ethanol. Because of this, some researchers are sceptical as to whether the use of fermentative ethanol can contribute to CO_2 reduction.

$$\underset{\text{D-Glucose}}{C_6H_{12}O_6} \longrightarrow \underset{\text{Ethanol}}{2\,CH_3CH_2OH} + \underset{\text{Carbon dioxide}}{2\,CO_2} \qquad \text{Equation 4.3.1}$$

Future-generation bioethanol via acetic acid fermentation

Research on bioethanol production by acetic acid fermentation is currently under way in the NEDO Development of Preparatory Basic Biomass Energy Technologies project (NEDO, 2009: 17). This bioethanol production involves three stages: decomposition of lignocellulosics by hot-compressed water; the conversion of decomposed products such as sugars etc. to acetic acid through fermentation; and the hydrogenolysis of

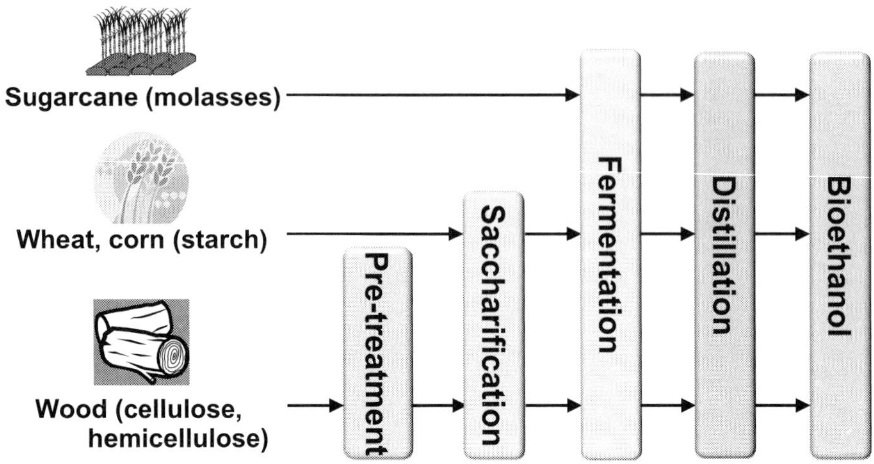

Figure 4.3.3 Various production types of bioethanol
Source: Saka (2006).

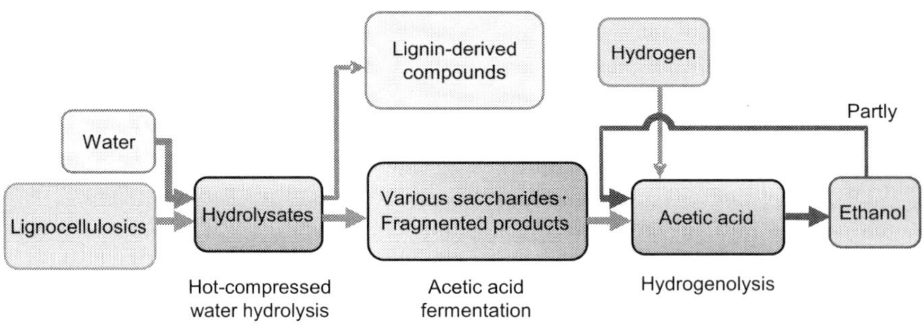

Figure 4.3.4 Eco-ethanol production from lignocellulosics with hot-compressed water treatment followed by acetic acid fermentation and hydrogenolysis
Source: NEDO (2009).

acetic acid. From these stages, the reaction shown in Equation 4.3.2 can be derived. Here it should be noted that all carbons that make up glucose are converted efficiently via acetic acid to bioethanol without releasing any CO_2, producing 1.5 times the amount of ethanol when compared with fermentative ethanol (Equation 4.3.1) as discussed previously. Figure 4.3.4 shows this ethanol production process studied in this project.

$$\underset{\text{D-Glucose}}{C_6H_{12}O_6} + \underset{\text{Hydrogen}}{6\,H_2} \longrightarrow \underset{\text{Ethanol}}{3\,CH_3CH_2OH} + \underset{\text{Water}}{3\,H_2O} \qquad \text{Equation 4.3.2}$$

4-3-4 Biodiesel

Biodiesel fuel (fatty acid methyl ester – FAME), being one good use of oil resources, has captured the world's attention as a clean energy alternative to petroleum, and has been commercially produced with an alkali-catalysed method. In Japan 5,000 litres/day of biodiesel is produced in Kyoto from waste oils/fats collected from sectors such as restaurants and individual homes (Figure 4.3.5).

The European Union uses biodiesel in a 5–30 per cent additive mixture with light diesel oil, and achieved production of 4.89 million tonnes for EU27 countries in 2006 (NEDO, 2007a: 64); however, use in Japan has stagnated at a level of only 4,000–5,000 tonnes, centred mainly in the city of Kyoto. Japan's yearly waste oil volume is 420,000–560,000 tonnes, although in reality only 40,000–50,000 tonnes of this is expected to be collected. This will account for no more than 0.1–0.2 per cent of the 41 billion litres of light diesel oil being used in Japan (as of 2003) (Imahara et al., 2007). Hence, one issue will be the best way to secure resources: whether to promote rapeseed cultivation as effective usage of fallow farmland, or turn our attention towards Southeast Asia for a supply of palm oil from oil palms. There is also a copious amount of oil contained in the seeds of trees such as the physic nut (*Jatropha curcas*), the sandbox (*Hura crepitans*) and the sea mango (*Cerbera manghas*) (Minami et al., 2005: 283–284).

Biodiesel is interconnected with global warming; its practical usage, based upon preferential tax treatment, is quite far advanced, mostly in the European Union. From August 2006, Germany went to a 9 per cent tax levy, with a 45 per cent tax to be imposed in a sequential manner by 2012, while in Japan quality standards have finally been decided, becoming taxable under local tax laws. It is hoped that biodiesel will be established in Japan as quickly as possible, through preferential tax treatment.

Biodiesel production technologies

Research on the conversion of vegetable oil/animal fat and their wastes to biodiesel is performed and put to practical use in many parts of the world, including Europe, the United States and Japan. While animal fat is solid, and vegetable oil has a viscosity of approximately 50 mm^2/s, they have a high flashpoint of 300°C and cannot be used as diesel fuel without further treatment. Therefore, under atmospheric pressure and at 50–60°C, methanol and alkaline catalysts are added to vegetable oil triglycerides for a transesterification reaction. In this way, the viscosity and flashpoint are brought down and FAME is produced.

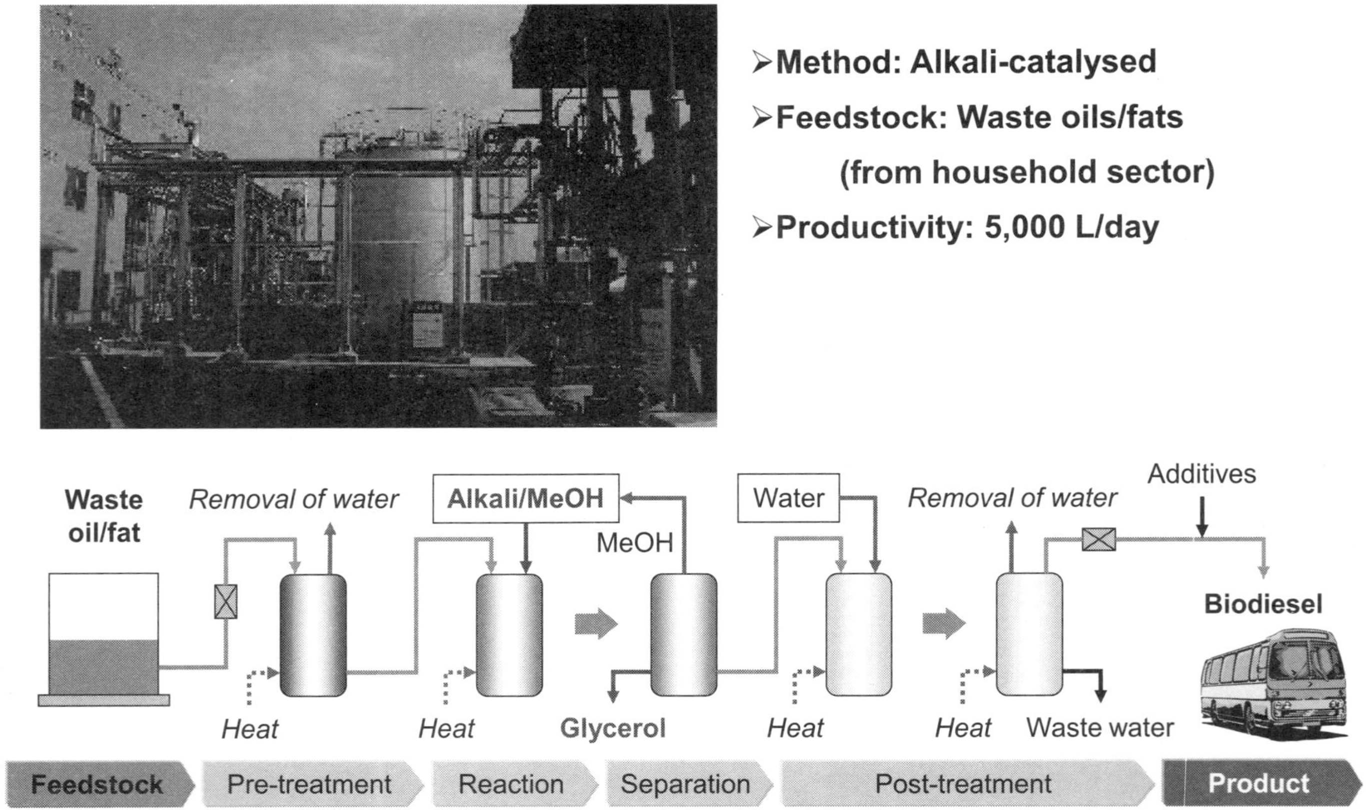

Figure 4.3.5 Kyoto municipal biodiesel production plant using the alkali-catalysed process

However, this process has a heavy environmental load. More specifically, sodium hydroxide and potassium hydroxide are used as alkaline catalysts, but several stages of water washing are required for catalyst removal after the reaction. Furthermore, a reaction with free fatty acids, which are contained in particular abundance in waste cooking oil, results in alkaline soap, which needs separation and purification and requires more catalysts. Alkaline catalytic methods are thus difficult to use for palm oil and waste oil, which contain a higher percentage of fatty acids, and the application of these methods for a wide variety of oils and fats is a difficult task.

In order to solve the various problems of these procedures, non-catalytic biodiesel manufacturing processes using the lipase method, ion-exchange resin catalyst method and supercritical methanol method (Saka and Kusdiana, 2001; Kusdiana and Saka, 2004) were developed (Figure 4.3.6). In the supercritical method, first the oil is treated with subcritical water leading to the hydrolytic degradation of triglycerides, which are converted to fatty acids and glycerin. Subsequently, the reaction liquid is allowed to stand, and the fatty acids containing an oily layer and the glycerin containing an aqueous layer are separated. Next, methanol is added to the oily layer under supercritical conditions to produce FAME in an esterification reaction of fatty acids. As the reaction conditions are comparatively mild – 270°C/7MPa – almost no degradation of unsaturated fatty acid occurs. This Saka-Dadan process is thus suited for practical application.

Future-generation biodiesel

In methanol-using processes such as those mentioned above, the development of glycerin as a by-product cannot be prevented. Therefore in recent years, along with the enlargement of the amount of biodiesel production, glycerin production has also drastically increased. However, in alkali-catalyzed methods glycerin is discharged as an admixture of methanol and water, as well as alkaline catalyst, etc. The sale value of such crude glycerin, approximately \$0.10/kg, is very low compared to purified glycerin, which costs around \$1.30–2.00/kg. When considering transport costs, disposal by sale is regarded as economically non-viable. It is thus expected that in the future the amount of disposed glycerin will increase, and as long as no effective utilization methods are established, this is likely to become a huge problem.

To deal with this problem, attention was focused on the interesterification reaction (one kind of transesterification reaction), and, under the NEDO Development of Preparatory Basic Bioenergy Technologies project (NEDO, 2007b: 20), a novel biodiesel manufacturing method was

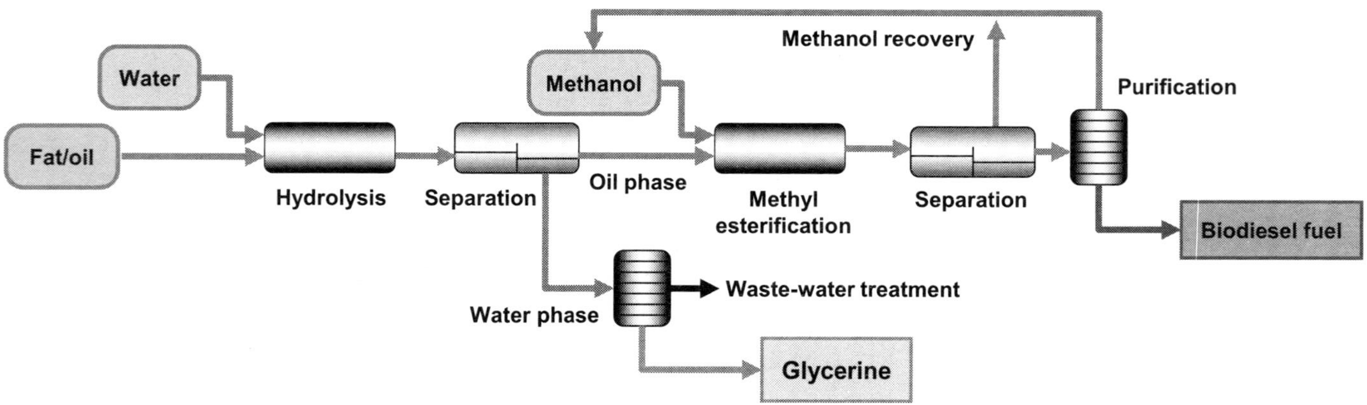

Figure 4.3.6 Biodiesel production by the two-step supercritical methanol method (Saka-Dadan process)
Source: Kusdiana and Saka (2004).

developed that does not produce any glycerin. As a result, it was found that in the supercritical state the interesterification reaction of methyl acetate and triglycerides proceeds non-catalytically, and FAME and triacetin are generated (Equation 4.3.3) (Saka and Isayama, 2009). In addition, for free fatty acid, it can be reacted with supercritical methyl acetate to be FAME (Equation 4.3.4) (ibid.).

$$\begin{array}{lcccccc} CH_2-OCOR^1 & & & & R^1COOCH_3 & & CH_2-OCOCH_3 \\ | & & & & & & | \\ CH-OCOR^2 & + & 3CH_3COOCH_3 & \rightarrow & R^2COOCH_3 & + & CH-OCOCH_3 \\ | & & & & & & | \\ CH_2-OCOR^3 & & & & R^3COOCH_3 & & CH_2-OCOCH_3 \\ \text{Triglyceride} & & \text{Methylacetate} & & \text{FAME} & & \text{Triacetin} \end{array}$$

Equation 4.3.3

$$\begin{array}{ccccccc} RCOOH & + & CH_3COOCH_3 & \rightarrow & RCOOCH_3 & + & 3CH_3COOH \\ \text{Fatty acid} & & \text{Methyl acetate} & & \text{FAME} & & \text{Acetic acid} \end{array}$$

Equation 4.3.4

To examine the effects of the triacetin obtained on the properties of fuel, triacetin was combined with methyl oleate, and after evaluating fuel properties we judged that when combined at a molar ratio of 1:3, which is theoretically obtainable from the interesterification reaction of oils and fats with methyl acetate, it has no adverse effect on the principal properties of fuel, but the admixture of triacetin enhances the oxidation stability of biodiesel and also exerts favourable effects on the current point. Furthermore, it was demonstrated that if biodiesel is defined as a mixture of FAME with triacetin, biodiesel will be 125 per cent in theoretical yield, which far exceeds previous manufacturing methods.

By focusing on "neutral ester" as a substitute for carboxylate ester, a biodiesel fuel manufacturing method was studied using a supercritical method under milder conditions that do not trigger corrosion of the reaction tube. This non-catalytic supercritical method, which uses dimethyl carbonate as neutral ester, is a new process that also received recognition due to the fact that glycerin is converted into highly useful chemicals with added value (Ilham and Saka, 2009).

These non-catalytic biodiesel production methods using supercritical fluid technologies are all the result of world-leading research that was exclusively conducted in Japan.

4-3-5 Concluding remarks

The chapter presents future trends and horizons of biomass use focusing on bioethanol and biodiesel, laying out issues and the current state of biofuels. Bioethanol production can provide a chance to produce independent "national fuel" from our own natural resources such as cedar trees. Although it is essential to import bioethanol from Brazil as a short-term strategy, for a long-term strategy it is important for Japan to establish its own production technologies as a "forest country" through development of new processes using woody biomass resources, which will foster employment, aid the economy and keep the environment in a healthy condition. In biodiesel production, waste oils available are insufficient, thus we need raw materials from Southeast Asian countries. However, to promote the use of biodiesel, tax exemption will be essential. It is very important to have our own production methods for both bioethanol and biodiesel, from an energy security viewpoint. To this end, future-generation of bioethanol and biodiesel production technologies was introduced.

REFERENCES

Biofuels Technology Innovation Council (2008) "The Biofuels Technology Innovation Plans", Agency for Natural Resources and Energy, Tokyo.

Ilham, Z. and S. Saka (2009) "Dimethyl Carbonate as Potential Reactant in Non-catalytic Biodiesel Production by Supercritical Method", *Bioresource Technology* 100(5), pp. 1793–1796.

Imahara, H., E. Minami, M. Hattori, H. Murakami, N. Matsui and S. Saka (2007) "Current Situation and Prospects of Oil/Fat Resources for Biodiesel Production", *Energy and Resources* 28(3), pp. 175–179.

Kusdiana, D. and S. Saka (2004) "Two-step Preparation for Catalyst-free Biodiesel Fuel Production", *Applied Biochemistry and Biotechnology* 115, pp. 781–791.

Minami, E. and S. Saka (2001) "Biomass·Energy·Environment: 2-2", in S. Saka (ed.) *Quantity of Biomass in Japan*. Tokyo: IPC, pp. 61–103.

——— (2002) "Survey on the Virgin Biomass and Its Unused and Waste Portions in Japan in Their Available Quantity", *Energy and Resources* 23(3), pp. 219–223.

Minami, E., H. Imahara, K. Sunandar, K. Abdullah and S. Saka (2005) "Biodiesel Production from Wood Oils/Fats", paper presented at IAWPS 2005, Yokohama, 27–30 November.

NEDO (2005) "High Efficiency Bioenergy Conversion Project", New Energy and Industrial Technology Development Organization, Kanagawa.

——— (2007a) "NEDO Kaigai Report", No. 1007, New Energy and Industrial Technology Development Organization, Kanagawa.

——— (2007b) "Development of Preparatory Basic Bioenergy Technologies", New Energy and Industrial Technology Development Organization, Kanagawa.

——— (2009) "Development of Preparatory Basic Bioenergy Technologies", New Energy and Industrial Technology Development Organization, Kanagawa.

Petroleum Association of Japan (2008) "The Present Petroleum Industry 2008", Petroleum Association of Japan, Tokyo.

Saka, S. (2006) "Current Technologies and Subjects for Bioethanol", *Chemistry* 61(11), pp. 12–16.

Saka, S. and Y. Isayama (2009) "A New Process for Catalyst-free Production of Biodiesel Using Supercritical Methyl Acetate", *Fuel* 88(7), pp. 1307–1313.

Saka, S. and D. Kusdiana (2001) "Biodiesel Fuel from Rapeseed Oil Prepared in Supercritical Methanol", *Fuel* 80(2), pp. 225–231.

4-4

Clean development mechanism policy and sustainable rural development in China

Akihisa Mori

4-4-1 Introduction

China's economic growth has been rapid since its economic reform and open-door policy of 1978. It tries to maintain an 8 per cent annual growth rate in the face of the worldwide economic downturn by ramping up government spending. On the other hand, it has been experiencing serious environmental pollution resulting from rapid industrialization and urbanization. In response, the central government has gradually initiated countermeasures, starting with a programme to combat water pollution in the Huai River basin in 1994.

Despite such efforts, the environmental problems are still serious. In addition, greenhouse gas (GHG) emission has been continuously rising. The average annual rate of increase since 1995 is approximately 8 per cent; the rate has exceeded 10 per cent since 2000 when economic growth accelerated again. In particular, the amount of CO_2 (carbon dioxide) emissions from electricity generation and heat has increased at an average annual rate of 15.7 per cent for the 11 years from 1995 to 2006 (Figure 4.4.1). As a result, in 2005 the amount of GHG emissions in China surpassed that in the United States, and it became the world's largest emitter (Figure 4.4.2). Moreover, China's CO_2 emission, which was ranked number two in the world in 2006, became number one in 2007.

Continued increase in GHG emissions in China is not only attributed to economic growth and an accompanying rise in energy consumption: lack of clear emission reduction targets and clear policies to achieve them

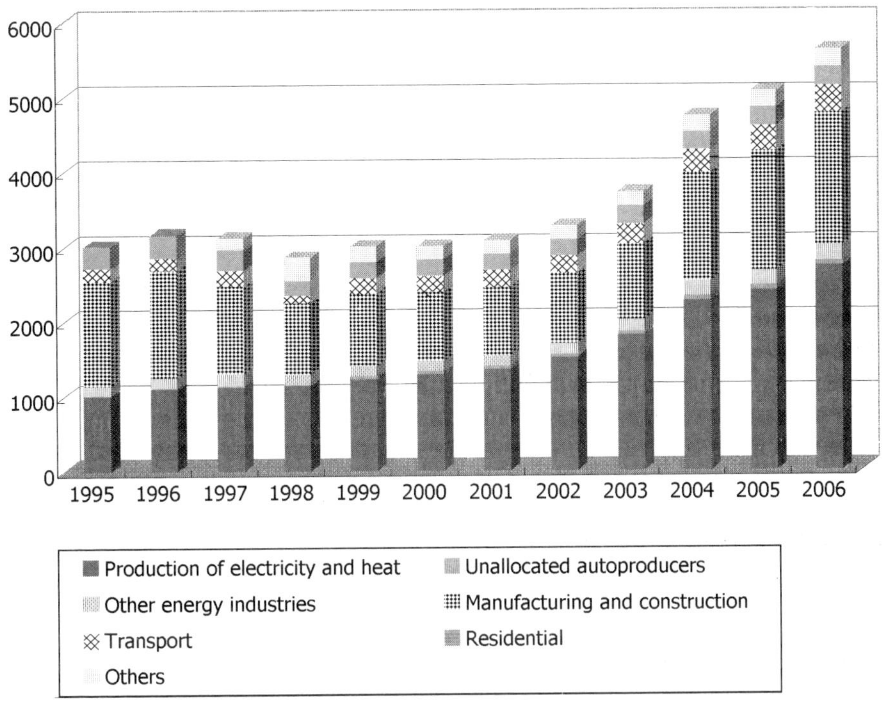

Figure 4.4.1 CO_2 emissions in China by sector, 1995–2006
Source: IEA (2009).

might have given little incentive for local governments and firms to reduce GHG emissions.

Even in such a policy climate, efficient energy use, greater use of renewable energies and the clean development mechanism (CDM) have been implemented to overcome the vicious cycle of increasing reliance on coal, inefficient energy supply and air pollution (Mori, 2011). The CDM is a mechanism in which the Annex I countries under the Kyoto Protocol organize projects to reduce emissions or increase sequestration by providing developing countries with technical or financial assistance, and count a certain portion of the resulting GHG reductions as part of what the Annex I countries themselves must achieve.

This "flexible" mechanism is established as a complement to reduce GHG emissions in Annex I countries. However, it is criticized for concentration in specific types of projects and specific nations, and little consideration for sustainable development in developing countries. To use the CDM as a tool for advancing sustainable development, SouthSouthNorth (2003) and Sutter and Parreño (2007) argue ways to improve its institutions.

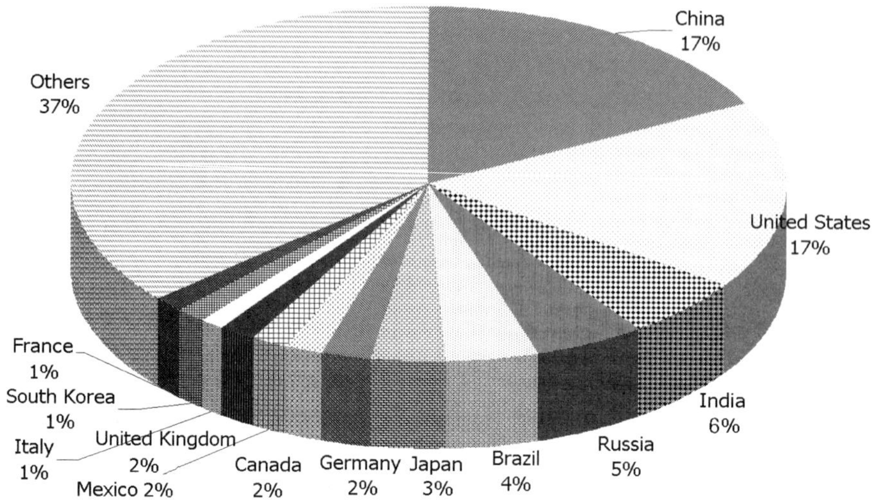

Figure 4.4.2 World greenhouse gas emissions, 2005
Source: OECD (2008).

The World Wildlife Fund proposed the Gold Standard that labels high-quality certified emissions reductions (CERs) in the carbon market. China has shown interest in contributions to sustainable development that CDM projects would make. However, the more emphasis developing countries put on such contributions, the less support from Annex I countries, which leads to few investments.

Assuming a trade-off between GHG reduction and sustainable development in host countries, domestic policies in the host country may have a large impact on the magnitude of contributions that CDM projects make to sustainable development. This chapter examines this potential by investigating a biogas CDM project for small-scale pig farms in rural areas, and agricultural policies in China.

4-4-2 CDM policy in China

In the 1990s the Chinese government was very cautious about the negotiation of the UN Framework Convention on Climate Change (UNFCCC): it may have mandated GHG reduction even in developing countries, including China, which would hinder its domestic economic growth. China judged that maintaining a representative role among the developing countries opposing such obligations (the G-77) would work advantageously in international politics (Kobayashi, 2002).

Once the CDM rules and regulations were specified at the UNFCCC Seventh Conference of the Parties, however, the Chinese government began to examine the effect of the CDM with support from the World Bank. Consequently, it recognized that the CDM would bring the country five benefits: an increase in net foreign direct investment amounting to US$475 million; improved efficiency in generation and consumption of electricity; a 0.5 per cent rise in GDP through investment in advanced technology and increased domestic production; development of local economies through technology transfers and tax revenues; and increased efficiency in energy use and the use of waste resulting from electricity generation (Nygard et al., 2004). With such research results, the country started to recognize that proactive use of the CDM would enable the achievement of policy goals such as stable energy supply and efficient use of energy.

In addition, the UNFCCC and the Kyoto Protocol take the principle of "common but differentiated responsibility", stating that they do not oblige developing countries to reduce GHG emissions. Hence, China ratified both the UNFCCC and the Kyoto Protocol in hope of additional funds from the Global Environment Facility as well as technological transfers and fund inflows through the CDM (Zhang, 2002).

China then announced the Interim Measures for the Operation and Management of CDM Projects in 2004 and the Measures for the Operation and Management of CDM Projects in 2005, declaring the government would actively promote CDM projects. It also announced a critical notification regarding the standardization of CDM projects, consulting services and evaluation activities in China.

Further, the government formulated China's National Climate Change Programme in 2007 to show targets, basic principles, focal areas and policy measures for climate change activities by 2010. As a goal of GHG emission reduction, the programme clearly states an increase of the share of renewable energy, including large-scale hydroelectric power plants in primary energy supply going up to 10 per cent and an increase in the extraction of coal-bed methane to 10 billion m^3, alongside a 20 per cent reduction in energy consumption per unit of GDP relative to its 2005 level described in the Eleventh Five-Year Plan. The programme also outlines a reduction of GHG emissions in 2010 by 200 million tonnes of CO_2-equivalent through coal-bed and coalmine methane CDM projects, and by 30 million tonnes of CO_2-equivalent through the promotion of biomass energy. The government is planning to have a target to improve energy consumption per unit of GDP by 17 per cent in the Twelfth Five-Year Plan (2011–2015).[1] By publicizing these active measures and plans globally, the Chinese government intends to avoid an obligation to reduce emissions in a post-2012 international framework for preventing climate change.

4-4-3 Features of CDM policy in China

There are three main features in CDM policy in China. First, it stipulates that profits made through transfers of CERs belong to the Chinese government and CDM project entities. Based on this provision, the Chinese government has a legal right to collect its share of revenue from the sales of CERs.

Second, the difference in the treatment of preferred and non-preferred subsectors in CDM projects is remarkably large. Three subsectors – improvement of energy efficiency; renewable energy; and recovery of methane, coal-bed methane and coalmine methane – are designated as key and receive preferential treatment in various procedures, plus tax of only 2 per cent of the revenue from the sales of CERs. In contrast, the government's share in the revenue from CER sales is set higher for hydrochlorofluorocarbon (HFC-23) and nitrous oxide (N_2O), at 65 and 30 per cent, respectively.

Third, entry by foreign entities is strictly restricted. The government limits the entities permitted to enter CDM projects to Chinese companies and firms with a Chinese holding company having 51 per cent or more of their shares. Reflecting this restriction, many CDM projects are proposed without a merger or technology partnership with a foreign company, and applications sent to the Chinese government or the CDM executive board for approval indicate that the participation of foreign companies tends to be limited to CER purchases.

4-4-4 The current state of CDM projects in China

China has become the nation with the largest number of CDM projects and amount of CERs. The number of CDM projects in China registered with the United Nations has drastically risen since 2007. As of May 2009 it had 564 registered projects, which surpassed India's 428 projects and dwarfed Brazil's 158. The amount of GHG emission reduction by 2012 rises to 887.86 million tonnes of CO_2-equivalent for China – almost four times the amount for India (Table 4.4.1).

This rapid increase is partly attributed to a unique feature of CDM projects in China. Until 2007 the majority of CERs came from HFC-23 reduction schemes that produced a large amount of CERs per project

Table 4.4.1 Number of CDM projects and volume of CERs by host country

	Number of projects	CERs up to 2012 (million tonnes of CO_2-equivalent)
China	564	888
India	428	239
Brazil	158	134
Mexico	114	48
Malaysia	46	17
Chile	32	29
South Korea	27	95
Indonesia	24	19
Argentina	15	27
Others	240	161
Total	1,648	1,657

with low project risks, and were thus regarded as the most cost-efficient CDM projects. However, no more HFC-23 reduction projects are expected to be proposed because all the feasible projects from existing factories producing HCFC-22 have been approved, and the UNFCCC Conference of Parties decided that it would no longer approve the reduction of HFC-23 from any new HCFC-22 producing factories. Subsequently, the reduction of nitrous oxide at factories and the recovery of coal-bed and coalmine methane are attracting attention due to perceived higher cost-effectiveness with lower risks.

CDM projects were also encouraged by the enactment of the Renewable Energy Law of the People's Republic of China in 2006. This law defines renewable energy as non-fossil (e.g. wind, solar, biomass, geothermal and ocean) energies, and does not include direct burning of straw, firewood or excreta in low-efficiency stoves. The law also states that the central government encourages renewable energies in rural areas, and that energy offices of local governments (above prefecture level) and relevant bureaucratic divisions must prepare plans for renewable energy development in rural areas and provide technical and financial support for the use of biogas from biomass, household solar energy and small-scale wind turbines and hydropower, taking into account different conditions in each region. Also, as a measure to promote renewable electricity, a *de facto* feed-in tariff is introduced to mandate power grids to conclude agreements to purchase all the renewable electricity generated by companies that obtain a government permit or are registered through submitting a report. If a grid operator does not purchase all the electricity, it faces a fine with an upper limit of twice the amount of economic losses sustained by power generation companies. The price for biomass electric power paid by the grid is set at an amount equalling each province's

Table 4.4.2 Sectoral allocation of number of CDM projects and volume of CERs in China

	Number of projects	CERs up to 2012 (million tonnes of CO_2-equivalent)
HFC reduction	11	366
N_2O reduction	26	103
Cement	3	3
Methane recovery	37	77
Methane avoidance	2	0
Afforestation	1	0
Fuel change	14	69
Waste gas and heat	63	70
Hydropower	267	118
Wind power	125	72
Biogas	3	1
Biomass	11	9
Other renewable energy	1	0
Total	564	888

2005 standard purchasing price for grid-produced electricity from desulphurized coal-fired plants plus 0.25 yuan/kWh. This led to a rapid increase in the number of CDM projects in renewable energy, including small-scale hydropower and biogas as well as wind power (Table 4.4.2).

Wind power and small-scale hydropower projects, however, do not necessarily improve the environment or advance sustainable development in the communities near the project site. They may cause noise problems and changes in land use, including the expropriation of farmland, and generated power is not always distributed at a price affordable to communities, thus perhaps worsening their standard of living.[2]

On the other hand, small-scale biogas or biomass projects are more likely to bring about the supply of electricity and gas to communities, a resulting decrease in deforestation, suppressed respiratory diseases due to reduced use of firewood and coal, and improvement in indoor pollution. Thus they have greater potential for improving the quality of life. Paying attention to these sustainable development impacts, the Chinese government has encouraged installing methane gas digesters for livestock at individual farms by providing a subsidy of 800 yuan per installation since 2000, when it entirely banned deforestation. The government provided an annual subsidy of 20–30 million yuan before 2000; this increased to 100 million yuan in 2000, 1 billion yuan in 2003 and 2.5 billion yuan in 2006 – a 100-fold increase. Despite this effort, in Hunan province, for example, only 30–40 out of 122 prefecture and district governments could obtain the subsidy annually, and the number was just 10–20 for county and village governments. These figures show that diffusion has been much slower than planned.[3]

The government therefore attempted to promote the existing measure by redesigning it as a CDM project and obtaining additional revenue from the acquisition of CERs. Two biogas CDM projects for pig farms were registered with the UNFCCC by June 2009: one is targeted at relatively large specialized pig farms; the other is for installing biogas digesters at rural small farms, which we examine in the following section.

4-4-5 Potential of a livestock-waste CDM project for sustainable rural development: The case of Enshi Tujia and Miao autonomous prefecture

The Eco-farming Biogas Project for Enshi Tujia and Miao autonomous prefecture, Hubei province, is designed to install biogas digesters at 33,000 farming households located in nationally designated impoverished areas in two county-level cities (Enshi and Lichuan) and six counties (Xuanen, Jianshi, Badong, Xianfeng, Laifeng and Hefeng) that are constituents of a prefecture in a poverty-stricken mountainous region. The project aims to reduce methane gas emissions by installing digesters to supplement the use of coal, and expects to cut the amount of GHG emission by 580,000 tonnes of CO_2-equivalent during a 10-year credit period. The biogas digesters used in this project are, in principle, those specified in the technological standards set by the Chinese government, and planning and construction are provided by engineers certified by the Ministry of Agriculture; there is no technology transfer from the Annex I countries.

As shown in the feasibility study for a CDM project in Dingcheng district in Changde city, Hunan province, biogas CDM projects for pig farms can produce large net benefits not only for the entire project but also for farmers, because they enable farmers to reduce expenditures due to the substitution for fossil fuel and chemical fertilizer and saving time that would have been used for collecting firewood or charcoal (Table 4.4.3). The study also shows that there is no incentive for private entities to invest in such projects because, assuming that they bear most of the investment costs, they cannot recover these. In order for private entities to recover their costs, project design must be adjusted so that farmers pay at least a portion of the investment. However, the initial cost is higher than farmers' annual income, while benefits are rather intangible – in the form of expenditure reductions. Therefore, farmers tend to perceive their own burden as higher and benefits as lower. In addition, the more remotely farmers are located from urban areas, the less opportunity they have to

Table 4.4.3 Cost-benefit matrix for the biogas CDM project at Chandu city, China (yuan)

	Project initiator	Farmer	Central government	Total
Revenue				
CER	908	0	19	927
Saving of fossil fuel	0	4,698	0	4,698
Saving of chemical fertilizer	0	5,813	0	5,813
Time saving	0	8,618	0	8,618
Cost				
Construction	1,600	0	800	2,400
Maintenance	0	0	0	0
Transaction	1,000	0	0	1,000
Profit	–1,692	19,129	–781	16,656

Notes:
CER price is assumed as US$10 per tonne of CO_2-equivalent.
Discount rate and credit period are assumed as 10 per cent and 10 years respectively.
Transaction cost is discussed in Michaelowa et al. (2003).

find a part-time job, which makes it difficult for them to take advantage of time saving by earning more income. Time saving may turn into additional leisure time, or give an incentive for young farmers to work in a large coastal city for long periods, leaving farming to the elders. In the latter case, installed biogas digesters do not get used sufficiently. For this reason farmers are reluctant to install digesters, even if the government provides a subsidy of 800 yuan, let alone bear part of the investment costs.

The Eco-farming Biogas Project for Enshi Tujia and Miao tries to overcome this challenge, being a CDM project led by local government. The project has four characteristics. First, farmers should bear construction and maintenance costs of biogas digesters. Second, to reduce the burden of initial investment costs borne by farmers, the credit union of the local government sets up a finance programme with the government's CER revenue as collateral. Third, to prevent insufficient maintenance by farmers to allow assured acquisition of CERs, the project operating entity, not farmers, does the actual installation and maintenance and receives compensation from farmers. Fourth, a project management office is established in the local government to utilize CER revenue to enhance technical assistance and instruction to village governments. According to the project design document, these measures can produce a positive net benefit for farmers and the entire project, and enable the project entity to recover costs even though benefits associated with time saving do not arise (Table 4.4.4).

Table 4.4.4 Cost-benefit matrix for the biogas CDM project at Enshi Tujia and Miao autonomous prefecture, China (yuan)

	Project initiator (local government)	Farmer	Central government	Total
Revenue				
CER	947	0	20	967
Saving of fossil fuel	0	4,698	0	4,698
Saving of chemical fertilizer	0	5,813	0	5,813
Cost				
Construction and maintenance	0	2,085	1,000	3,085
Reserve for write-off	<947	0	0	<947
Profit	>0	8,426	–980	>7,445

Notes:
CER price is assumed as US$10 per tonne of CO_2-equivalent.
Discount rate and credit period are assumed as 10 per cent and 10 years respectively.
Transaction cost is assumed as zero with consideration to the local-government-initiated CDM project, while collateral is counted on as a reserve for write-off.
Savings of fossil fuel and chemical fertilizer are assumed to be the same as Table 4.4.3, while time saving is assumed to be zero due to few opportunities to get part-time jobs.

This project is, however, merely government coercion to achieve its policy goal of diffusing biogas digesters in which it installs biogas digesters first, and forces farmers to pay compensation for the cost afterwards. In order to pay compensation, a farmer has two options: sustain operation of biogas digesters to save enough from reduced use of coal, briquettes and chemical fertilizers; or let young generations work in large cities for a period long enough to earn income exceeding the amount of loan repayment. The former choice increases the risk of pests emerging due to the transition to organic fertilizers in circumstances where a farmer cannot expect increased productivity by expanding farm size (Takahashi, 2009). There is also a risk of not getting biogas if swine influenza spreads.[4] To avoid such risks, farmers continue to use fossil fuel and chemical fertilizers and are not inclined to install biogas digesters, nor completely replace production and consumption as shown in Table 4.4.4. The latter choice depends on the availability of jobs in large cities.

If farmers cannot repay their loan, they have no choice but to sell their right to use land to large agricultural corporations in the process of liquidating their assets.[5] Traditionally, land-use rights have been the last resort that have guaranteed work and subsistence-level living for farmers with no social security from the government. Farmers who have sold their land-use right become employed workers without social security, and are more dependent on their employers and more vulnerable to external conditions (Shimizu, 2005).

We can draw two findings from this case. First, small-scale livestock-waste CDM projects can be financially viable only when the government can build institutions that prohibit farmers from migration in the current context of China. Second, farmers can improve their living standard only when they can manage various kinds of risks, including price fluctuations for their agricultural products and natural disasters.

4-4-6 Agricultural policies and sustainable development

Since the establishment of the People's Republic of China, the government has discriminated against farmers through policies and institutions, such as the policy to keep agricultural prices low and prohibition of urban migration under the household registration system. The repressed agricultural price was abolished in 1980 and there was official acceptance of the sale of surplus harvest, which increased farmers' income in the 1980s. But agricultural prices fell drastically in the 1990s because of excessive production. Land has been segmented and productivity reduced since 1980, because farmland area has decreased while the agrarian population has continued to grow. Underdeveloped distribution systems, such as lack of a credible appraisal mechanism, insufficient functioning of price adjustment systems and weak storage capability reflected in the lack of storage space and refrigerators, make it difficult for farmers to sell their products at the most favourable terms (ibid.). As a result, farmers' absolute income has declined after a peak in 1997 (Shimizu, 2006).

To supplement agricultural income, many farmers have a second job at medium- or small-scale companies or work as manual labourers for long periods. However, the household registration system makes it difficult for farmers to move to large cities to obtain urban household registration that would give them access to various public services there. Central government developed a plan to abolish the differentiation between agricultural and non-agricultural (urban) household registration in approximately five years from 2000 and put an end to the planned management of farmers' transfer to small cities. Accordingly, in 2001 several provinces ended rural and urban household registration and unified them into resident household registration. However, since the government of a large city can set its own conditions for issuing permits to incoming migrants, the acquisition of an urban household registration is still difficult. Therefore, types of jobs that incoming farmers can find are limited to contract labour at factories or manual labour with high risks and severe working conditions, such as construction work. Such jobs provide minimal wages and do not offer social insurance. Knowing that only unstable and risky jobs are available, farmers working in a city do not sell their land-use right, thereby securing their living. Hence, no agricultural productivity improvement is potentially gained by expanding the scale of production, while more farmland is left unattended and barren. In addition, no group to represent the interests of farmers is allowed to organize, and the proportion of farmers in the population is small compared to that of bureaucrats in the People's Congress: there are few institutions that incorporate farmers' opinions into policy-making processes (Korogi, 2005).[6]

To make CDM projects advance sustainable development in rural areas, it is necessary to modify the existing policies further to overcome the problems of farmers, rural areas and agriculture. As a first step, it is important to establish political institutions that reflect the opinions of farmers, and allow farmers, without regard to their type of household registration, to receive the same public services enjoyed by urban people, such as social security, healthcare and education.[7]

Such reforms have been advanced, however, only in policy areas that central government can deal with by increasing public expenditure. Redistribution policies such as property tax, inheritance tax and the establishment of a social security fund have not been realized because of disagreements within the Communist Party, backed by fierce opposition from wealthier people. Also, a stamp tax hike for stock transactions, which was passed in 2007, was cancelled to prevent stock prices falling at the beginning of 2008.

In addition, there seems to be no end to forced expropriations and development of land by local governments, ignoring environmental impact assessments and farmers' resistance to such actions. The forced land expropriation is pushed by the fact that local governments receive far greater income from property development than from taxes, and heads and officials of local governments are evaluated by economic performance in their jurisdiction. To mitigate the latter incentive, central government is debating the use of an integrated environmental and economic indicator such as green GDP as an index for performance evaluation. In reality, however, only three environmental indicators are taken into account: total amount of sulphur dioxide emissions, total amount of chemical oxygen demand discharge and energy consumption per unit of GDP. Environmental deterioration caused by forced expropriations and land redevelopment is not properly taken into account: rather, these actions receive high marks in economic performance indicators.

When these problems are overcome, a greater number of CDM projects in rural areas would be proposed and implemented, providing ideas and opportunities for promoting sustainable development in these areas.

4-4-7 Conclusion

This chapter has shown that the Chinese government became active in CDM projects after recognizing these would advance the sustainable development that the country wants to realize. It has promoted biogas projects for small-scale pig farms as a way of promoting renewable energy and preventing deforestation, as well as reducing poverty in rural areas. Recently, a CDM project was introduced to diffuse biogas digestion to small-scale farmers over a wider area. Despite the project's potentially large positive net profit, uptake is slow due lack of profitability to project developers and financiers, high installation costs to farmers and their migration to cities as contract or manual labourers. To ensure profits to them and sustainability of the project, local governments have to implement the project by themselves, provide loans to farmers and recover the costs, as seen in the case of Enshi Tujia and Miao. This chapter finds that this is due mainly to farmers' perceived substantially high risks, which are ascribed not only to the size of initial investments but also to institutions that discriminate against farmers, such as the existing agricultural policies, the household registration system and a performance evaluation system that cannot reduce local governments' appetite for development nor provide incentives to promote environmental preservation actively.

Notes

1. *Jiji Tsushin*, 17 June 2009 (www.jiji.com/jc/zc?k=200906/2009061700048).
2. In Shanwei, Guangdong province, there was a protest by farmers opposing land expropriation for a wind power plant, which was subsequently quelled by a large-scale police action (Shimizu, 2006: 350–352).
3. Interview at Hunan Province Development and Reform Commission, March 2006.
4. Swine influenza emerged in vast area of China during the period 2005–2006, forcing many farmers to sell their hogs at a low price. According to an interview conducted by the author and other researchers in Liuan, Anhui province, in 2007–2008 swine influenza was one of the major reasons why farmers abandoned small-scale farming and hog farming and went to large cities for long-term work.
5. All land in China is state owned. However, the Property Law of 2007 allows automatic continuation of a land-use right after its predetermined lease period ends, as well as its sale and purchase.
6. This is due to the disparity in the ratio of representatives per head of population in urban and rural areas. It was decided in 1992 that one representative for the National People's Congress should be elected for every 960,000 people in rural areas and for every 240,000 people in urban areas,
7. The tax reform implemented in Anhui province reduced the "unreasonable" fees on farmers by simplifying various fees. However, it led to shortage of revenues for local governments despite the 20 billion yuan subsidies from the central government. This delayed and stopped salary payments to schoolteachers and made the operation of com-

pulsory education in rural areas difficult. As a result, such reforms did not spread nationwide (Yan, 2002).

REFERENCES

IEA (2009) *CO_2 Emissions from Fuel Combustion*. Paris: International Energy Agency.

Kobayashi, Yuka (2002) "Navigating between "Luxury" and "Survival" Emissions: Tensions in China's Multilateral and Bilateral Climate Change Policy", in Paul G. Harris (ed.) *Global Warming and East Asia: The Domestic and International Politics of Climate Change*. London: Routledge, pp. 86–108.

Korogi, Ichiro (2005) *Turbulent China: The Future of 1.3 Billion People*. Tokyo: Iwanami Shinsho (in Japanese).

Michaelowa, Axel, Jusen Asuka-Zhang, Karsten Lrause, Bernhard Grimm and Tobisa Koch (2003) "The Clean Development Mechanism and China's Energy Sector", in Paul G. Harris (ed.) *Global Warming and East Asia: The Domestic and International Politics of Climate Change*. London: Routledge, pp. 109–129.

Mori, Akihisa (2011) "Can CDM Be an Instrument for Mitigating Conflicting Environmental Concerns between China and Japan?", in Kazuhiro Ueta (ed.) *CDM and Sustainable Development: China and Japan*. Kyoto: Kyoto University Press.

Nygard, Jostein, Holger Liptow, Deshun Liu, Robert Livernash and Xuedu Lu (2004) *Clean Development Mechanism in China: Taking a Proactive and Sustainable Approach*. Washington, DC: World Bank.

OECD (2008) *CO_2 Emissions from Fuel Combustion 2008*. Paris: OECD Publishing.

Shimizu, Yoshikazu (2005) *Farmer Uprisings in China*. Tokyo: Kodansha + α Bunnko (in Japanese).

——— (2006) *The End of People's China*. Tokyo: Kodansha + α Bunnko (in Japanese).

SouthSouthNorth (2003) *Climate Change and the Kyoto Protocol's Clean Development Mechanism*. London: ITDG Publishing.

Sutter, C. and J. C. Parreño (2007) "Does the Current Clean Development Mechanism (CDM) Deliver Its Sustainable Development Claim? An Analysis of Officially Registered CDM Projects", *Climatic Change* 84, pp. 75–90.

Takahashi, Goro (2009) *Agriculture in China: Abused Farmers, Land, and Water*. Tokyo: Asahi Shinsho (in Japanese).

Yan, Zenping (2002) *The Current Chinese Economy 2: Issues Facing the Agricultural State*. Nagoya: University of Nagoya Press (in Japanese).

Zhang, Zhihong (2002) "The Forces behind China's Climate Change Policy", in Paul G. Harris (ed.) *Global Warming and East Asia: The Domestic and International Politics of Climate Change*. London: Routledge, pp. 66–85.

4-5

Conservation of peat bog and agro-forestry in Indonesia

Kosuke Mizuno and Haris Gunawan

4-5-1 Background to the issues – Letter in *Nature* magazine and the third-largest carbon emissions in the world

A letter, "The Amount of Carbon Released from Peat and Forest Fires in Indonesia in 1997", was published in *Nature* in 2002 (Page et al., 2002). In the letter, the amount of carbon released by the burning of peatland forests throughout Indonesia during the 1997 El Niño event was estimated to be between 0.81 and 2.57 gigatonnes (Gt). This is equivalent to 13–40 per cent of the 6.4 Gt average annual carbon emissions caused by the burning of fossil fuels worldwide during the same period.[1]

According to Hooijer et al. (2006) of the Wetland International Group, the amount of carbon released from peatlands in Indonesia includes not only carbon released by fire, but also from the degradation of peatlands caused by their draining and drying for oil palm and eucalyptus planting and deforestation due to road construction. Accordingly, the most conservative estimate of the annual amount of carbon released due to the degradation of peatlands in the Kalimantan Indonesia, Sumatra and Papua areas is 0.63 Gt, and carbon released in the burning of peatlands from 1997 to 2006 was 1.40 Gt. By adding these two, the annual amount of carbon released from Indonesian peatlands is approximately 2 Gt, estimated to be equivalent to 8 per cent of the carbon emissions due to the global burning of fossil fuels in 2000. As a result, Indonesia is the third-largest emitter of carbon in the world, following the United States and

China. This is significantly different from its current ranking of 21 when the amount of carbon released by peatlands is not included (ibid.: 29).

Hooijer et al. (ibid.: 31) stressed the importance of forest conservation and drainage avoidance in remaining peat swamp forests; restoration of degraded peatland hydrological systems and peat forests or other sustainable vegetation cover where possible; and improved water management in peatland plantation, incorporated in water management master plans for peatland areas.

These reports had a significant impact on Indonesian society. In identifying Indonesia as the world's third-largest carbon emitter, the credibility of the data was doubted, and there was worry that such criticism would reduce the range of technological choices for the country's industrialization (for example, limits on the use of coal, etc.), consequently impeding development. Furthermore, if the amount of carbon emissions is recognized as the third largest in the world, Indonesia might be classified as a participating nation to which Annex I of the UN Framework Convention on Climate Change (UNFCCC) would apply, and might then be subject to certain responsibilities to carry out quantified commitments for the control and reduction of carbon emissions. There are various viewpoints in this regard, including that this would go against national interests, that Indonesia should carry out technological development using clean energy instead, or should actively participate in emissions trading through the clean development mechanism (see www.technologyindonesia.com/download.php?file=pemanasan.pdf).

This chapter considers policies for Indonesia in such conditions, focusing on the issue of carbon released by peatlands and efforts to create a low-carbon society, especially with regard to the processes of forest engineering and peatlands. Efforts in creating a low-carbon society in Indonesia based on the Kyoto Protocol are explained, and the background of forest exploitation and conversion to farmland is described. After this, development and conservation of peatlands and issues regarding carbon emissions are discussed.

4-5-2 Efforts leading to a low-carbon society in Indonesia

Indonesia ratified the Kyoto Protocol and the UNFCCC by Act No. 17 of 2004, and incorporated them as part of domestic law. Indonesia is a developing country party which is not included in Annexes I and II of the UNFCCC, and "the extent to which developing country parties will effectively implement their commitments under the Convention will depend on the effective implementation by developed country parties of their commitments under the Convention related to financial resources and transfer of technology".

The government issued Presidential Decree No. 5 in 2006 regarding the national energy policy, and has set goals that should be attained by 2025. These include that energy consumption elasticity to national income will be less than 1, and efforts will be made towards diversification and optimization of energy sources; as a result, the share of crude oil in national energy consumption would be kept to less than 20 per cent. Furthermore, a target was set to supply over 5 per cent in biofuels, over 5 per cent in geothermal energy and a total of over 5 per cent in biomass, nuclear, small-scale hydroelectric power generation and wind power as new energy sources.

Moreover, according to Act No. 30 of 2007 on Energy, since energy for economic activities and national defence is extremely important, energy administration – which includes supply, use and management – is to be carried out fairly, sustainably, optimally and uniformly. Attention is given to geothermal energy, wind power, bioenergy, solar energy, small and large hydropower and ocean thermal gradient and other ocean power, which can be sustainable if properly used.

Furthermore, Instruction of the President No. 1 of 2006 regarding the supply and use of biofuels as alternative fuel sources ordered 13 related ministries and provinces, districts and cities to promote their supply and use. As a result, biofuel use has advanced somewhat, and the supply and use of biofuels made from palm oil or the pressed pulp of sugarcane have been promoted.

As seen from the above, although efforts to change over to a low-carbon society in Indonesia have been implemented, these efforts have not exceeded this level of middle- and long-term goals because Indonesia is a developing country without carbon emission reduction commitments and assignments in terms of the UNFCCC, and has no specific carbon emission reduction goals set in this path.

Against this background, as described earlier it has been asserted that Indonesia is the world's third-largest emitter of carbon, and the main causes are the degradation and burning of peatlands, so the government must now respond quickly. To determine this response, policies regarding the use of Indonesian peatlands and forests, including peatland forest, must be considered.

4-5-3 Development of forests and peatland

Study of peatlands and government regulations

The existence of peatlands in Indonesia has been well known since colonial times, and various studies have been undertaken since the late nineteenth century. For example, Polak (1941) carried out research on the distribution of peatlands in the Dutch East Indies, examining chemical characteristics such as oligotrophy and strong acidity, and physical and biological characteristics of the area's vegetation. Polak also determined that peatlands do not have soil and have trees growing in them, and that oxidization and sinkage rapidly occur by the draining of the water, etc. Moreover, regarding sinkage and disappearance of peatland due to use and drainage, Furukawa (1992: 25–38) explained that the local Malay have adjusted themselves to the conditions: they prefer to move frequently from one place to other as shifting cultivators, and engage in many kinds of occupations such as collecting non-timber products, trade and so on.

However, the Indonesian government, including colonial government, has viewed peatland forest as a part of the general forest, or part of the forest reserved for hydrological, climatological or cultural reasons, without any specific established rules regarding peatland.[2] It was not until 1990 that it established a conservation standard regarding peatlands. Presidential Decision No. 32 of 1990 regarding conservation areas (*kawasan lindung*) defined conservation forest (*kawasan hutan lindung*), protected peatland (*kawasan bergambut*) and water catchment areas (*kawasan resapan air*) as the conservation areas in Article 4. Regarding peatland, Article 9 stipulates "Conservation of peatland area which functions as flood control area in water conservation and flood prevention, and conservation of the special ecology of the designated peatland district." Article 10 stipulates that "the standard for a peatland area is peatland which has more than 3 meters depth of peat deposit and located in the upstream of the river and swamp". Article 37 prohibits cultivation activities (*kegiatan budidaya*) except when such activities do not hinder the preservation and conservation function in the area.

Progress of forest development

The history of the administration of forest development dates back far before the regulation in 1990 regarding peatlands. To understand peatland development, it is necessary first to understand the background of the administration of forest development.

Indonesia's forest management has a long history, but considering it from the time of the Suharto administration, the standard of conservation and use was regulated by the Basic Forestry Act of 1967. The Act classifies forests into owned forests, with established private and organization rights (*hutan hak*), and state forests where such rights have not been established (*hutan negara*). State forests are classified into conservation forests (*hutan lindung*), production forests (*hutan produksi*), natural protected forests (*hutan suaka alam*) and tourism forests (*hutan wisata*).

The Basic Forestry Act of 1967[3] regulates forest concession rights (*hak pengusahaan hutan*) in Article 8, and acquisition of timber is permitted on the condition of reforestation and maintenance. Also, an industrial forest plantation permit (*hak pengusahaan hutan tanaman industri*) was stipulated for one-time clear-cutting rights and reforestation for industrial purposes.

Next, in 1983, the Consensus on Forest Zoning was established as the forest zoning classification by the Department of Forestry. State forests were then classified as conservation forests (*hutan konservasi*) and protected forests (*hutan lindung*), consisting of natural protected forests, tourism forests and national parks, and production forests, consisting of permanent production forests (*hutan produksi tetap*), limited-use production forests (*hutan produksi terbatas*) and convertible production forests (*hutan produksi yang dapat dikonversi*). As a result of this classification, protected forests throughout Indonesia covered 19.15 million ha (14 per cent), conservation forest 29.64 million ha (21 per cent), limited-use production forest 29.57 million ha (21 per cent), permanent production forest 33.40 million ha (23 per cent) and convertible production forest 30.00 million ha (21 per cent) (Colchester et al., 2006: 67).

For these forests, the forest concession rights and industrial forest plantation permits, as described above, were rendered to companies. For example, in Jambi province, according to the Consensus on Forest Zoning agreed at provincial level in 1987, the area of natural protected forest and tourism forest was 603,000 ha, conservation forest was 181,000 ha, limited-use production forest was 363,000 ha, permanent production forest was 1.07 million ha, convertible production forest was 727,000 ha and land for other purposes was 2.15 million ha, giving a total area in the whole province of 5.10 million ha. For these lands, 15 forest concession rights were rendered in 1997, totalling 1.22 million ha, which consisted of 643,000 ha of permanent production forest, 196,000 ha of limited-use production forest, 157,000 ha of convertible production forest, 49,000 ha of conservation forest, 1,000 ha of natural protected forest and 180,000 ha of other forest.[4]

As previously stated, development/utilization of all state forests is under a permit system, and forest concession rights to allow timber logging were stipulated in 1967. Plywood factories and sawmills were established in the 1970s, as logging companies were obliged to set up factories. In particular, plywood became one of the most important export commodities in the 1980s and 1990s.

In Riau province, for example, which has a total area of 9.45 million ha, forest concession rights were issued for 5.35 million ha by 1994, and there were 32 sawmills and 18 plywood factories. However, forest resources declined during the 2000s, so forests covered by concession rights were reduced. In 2002 forest concession rights were granted for 3.21 million ha, and there were 14 sawmills and six plywood factories.[5]

On the other hand, although industrial forest plantation permits have been issued since the 1970s, the area covered by such permits has rapidly increased since the 1990s. The industrial plantation permit area in Riau in 1994 was 269,000 ha, and this had increased to 873,000 ha by 2003.[6] This was due to an increase of afforestation of eucalyptus trees to supply the pulp industry, which significantly increased production during that period.

Forest use was also promoted by the increase of oil palm plantations. Plantation owners must acquire rights from the government for this land use, such as long-term usufruct rights. In Riau province in 1994, 473,000 ha of land rights were given for business by plantation companies, including 363,000 ha of long-term usufruct rights to 62 companies. In 1998 rights to establish an agricultural plantation increased to cover 789,000 ha of land, including 593,000 ha of long-term usufruct rights for 89 companies.[7]

According to the Consensus on Forest Zoning in Riau province, the area of conservation forest was 229,000 ha (2.7 per cent of its total forest), natural protected forest and tourism forest was 532,000 ha (6.3 per cent), permanent production forest was 1.60 million ha (19.0 per cent), limited-use production forest was 1.81 million ha (21.5 per cent) and convertible production forest was 4.28 million ha (50.6 per cent).

The area of land covered by forest concession rights in Riau province was 3.47 million ha (1997), and land with industrial forest plantation permits was 688,000 ha (1998). The area of land acquired by plantation companies was 789,000 ha.[8] Combining these three exceeds the total land designated by the Consensus on Forest Zoning as limited-use production and permanent production forest. This is considered possible as a result of the conversion of convertible production forest.

For oil palm plantation cultivation planned in convertible forests, a forest release permit (*pelepasan* – release from state forest) is required prior to receiving long-term usufruct rights. This has been covered in various regulations since the establishment of Forestry Minister Decision No. 145 of 1986.[9] To convert more than 100 ha of forest to farmland, an application must be submitted to the Ministry of Forestry, and for less than 100 ha to the province governor; in either case, the release must be approved under the Forestry Minister Decision (Salim, 2003: 94–99).

Vast areas of forest have been released or converted to plantations in this way: 1.65 million ha by 1988, 3.8 million ha by 1993 and 8.2 million ha up to March 1998 nationwide. Riau province is one of the most converted areas, with 1.98 million ha converted from forest to plantation up to March 1998. While the purpose of such conversion is of course to operate plantations, there are still many areas which have not yet been converted to plantations and are simply logged as released forest areas

(Basyar, 2008: 2–6). For this reason, it is assumed that data for converted plantation sites and acquisition of land rights such as long-term usufruct rights do not agree. Looking at land-use data in Riau province, there were 838,000 ha of plantation in 1988, increasing to 1.92 million ha in 2000 and 2.32 million ha in 2005.[10] Although some data sources differ, it is clear that the plantation area rapidly increased due to the conversion of forest since the end of the 1980s.

4-5-4 Progress in use and issues of conservation for peatlands

Progress in the use of peatland

The government regulates peatlands with a thickness exceeding 3 m located in upstream river and swamp areas as conservation forest, according to the 1990 Presidential Decision. This policy was confirmed in Government Decree No. 47 of 1997 regarding the national zoning plan.

However, peatland issues are hardly mentioned in various laws granting land rights, and are hardly considered when rights are issued. For example, the Act on Forestry of 1999 does not mention issues regarding peatland at all.

Due to advances in general forest development and the depletion of high-quality land, forest concession rights, industrial forest plantation permits, conversion permits for agricultural plantations and land rights for management plantations have been issued for a wide range of peatland. According to Hooijer et al. (2006: 12–14), there are 3.83 million ha of peatlands in Riau, making up 42 per cent of the province. Various rights were established on this land: forest concession rights have been granted to 13 per cent of the peatlands, industrial forest plantation permits to 20 per cent and rights for oil palm plantation to 23 per cent. Companies acquiring industrial forest plantation permits or rights for oil palm plantation will clear-cut the entire forest at once, greatly affecting the peatland.

Furthermore, according to Raflis (2007), who studied the local land-use planning in Riau, by the year 2000 1.96 million ha of peatland in the province had been converted to plantations or granted industrial forest plantation permits; of these, 864,000 ha were estimated to be peatland more than 3 m deep. Also, 230,000 ha of the peatlands, which corresponds to 70 per cent of the industrial forest plantation land given by the province governor, were more than 3 m deep.

Timber logging since the time of the Dutch East Indies Company, promotion of a transmigration policy among islands, colonization by plantation companies since colonial times, large-scale logging and development of the plywood industry since the 1970s, promotion of industrial reforestation and the rapid increase of plantation cultivation after the 1980s have encouraged the use of Sumatran forests and their conversion to farmland, etc. This has led to a lack of suitable sites and a massive wave of development in peatlands, although such areas are not necessarily suitable for their intended use.

Although government policy regarding peatland development was established in the 1990s, this policy is not effective in the midst of skyrocketing prices and a rapid increase of palm oil exports, the increase in global demand for palm oil and the development of the paper industry in Indonesia. Thus the estimated amount of carbon released due to fires occurring in peatland forests in Indonesia (Page et al., 2002) and the amount of carbon released due to the draining and degradation of the peatland (Hooijer et al., 2006) have increased enormously. As a result, the situation has completely changed, and Indonesia has become the world's third-largest carbon-emitting country.

Countermeasures for peatland carbon emissions

The government is under pressure to establish countermeasures regarding carbon released from peatlands. As a result, it has first used the laws to address this issue. Fundamentally, development of peatlands with a depth of more than 3 m, which are designated as conservation areas, would be considered a violation of the law, so one countermeasure can be to limit development to peatlands with a depth of less than 3 m.

The Indonesian government has carefully worked to resolve the issues by using peatlands with a depth of less than 3 m under various conditions. Regulation of the Minister of Agriculture No. 14 of 2009, Guidelines on the Use of Peatland for Oil Palm Plantations, encourages the use of non-peatland as much as possible, and stipulates that even in peatland with a depth of less than 3 m, peatland of lower-level maturity and the most undecomposed fibrik peat should not be used. Moreover, the depth and width of the drainage ditches are regulated, in order to prevent the peat from drying and burning, because the peatland cannot return to its original condition once the peat has dried and degraded. The adjustment of groundwater levels in peatland is regulated by the installation of automatic water sluices, and companies which violate these rules will have their long-term usufruct rights revoked.

Furthermore, the government enacted the 2009 Regulation of the Minister of Forestry No. P-30/Menhut-II/2009 regarding Implementation Procedures of Reducing Emissions from Deforestation and Forest Degradation, and regulated the rights and obligations of the parties involved with regard to activities to reduce carbon emissions brought about by deforestation and degradation, especially those for emissions trading.

Policies related to carbon emissions caused by the use of peatland are now discussed. Regarding peatland with a depth more than 3 m, use has largely advanced as described above. Many advocates and NGOs conclude that these uses are clearly illegal, so the government should take strict measures. The government has not clearly defined its policy in this matter yet.

Regarding peatland with a depth of less than 3 m, the depth standard was set in 1990 when there was no awareness of carbon emissions from peatlands. However, data from many studies show that large amounts of carbon can be released by draining, even in peatlands with depths less than 3 m. According to the study by Hooijer et al. (2006: 18), 60 kg of carbon is released from the subsidence of one cubic metre of peatland, and correlation of drained peat depth with amount of carbon released shows an estimated figure with an almost linear function. It is assumed that once the peatland is drained, carbon will be released without any significant difference between peatlands with depths of more or less than 3 m. So there is no significant difference in the estimation according to the depth of the peatland.

According Dr Supiandi of Bogor Agricultural University, a researcher of peatland issues, the government defined a depth of 3 m in 1990 because it was assumed that if the swamp was more than 3 m, even if a tree was planted on the ground the roots would not be able to go through the peat layer and it would be unable to grow.[11] If this is so, abiding by this 3 m standard may have meaning in terms of path dependency, but other measures need to be considered to resolve issues regarding carbon emissions from peatland.

Moreover, the government has issued guidelines for the cultivation of oil palms in peatlands with a depth of less than 3 m. However, according to a study by Agus, Suyanto and van Noordwijk (2007: 3–5), oil palm releases more than 100 tonnes of carbon per year per ha from cultivation of peatland. Even if the amount of biomass fixing by oil palms is deducted, there would still be 87 tonnes of carbon released, and is said to have a higher amount of carbon release than rubber (less than 40 tonnes) or rice fields. According to this study, no kind of agriculture can fix carbon as biomass sufficiently to offset the amount released by the subsidence of peatland. This also applies to slash-and-burn and traditional agriculture cultivating vegetables and upland rice.

Basically, trees that grow without releasing carbon in the peatland are those species which grow in original pristine peatland forest. Among these, trees with higher economic values are jelutung (*Dyera lowii*), terentang (*Camnospermo coriaeceum*), sago palm (*Melroxylon sago*), ramin

(*Gonystylus banconus*) and meranti bunga (*Shorea teysmanniana*); some other promising native species can grow well without changing the basic characteristics of this ecosystem.

These trees grow naturally and are not planted by the local people. Jelutung resin can be harvested and sold, and the trees can be logged. Jelutung and ramin can be used to make furniture, and the meranti group has been used to manufacture plywood.

Favourable measures for peatland conservation and the reduction of carbon released from peatlands are needed. To realize these, the avoidance of draining and drying of peatlands is essential: when constructing a drainage ditch, installing the appropriate sluice gates can prevent the reduction of peat subsurface water. Furthermore, in addition to promoting the cultivation of jelutung, which has high economic value, developing a market to increase its utilization and economic value is desirable, as this will promote conservation of peatland forests and support the livelihood of the local people. Jelutung latex is exported to Japan as chewing gum material, and this market should be developed. Also, to promote cultivation of these trees by the local people, the establishment of simple cultivation methods, ideas to use the trees and an organization and institution for cultivation are necessary.

We turn now to the possibility of emissions trading. At COP13 held in Bali, Indonesia, in December 2007, a possible price of CO_2 emissions of \$4–18 per tonne was discussed. Agus, Suyanto and van Noordwijk (ibid.: 4–5) calculated the opportunity cost of CO_2 in cultivating oil palm by estimating profit minus total cost over 25 years, divided by CO_2 emitted during that period (reduced by fixed carbon), resulting in \$4.1 per tonne of CO_2 emissions. This shows that promoting emissions trading can greatly influence the carbon emission issue caused by peatland subsidence.

Moreover, if emission trading is possible, it becomes possible to consider an amount of subsidy payment to the local people and companies for the cultivation of jelutung, which does not release carbon, as described above.

4-5-5 Conclusion

Indonesia has worked towards a low-carbon society in response to the Kyoto Protocol, by efforts such as the promotion of biofuel use and development of clean energies such as geothermal and solar. However, these are only middle- and long-term efforts as a developing country participant in the UNFCCC, and are dependent on effective implementation of commitments regarding economic and technological transfer by advanced participant countries.

However, studies showed that estimated amounts of carbon released by peatland forest burning and drainage and degradation of peatland in Indonesia were huge, identifying Indonesia as the world's third-largest carbon-emitting country. As a result, the situation regarding Indonesia's carbon emissions, especially involving peatlands, has completely changed.

Economic development in Indonesia, timber logging, the development of the plywood industry, promotion of industrial reforestation and the development of plantation cultivation have encouraged the use of Sumatran forests and their conversion to farmland. This has led to massive peatland exploitation, although such areas are not suitable for their intended application. Although Indonesia established a policy regarding peatland development after the 1990s, this policy was ineffective, and in fact is not mentioned in the 1999 Act on Forestry.

However, with the appearance of the carbon emissions issue regarding peatlands, the government is under pressure to establish measures to address this issue. Fundamentally, development of peatlands more than 3 m deep, which are designated as a conservation area, can be considered to be illegal, so one action can be to limit development to peatlands with a depth of less than 3 m. Moreover, regulations applying to oil palm plantations require careful work to resolve issues by using peatlands with a depth of less than 3 m only under various conditions and adjustment of the groundwater level by the installation of automatic water sluices. Companies violating these requirements must have their long-term usufruct rights revoked.

Furthermore, the government regulated the rights and obligations of the parties involved in emissions trading in regards to activities to reduce carbon emissions brought about by forest loss and peatland degradation.

Problems regarding these policies include the actual continued exploitation of wide areas of peatland with a depth of more than 3 m, the government's unclear policies to cope with this and the fact that large-scale carbon emissions cannot be avoided even if the 3 m regulation is enforced.

Regarding countermeasures for these problems, in addition to measures to implement stricter water sluice management in drainage ditches within current peatlands, active cultivation of tree species which grow naturally in pristine forests, such as jelutung and ramin, was considered. Reforestation technologies to meet these goals, ideas to use the trees, development of a product market, etc., should be promoted, while organizations and institutions that enable the local people to participate actively should be established and put in place. In this regard, emissions trading has big potential to resolve the conservation issues of peatlands, by making use of the proceeds of trade to give subsidies to cultivators of tree species which naturally grow in pristine peatland forests, and to companies which promote technological innovation for tree breeding and development of simple methods to plant the trees.

Notes

1. In the study, 2.5 million ha of forest were surveyed, including 1 million ha of converted rice fields, of which 86.4 per cent were peatland drained under the policy pursued by the Suharto administration in Central Kalimantan province. Wide-range fires were observed within the 1 million ha where the peatlands had been drained and converted to rice fields and had lost their original form (fires occurred in 51.3 per cent of the 1 million ha); in comparison, fires occurred in only 14.1 per cent of areas where the peatlands were untouched. Moreover, it was estimated that the amount of carbon released from this 2.5 million ha of peatland was 0.19–0.23 Gt, and an additional 0.05 Gt from the burning of the overlying vegetation. Extrapolating from this, the amount of carbon emissions due to fires occurring in Indonesia as a whole was estimated on the basis of an affected land area of up to 20.07 million ha. Moreover, when considering the increase in fires in peatland forest and grassland in recent years, the increase in the amount of carbon released from Indonesia's peatland is considered to be an important cause in the increase in global carbon emissions, from an annual average of 3.2 Gt between 1990 and 1999 to 6 Gt in 1998.
2. Colonial government always paid much attention to the teak forest; other forest was categorized as wild wood forest (*wildhoutbosschen*). This wild wood forest consisted of two categories on Java Island: the preserved forest (*in stand te houden*) that was designated by the governor-general for climatological and hydrological concerns, for use by local industry or for the purpose of public interests; and the unpreserved wild wood forest (*niet in stand to houden wildhoutbosschen*) that could be subject to rights of ownership, rights of land surface and so on. In outer islands, until 1910 the local authority in each region designated forest that would be forbidden from exploitation and arbitrary cutting for reasons of hydrology or in consideration of current or foreseeable future need for the forest (Paulus, 1917). However, there was no particular policy for peatland or peatland forest.
3. Lands where rights of ownership cannot be proven are designated as state-owned land in the Declaration of State as State Land (*domeinverklaring*), according to the Land Law (Agrarische Wet) issued in 1870 in colonial times. As such, much mountain forest became state owned. On the other hand, property rights etc. (based on Western law – *eigendom*) were set for land where rights could be proven. However, the 1960 Basic Land Act that determines the land rights in Indonesia is based on customary law, and the government, which holds the top position in the hierarchy in customary law, has the right to control all lands. Forest land that is not covered by personal property rights is determined to be "land directly controlled by the state" (*tanah yang lansung dikuasai negara*), and is called state forest (*hutan negara*). This state forest differs from forest owned by the state. See Harsono (2003).
4. See www.dephut.go.id/INFORMASI/Propinsi/JAMBI/hutan_jambi.html.
5. Data taken from various annual editions of *Statistik Perusahaan Hak Pengusahaan Hutan*, Badan Pusat Statistik, Jakarta.
6. Data taken from various annual editions of *Statistik Hak Tanaman Industri*, Badan Pusat Statistik, Jakarta.
7. Data taken from various annual editions of *Statistik Perusahaasn Perkebunan*, Badan Pusat Statistik, Jakarta.

8. According to various statistical data from the sources in notes 5–7 above.
9. The purpose of releasing forest areas from state forest, in addition to plantations, is to convert forests, transmigration among islands and other purposes.
10. Data taken from various annual editions of *Statistik Penggunaan Tanah* and *Statistik Indonesia*, Badan Pusat Statistik, Jakarta.
11. Interview by the author with Dr Supiandi Sabiham, 11 July 2009.

REFERENCES

Agus, Fahmuddin, Wahyuno Suyanto and Meine van Noordwijk (2007) "Reducing Emissions from Peatland and Deforestation and Degradation: Carbon Emission and Opportunity Costs", paper presented at international symposium and workshop on Tropical Peatland Carbon–Climate–Human Interaction–Carbon Pools, Fire Mitigation, Restoration and Wise Use, Yogyakarta, 27–31 August.

Basyar, A. Hakim (2008) "Evaluasi Penerapan Kebijakan Konversi Hutan untuk Perkebunan Besar Kelapa Sawit"; available at www.bappenas.go.id/evaluasi-penerapan-kebijakan-konversi-hutan-untuk-perkebunan-besar-kelapa-sawit---oleh-a-hakim-basyar-/.

Colchester, Marcus, Norman Jiwan, Andiko, Martua Sirait, Asep Yunan Firdaus, A. Surambo and Herbert Pane (2006) *Promised Land. Palm Oil and Land Acquisition in Indonesia: Implications for Local Communities and Indigenous Peoples*. New Queensland and Bogor: Forest Peoples Programme/Sawit Watch.

Furukawa, Hisao (1992) *Indoneshia no Teishitchi* (*Coastal Wetlands of Indonesia*). Tokyo: Keiso Shobo.

Harsono, Budi (2003) *Hukum Agraria Indonesia, Sejarah Pembentukan Undang-undang Pokok Agrarian, Isi dan Pelaksanaannya*. Jakarta: Djambatan.

Hooijer, Aljosja, Marcel Silvius, Henk Wosten and Susan Page (2006) "PET-CO_2, Assessment of CO_2 Emissions from Drained Peatlands in SE Asia", Report Q3943, Delft Hydraulics, Delft.

Page, Susan, Florian Siegert, John O. Rieley, Hans-Dieter V. Boehm, Adi Jaya and Suwido Limin (2002) "The Amount of Carbon Released from Peat and Forest Fires in Indonesia during 1997", *Nature* 420, 7 November, pp. 61–65.

Paulus, J. (1917) *Encyclopaedie van Nederlandsche-Indië*. The Hague and Leiden: Martinus Nijhoff/E. J. Brill.

Polak, B. (1941) "Veenonderzoek in Nederlandsch Indië, Stand en expose der vraagstukken", *Landbouw* XVII(12), pp. 1033–1067.

Raflis (2007) "Draft Analysis Rencana Tata Ruang Wilayah Provinsi Riau Tahun 2001–2015, Perbandingan RTRWP Riau 2001–2015 Dengan RTRWK 7 Kabupaten"; available at www.slideshare.net/raflis/analisis-rtrwp-riau-2007.

Salim, H. S. (2003) *Dasar-dasar Hukum Kehutanan*. Jakarta: Sinar Grafika.

4-6

Do markets matter? The role of markets in the post-2012 international climate regime

Yukari Takamura

4-6-1 Introduction

The Fourth Assessment Report (AR4) of the Intergovernmental Panel on Climate Change (IPCC) indicates that climate change is occurring, and most of the observed increase in globally averaged temperatures since the mid-twentieth century is very likely due to the increase in anthropogenic greenhouse gas (GHG) concentrations (IPCC, 2007a: 10). It is likely that anthropogenic warming has had a discernible influence on many physical and biological systems, and thus impacted upon our ecosystems, lives and economies. The AR4 makes it clear that while the impacts of future climate change will vary across regions, it is very likely that all regions will experience a net decline in benefits or net increase in costs from a rise in temperature greater than 2–3°C and that developing countries are expected to experience larger percentage losses (IPCC, 2007b: 16).

In terms of its causes and effects, climate change is global in nature. In order to avoid adverse effects and tackle climate change effectively, we need cooperation and coordination at the global level to reduce GHG emissions.

Climate change has now become one of the top issues on the agenda of international forums. The international community has cooperated in tackling it within the framework of the UN Framework Convention on Climate Change (UNFCCC) and its Kyoto Protocol. The protocol puts in place the Kyoto mechanisms, and allows developed countries to use market mechanisms to achieve their reduction target under the protocol. Many developed countries have been implementing various policies and measures, including emissions trading schemes, with a view to combating climate change; these, together with the Kyoto mechanisms, have led to the emergence of a "carbon market". Another process started to produce a new and more comprehensive international regulatory framework – a "post-Kyoto" framework – under the Bali Action Plan adopted at the thirteenth Conference of Parties (COP13) of the UNFCCC, held in 2007.

This chapter will first briefly outlined the current climate regime and introduce the evolution of carbon markets under the regime. Second, having presented the state of affairs of and challenges for post-2012 negotiations, it will explore what role the market mechanisms have played and will play in a future climate regulatory framework, and how they should be designed to deliver expected functions, in hopes of contributing to realization of a more effective climate regime. (Note that this chapter was submitted before COP15 held in Copenhagen, the outcome of which is not reflected.)

4-6-2 The current climate regime and state of the emerging carbon market

The current climate regime: The UNFCCC and its Kyoto Protocol

Following the resolution by the UN General Assembly to launch negotiations towards a legal instrument on climate change, immediately before the UN Conference on Environment and Development, countries agreed to adopt the first international treaty dealing with climate change, the UNFCCC. The UNFCCC stipulates in Article 2 the ultimate objective of its own and any related legal instruments that its COP may adopt: stabilization of GHG concentrations in the atmosphere at a level that would prevent dangerous anthropogenic interference with the climate system. While the convention provides for some action by all parties, including commitment to formulate and implement national programmes containing measures to mitigate climate change (Article 4(1)(b)), commitments and their stringency differ depending on categories of countries – Annex I parties (developed countries) and non-Annex I parties (developing countries). Annex I parties are obliged to adopt national policies and take measures on the mitigation of climate change and communicate detailed relevant information (Article 4(2)). In addition, Annex II parties (OECD countries) have obligations to provide new and additional financial resources to meet the agreed full costs incurred by developing country parties in complying with their obligations under the convention

(Article 4(3)), and take all practicable steps to promote, facilitate and finance, as appropriate, the transfer of or access to environmentally sound technologies to other parties to enable them to implement the provisions of the convention (Article 4(5)).

The Kyoto Protocol to the UNFCCC, adopted at the third COP held in Kyoto in 1997, stipulates that Annex I parties ensure that their aggregate anthropogenic carbon dioxide (CO_2) equivalent emissions of GHGs do not exceed their assigned amounts, calculated pursuant to their quantified emission limitation and reduction commitments inscribed in Annex B (Article 3(1)). Developed countries can fulfil their commitment by reducing their emissions domestically and/or acquiring carbon credits from outside their territory through the Kyoto mechanisms. The protocol provides three such market-based mechanisms for Annex I parties: joint implementation (Article 6), the clean development mechanism (CDM) (Article 12) and emissions trading (Article 17).[1] Although the use and carry-over of some types of units are subject to conditions, units issued under these mechanisms are in principle fungible with each other. Annex I countries can use these units to meet their quantified targets under the Kyoto Protocol in a cost-effective way; these parties may also authorize legal entities to participate in the Kyoto mechanisms and, *inter alia*, trade units. Annex I parties and authorized legal entities can sell excess units to other Annex I countries and legal entities. The expectation of profits through trade provides incentive to reduce emissions further.

The expanding carbon market

The carbon market has been vigorously expanding (Table 4.6.2). First of all, the development of the CDM has been remarkable. According to data provided by the UNEP Risø Centre (2010), 2,221 CDM projects have already been registered and about 3,000 projects are in the pipeline. A reduction of more than 2.8 billion tonnes of CO_2-equivalent is expected through the CDM by the end of 2012, which corresponds to more than two years' aggregated emissions from Japan or almost half of the US annual emissions. Although developing countries have no quantified targets under the Kyoto Protocol, their emissions have also been significantly reduced through the CDM.

A World Bank report (Capoor and Ambrosi, 2009: 1–2) indicates that the overall carbon market continued to grow in 2008, reaching a total value transacted of about US$126 billion (€86 billion) at the end of the year, double its 2007 value, of which approximately US$92 billion was traded under the EU Emissions Trading Scheme (ETS). CERs (certified emission reductions) issued by CDM projects were directly transacted to a value of about US$70 billion. The amount is nearly equivalent to three

Table 4.6.1 Implications of long-term targets

Category	CO_2 concentration (ppm)	CO_2-e concentration (ppm)	Global mean temperature increase above pre-industrial level (°C)	Peaking year for CO_2 emissions	Change in global CO_2 emissions in 2050 (% of 2000 emissions)
I	350–400	445–490	2.0–2.4	2000–2015	–85 to –50
II	400–440	490–535	2.4–2.8	2000–2020	–60 to –30
III	440–485	535–590	2.8–3.2	2010–2030	–30 to +5
IV	485–570	590–710	3.2–4.0	2020–2060	+10 to +60
V	570–660	710–855	4.0–4.9	2050–2080	+25 to +85
VI	660–790	855–1,130	4.9–6.1	2060–2090	+90 to +140

Source: IPCC (2007c).

times the four-year funding (2002–2006) granted to developing countries under the Global Environment Facility (Global Environment Facility, 2002: 3).[2] The CDM executive board reported that the amount of investment made in developing countries under the CDM was, by the end of 2006, over US$25 billion (UNFCCC, 2007a: 4, para. 10). These values and volumes of transaction were driven by demand, coming mainly from private entities in the European Union that need CERs to meet their targets under the ETS, but also from EU countries and Japan for their compliance with Kyoto targets (Capoor and Ambrosi, 2009: 1–2).

In addition, a recent report released by the UNFCCC secretariat reveals that the CDM may contribute to technology transfer by financing emission reduction projects using technologies currently not available in the host countries: while technology transfer varies across project types, about 39 per cent of all CDM projects accounting for 64 per cent of annual emission reductions, especially projects with foreign participants, claim to involve technology transfer (Seres, 2007).

Hence, market mechanisms have now become a window for significant emission reduction in developing countries as well as for transferring technologies and funds to developing countries necessary for "decarbonizing" their economies and society.

4-6-3 Challenges for the post-2012 climate regime

A more rapid move to decarbonized society: Implications of the emergent long-term target

The IPCC AR4 indicates that global GHG emissions need to peak in the next 10–15 years and be reduced to very low levels, well below half the levels recorded in 2000, by the middle of the twenty-first century. This is necessary to stabilize the concentration of GHGs in the atmosphere to attain the most stringent mitigation levels reviewed by the IPCC (2007c: 39 and 90).[3] At the Hokkaido Toyako summit in 2008, G8 countries endorsed "the goal of achieving at least 50 per cent reduction of global emissions by 2050" as the target they want to "share with all Parties to the UNFCCC" and "to consider and adopt in the FCCC negotiations" (G8, 2008) on a post-Kyoto (that is, post-2012) regime; this was reconfirmed at the L'Aquila summit in 2009 (G8, 2009). While this goal is shared by industrialized countries, including the United States, emerging economies such as China and India appear reluctant to agree upon such a numerical global target.

The implications that the long-term goal suggests are striking. The AR4 shows that the target of 50 per cent reduction by 2050 corresponds to a

Table 4.6.2 Expansion of carbon market

	2007		2008	
	Volume ($MtCO_2$-e)	Value (MUS$)	Volume ($MtCO_2$-e)	Value (MUS$)
Project-based transactions				
Primary CDM	552	7,433	389	6,519
Joint implementation	41	499	20	294
Voluntary market	43	263	54	397
Subtotal	636	8,195	463	7,210
Secondary CDM				
Subtotal	240	5,451	1,072	26,277
Allowances markets				
EU ETS	2,060	49,065	3,093	91,910
New South Wales	25	224	31	183
Chicago Climate Exchange	23	72	69	309
RGGI	na	na	65	246
AAU	na	na	18	211
Subtotal	2,108	49,361	3,276	92,859
Total	2,984	63,007	4,811	126,345

Source: Capoor and Ambrosi (2009).

peak in the level of global emissions by 2020 at the latest – that is, in about 10 years (Table 4.6.1) (IPCC, 2007c: 39 and 90). It should also be noted that even this goal could not avoid an increase in temperature by more than 2°C (ibid.), as a result of which every part of the globe would experience adverse climate change impacts, as mentioned above.

However, the challenge to achieve such a goal is not easy. According to the AR4, for 2030, projections of total GHG emissions (Kyoto gases) consistently show an increase of 25–90 per cent compared with 2000 (ibid.: 30–32). Such an increase is attributed to increases in emissions from both developed and developing countries. The International Energy Agency (2004: 74–77) projects that global energy-related CO_2 emissions will increase by 1.7 per cent per year over 2002–2030, reaching 62 per cent over the 2002 level, and that more than two-thirds of the increase will come from developing countries.

Accordingly, the emerging long-term target requires us to reduce emissions more drastically and rapidly and to move as quickly as possible towards a low-carbon society. As 2020 is somehow considered the target year for ongoing negotiations towards a post-2012 climate regime, the regime should deliver significant reductions to make global emission peak out by 2020 in order to avoid dangerous climate change. Failure to establish an effective regime would lead to a failure in achieving the long-term target. To make the post-2012 regime effective, more drastic reduction by developed countries is needed, but mitigation efforts by major emitting developing countries are also necessary in light of their share in global emissions and the projected increase in emissions from such countries.

Scaling up investment and financial flows for decarbonzation

Although the share of developing countries in global emissions and the projected increase in the emissions from major emitting developing countries are both significant, their per capita emission is still very low compared to industrialized countries. In 2004 Annex I developed countries had 20 per cent of the world's population but accounted for 46 per cent of global GHG emissions, and the non-Annex I developing countries, with 80 per cent of the world's population, accounted for only 54 per cent of global emissions. The contrast between regions is even more pronounced: 5 per cent of the world's population (North America) emit 19.4 per cent, while 30.3 per cent (non-Annex I South Asia) emit 13.1 per cent (IPCC, 2007c: 30). This trend will still continue in 2030. Bearing in mind that over 1.6 billion people, a little over a quarter of the world's population, in developing countries did not have access to electricity in their homes in 2002, meeting basic needs, such as improving access to energy, is one of the global priorities. Simply requesting developing countries to accept emission limitations and reductions at the cost of sacrificing imminent and legitimate development needs is not a politically feasible solution, nor is it one that will bring developing countries on board. What we need is to find a solution by which developing countries will succeed in decarbonizing their society and economy while meeting their development needs. The question of how to support decarbonization efforts by developing countries is thus key.

Investment and financial flows to address climate change are crucial from this point of view. According to estimates presented by the UNFCCC secretariat (UNFCCC, 2007b), the funding needed to reduce global CO_2-equivalent emissions by 25 per cent below 2000 levels by 2030[4] requires additional investment and financial flows of US$200–210 billion in 2030 compared to the amount expected to be available under a business-as-usual scenario. Additional investment flows in non-Annex I parties are estimated at more than 50 per cent of the total needed in 2030, by which the emission reductions achieved by the countries amount to 68 per cent of global emission reductions. The secretariat's update in 2008 (UNFCCC, 2008a) presents estimates of additional investment and financial flows needed that are about 170 per cent higher than the 2007 estimate. In considering the means to enhance investment and financial flows, it is important to focus on the role of private sector investments, which will constitute the largest share of financial flows (86 per cent) (UNFCCC, 2008b: 2). The carbon market could channel significant investment and financial flows from the private sector to deliver significant emission reductions in developing countries.

Market mechanisms are also important in light of the incentive they have provided to developing countries. These countries, which were initially distrustful of market mechanisms,[5] are now strongly supportive of the continuation of the CDM beyond 2012 because of its potential financial and investment flows. Operationalizing the Adaptation Fund,[6] which depends on proceeds from CDM projects, has further strengthened developing countries' support for the CDM. Without the CDM, it would be very difficult to keep these countries even seated in the negotiations.

4-6-4 Market mechanisms and their potential in the post-2012 climate regime

Ongoing negotiations towards the post-2012 climate regime

Under the UNFCCC process, ongoing negotiation towards a post-2012 regime has been progressing on two tracks. The first is negotiation on further commitments of Annex I countries beyond 2012 under the Kyoto Protocol, which started at COP11 in Montreal in 2005 by establishing an *ad hoc* working group (AWG-KP). The other track is negotiation through the *ad hoc* working group on long-term cooperative actions (AWG-LCA), launched at COP13 held in Bali in 2007. Both tracks aimed to reach an agreement at COP15 held in 2009 (Figure 4.6.1).

The first track of negotiation was based on Article 3(9) of the Kyoto Protocol, stating that the COP serving as the meeting of the parties to the protocol shall initiate the consideration of commitments for subsequent periods for Annex I parties at least seven years before the end of the first commitment period. The AWG-KP was established to progress the negotiation, the terms of reference of which are so broad as to cover possible revision of all relevant rules, including the Kyoto mechanisms, land use, land-use change and forestry, and coverage of gases (UNFCCC, 2006e: 5, para. 16). The second track of negotiation aims to examine commitments of developed countries, including the United States, as well as actions of developing countries, and to reach an agreed outcome on these matters at COP15 based on the Bali Action Plan (UNFCCC, 2008c: 3). Although the scope of these two tracks substantially overlaps, they are deemed separate and independent.

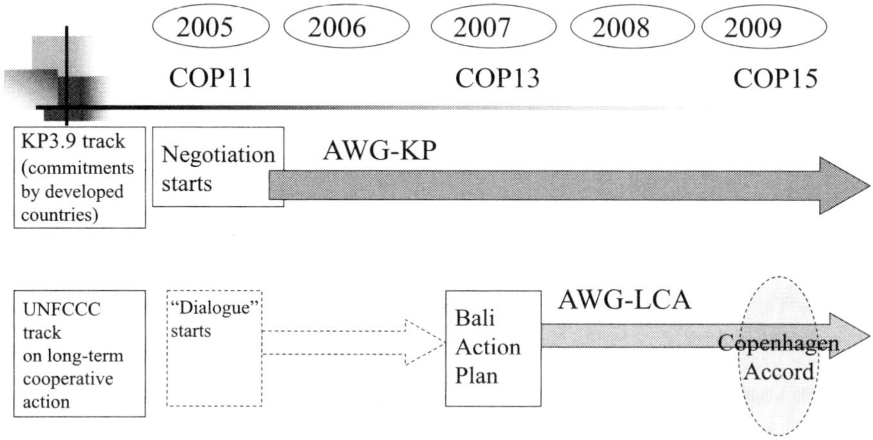

Figure 4.6.1 Two-track negotiations under the UNFCCC and its Kyoto Protocol

Market mechanisms supporting mitigation efforts by developing countries

There is increasing support for a future climate policy centring on continuation and expansion of the emerging carbon market, which is the main feature of ongoing climate negotiation. At the first AWG-KP meeting in Bangkok in March–April 2008 after the Bali conference in 2007, parties to the Kyoto Protocol agreed that "emissions trading and the project-based mechanisms under the Kyoto Protocol should continue to be available to Annex I Parties as means to meet their emission reduction targets and could be appropriately improved", while agreeing that use of these market mechanisms should be supplemental to domestic reduction (UNFCCC, 2008d: 6).[7]

The negotiations of the AWG-KP suggested, based on the IPCC AR4, that developed countries as a whole will achieve emission reduction on a scale of 25–40 per cent below 1990 emissions in 2020. In all cases, to achieve the long-term target that would avoid dangerous climate change, significant emission reduction by developed countries is necessary. Increasing attention has been focused on the importance of market mechanisms as a tool of cost-effective mitigation.

In reality, many proposals to introduce new market mechanisms to support mitigation actions by developing countries have been put forward in both the AWG-KP and the AWG-LCA. One example is NAMA (nationally appropriate mitigation actions) crediting. In the Bali Action Plan, countries decided to consider "Nationally appropriate mitigation actions by developing country Parties in the context of sustainable development, supported and enabled by technology, financing and capacity-building, in a measurable, reportable and verifiable manner" as enhanced actions on mitigation. Based on this provision, NAMA has gained undeniable support as a pivotal concept for institutionalizing mitigation actions by developing countries in a post-2012 regime, although there is still divergence of views on several points, such as legal nature and methods of support, even among these countries. Developing countries, in the context of pursuing sustainable development, will register their voluntary mitigation actions in the international registry, thus their mitigation actions will be enhanced through gaining international recognition and support. One option for supporting mitigation actions by developing countries is to credit their reductions through use of market mechanisms. The NAMA concept is based on the South African proposal of "sustainable development policies and measures" (UNFCCC, 2006c).[8] Although the definition of NAMA and how the concept will be operationalized have not yet been agreed, the idea has been moving towards internationally recognizing, supervising and enhancing various mitigation actions according to the circumstances of each developing country, which is clearly going beyond the current situation, while leaving mitigation actions by developing countries up to them.

Creating a global regulatory regime by simply expanding Kyoto targets to major emitting developing nations such as China and India is not politically feasible for the moment: political reality will not be able to keep up with such a simple top-down approach. In addition, as most large emitting developing countries do not have precise economy-wide emission data, it is difficult, if not impossible, to set an emission target similar to the Kyoto targets. A drastic increase in projected emissions adds another difficulty: a stringent target will not be acceptable for developing countries, and a loose target will not be appropriate as it could discourage them from taking actions even when they are capable of doing so. It is therefore wiser to establish a mechanism ensuring real reduction rather than struggle to set a meaningless numerical target. China, for instance, although still reluctant to be reviewed internationally, will suggest committing itself to some mitigation policies and measures (see, for instance, UNFCCC, 2008e: 19). China is actually implementing a wide range of energy and industrial policies that are not driven by climate change concerns but are contributing to mitigation by slowing its GHG growth. China's Eleventh Five-Year Plan includes a major programme to improve energy efficiency nationwide, including a goal of reducing energy intensity (energy consumption per unit of GDP) by 20 per cent below 2005 levels by 2010. The government projects that meeting this target would reduce China's GHG emissions 10 per cent below business as usual; researchers estimate that over 1.5 billion tonnes of CO_2 reductions would be achieved (Pew Center on Global Climate Change, 2007). Under such circumstances, encouraging China to pledge to follow policies and measures with mitigation effects and supporting such efforts internationally are the most feasible and possibly the most effective option for a post-2012 regime. A bottom-up approach could respond to such realities and a wide variety of national circumstances. And some supporting mechanisms, including market mechanisms, will be necessary so that NAMA can deliver effective reduction.

Another proposal to enhance mitigation action by developing countries is to set them a sectoral target, not a target on economy-wide emissions like that for developed countries. A typical proposal is the one put forward by the US-based Center for Clean Air Policy (CCAP) think-tank (Schmidt et al., 2008). According to this proposal, while developed countries will take on national economy-wide emission, developing countries will voluntarily set a carbon intensity target on one or more sectors. Developing countries will be given incentives to set targets in such a way that emission reductions achieved beyond the target would be eligible for sale as credits to developed countries. However, failure to meet the target would not involve any penalties or requirement to purchase credits from other countries. For that reason, the target under the CCAP proposal is characterized as a "no-lose target". The European Union has put forward a "sectoral crediting mechanism", which combines setting sectoral targets with support through market mechanisms.

This approach clearly has advantages. For instance, even with their relatively limited capacity to take mitigation actions, such sectoral targets would give incentive for developing countries to take on a target voluntarily while enhancing their capacity through a learning-by-doing approach. And a sectoral approach would enhance decarbonization of the targeted sector as a whole and promote emission limitation policies in developing countries. However, it would be difficult to expect an effective reduction if the selection of the targeted sector and/or the target level is not appropriate, or if no measure is taken in response to non-compliance with the target. In particular, sector-based market mechanisms might lead to increased global emission and obstruct effective operation of carbon markets because of difficulty in providing an appropriate baseline and meeting requirements of additionality in emission reduction. For that reason, some authors have emphasized that it would be desirable not to depend on a market mechanism and rather to strengthen bilateral and multilateral public financial support (Heller and Shukla, 2003: 111).

Raising funds for supporting efforts to tackle climate change

As indicated above, enormous amounts of additional financial and investment flows are estimated to be required for achieving a long-term emission reduction goal, such as "at least 50 per cent reduction by 2050". In a communication issued in September 2009, the European Commission estimated that finance requirements for adaptation and mitigation actions in developing countries could reach roughly €100 billion per year by 2020 (Commission of the European Communities, 2009: 3). While ensuring stable public funding is far more important, it should be noted that market mechanisms have been recognized as capable of raising a considerable amount of financial and investment flows from the private sector necessary to deliver a drastic cut of emissions and respond to increasing needs for adaptation.

The ongoing climate negotiation towards a post-2012 regime has seen a significant number of proposals to raise the funds necessary to meet mitigation and adaptation needs, through innovative use of evolving market mechanisms (UNFCCC, 2009, 2008f; Müller, 2008). For instance, learning from the experience of the Adaptation Fund established under the Kyoto Protocol that automatically receives 2 per cent of credits issued from CDM project activities without depending on voluntary pledges by developed countries (UNFCCC, 2006b: 19, para. 66(a)), developing countries have advocated extension of a similar method to the other Kyoto mechanisms, namely joint implementation and emissions trading. In the AWG-LCA context, Norway has proposed ensuring funds for financial support to developing countries through auctioning of a portion of assigned amounts, which are allocated free of charge to developed country parties of the Kyoto Protocol for the first commitment period (UNFCCC, 2008g: 48–49). Tuvalu has advocated raising necessary revenues through auctioning credits under an emissions trading scheme to be introduced in the international aviation sector. It is possible that proposals for sectoral crediting mechanisms and improvement of the CDM also have potential to contribute to providing financial support for mitigation efforts by developing countries.

4-6-5 Challenges for use of market mechanisms in the post-2012 regime

It would be unwise to deny the role of the market in the post-2012 climate regime, given its potential for delivering emission reductions and financial and investment flows to attain the ultimate objective of saving the climate and achieving sustainable development. The question is how the regime should be designed to use market mechanisms.

Stewart and Wiener (2003) suggest a future climate regime based on an international GHG cap-and-trade system, which would include the

United States and major developing countries. In this system, developing countries would receive generous emissions allowances so they have the space to pursue development. However, it is unlikely that these countries will accept emissions caps in the near future. Stewart and Wiener suggest that, as an initial step, other strategies for engaging developing countries in cooperative arrangements should be explored, including arrangements for technology transfer and cooperation, pledge and review systems, sectoral arrangements and no-lose targets, use of emissions intensity targets and others that could eventually lead to a global post-2012 climate regulatory regime.

In light of the current status of climate negotiations, it is likely that the general outline and elements presented by Stewart and Wiener (ibid.) will be seen in the core of the future climate regime. Still, two questions remain: whether adopting such a "bottom-up approach" on a short-term basis is effective and sufficient to achieve long-term goals; and how the regime should be designed to maximize the potential of the market and meet its challenges.

In general, the market by nature requires a strong regulatory and enforcement framework to ensure an equal footing among players and keep the market operating soundly. Further expansion of the carbon market requires that someone must have, and continue to have, binding stringent emission obligations to generate a demand for emission credits (Bosi and Ellis, 2005: 13). The more ambitious the targets, the higher the price of carbon, which gives developing countries more incentive to participate in the cap-and-trade system and leads to more investment and transfer of technologies. From a regulatory perspective, keeping the carbon market operating soundly requires a specific regulatory framework: deeper cuts than the current level of emissions by some, and effective enforcement sufficient to deter non-compliance. That has been broadly recognized by scholars (Haites, 2005: 329), and seen in lessons from precedents such as the US SO_x emissions trading scheme and the ETS (Ellerman, Joskow and Harrison, 2003; Commission of the European Communities, 2001).

Despite many advantages of using market mechanisms, they still face challenges. In theory, the market works in a cost-effective manner. Through the market, funds and technology are allocated to places where the more cost-effective emission reduction options are possible. This may lead to an unbalanced distribution of financial and technology flows among countries, exacerbating existing disparity in economic power. Actually, more than 90 per cent of CERs are so far being – and are expected to be after 2012 – issued from CDM projects in four countries: China (49.0 per cent), India (18.9 per cent), South Korea (13.2 per cent) and Brazil (9.9 per cent) (UNEP Risø Centre, 2010). The market is not a panacea for addressing development problems and disparities in economic power and wealth; it might even widen such disparities among developing countries.

Second, as individual countries and economic actors tend to behave in ways to maximize their own short-term profits and minimize their costs, their decisions do not necessarily contribute to collective long-term objectives of tackling climate change and achieving sustainable development. One example can be found in the reality of the CDM. More than half the total CERs are generated by projects for destroying HFC-23 (ibid.),[9] a very potent GHG resulting from the production of HCFC-22, whose reduction cost is estimated to be very low (US\$0.2–0.5/tCO_2) (IPCC/TEAP, 2005; Schneider, Graichen and Matz, 2005). In this sense, these projects provide "cost-effective" reduction. However, due to using end-of-pipe technology, they cannot produce positive effects to contribute to decarbonization and sustainable development in developing countries. Their short-term cost-effectiveness may divert the CDM from other types of projects contributing more to decarbonization in the long run, such as renewable energy projects, which are not considered attractive because of relatively higher initial investment. In addition, the enormous profit resulting from such CDM projects practically subsidizes production of HCFC-22, which is itself both an ozone-depleting substance and a GHG, and would discourage developing countries from taking more action to phase out or even halt increased production of HCFC-22.[10] The current project status actually shows that participants have been attracted by such non-CO_2 projects because of their short-term cost-effectiveness, and that financial and investment flows through the CDM to energy efficiency and adoption of renewable sources of energy are insufficient, despite being essential for decarbonization.

Another example is the case of CDM afforestation and reforestation projects. The rules on these activities leave the judgement of whether the projects will cause significant negative socio-economic and environmental impacts to the host country's discretion (UNFCCC, 2006d: 64, para. 12(c)). Host countries, attracted by short-term economic interest generated through the CDM, might disregard environmental and social values such as biodiversity, fearing that too-stringent procedures might be perceived as incurring higher costs, and thus possible obstacles to attracting investment.

Market mechanisms are based on the idea of market liberalism, which tends to focus on short-term cost-effectiveness. Private actors might lose sight of long-term effects and other environmental and social values in their decision-making, although it is crucially important and necessary to promote such long-term effects and values in the context of our goal of saving the climate and achieving sustainable development. Market mechanisms should be designed to induce market participants to make decisions that take regard of factors other than short-term efficiency. Infusing public policy elements into markets is essential for markets to play an adequate role (Kysar, 2005: 2156).

4-6-6 Conclusion

To achieve the ultimate objective of combating climate change, a regime centring on the carbon market might be the only way forward. The carbon market could provide cost-effective mitigation options and thus realize greater and more rapid reduction of GHG emissions. It could also deliver significant emission reductions in developing countries by transferring necessary funds and technologies through chanelling private sector investment and financial flows, and thus could secure the involvement of major emitting countries in mitigation actions.

Adopting simply a top-down approach in the post-2012 climate regime would not be in consonance with political reality. Starting and accelerating mitigation efforts in various settings could be more effective. However, without a regulatory framework, the carbon market does not work effectively. As pointed out by Diringer (2003: 3), "only markets can mobilize capital and technological prowess on the scale needed" to reduce GHG emissions dramatically, but "the direction and imperative must come from governments". A global regulatory regime is still needed to deliver the global emission reductions required for climate protection. It could also assist in enhancing the consideration given by market participants to long-term interests of climate protection and sustainable development.

However, the question is not one of a choice between bottom-up and top-down approaches. As practices under the Kyoto Protocol show, a global regulatory regime can be a good driver of, and provide a learning opportunity for, bilateral and regional arrangements. The CDM has successfully encouraged establishment of administrative bodies for managing projects in developing countries, and inspired these countries' interest in climate change issues (IGES, 2008). At the same time, global regulatory regimes are often influenced and supported by other regulatory regimes. Emission trading under the Kyoto Protocol was inspired by the SO_x trading system in the United States; especially before entry into force of the Kyoto Protocol, activities of other organizations outside the UNFCCC, such as the World Bank, provided incentives for establishment of a carbon market (Carr and Rosembuj, 2008: 52); and continuation of the market mechanisms under the Kyoto Protocol, and proliferation of emissions trading schemes in various countries and regions, are driven by the success of the EU carbon market. Such proliferation of emissions trading schemes might lead to a global regulatory regime by linking them to each other and standardizing some of their basic components (Haites, 2004, 2005). The evolution of the regulatory regime in the field of climate change is therefore quite dynamic.

There is increasing expectation that market mechanisms will facilitate climate protection by seeking cost-effective reductions but also by responding to multiple needs – such as distributing funds, diffusing technologies and raising money necessary for climate protection and adaptation – while respecting other environmental and social values. To achieve these purposes, a regulatory regime must intervene even at the sacrifice of market efficiency.

The carbon market has emerged from a regulatory framework, evolution of which has been influenced by market developments. A well-designed regulatory regime is necessary for the market to reach its full potential and deliver its expected function. This dynamic interaction between regulation and market will determine the creation of a future climate regime.

Acknowledgements

For very helpful comments and contributions, the author thanks all the members of IR3S and the Kyoto Sustainability Initiative as well as reviewers of the chapter. The author also expresses special thanks to Hirotaka Matsuda and Akiko Kusubayashi-Miyoshi for their indispensable support.

Notes

1. Detailed rules on the Kyoto mechanisms were officially adopted in COP/MOP1, the first meeting of parties to the Kyoto Protocol after its entry into force. For details see Yamin (2005) and Yamin and Depledge (2004, especially Ch. 6).
2. The total size of the Third Replenishment (2002–2006) agreed in the Second GEF Assembly was SDR 2,341 million (US$2,970 million). The GEF funds projects in six focal areas: climate change, biodiversity, international waters, ozone depletion, land degradation and persistent organic pollutants.
3. For recognition of such scientific findings by parties to the Kyoto Protocol, see UNFCCC (2008a: 5, para. 16).
4. Under this scenario, energy-related CO_2 emissions would return to current levels by 2030, while other GHG emissions would be reduced and CO_2 removals increased substantially.
5. One typical example could be found in the submission put forward to the Ad Hoc Group on the Berlin Mandate (UNFCCC, 1997). The G77 and China emphasized their opposition to emissions trading, on the grounds, among other concerns, of its complex-

ity, that it implied the creation of "emission rights" and was outside the scope of the Berlin Mandate, and that it would transform emission reduction obligations into commercial transactions; the G77 also stated that quantified commitments should be met "primarily through domestic action" (Depledge, 2000: 83, para. 387).

6. The Adaptation Fund was established by Decision 10/CP.7 in 2001 to finance concrete adaptation projects and programmes in developing countries that are parties to the protocol, as well as activities agreed by Decision 5/CP.7. The fund is financed mainly by a share of the proceeds of CDM project activities: upon the issuance of CERs, 2 per cent of the CERs issued for a CDM project activity are automatically forwarded to the fund. See UNFCCC (2006a: 3, 2006b: 19, para. 66(a)).
7. The quantified emission reduction and limitation objectives based on such agreed premises imply that the objectives consist of domestic reduction and support for developing countries through use of the Kyoto mechanisms.
8. For details see Kameyama (2005).
9. For these project activities see Matsumoto (2006), Driesen (2008: 21) and Voigt (2008: 18).
10. A decision made in 2007 by the meeting of the parties of the Montreal Protocol to accelerate phase-out of HCFC-22 by developing countries might correct such problems.

REFERENCES

Bosi, M. and J. Ellis (2005) "Exploring Options for Sectoral Crediting Mechanisms", COM/ENV/EPOC/IEA/SLT(2005)1, OECD/IEA, Paris.

Capoor, K. and P. Ambrosi (2009) *State and Trends of the Carbon Market 2009*. Washington, DC: World Bank.

Carr, C. and F. Rosembuj (2008) "Flexible Mechanisms for Climate Change Compliance: Emission Offset Purchases under the Clean Development Mechanism", *New York University Environmental Law Journal* 16(1), pp. 44–62.

Commission of the European Communities (2001) "Proposal for a Directive of the European Parliament and of the Council Establishing a Scheme for Greenhouse Gas Emission Allowance Trading within the Community and Amending Council Directive 96/61/EC", COM(2001) 581 final, 23 October.

——— (2009) "Communication from the Commission to the European Parliament, the Council, the European Economic and Social Committee and the Committee of the Regions, Stepping Up International Climate Finance: A European Blueprint for the Copenhagen Deal", COM(2009) 475/3, 10 September.

Depledge, J. (2000) "Tracing the Origins of the Kyoto Protocol: An Article-by-article Textual History", UNFCCC Technical Paper FCCC/TP/2000/2, 25 November.

Diringer, E. (2003) "Overview: Climate Crossroads", in *Beyond Kyoto: Advancing the International Effort against Climate Change*. Washington, DC: Pew Center on Global Climate Change, pp. 1–10.

Driesen, D. M. (2008) "Sustainable Development and Market Liberalism's Shotgun Wedding: Emissions Trading under the Kyoto Protocol", *Indiana Law Journal* 83(1), pp. 21–69.

Ellerman, A. D., P. L. Joskow and D. Harrison Jr (2003) *Emissions Trading in the US: Experience, Lessons, and Considerations for Greenhouse Gases*. Washington, DC: Pew Center on Global Climate Change.

G8 (2008) "G8 Hokkaido Toyako Summit Leaders Declaration", 8 July; available at www.mofa.go.jp/policy/economy/summit/2008/doc/doc080714__en.html.

——— (2009) "G8 Leaders Declaration: Responsible Leadership for a Sustainable Future", 8 July; available at www.g8italia2009.it/static/G8_Allegato/G8_Declaration_08_07_09_final,0.pdf.

Global Environment Facility (2002) "Summary of Negotiations on the Third Replenishment of the GEF Trust Fund", GEF/A.2/7, 19 September, Global Environment Facility, Washington, DC.

Haites, E. (2004) "Harmonisation between National and International Tradeable Permit Schemes", in *Greenhouse Gas Emissions Trading and Project-based Mechanisms*, Proceedings of OECD Global Forum on Sustainable Development: Emissions Trading and CATEP Country Forum, Paris, 17–18 March 2003. Paris: OECD, pp. 105–118.

——— (2005) "Conclusion: Mechanisms, Linkages and the Direction of the Future Climate Regime", in F. Yamin (ed.) *Climate Change and Carbon Markets*. London: Earthscan, pp. 321–352.

Heller, T. and P. R. Shukla (2003) "Development and Climate: Engaging Developing Countries", in *Beyond Kyoto: Advancing the International Effort against Climate Change*. Washington, DC: Pew Center on Global Climate Change, pp. 111–140.

IGES (2008) "Climate Change Policies in the Asia-Pacific: Reuniting Climate Change and Sustainable Development", White Paper, Institute for Global Environmental Strategies, Hayama.

International Energy Agency (2004) *World Energy Outlook 2004*. Paris: OECD.

IPCC (2007a) *Summary for Policymakers, Climate Change 2007: The Physical Science Basis*, Contribution of Working Group I to the Intergovernmental Panel on Climate Change Fourth Assessment Report. Geneva: IPCC.

——— (2007b) *Summary for Policymakers, Climate Change 2007: Impacts, Adaptation and Vulnerability*, Contribution of Working Group II to the Intergovernmental Panel on Climate Change Fourth Assessment Report. Geneva: IPCC.

——— (2007c) *Technical Summary*, Contribution of Working Group III to the Intergovernmental Panel on Climate Change Fourth Assessment Report. Geneva: IPCC.

IPCC/TEAP (2005) "Safeguarding the Ozone Layer and the Global Climate System: Special Report", IPCC, Geneva; available at www.ipcc.ch/publications_and_data/publications_and_data_reports.htm#2.

Kameyama, Y. (2005) "Sustainable Development Policies and Measures (SD-PAMs)", in Y. Takamura and Y. Kameyama (eds) *Where Will Global Warming Negotiations Lead? The Prospect of International Climate Change Regime beyond 2012*. Tokyo: Daigaku tosho, pp. 190–194 (in Japanese).

Kysar, D. A. (2005) "Sustainable Development and Private Global Governance", *Texas Law Review* 83, pp. 2109–2166.

Matsumoto. Y. (2006) "Causes of Policy Contradictions Arising between Environmental Regimes through the Clean Development Mechanism, from a Policy-interlinkage Perspective", *Research on Environmental Destruction* 35(4), pp. 53–59 (in Japanese).

Müller B. (2008) *International Adaptation Funding. The Need for an Innovative and Strategic Approach.* Oxford: Oxford Institute for Energy Studies.

Pew Center on Global Climate Change (2007) "Climate Change Mitigation Measures in the People's Republic of China", International Brief 1; available at www.pewclimate.org/docUploads/Internationalpercent20Briefpercent20 percent20China.pdf.

Schmidt, J., N. Helme, J. Lee and M. Houdashelt (2008) "Sector-based Approach to the Post-2012 Climate Change Policy Architecture", *Climate Policy* 8, pp. 494–515.

Schneider, L., J. Graichen and N. Matz (2005) "Implications of the CDM on Other Conventions. The Case of HFC-23 Destruction", Discussion Paper, Öko-Institut, Berlin; available at http://unfccc.int/resource/docs/2005/smsn/ngo/002.pdf.

Seres, S. in consultation with E. Haites (2007) "Analysis of Technology Transfer in CDM Projects, Final Report Prepared for the UNFCCC Registration & Issuance Unit CDM/SDM"; available at http://cdm.unfccc.int/Reference/Reports/TTreport/report1207.pdf.

Stewart, R. B. and J. B. Wiener (2003) *Reconstructing Climate Policy: Beyond Kyoto*. Washington, DC: American Enterprise Institute.

Takamura, Y. and Y. Kameyama (eds) (2005) *Where Will Global Warming Negotiations Lead? The Prospect of International Climate Change Regime beyond 2012*. Tokyo: Daigaku tosho (in Japanese).

UNEP Risø Centre (2010) "CDM Pipeline Overview"; available at www.uneprisoe.org/.

UNFCCC (1997) "Submission to Ad Hoc Group on the Berlin Mandate (AGBM8)", FCCC/AGBM/1997/MISC.1/Add.8, 30 October.

——— (2006a) "Decision 28/CMP.1 Initial Guidance to an Entity Entrusted with the Operation of the Financial Mechanism of the Convention, for the Operation of the Adaptation Fund", FCCC/KP/CMP/2005/8/Add.4, 30 March.

——— (2006b) "Decision 3/CMP.1 Modalities and Procedures for a Clean Development Mechanism as Defined in Article 12 of the Kyoto Protocol", FCCC/KP/CMP/2005/8/Add.1, Annex, 30 March.

——— (2006c) "Submission from South Africa", Dialogue Working Paper 18.

——— (2006d) "Decision 5/CMP.1 Modalities and Procedures for Afforestation and Reforestation Project Activities under the Clean Development Mechanism in the First Commitment Period of the Kyoto Protocol", FCCC/KP/CMP/2005/8/Add.1, Annex, 30 March.

——— (2006e) "Report of the Ad Hoc Working Group on Further Commitments for Annex I Parties under the Kyoto Protocol on Its Second Session", FCCC/KP/AWG/2006/4, 14 December.

——— (2007a) "Annual Report of the Executive Board of the Clean Development Mechanism to the Conference of the Parties Serving as the Meeting of Parties to the Kyoto Protocol, Part 1", FCCC/KP/CMP/2007/3, 6 November.

——— (2007b) "Report on the Analysis of Existing and Potential Investment and Financial Flows Relevant to the Development of an Effective and Appropriate

International Response to Climate Change", Dialogue Working Paper 8, 31 August.

——— (2008a) "Investment and Financial Flows to Address Climate Change: An Update", FCCC/TP/2008/7, 26 November.

——— (2008b) "Report of the Ad Hoc Working Group on Further Commitments for Annex I Parties under the Kyoto Protocol on Its Resumed Fourth Session", FCCC/KP/AWG/2007/5, 5 February.

——— (2008c) "Decision 1/CP.13 Bali Action Plan", FCCC/CP/2007/6/Add.1, 14 March.

——— (2008d) "Report of the Ad Hoc Working Group on Further Commitments for Annex I Parties under the Kyoto Protocol on the First Part of its Fifth Session, Held in Bangkok from 31 March to 4 April 2008", FCCC/KP/AWG/2008/2, 15 May.

——— (2008e) "Submission from China to Ad Hoc Working Group on Long-term Cooperative Action under the Convention", FCCC/AWGLCA/2008/MISC.1, 3 March.

——— (2008f) "Funding Adaptation in Developing Countries: Extending the Share of Proceeds Used to Assist in Meeting the Costs of Adaptation; and Options Related to Assigned Amount Units of Parties Included in Annex I to the Convention", Technical Paper FCCC/TP/2008/6, 13 October.

——— (2008g) "Ideas and Proposals on the Elements Contained in Paragraph 1 of the Bali Action Plan, Submissions from Parties, Paper No. 4B: Norway Auctioning Allowances", FCCC/AWGLCA/2008/MISC.2, 14 August.

——— (2009) "Ideas and Proposals on Paragraph 1 of the Bali Action Plan, Revised Note by the Chair", FCCC/AWGLCA/2008/16/Rev. 1, 15 January.

Voigt, C. (2008) "Is the Clean Development Mechanism Sustainable? Some Critical Aspects", *Sustainable Development Law & Policy* 8, pp. 15–21.

Yamin, F. (2005) "The International Rules on the Kyoto Mechanisms", in F. Yamin (ed.) *Climate Change and Carbon Markets: A Handbook of Emission Reduction Mechanisms*. London: Earthscan, pp. 1–74.

Yamin, F. and J. Depledge (2004) *The International Climate Change Regime: A Guide to Rules, Institutions and Procedures*. Cambridge: Cambridge University Press.

5

Adaptation to environmental change

5-1

Adaptation in global integrated assessment models of climate change

Hans-Martin Füssel

5-1-1 Introduction

Integrated assessment models (IAMs) of climate change combine dynamic descriptions of the energy-economy system, the climate system and climate impacts to support the formulation of global, and possibly regional, climate policy. Originally they were designed to inform mitigation policy, but some are now applied in the context of adaptation policy as well. This chapter reviews the modelling of climate impacts and adaptation in global IAMs, including both models with an economic focus and those with a science focus. Key advances in the representation of climate impacts in IAMs during the last decade include improved consideration of differences in impacts across regions, the development of non-monetary reduced-form models and coupling global IAMs with regional and sectoral impact models to assess climate change together with other sustainability issues. Further advances include a stronger focus on probabilistic analysis and attempts at considering large-scale climate instabilities. Adaptation has received only limited attention in global IAMs so far, mostly due to the mismatch in spatial scales at which mitigation and adaptation decisions are generally made. Some recent IAMs attempt to identify optimal levels of adaptation in climate-sensitive sectors or do include adaptation to climate change explicitly as a decision variable. The main reason for the consideration of adaptation in global welfare-maximizing IAMs is to assess the sensitivity of mitigation targets to different assumptions about the magnitude and effectiveness of adaptation.

IAMs with geographically explicit impact models may also provide information that is useful for adaptation planning.

There is a wide variety of IAMs, which reflects the diversity of decision contexts in global climate policy as well as the range of underlying scientific disciplines. IAMs differ in their use of monetary values, spatial resolution, consideration of uncertainty and the underlying decision-making framework.

Applications of IAMs can be broadly distinguished into policy optimization, policy evaluation and policy guidance. Because IAMs have generally been designed to be applied in one of these decision-analytical frameworks, it is common to speak of policy optimization models, policy evaluation models and policy guidance models, respectively. There is, however, some overlap between these categories, as witnessed by the application of some policy evaluation models (e.g. PAGE) and policy guidance models (e.g. ICLIPS) in policy optimization mode. Policy optimization models are designed to determine the "best" climate policy as defined by an aggregated welfare function over time, possibly considering user-specified climatic constraints. Their complexity is severely limited by the numerical algorithms used to solve optimization problems. Furthermore, wide-ranging subjective assumptions are necessary to aggregate all consequences of alternative policies in a social welfare function to be maximized. Policy evaluation models (also known as simulation models) evaluate the effects of specific policies on various social, economic and environmental parameters. Since these models are not subject to the computational constraints of optimizing models, they can include a much higher level of process and regional detail and provide more detailed information on the consequences of alternative policies. Policy guidance models determine all policies that are compatible with a set of subjectively specified constraints ("guardrails"). Their ability to consider multiple independent criteria in evaluating the acceptability of a given policy strategy does not require the heroic assumptions necessary for formulating an aggregated welfare function in policy optimization models. Because the algorithms applied by policy guidance models are similar to those of optimization models, they also require a highly simplified representation of dynamic system components.

Another important distinction of IAMs is their degree of spatial detail. Optimizing models either apply global averages or distinguish a limited number of geopolitical regions. Most policy evaluation models, in contrast, determine climate impacts on a geographical grid (often 0.5° latitude by 0.5° latitude). Some IAMs use different spatial resolutions in different submodules.

IAM analyses can also be distinguished according to their consideration of uncertainty. Deterministic analyses apply best-guess values for all model parameters. The simplest and most common approach to consider uncertainty is sensitivity analysis, where uncertain parameters are varied one at a time. A more thorough treatment of uncertainty is through stochastic simulation, where probability distributions are specified for several uncertain model parameters and inputs, and the results are determined as a probability distribution. Some models have been developed to address uncertainties from the outset, whereas others are modified later to allow for probabilistic analysis. Finally, adaptive analyses (also known as sequential decision-making under uncertainty) denote probabilistic applications of optimizing models that allow for future learning about key scientific or policy uncertainties. Note that the term "adaptive" in this context is not related to "adaptation to climate change".

This chapter reviews the modelling of climate impacts and adaptation in IAMs, focusing on the development in these areas during the last decade. Section 5-1-2 presents the recent literature on impacts and adaptation in IAMs and provides an overview of all recent IAMs. Based on this overview, Section 5-1-3 reviews the development and state of the art of climate impact modelling in IAMs, and Section 5-1-4 reviews the development and state of the art of adaptation modelling. Section 5-1-5 discusses possible ways forward for climate impact and adaptation modelling in IAMs. Section 5-1-6 concludes.

5-1-2 Review of recent IAMs

Several reviews of IAMs have been published recently. General reviews were conducted by Hope (2005) and Füssel and Mastrandrea (2010). Tol and Fankhauser (1998) reviewed the modelling of impacts in 18 IAMs that participated in the Stanford Energy Modeling Forum 14, discussing the level of spatial detail, the damage categories considered, the impact metrics, the climatic and non-climatic drivers of impacts, the functional specification and benchmarks of monetized damage functions, the feedback of impacts on other model variables and the representation of adaptation. Yohe (1999) briefly reviewed the representation of impacts in 20 IAMs, including most of the models considered by Tol and Fankhauser (1998). Stanton, Ackerman and Kartha (2009) review 30 climate-economy models, focusing on the treatment of four critical issues. They conclude that none of the existing models incorporates the best practices on all or most of the questions examined in their review.

Hitz and Smith (2004) surveyed studies that address global impacts of climate change as a function of the increase in global mean temperature (GMT). Their review includes biophysical modelling studies in sea-level rise, agriculture, water resources, human health, energy, terrestrial ecosystems productivity, forestry, biodiversity and marine ecosystem productivity as well as the monetized damage functions of three IAMs. Lecocq and Shalizi (2007b) review the empirical and theoretical literature on economic growth to examine how the four components of the climate change bill, namely mitigation, proactive and reactive adaptation, and climate impacts, affect economic growth, especially in developing countries. They include nine optimizing IAMs, but the focus is on the feedback of economic damages on future economic growth rather than on impact modelling.

de Bruin, Dellink and Agrawala (2009) and Patt et al. (2010) review the consideration of adaptation in IAMs, focusing on models for intertemporal cost-benefit analysis at a global scale. The latter paper also suggests ways for an improved treatment of adaptation by considering more of its bottom-up characteristics. Finally, Dickinson (2007) presents a review of different types of adaptation models, including some global IAMs, but most of the models are concerned with the evaluation of regional and/or sectoral adaptation options.

This chapter adds to this body of literature by reviewing recent developments in the modelling of impacts and adaptation in global IAMs. It includes all recent IAMs that allow for the comparison of mitigation targets and specific impacts of climate change. The criteria for the inclusion of a model are as follows.

- *Global coverage*. The model must be global or include regions that together cover the whole world. Models focusing on regional impacts or adaptation (e.g. IGEM, CLIMPACTS, CanCLIM, RegIS2) and other models reviewed in Dickinson (ibid.) are not included.
- *Full vertical integration*. The model must include an energy/economy module, a climate module and a representation of climate impacts. Hence, climate-economy models without explicit representation of impacts (e.g. most general equilibrium and cost minimization models reviewed in Stanton, Ackerman and Kartha, 2009) and models that only assess the probability of triggering a specific tipping element (e.g. dimrise – Zickfeld and Bruckner, 2003) are not included. The same applies to the coupling of exogenous climate scenarios with sector-specific impact models, e.g. GIM (Mendelsohn, Schlesinger and Williams, 2000), DIVA (Hinkel and Klein, 2009) and the UK "fast-track" studies (Arnell et al., 2002; Parry et al., 2004).
- *Real-world data*. The model must include quantitative data aimed at resembling the real world. Purely theoretical or conceptual models, e.g. ISIS (Grossmann, Magaard and von Storch, 2003), NeDym (Hallegatte, Hourcade and Dumas, 2007) and the unnamed partial equilibrium model presented in Lecocq and Shalizi (2007a), are not included.

- *Active development.* The model must have been in active development since the review by Tol and Fankhauser (1998). Inactive models (e.g. CONNECTICUT, SLICE, CETA, CSERGE, MARIA, PEF, PGCAM, DIAM, AS/ExM, FARM, TARGETS, HCRA, PGCAM) are not included to avoid duplication with Tol and Fankhauser (ibid.). In addition, variants of existing models are only included if the representation of impacts and/or adaptation differs from the earlier model. For instance, PRICE (Nordhaus and Popp, 1997), ENTICE (Popp, 2004) and ENTICE-BR (Popp, 2006) are not included because they apply the original DICE damage function, but AD-DICE is included.
- *Peer-reviewed.* The model must be described in the peer-reviewed literature. If an earlier model version is described in a peer-reviewed article, presentation of the most recent version in a working paper or conference proceeding is considered sufficient.

Note that the requirement for full vertical integration excludes several models that are regarded as IAMs in other reviews (Dickinson, 2007; Stanton, Ackerman and Kartha, 2009; Patt et al., 2010). Table 5.1.1 presents an overview of all IAMs that match the criteria above. An asterisk marks those models where an earlier version has already been reviewed (Tol and Fankhauser, 1998; Yohe, 1999). A detailed review of these IAMs will be presented in the following sections.

5-1-3 Impact modelling in IAMs

Various approaches have been pursued for representing climate change impacts in IAMs. The main representations of impact in IAMs include geographically explicit biophysical impact models (e.g. for climate-related yield changes, disease incidence and flooding of coastal areas) on the one hand and globally aggregated or regional monetary damage functions on the other. Monetary damage functions have been derived from a combination of case studies for selected regions or countries (most often the United States), cross-sectional analysis (i.e. studies that extrapolate current variations in economic productivity or other relevant variables across climate zones into the future), formal expert assessment and "guesstimates" by the modeller.

The choice of impact metrics in an IAM is largely determined by the underlying decision-analytical framework. Dynamic welfare maximization models, the most common category of policy optimization models, require an intertemporal social welfare function that aggregates all climate impacts across time, regions, impact domains and uncertain states of the world (in stochastic analysis). While climate impacts do not necessarily have to be monetized (the welfare function could aggregate monetary

Table 5.1.1 Modelling of climate impacts and adaptation in recent IAMs

Model			Approach		Drivers of impacts			Representation of impacts				Adaptation
Name	Reference	Notes	Type	Uncertainty	Change in mean climate	"Other" climate change	Non-climatic	Resolution	Metrics	Sectors	Feedback	
DICE-2007*	Nordhaus, 2008	Uses impact information aggregated from RICE-2004	Opt	Det, Prob, Adapt	glTemp	–	–	Global	Mon	–	GDP	Imp
AD-DICE	de Bruin, Dellink and Tol, 2009	Global damage function for optimal adaptation identical to DICE-99	Opt	Det	glTemp	–	–	Global	Mon	–	GDP	Con (continuous): Reallocation of production factors and budgets
MERGE 5.1*	Manne and Richels, 2004a, 2004b	Damage function derived from DICE-92	Opt	Det, Prob	glTemp	–	–	9 regions	Mon	Mar, nMar	GDP, utility	Imp
RICE-2004*	Nordhaus and Boyer, 2000 Yang and Nordhaus, 2006		Opt	Det	glTemp	–	–	13 regions	Mon	–	GDP	Imp
WITCH	Bosetti et al., 2006 Bosetti, Massetti and Tavoni, 2007	Regional damage functions identical to RICE-99	Opt	Det	glTemp	–	–	12 regions	Mon	–	GDP	Imp
AD-RICE	de Bruin, Dellink and Agrawala, 2009	Regional damage functions for optimal adaptation identical to RICE-99	Opt	Det	glTemp	–	–	13 regions	Mon	–	GDP	Con (continuous): Reallocation of production factors and budgets

Table 5.1.1 (cont.)

Model			Approach		Drivers of impacts			Representation of impacts				Adaptation
Name	Reference	Notes	Type	Uncertainty	Change in mean climate	"Other" climate change	Non-climatic	Resolution	Metrics	Sectors	Feedback	
AD-FAIR	Hof et al., 2009	Impacts and adaptation identical to AD-RICE	Opt	Det	glTemp	–	–	17 regions	Mon	–	GDP	Con (continuous): Reallocation of production factors and budgets
GRAPE	Kurosawa et al., 1999	Damage function is very similar to RICE	Opt	Det	glTemp	–	–	10 regions	Mon	–	GDP	Imp
FUND 3.3*	Tol, 2007 Anthoff and Tol, 2008	Some impact modules (e.g. for health) include non-monetary impact representations	Opt	Det, Prob	glTemp (level, rate), gSea, CO_2	Wind storms, river floods	Income per capita, urban population	16 regions	Mon, (Bio)	Wat, Ag, For, En, Co, He, Set	GDP (including investment), population	Ind: agriculture Opt: coasts
WIAGEM	Kemfert, 2002 Tol, 2002	Applies impact functions from FUND 2.0 in a disputed way (Roson and Tol, 2006; Kemfert, 2006)	Opt	Det, Prob	glTemp (level, rate), gSea, CO_2	Wind storms, river floods	–	11 regions	Mon	Wat, Ag, For, Eco, Co	Investment, population	Ind
PAGE2002*	Hope, Anderson and Wenman, 1993 Hope, 2006, 2008, 2009 Ackerman et al., 2008	Adaptation increases tolerable level and rate of temperature rise	Eval, Opt	Prob	regTemp (level, rate)	Unspecific large-scale discontinuity	–	8 regions	Mon	Mar, nMar	–	Scen (binary)

MiniCAM*	Brenkert et al., 2003 Sands and Leimbach, 2003	Impacts and adaptation only considered when MiniCAM is coupled with AgLU	Eval, Opt	Det	regTemp, regPrec	–	Technology	11 regions	Bio, Mon	Ag, For	GDP	Rule: Land allocation
AIM (2003)*	Kainuma, Matsuoka and Morita, 2003	AIM/Impact: [Food], [Health], [Veg], [Hydro], [Water]	Eval	Det	locTemp, locPrec, locCloud	–	Urban/rural population density, income per capita, technology, dietary preferences	Grid; 30 regions, selected countries	Bio, Mon	Wat, Ag, For, Eco, He	–	Pol: Water-use efficiency improvement, flood mitigation, land use (only in [Country] model)
IMAGE 2.4*	Bouwman, Kram and Klein Goldewijk, 2006	Soft links to Water GAP, LPJ, and GLOBIO 3	Eval	Det	locTemp, locPrec, locCloud, CO_2	–	Land use, population density, dietary preferences	Grid; 24 regions	Bio	Wat, Ag, For, Eco, En	Carbon cycle, albedo	Rule: Land allocation Pol: Trade policies
ICLIPS	Toth et al., 2002, 2003 Füssel et al., 2003 Sands and Leimbach, 2003	Uses impact modules from IMAGE 2.1 (TVM) and WaterGAP 1.1, aggregated to CIRFs	Guard	Det, Prob	locTemp, locPrec, locCloud, CO_2	–	–	Grid, 11 or more regions	Bio	Wat, Ag, For, Eco	–	Rule: Crop switching (some aggregated indicators); land allocation (when linked with AgLU)
CIAS	Warren et al., 2008	Initial version includes ecosystem CIRFs from ICLIPS and a hydrological module	Eval	Det, Prob	locTemp, locPrec, locCloud, CO_2	–	–	Grid, 11 or more regions	Bio	Wat, Eco	–	N.A.

Table 5.1.1 (cont.)

Model			Approach		Drivers of impacts			Representation of impacts				Adaptation
Name	Reference	Notes	Type	Uncertainty	Change in mean climate	"Other" climate change	Non-climatic	Resolution	Metrics	Sectors	Feedback	
IGSM2*	Sokolov et al., 2005 Schlosser, Sokolov and Kicklighter, 2007	Global Land System (GLS)	Eval	Det	regTemp, regPrec, regCloud, CO_2, O_3	–	Land-use change	34 latitude bands	Bio	Wat, Ag, For, Eco, (He)	GDP, agricultural trade, land vegetation change, carbon cycle	Rule: Land use, agricultural trade
ICAM 3*	Dowlatabadi, 1998, 2000	Taken from Tol and Fankhauser (1998) because insufficient information is available on ICAM 3	Eval	Prob	regTemp (level, rate), regPrec	–	Population density	11 regions	Mon, Bio	Co, He, other Mar, other nMar	GDP, utility	Ind

Notes:

* Earlier version of the model reviewed in Tol and Fankhauser (1998).

Non-climatic includes dynamic variables that are modelled endogenously other than GDP, consumption and income for monetary impact metrics.

Type: policy **opt**imization, policy **eval**uation, **guard**rail analysis.

Uncertainty: deterministic, **prob**abilistic, **adapt**ive.

Climate variables: global or **reg**ional or **loc**al (i.e. gridded) **temp**erature, **prec**ipitation, **cloud**iness/insolation, **sea** level, $\mathbf{CO_2}$ concentration, $\mathbf{O_3}$ concentration.

Metrics: monetary damages, **bio**physical units.

Sectors: market, **n**on-**mar**ket, **wat**er, **ag**riculture, **for**est, natural **eco**systems, **co**astal zones, **he**alth, **en**ergy, **set**tlements and infrastructure.

Adaptation: implicit, **ind**uced (transition time and/or costs), **scen**ario variable (without costs), **opt**imizing (considering costs and benefits), **con**trol variable (with costs), **n**ot **a**pplicable, **rule**-based (non-monetary optimization), **pol**icy variable (non-monetary choice).

and non-monetary welfare components), all recent IAMs based on this framework apply monetary damage functions. Cost minimization models, another category of policy optimization models, generally specify a greenhouse gas concentration target or a climate stabilization target rather than an impacts target. One exception concerns the ICLIPS model, a policy guidance model that has been applied in cost minimization mode with a biophysical impacts target. Most climate-economy models based on a general or partial equilibrium approach do not include an impacts module. Policy evaluation models can represent climate impacts in different ways: most include complex, geographically explicit impact models, while others apply monetary damage functions. Policy guidance models require aggregated but not necessarily monetized impacts for the specification of guardrails for maximum tolerable climate impacts. The only available policy guidance model refrains from monetizing climate impacts.

Several other impact metrics have been applied or suggested in the literature. The UK fast-track assessment (Parry et al., 2001) describes climate impacts by the number of people severely affected ("millions at risk"), but this aggregated impact metric has not been taken up by any IAM. Schneider, Kuntz-Duriseti and Azar (2000) suggested five impact metrics: monetary loss, loss of life, quality of life, biodiversity loss and distribution/equity. Monetary losses are most widely included in IAMs. Interestingly, even when IAMs do estimate loss of life from climate change (e.g. FUND), their developers have chosen to include these impacts in the monetary damage estimates rather than reporting mortality figures separately. There has been some attention to the distributional aspects of climate impacts across regions in analyses with FUND (Tol and Verheyen, 2004) and GIM (Mendelsohn, Schlesinger and Williams, 2000), whereby the latter is not a full IAM. Biodiversity loss is difficult to quantify, but several non-optimizing IAMs have considered ecosystem transformation, including IMAGE (Alcamo and Kreileman, 1998) and ICLIPS (Füssel and van Minnen, 2001; Toth et al., 2002).

The most recent comprehensive review of impacts modelling in IAMs is already more than a decade old (Tol and Fankhauser, 1998). The IAMs included in that review differ widely with respect to the damage categories considered, measurement unit and level of spatial detail. All optimizing models represented climate impacts by globally aggregated or regionally specific monetary damage functions, which show climate damages as a fraction of (global or regional) gross domestic product (GDP). The functional relationship between climate indicators and (market) impacts was typically devised by the authors and fitted to a limited number of impact assessments. Despite the impressive number of optimizing IAMs considered, monetized impact estimates were found to be "based on a rather narrow set of studies" and "Damage modules are often not more than ad hoc extrapolations around the 2*CO_2 benchmark" (ibid.). Table 5.1.1 reveals that this characterization largely applies to more recent IAMs as well.

The damage functions of DICE-2007, AD-DICE, MERGE 5.1, RICE-2004, WITCH, AD-RICE and AD-FAIR are all derived from damage estimates of Nordhaus and co-authors. They represent climate damages as a second-order polynomial of the increase in GMT. The main progress compared to earlier versions of the DICE/RICE models and their derivatives is that the recent damage estimates are based on a broader range of studies, including more impact assessments outside the United States. Furthermore, several scholars have modified DICE to account for large-scale climate instabilities, in particular a breakdown of the thermohaline ocean circulation (THC) (Gjerde, Grepperud and Kverndokk, 1999; Roughgarden and Schneider, 1999; Keller et al., 2000; Mastrandrea and Schneider, 2001; Azar and Lindgren, 2003; Keller, Bolker and Bradford, 2004; Yohe, Schlesinger and Andronova, 2006). The damage function of GRAPE has the same form as that of RICE but applies somewhat different (and only partly documented) parameters (Kurosawa et al., 1999). Even though the title of the paper (ibid.) suggests that GRAPE addresses adaptation, this is not actually the case.

The damage functions of FUND 3.3 and WIAGEM are based on estimates by Tol and co-authors. There are a number of important differences between the DICE/RICE and FUND damage functions. First, climate impacts in DICE/RICE are driven exclusively by the change in GMT, and a single damage function attempts to represent climate impacts on all sectors considered, assuming optimal adaptation. FUND, in contrast, estimates separate damage functions for the sectors of water, agriculture and forestry (including CO_2 fertilization), energy consumption (space heating and cooling), coasts (wetland and dryland loss and protection costs), human health (diarrhoea, vector-borne diseases, cardiovascular and respiratory mortality) and settlements and infrastructure. These damage functions are based on the combination and extrapolation of globally comprehensive studies using scenarios based on general circulation models. Second, climate impacts in FUND are driven by the level and rate of GMT change, sea-level change, wind storms, river floods (whereby the last three climate variables are assumed to change linearly with GMT) and CO_2 concentration. Third, most welfare-optimizing IAMs represent climate damages as losses to income even though many impacts entail losses in capital stocks and reductions in productivity. FUND is unusual in that it models damages as reductions to both consumption and investment. Fourth, FUND describes health impacts using biophysical as well as monetary metrics. Literature-based estimates of deaths and disease incidence caused by climate change are converted into monetary damages based on the per capita income in the affected region. The functional forms of the relationship between climate variables and damages in each sector covered by FUND are largely based on expert judgement by Tol. FUND has also been applied to consider large-scale climate instabilities, such as a THC breakdown (Link and Tol, 2004) and a collapse of the West Antarctic ice-sheet (Nicholls, Tol and Vafeidis, 2008), and to compare the effects of different weighting schemes for regional impacts on the total damages from climate change (Anthoff, Hepburn and Tol, 2009).

PAGE2002 is the third widely used IAM that applies monetized damage functions. In contrast to DICE/RICE and FUND, PAGE2002 was originally developed as a policy evaluation model. More recently, however, it has also been applied to determine "optimal" climate mitigation policies (Hope, 2008, 2009). Climate damages in PAGE2002 depend on the level and rate of regional rather than global temperature change to account for the regional cooling effect of aerosols. The empirical basis comprises impact studies from the early 1990s, whereby an unspecified climate discontinuity has been included in PAGE2002. Because PAGE2002 has been specifically developed for probabilistic assessment of climate change, all parameters of the damage function are characterized by probability distributions rather than single best estimates.

MiniCAM is distinguished from other optimizing IAMs because it does not attempt to cover all major impacts of climate change. It can be coupled to the AGLU model, which calculates biophysical and monetized impacts of climate change on crop yields and forestry. Other climate-sensitive sectors are not mentioned in the most recent description of MiniCAM (Brenkert et al., 2003) even though they were apparently included in earlier model versions (Edmonds et al., 1996).

Figure 5.1.1 compares monetized global damage functions from different IAMs. The top diagram is derived from GIM (Mendelsohn, Schlesinger and Williams, 2000), RICE-99 (Nordhaus and Boyer, 2000) and FUND 2.0 (Tol, 2002). The bottom diagram is from the Stern Review (Stern, 2007), which applied PAGE2002 (Hope, 2006). Note that a recent (unnamed) update of PAGE2002 (Ackerman et al., 2008) models even higher damages from climate change. Figure 5.1.2 shows some of the key factors that influence estimates of the social costs of carbon (i.e. the marginal damage for an additional unit of carbon emitted), which is one of the main applications of IAMs with monetized damage functions (Downing et al., 2005).

Some of the limitations of aggregated damage functions in IAMs include the often arbitrary or under-explained choice of exponents and other parameters, and the common representation of damages in terms of losses to income, not capital (Stanton, Ackerman and Kartha, 2009).

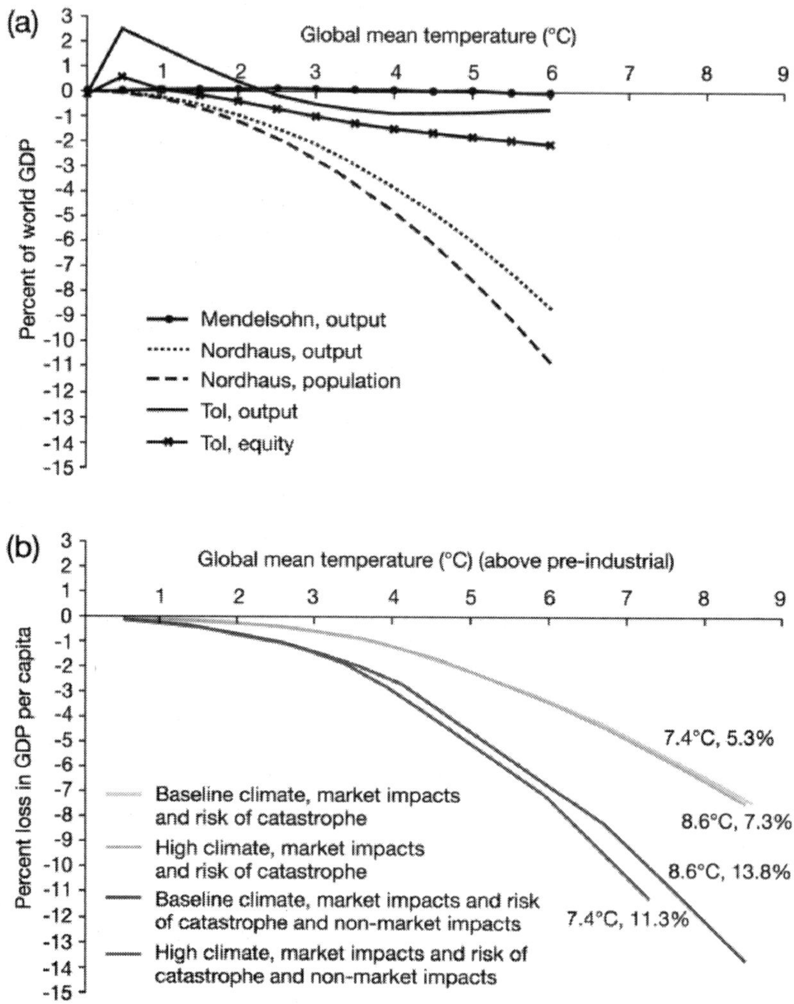

Figure 5.1.1 Global damage functions, as a percentage of global GDP, derived from different IAMs
Source: Yohe and Lasco (2007).

Another limitation concerns a seemingly subtle but important incongruence at the interface between reduced-form climate models, which estimate the expected temperature change for a given emission scenario, and damage functions, which report damages for an actual level of temperature change. Because all damage functions applied in IAMs rise faster than linear (generally quadratic) with the level of climate change, the damages for the expected level of temperature change substantially

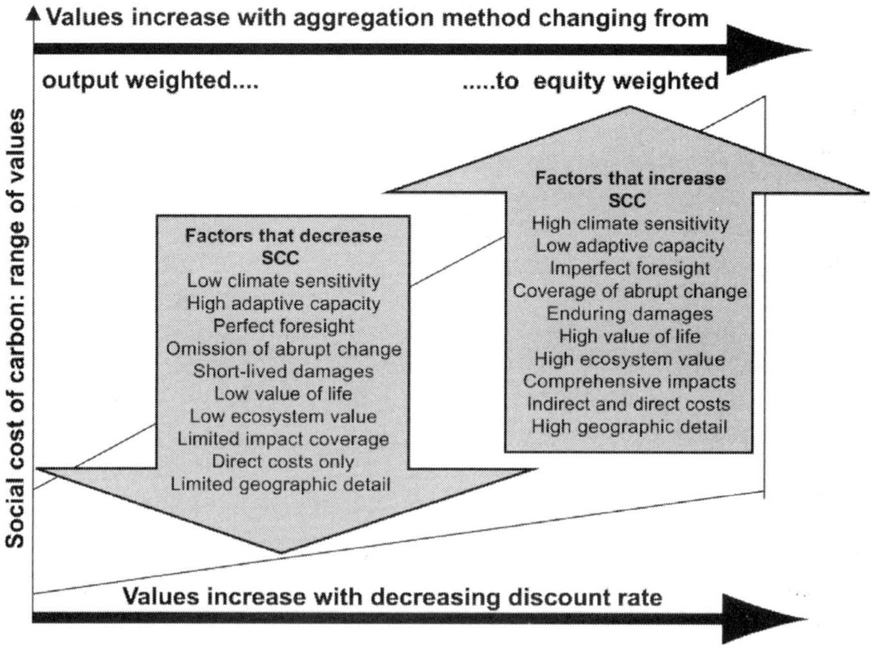

Figure 5.1.2 Factors influencing the social costs of carbon
Source: Fisher and Nakicenovic (2007).

underestimate the expected damages from climate change. Further limitations include the necessity for subjective choices in the aggregation of climate impacts across time and – in regionalized models – across space. The latter aggregation often applies Negishi (1972) welfare weights that implicitly impose an assumption that human welfare is more valuable in richer parts of the world (Stanton, Ackerman and Kartha, 2009).

Most policy evaluation models reviewed by Tol and Fankhauser (1998), with the exception of PAGE, include complex climate impact modules driven by gridded climate projections. This is still the case for many recent policy evaluation IAMs (AIM, IMAGE and CIAS). These models simulate geographically explicit impacts of climate change on a similar range of sectors – water, agriculture, forestry and natural ecosystems, and sometimes human health and energy demand – driven by gridded projections of changes in temperature, precipitation, cloudiness and possibly CO_2 concentration.

AIM is distinguished from the other policy evaluation models by two features. First, biophysical impacts of climate change on agriculture are monetized and used as input to a trade model to assess higher-order social impacts, in particular on food security. The combination of crop yield estimates with trade models has been common in sector-specific climate impact and adaptation studies, but not in IAMs. Second, the global AIM model is extended by various national models (AIM/COUNTRY) that allow assessing the combined impacts of global climate change and national policies at a much higher resolution than is possible with a uniform global model.

IGSM2 differs from other policy evaluation models by its coarser spatial resolution. Whereas the biosphere module of IGSM1 was applied at the "usual" 0.5° by 0.5° resolution, the GLS module of the more recent IGSM2 simulates biosphere and hydrology within 34 latitudinal bands defined by the IGSM2 atmosphere dynamics and chemistry submodel. IGSM2 considers human health, but focuses on the indirect impacts of climate change policies via air pollution rather than on the direct impact of climate change on human health.

The characterization of ICAM in Table 5.5.1 has been taken from Tol and Fankhauser (ibid.) because the only description of its climate impact module available in publications on ICAM-3 provides insufficient detail: "the impact from climate change is calculated as a function of temperature change, its rate of increase, an estimate of the agricultural sector as a fraction of the economy, and coastal zone damages due to sea level rise" (Dowlatabadi, 1998: 476).

The ICLIPS model is the only IAM that implements a policy guidance approach. It applies existing biophysical models (notably from IMAGE 2.1 and WaterGAP 1.1) at the "usual" 0.5° by 0.5° resolution and aggregates their results to climate impact response functions (CIRFs) defined at the global level or at the level of geopolitical or ecological regions. CIRFs represent non-monetary aggregated damage functions that can be used to establish guardrails for climate policy. ICLIPS has also been used to assess the relationship between emission pathways and the likelihood of large-scale climate instabilities, such as a THC breakdown (Zickfeld and Bruckner, 2003). CIAS differs from the other IAMs by its modular structure. Rather than being a monolithic model built by one group, CIAS was developed to provide a framework that enables the linking of different modules in a flexible manner. The initial version includes ecosystem CIRFs from the ICLIPS model as well as a global hydrological model. A related approach is followed by AIM, which uses 20 modules, including modules for regional climate impacts (AIM [Country]).

In summary, the main developments in impacts modelling since the review by Tol and Fankhauser (1998) are as follows.

- Several IAMs have been applied to consider large-scale climate instabilities, either by *ad hoc* modifications to the damage function (DICE, FUND and PAGE) or by coupling with a dynamic reduced-form model (DICE and ICLIPS). In contrast, none of the geographically explicit

IAMs considers large-scale climate instabilities because detailed climate scenarios of these hypothetical events are not generally available.

- Increasing numbers of IAMs have been applied for probabilistic assessments using Monte Carlo analysis. These studies have determined monetized damage functions that consider climate change uncertainties, optimal decision policies considering uncertain damage functions and the probability of triggering large-scale climate instabilities (Mastrandrea and Schneider, 2001, 2004, 2005; Azar and Lindgren, 2003; Wright and Erickson, 2003; Keller, Bolker and Bradford, 2004; O'Neill and Oppenheimer, 2004; Yohe, Andronova and Schlesinger, 2004; Downing et al., 2005; McInerney and Keller, 2008). Monte Carlo analysis is not currently feasible for geographically explicit IAMs due to computational constraints.
- The development of an IAM that implements the policy guidance approach has motivated the development of CIRFs, which are non-monetary reduced-form impact models.
- Various efforts have been made to develop modular IAM systems. The CIAS framework has been specifically designed to enable the coupling of modules developed by different groups. Several other IAMs have been coupled with global or regional impact models that are not part of the "core" model (MiniCAM, AIM and IMAGE).
- Several recent IAMs consider climate change in combination with other environmental and sustainability issues, such as air pollution and land use (AIM, IMAGE and IGSM).
- Several modelling groups have developed visualization tools that present results of geographically explicit climate impact simulations without the need for running the full IAM. Examples include the IMAGE user support system (Leemans et al., 1998), the ICLIPS impacts tool (Füssel, 2003) and AIM/Impact [Country] (Kainuma, Matsuoka and Morita, 2003).

5-1-4 Adaptation modelling in IAMs

Adaptation is generally understood as any action aimed at reducing impacts or exploiting beneficial impacts of climate change. It can reduce many adverse social and economic impacts from climate change (compared to a hypothetical no-adaptation case), but it generally comes at a cost. The potential for human adaptation to prevent or reduce biophysical changes is much more limited. For instance, the continued existence of the Great Barrier Reef cannot be ensured once temperature and ocean acidity become unsuitable for the key organisms that compose it. Note that the distinction between human impacts and adaptation is not always clear – thus outmigration from regions at risk of coastal flooding may be considered as a human impact by some and as human adaptation by others.

Virtually all IAMs reviewed by Tol and Fankhauser (1998) focus on a trade-off between damages due to climate change and the costs of mitigation. Adaptation is either ignored or treated only implicitly as part of the damage estimate. According to de Bruin, Dellink and Agrawala (2009), the situation has not evolved much since then, with the exception of several IAMs co-developed by the first author of that study: AD-DICE, AD-RICE and AD-FAIR. The situation is not that bleak, however, because IAMs with non-monetary impact metrics were not considered in this review. Table 5.1.1 distinguishes the following categories for consideration of adaptation in IAMs with monetary damage functions (1–4) and biophysical impact functions (5–7).

1. *Implicit: DICE, RICE, MERGE and WITCH.* The DICE model originally based its damage estimates on Ricardian analysis, using data from the United States to calculate damages as a function of the degree of warming, and then applied that function globally. The regional version of DICE, RICE, applies on a region-by-region basis either Ricardian analysis or a production function approach within a general equilibrium framework, which again assumes shifts in production to minimize losses. Hence the damage functions of DICE, RICE, MERGE and WITCH implicitly assume optimal adaptation and tend to ignore the costs of adapting.
2. *Induced, optimizing: FUND and WIAGEM.* FUND has developed damage functions from a large number of regional studies, each of which minimizes losses through adaptation wherever considered feasible. The reduced-form damage function for agriculture in FUND represents adaptation explicitly through transition time and costs. This is possible because the damage functions in FUND consider level and rate of global climate change, whereas those in DICE/RICE consider only its level. The damage function for sea-level rise in FUND treats coastal protection as a continuous decision variable, which is optimized based on a cost-benefit approach developed by Fankhauser (1994). The assumption of optimal adaptation to sea-level rise has been relaxed in one analysis to assess the trade-off between adaptation and mitigation for this sector (Tol, 2007). Adaptation in other sectors is not modelled explicitly in FUND.
3. *Scenario variable: PAGE.* PAGE represents adaptation as a scenario variable by allowing a binary choice between no adaptation and aggressive adaptation. This representation is based on the simple assumption that aggressive adaptation increases the tolerable level and rate of climate change and decreases the residual impacts. The specifi-

cation of adaptation is unchanged through all model versions up to and including PAGE2002. A recent review has suggested that the assumptions regarding the effectiveness of adaptation in PAGE have been overly optimistic (de Bruin, Dellink and Tol, 2009). In response to this critique, a more recent (unnamed) variant of PAGE2002 makes less optimistic assumptions (Ackerman et al., 2008).

4. *Control variable: AD-DICE, AD-RICE and AD-FAIR.* AD-DICE, AD-RICE and AD-FAIR treat adaptation explicitly, by considering it as a control variable. The AD-DICE model separates the global damage function of DICE-99, which assumes optimal adaptation, into an adaptation cost and a residual damage cost component. The calibration applies assumptions on the fraction of adaptation costs in total damages and the level of avoided damages from Tol, Fankhauser and Smith (1998) in the calibration point of the DICE damage function. A similar approach is applied for AD-RICE, which is based on the regional damage functions of RICE-99. Using these calibrations, adaptation and mitigation decisions become separable in AD-DICE and AD-RICE. AD-FAIR uses the same damage function as AD-RICE.
5. *Not applicable: CIAS.* Because CIAS is designed to link modules (including impact modules) flexibly, the inclusion of adaptation is dependent on its representation in those impact modules. The original version of CIAS includes CIRFs from ICLIPS that describe the climate-induced changes in natural ecosystems. Human adaptation is considered to be irrelevant for this impact domain, as it is impossible to ensure the continued existence of an ecosystem after the climate has become unsuitable to sustain it.
6. *Rule-based: ICLIPS, MiniCAM, IMAGE and IGSM.* IAMs with geographically explicit impact models for human-managed systems generally contain rules that describe how the management changes ("adapts") in response to changing climatic and/or socio-economic conditions. Agricultural adaptations in ICLIPS are limited to changes in planting dates, cultivars and crop switching (for some aggregated impact indicators only). MiniCAM/AgLU, IMAGE and IGSM additionally allow for changes in land use, some of which also have implications for mitigation policy. It is not clear whether other adaptations, such as changes in fertilizer use and expansion of irrigation, have been considered by any of these models.
7. *Policy variable: IMAGE and AIM.* IMAGE can be applied to assess the combined effect of climate change and changes in trade policies on food supply. The national extensions of AIM/Impact are able to assess the interaction between climate impacts and several national policies, including water-use efficiency improvement, flood mitigation and land-use change. Since both models consider climate change in the context

of other drivers, including demographic and socio-economic change, these "adaptation" policies are not primarily assessed on their ability to reduce the impacts of climate change, but to achieve broader sustainability goals.

Two developments in adaptation modelling since the review by Tol and Fankhauser (1998) are worth highlighting. First, an approach has been developed to consider adaptation in policy optimization IAMs based on DICE/RICE. However, wide-ranging assumptions are required to determine the five parameters of the residual damage and adaptation cost functions of AD-DICE, based on the single calibration point of the original DICE damage function. Second, most policy evaluation models now consider several policies that may be regarded as adaptation to climate change, in particular regarding land allocation, crop management, international trade and producers' and consumers' behaviour. The treatment of adaptation in policy optimization IAMs with monetary impact metrics emphasizes adaptation activities that are additional and largely separable from current activities. In contrast, the treatment of adaptation in policy evaluation IAMs with non-monetary impact metrics emphasizes that climate change is one among many determinants of human actions, some of which contribute to successful adaptation to climate change.

5-1-5 Challenges and opportunities

There are various challenges for modelling climate impacts in IAMs. Projections of biophysical impacts are affected by large uncertainties about future climate change (including potential large-scale climate instabilities and changes in extreme climate events) and other environmental changes (e.g. land-use change). Projections of human impacts are additionally affected by uncertainties about socio-economic and technological development, and the adaptive capacity of societies. These challenges are due to limitations of the underlying science, and improved representation of impacts in IAMs must therefore come primarily out of disciplinary studies in climate-sensitive sectors. The systematic assessment and communication of uncertainties associated with specific model simulations should be key concerns for all IAM applications, particularly those of policy evaluation models.

Even if biophysical and social impacts of climate change were known with certainty, monetary impact projections would still be strongly affected by subjective choices regarding the aggregation of costs and benefits across time, space, social groups, market and non-market impact categories and uncertain states of the world. These choices often dominate the outcome of the aggregation (Azar, 1998; Downing et al., 2005).

The challenge of aggregation is inherent to policy optimization IAMs, which require the aggregation of all climate impacts despite the unprecedented spatial and temporal scope of the climate problem. (For a more detailed critique of the application of aggregated monetary damage functions for climate change, see Schneider, 1997; Smith, Schellnhuber and Mirza, 2001; Kuntz-Duriseti, 2004; Hall and Behl, 2006; Jaeger, Schellnhuber and Brovkin, 2008; Stanton, Ackerman and Kartha, 2009.) At the least, their responsible use requires a "traceable account" of the main value judgements involved in the aggregation and an analysis of their sensitivity to alternative judgements (Schneider, Kuntz-Duriseti and Azar, 2000).

Adaptation is much more difficult to address in global IAMs than mitigation, for several reasons. First, adaptation is highly localized, and it is very hard for IAMs to capture the diversity of climate impacts, adaptive capacity and costs within diverse regions and countries. Second, adaptation involves a more diverse range of actors and actions, which complicates the representation of adaptation in highly aggregated models. Third, adaptation is more difficult to separate from current activities, and there is no common performance indicator. As a result, it is difficult to determine its costs and effectiveness. Fourth, adaptation is often constrained by non-economic factors, including cultural preferences and the non-optimal use of information by agents, which complicates modelling of likely or optimal adaptation. Finally, mitigation benefits are global, and mitigation costs can be shared globally through emissions trading; in contrast, the benefits and costs of adaptation occur mainly at the local or regional level, which severely limits the usefulness of globally aggregated analysis.

For a more detailed discussion of the challenges and opportunities for modelling adaptation in IAMs, it is useful to distinguish different purposes for including adaptation in IAMs.

- *Analysing the trade-off between mitigation costs, adaptation costs and residual impacts ("modelling adaptation to guide global mitigation").* This type of analysis intends to assess alternative global climate policies by considering the costs and benefits of different levels of global mitigation and adaptation. The results are most relevant for guiding mitigation efforts whose public good characteristics suggest that targets should be set centrally. Any policy-optimizing assessment of adaptation and mitigation faces the challenges inherent in monetary damage functions discussed above. In addition, it must express all adaptation efforts in monetary terms, even though many of them represent non-market costs, such as loss of cultural traditions and forced changes in social structure and individual behaviour. Given these difficulties, Patt et al. (2010) argue that the most important question policy optimization

IAMs can help to answer is how sensitive the choice of an optimal or appropriate mitigation target is to the range of potential future adaptations. They note that varying adaptation between nothing and its optimal level in AD-DICE moves the optimal mitigation target from a 22 per cent to a 16 per cent reduction from baseline emissions by 2100, which is marginal compared to the range of mitigation targets currently being considered by policy-makers. The gap between these two mitigation levels implies that these policy-makers either (implicitly) apply other damage and mitigation cost functions than DICE-99 or do not choose the mitigation target based on a maximization of the net benefits of climate policies. It would be worth testing whether the conclusion that different adaptation strategies in AD-DICE have a relatively limited effect on the optimal level of mitigation is robust under alternative specifications of damage, adaptation and mitigation cost functions.

- *Analysing the trade-offs between mitigation and adaptation financing ("modelling mitigation and adaptation to guide international adaptation funding").* The Kyoto Protocol establishes a link between mitigation policies and international adaptation financing by using a levy on the clean development mechanism to provide resources to the Adaptation Fund. IAMs can assess international adaptation funding by comparing the resources raised by alternative financing mechanisms with the financial adaptation needs determined either exogenously or endogenously depending on the level of mitigation. An analysis with AD-FAIR found that current mechanisms for financing adaptation to climate change are clearly inadequate to provide the level of resources in developing countries determined by the AD-RICE adaptation cost functions (Hof et al., 2009). Such analyses could be extended by considering the costs of residual impacts in addition to adaptation costs, noting that any such cost estimates are highly controversial.
- *Assessing adaptation costs across regions ("modelling adaptation to guide international adaptation spending").* IAMs may, in principle, inform the allocation of resources from a global adaptation fund across countries by providing information on their respective adaptation needs. In addition to the scientific uncertainties regarding regional climate impacts and corresponding adaptation needs, however, such an application raises important normative issues. First, the adaptation costs of a country depend crucially on the level of residual impacts deemed acceptable. Determining adaptation costs on the basis of cost-benefit analysis (e.g. as done in FUND for coastal protection) could result in particularly unjust outcomes when residual impacts are not considered. For instance, a poor country that is relatively easy to protect against sea-level rise could "claim" the costs for full protection of its coastline, whereas a country that is more difficult to protect may be

left without assistance if coastal protection is modelled as not cost-effective there. Second, international support for adaptation will depend not only on the level of adaptation costs of a country, but also on its ability to shoulder (part of) these costs.

- *Assessing the effects of adaptation on residual impacts of climate change ("modelling adaptation to guide the level of regional adaptation").* IAMs can, in principle, be applied to assess the trade-off between adaptation and residual impacts at the regional level. For example, FUND has been applied to determine residual impacts of sea-level rise for different levels of coastal protection. Patt et al. (2010) argue, however, that policy optimization IAMs are unsuitable for guiding adaptation because of the mismatch in spatial scale between global models and local adaptation needs, and the irrelevance of adaptation targets for the design of efficient and equitable adaptation policies. Sectoral and regional models are generally more appropriate tools to assist the design and prioritization of regional adaptation measures.
- *Identify good adaptation policies ("modelling adaptation to guide the design of adaptation").* Geographically explicit IAMs can help designing adaptation strategies by assessing the effectiveness of proposed adaptation measures in reducing adverse climate impacts and their interaction with other policy domains. For instance, land-use models can analyse the interaction between shifts in cropping areas ("adaptation"), potential increases in bioenergy production ("mitigation") and expansions of protected areas ("biodiversity protection"), including potential synergies, areas of conflict and trade-offs between different goals. IAMs with non-monetary representation of impacts have been coupled to sectoral (e.g. IMAGE) or regional (e.g. AIM) impact models, but many impact domains and adaptation policies are not currently covered by any IAM. This coupling approach can combine the strengths of global IAMs to analyse the relationship between global mitigation efforts and regional impacts with those of more detailed models to assess the relationship between specific regional policies and residual impacts. Specific model applications, however, would likely focus either on mitigation or on adaptation.
- *Identify likely adaptations ("modelling adaptation to understand the level of adaptation").* Adaptation modelling in IAMs has been concerned with either determining optimal levels of adaptation or assessing alternative adaptation strategies. Models can also be used to understand the likely level and effectiveness of adaptation under different scenarios and assumptions. Such models would focus on the process of adaptation, including decision processes, transition costs, non-economic constraints and lag times (ibid.). It is currently not clear, however, how detailed "adaptation process models" could be integrated with global IAMs.

5-1-6 Conclusion

Climate impact modelling in early IAMs could largely be distinguished into two categories. Policy optimization models based on a cost-benefit paradigm applied aggregated monetary damage functions driven by smooth changes in global mean temperature (dubbed "the same, only warmer"), whereas policy guidance models applied geographically explicit biophysical climate impact models. This characterization is still largely correct, but the picture has become more differentiated recently. One policy optimization model (FUND) includes biophysical representations of some climate impacts, and several of these models have been modified to consider the possibility of large-scale climate instabilities. Most recent policy evaluation models consider climate change in combination with other environmental and sustainability issues, and they are increasingly coupled with sectoral and regional impact models to extend the capabilities of the core model for specific applications. The only policy guidance model (ICLIPS) applies non-monetary reduced-form impact models, which combine elements of the two earlier model categories.

The consideration of adaptation also differs substantially across model categories. Until recently, all policy optimization models implicitly assumed optimal adaptation in their damage function. Considering the various non-economic constraints to adaptation, these models likely underestimate the full costs of climate change. This assumption has recently been relaxed in some IAMs. In particular, AD-DICE and AD-RICE attempt to separate the residual damage and adaptation cost functions implicitly contained in the aggregated damage functions of DICE and RICE, respectively. Doing so, these models can treat mitigation and adaptation as separate control variables. Initial results of AD-DICE suggest that the optimal mitigation target is rather insensitive to the explicit consideration of adaptation. FUND has been applied to investigate the trade-offs between mitigation and adaptation for the impacts of sea-level rise on coastal zones. The consideration of adaptation in policy optimization models is, however, severely hampered for two reasons in addition to the empirical and normative challenges faced by earlier policy optimization IAMs. First, it is confronted with large uncertainties about the costs and benefits of adaptation where few empirical data are available in most sectors (Agrawala and Fankhauser, 2008). Second, the separation of efficiency and equity aspects that is possible for mitigation due to its public good characteristics cannot be applied to adaptation, which yields mostly local benefits. Considering these challenges, the most promising way forward appears to be improving the theoretical understanding of adaptation by means of conceptual models (such as those considered in Lecocq and Shalizi, 2007a, 2007b) and improving the empirical aspects of adaptation by a systematic collection of costs and effectiveness of adaptation measures from bottom-up studies.

Policy evaluation models increasingly consider management strategies that may be viewed as adaptation to climate change. Their effectiveness in reducing the impacts of climate change is often difficult to assess, because these management strategies usually respond to a broad set of environmental and socio-economic conditions rather than to climate change only. Further coupling of global IAMs with regional and sectoral models would enable assessing the effects of various management strategies under different climate scenarios. Analyses with policy guidance models may be surprisingly insensitive to the consideration of adaptation because impact guardrails have generally been defined for sectors where human adaptation has little potential (e.g. transformation of natural ecosystems) or on the basis of large-scale climate instabilities (e.g. breakdown of the thermohaline ocean circulation).

REFERENCES

Ackerman, F., E. A. Stanton, C. Hope and S. Alberth (2008) "Did the Stern Review Underestimate US and Global Climate Damages?", Working Paper WP-US-0802, Stockholm Environment Institute, Stockholm.

Agrawala, S. and S. Fankhauser (eds) (2008) *Economic Aspects of Adaptation to Climate Change: Costs, Benefits and Policy Instruments*. Paris: OECD.

Alcamo, J. and E. Kreileman (1998) "Emission Scenarios and Global Climate Protection", in J. Alcamo, R. Leemans and E. Kreileman (eds) *Global Change Scenarios of the 21st Century. Results from the IMAGE 2.1 Model*. Oxford: Pergamon Press, pp. 163–192.

Anthoff, D. and R. S. J. Tol (2008) "The Climate Framework for Uncertainty, Negotiation and Distribution (FUND), Technical Description, Version 3.3".

Anthoff, D., C. Hepburn and R. S. J. Tol (2009) "Equity Weighting and the Marginal Damage Costs of Climate Change", *Ecological Economics* 68(3), pp. 836–849; available at www.sciencedirect.com/science/article/B6VDY-4T4108R-1/2/cee17de6cd7ef5bf51d9b12b175f4c09.

Arnell, N. W., M. G. R. Cannell, M. Hulme, R. S. Kovats, J. F. C. Mitchell, R. J. Nicholls, M. L. Parry, M. T. J. Livermore and A. White (2002) "The Consequences of CO_2 Stabilisation for the Impacts of Climate Change", *Climatic Change* 53, pp. 413–446.

Azar, C. (1998) "Are Optimal CO_2 Emissions Really Optimal? Four Critical Issues for Economists in the Greenhouse", *Environmental and Resource Economics* 11, pp. 1–15.

Azar, C. and K. Lindgren (2003) "Catastrophic Events and Stochastic Cost–benefit Analysis of Climate Change", *Climatic Change* 56, pp. 245–255.

Bosetti, V., E. Massetti and M. Tavoni (2007) "The WITCH Model: Structure, Baseline, Solutions", FEEM Working Paper No. 10.2007; available at http://ssrn.com/abstract=960746.

Bosetti, V., C. Carraro, M. Galeotti, E. Massetti and M. Tavoni (2006) "WITCH: A World Induced Technical Change Hybrid Model", *Energy Journal* 27(Special Issue), pp. 13–38.

Bouwman, A. F., T. Kram and K. Klein Goldewijk (eds) (2006) *Integrated Modelling of Global Environmental Change*. Bilthoven: Netherlands Environmental Assessment Agency (MNP).

Brenkert, A. L., S. J. Smith, S. H. Kim and H. M. Pitcher (2003) "Model Documentation for the MiniCAM", Technical Report PNNL-14337, Pacific Northwest National Laboratory, College Park, MD.

de Bruin, K. C., R. B. Dellink and S. Agrawala (2009) "Economic Aspects of Adaptation to Climate Change: Integrated Assessment Modelling of Adaptation Costs and Benefits", Environment Working Paper No. 6, OECD, Paris.

de Bruin, K. C., R. B. Dellink and R. S. J. Tol (2009) "AD-DICE: An Implementation of Adaptation in the DICE Model", *Climatic Change* 95, pp. 63–81.

Dickinson, T. (2007) "The Compendium of Adaptation Models for Climate Change", Environment Canada; available at www.preventionweb.net/files/2287_CompendiumofAdaptationModelsforCC.pdf.

Dowlatabadi, H. (1998) "Sensitivity of Climate Change Mitigation Estimates on Assumptions about Technical Change", *Energy Economics* 20, pp. 473–493.

——— (2000) "Bumping against a Gas Ceiling", *Climatic Change* 46, pp. 391–407.

Downing, T. E., D. Anthoff, R. Butterfield, M. Ceronsky, M. Grubb, J. Guo, C. Hepburn, C. Hope, A. Hunt, A. Li, A. Markandya, S. Moss, A. Nyong, R. S. J. Tol and P. Watkiss (2005) *Social Cost of Carbon: A Closer Look at Uncertainty*. London: DEFRA.

Edmonds, J., M. Wise, H. Pitcher, P. Richels, T. Wigley and C. MacCracken (1996) "An Integrated Assessment of Climate Change and the Accelerated Introduction of Advanced Energy Technologies: An Application of MiniCAM 1.0", *Mitigation and Adaptation Strategies for Global Change* 1, pp. 311–319.

Fankhauser, S. (1994) "Protection vs. Retreat – The Economic Costs of Sea Level Rise", *Environment and Planning A* 27, pp. 299–319.

Fisher, B. and N. Nakicenovic (2007) "Issues Related to Mitigation in the Long-term Context", in IPCC (ed.) *Climate Change 2007: Mitigation of Climate Change*. Cambridge: Cambridge University Press, pp. 169–250.

Füssel, H.-M. (2003) "The ICLIPS Impacts Tool: A Graphical User Interface to Climate Impact Response Functions for Integrated Assessments of Climate Change", *Integrated Assessment* 4, pp. 116–125.

Füssel, H.-M. and M. D. Mastrandrea (2010) "Integrated Assessment Modeling of Climate Change", in S. H. Schneider, A. Rosencranz and M. D. Mastrandrea (eds) *Climate Change Science and Policy*. Washington, DC: Island Press, pp. 150–161.

Füssel, H.-M. and J. G. van Minnen (2001) "Climate Impact Response Functions for Terrestrial Ecosystems", *Integrated Assessment* 2, pp. 183–197.

Füssel, H.-M., F. L. Toth, J. G. van Minnen and F. Kaspar (2003) "Climate Impact Response Functions as Impact Tools in the Tolerable Windows Approach", *Climatic Change* 56, pp. 91–117.

Gjerde, J., S. Grepperud and S. Kverndokk (1999) "Optimal Climate Policy under the Possibility of a Catastrophe", *Resource and Energy Economics* 21, pp. 289–317.

Grossmann, W. D., L. Magaard and H. von Storch (2003) "Using Economic Change for Adaptation to Climate Risks – A Modeling Study", GKSS 2003/3, GKSS, Geesthacht.

Hall, D. C. and R. J. Behl (2006) "Integrating Economic Analysis and the Science of Climate Instability", *Ecological Economics* 57, pp. 442–465.

Hallegatte, S., J.-C. Hourcade and P. Dumas (2007) "Why Economic Dynamics Matter in Assessing Climate Change Damages: Illustration on Extreme Events", *Ecological Economics* 62, pp. 330–340.

Hinkel, J. and R. J. T. Klein (2009) "Integrating Knowledge to Assess Coastal Vulnerability to Sea-level Rise: The Development of the DIVA Tool", *Global Environmental Change* 19, pp. 384–395.

Hitz, S. and J. Smith (2004) "Estimating Global Impacts from Climate Change", *Global Environmental Change* 14, pp. 201–218.

Hof, A. F., K. C. de Bruin, R. B. Dellink, M. G. J. den Elzen and D. P. van Vuuren (2009) "The Effect of Different Mitigation Strategies on International Financing of Adaptation", *Environmental Science & Policy* 12(7), pp. 832–843; available at www.nccr-climate.unibe.ch/conferences/climate_policies/working_papers/Hof.pdf.

Hope, C. (2005) "Integrated Assessment Models", in D. Helm (ed.) *Climate Change Policy*. Oxford: Oxford University Press, pp. 77–98.

——— (2006) "The Marginal Impact of CO_2 from PAGE2002: An Integrated Assessment Model Incorporating the IPCC's Five Reasons for Concern", *Integrated Assessment* 6, pp. 19–56.

——— (2008) "Optimal Carbon Emissions and the Social Cost of Carbon over Time under Uncertainty", *Integrated Assessment* 8, pp. 107–122.

——— (2009) "How Deep Should the Deep Cuts Be? Optimal CO_2 Emissions over Time under Uncertainty", *Climate Policy* 9, pp. 3–8.

Hope, C. W., J. Anderson and P. Wenman (1993) "Policy Analysis of the Greenhouse Effect – An Application of the PAGE Model", *Energy Policy* 15, pp. 328–338.

Jaeger, C., H.-J. Schellnhuber and V. Brovkin (2008) "Stern's Review and Adam's Fallacy", *Climatic Change* 89, pp. 207–218.

Kainuma, M., Y. Matsuoka and T. Morita (eds) (2003) *Climate Policy Assessment: Asia-Pacific Integrated Modeling*. Tokyo: Springer.

Keller, K., K. Tan, F. M. M. Morel and D. F. Bradford (2000) "Preserving the Ocean Circulation: Implications for Climate Policy", *Climatic Change* 47, pp. 17–43.

Keller, K., B. M. Bolker and D. F. Bradford (2004) "Uncertain Climate Thresholds and Optimal Economic Growth", *Journal of Environmental Economics and Management* 48, pp. 723–741.

Kemfert, C. (2002) "An Integrated Assessment Model of Economy-Energy-Climate – The Model WIAGEM", *Integrated Assessment* 3, pp. 281–298.

——— (2006) "An Integrated Assessment of Economy, Energy and Climate. The Model WIAGEM – A Reply to Comment by Roson and Tol", *Integrated Assessment* 6(3), pp. 45–49.

Kuntz-Duriseti, K. (2004) "Evaluating the Economic Value of the Precautionary Principle: Using Cost-benefit Analysis to Place a Value on Precaution", *Environmental Science & Policy* 7, pp. 291–301.

Kurosawa, A., H. Yagita, W. Zhou, K. Tokimatsu and Y. Yanagisawa (1999) "Analysis of Carbon Emission Stabilization Targets and Adaptation by Integrated Assessment Model", *Energy Journal* 20(Special Issue), pp. 157–175.

Lecocq, F. and Z. Shalizi (2007a) "Balancing Expenditures on Mitigation of and Adaptation to Climate Change: An Exploration of Issues Relevant to Developing Countries", Policy Research Working Paper 4299, World Bank, Washington, DC; available at www-wds.worldbank.org/servlet/WDSContentServer/WDSP/IB/2007/08/02/000158349_20070802095523/Rendered/PDF/wps4299.pdf.

——— (2007b) "How Might Climate Change Affect Economic Growth in Developing Countries? A Review of the Growth Literature with a Climate Lens", Policy Research Working Paper 4315, World Bank, Washington, DC; available at www-wds.worldbank.org/external/default/WDSContentServer/WDSP/IB/2007/08/13/000158349_20070813145822/Rendered/PDF/wps4315.pdf.

Leemans, R., E. Kreileman, G. Zuidema, J. Alcamo, M. Berk, G. J. Born, M. den Elzen, R. Hootsmans, M. Janssen, M. Schaeffer, S. Toet and B. de Vries (1998) "The IMAGE User Support System. Global Change Scenarios from IMAGE 2.1", Report 481508006, RIVM, Bilthoven.

Link, P. M. and R. S. J. Tol (2004) "Possible Economic Impacts of a Shutdown of the Thermohaline Circulation: An Application of FUND", *Portuguese Economic Journal* 3, pp. 99–114.

Manne, A. and R. Richels (2004a) "The Impact of Learning-by-doing on the Timing and Costs of CO_2 Abatement", *Energy Economics* 26, pp. 603–619.

——— (2004b) "MERGE: An Integrated Assessment Model for Global Climate Change"; available at www.stanford.edu/group/MERGE/GERAD1.pdf.

Mastrandrea, M. D. and S. H. Schneider (2001) "Integrated Assessment of Abrupt Climatic Changes", *Climate Policy* 1, pp. 433–449.

——— (2004) "Probabilistic Integrated Assessment of 'Dangerous' Climate Change", *Science* 304, pp. 571–575.

——— (2005) "Probabilistic Assessment of 'Dangerous' Climate Change and Emissions Scenarios", *Proceedings of the National Academy of Sciences* 102, pp. 15728–15735.

McInerney, D. and K. Keller (2008) "Economically Optimal Risk Reduction Strategies in the Face of Uncertain Climate Thresholds", *Climatic Change* 91, pp. 29–41.

Mendelsohn, R., M. Schlesinger and L. Williams (2000) "Comparing Impacts across Climate Models", *Integrated Assessment* 1, pp. 37–48.

Negishi, T. (1972) *General Equilibrium Theory and International Trade.* Amsterdam: North-Holland.

Nicholls, R., R. S. J. Tol and A. Vafeidis (2008) "Global Estimates of the Impact of a Collapse of the West Antarctic Ice Sheet: An Application of FUND", *Climatic Change* 91(1), pp. 171–191.

Nordhaus, W. D. (2008) *A Question of Balance: Weighing the Options on Global Warming Policies.* New Haven, CT: Yale University Press.

Nordhaus, W. D. and J. Boyer (2000) *Warming the World: Economic Models of Global Warming*. Cambridge, MA: MIT Press.

Nordhaus, W. D. and D. Popp (1997) "What Is the Value of Scientific Knowledge? An Application to Global Warming Using the PRICE Model", *Energy Journal* 18, pp. 1–45.

O'Neill, B. and M. Oppenheimer (2004) "Climate Change Impacts Are Sensitive to the Concentration Stabilization Path", *Proceedings of the National Academy of Sciences* 101, pp. 16411–16416.

Parry, M. L., C. Rosenzweig, A. Iglesias, M. Livermore and G. Fischer (2004) "Effects of Climate Change on Global Food Production under SRES Emissions and Socio-economic Scenarios", *Global Environmental Change* 14(1), pp. 53–67.

Parry, M. L., N. Arnell, T. McMichael, R. Nicholls, P. Martens, S. Kovats, M. Livermore, C. Rosenzweig, A. Iglesias and G. Fischer (2001) "Millions at Risk: Defining Critical Climate Change Threats and Targets", *Global Environmental Change* 11, pp. 181–183.

Patt, A. G., D. P. van Vuuren, F. Berkhout, A. Aaheim, A. F. Hof, M. Isaac and R. Mechler (2010) "Adaptation in Integrated Assessment Modeling: Where Do We Stand?", *Climatic Change* 99(3/4), pp. 383–402.

Popp, D. (2004) "ENTICE: Endogenous Technological Change in the DICE Model of Global Warming", *Journal of Environmental Economics and Management* 48(1), pp. 742–768.

——— (2006) "ENTICE-BR: The Effects of Backstop Technology R&D on Climate Policy Models", *Energy Economics* 28(2), pp. 188–222.

Roson, R. and R. S. J. Tol (2006) "An Integrated Assessment Model of Economy-Energy-Climate – The Model WIAGEM: A Comment", *Integrated Assessment* 6(1), pp. 75–82.

Roughgarden, T. and S. H. Schneider (1999) "Climate Change Policy: Quantifying Uncertainties for Damages and Optimal Carbon Taxes", *Environment* 27, pp. 415–429.

Sands, R. D. and M. Leimbach (2003) "Modeling Agriculture and Land Use in an Integrated Assessment Framework", *Climatic Change* 56, pp. 185–210.

Schlosser, C. A., A. P. Sokolov and D. W. Kicklighter (2007) "A Global Land System Framework for Integrated Climate Change Assessments", Report No. 147, MIT Joint Program on Science and Policy of Global Change, Cambridge, MA.

Schneider, S. H. (1997) "Integrated Assessment Modeling of Global Climate Change: Transparent Rational Tool for Policy Making or Opaque Screen Hiding Value-laden Assumptions?", *Environmental Modeling and Assessment* 2, pp. 229–249.

Schneider, S. H., K. Kuntz-Duriseti and C. Azar (2000) "Costing Non-linearities, Surprises, and Irreversible Events", *Pacific and Asian Journal of Energy* 10, pp. 81–106.

Smith, J. B., H.-J. Schellnhuber and M. M. Q. Mirza (2001) "Vulnerability to Climate Change and Reasons for Concern: A Synthesis", in J. J. McCarthy, O. F. Canziani, N. A. Leary, D. J. Dokken and K. S. White (eds) *Climate Change 2001:*

Impacts, Adaptation and Vulnerability. Cambridge: Cambridge University Press, pp. 913–967.

Sokolov, A. P., C. A. Schlosser, S. Dutkiewicz, S. Paltsev, D. W. Kicklighter, H. D. Jacoby, R. G. Prinn, C. E. Forest, J. Reilly, C. Wang, B. Felzer, M. C. Sarofim, J. Scott, P. H. Stone, J. M. Melillo and J. Cohen (2005) "The MIT Integrated Global System Model (IGSM) Version 2: Model Description and Baseline Evaluation", Report No. 124, MIT Joint Program on Science and Policy of Global Change, Cambridge, MA.

Stanton, E. A., F. Ackerman and S. Kartha (2009) "Inside the Integrated Assessment Models: Four Issues in Climate Economics", *Climate & Development* 1, pp. 166–184.

Stern, N. (2007) *The Economics of Climate Change*. Cambridge: Cambridge University Press.

Tol, R. S. J. (2002) "Estimates of the Damage Costs of Climate Change. Part II: Dynamic Estimates", *Environmental and Resource Economics* 21, pp. 135–160.

——— (2007) "The Double Trade-off between Adaptation and Mitigation for Sea-level Rise: An Application of FUND", *Mitigation and Adaption Strategies for Global Change* 12(5), pp. 741–753.

Tol, R. S. J. and S. Fankhauser (1998) "On the Representation of Impact in Integrated Assessment Models of Climate Change", *Environmental Modeling and Assessment* 3, pp. 63–74.

Tol, R. S. J. and R. Verheyen (2004) "State Responsibility and Compensation for Climate Change Damages – A Legal and Economic Assessment", *Energy Policy* 32, pp. 1109–1130.

Tol, R. S. J., S. Fankhauser and J. B. Smith (1998) "The Scope for Adaptation to Climate Change: What Can We Learn from the Impact Literature?", *Global Environmental Change* 8, pp. 109–123.

Toth, F. L., T. Bruckner, H.-M. Füssel, M. Leimbach and G. Petschel-Held (2003) "Integrated Assessment of Long-term Climate Policies: Part 1 – Model Presentation", *Climatic Change* 56, pp. 37–56.

Toth, F. L., T. Bruckner, H.-M. Füssel, M. Leimbach, G. Petschel-Held and H.-J. Schellnhuber (2002) "Exploring Options for Global Climate Policy: A New Analytical Framework", *Environment* 44(5), pp. 22–34.

Warren, R., S. de la Nava Santos, N. W. Arnell, M. Bane, T. Barker, C. Barton, R. Ford, H.-M. Füssel, R. K. S. Hankin, R. Klein, C. Linstead, J. Kohler, T. D. Mitchell, T. J. Osborn, H. Pan, S. C. B. Raper, G. Riley, H.-J. Schellnhuber, S. Winne and D. Anderson (2008) "Development and Illustrative Outputs of the Community Integrated Assessment System (CIAS), a Multi-institutional Modular Integrated Assessment Approach for Modelling Climate Change", *Environmental Modelling and Software* 23(5), pp. 592–610.

Wright, E. L. and J. D. Erickson (2003) "Incorporating Catastrophes into Integrated Assessment: Science, Impacts, and Adaptation", *Climatic Change* 57, pp. 265–286.

Yang, Z. and W. D. Nordhaus (2006) "Magnitude and Direction of Technological Transfers for Mitigating GHG Emissions", *Energy Economics* 28(5/6), pp. 730–741.

Yohe, G. W. (1999) "The Tolerable Windows Approach: Lessons and Limitations. An Editorial Comment", *Climatic Change* 41, pp. 283–295.

Yohe, G. W. and R. D. Lasco (2007) "Perspectives on Climate Change and Sustainability", in IPCC (ed.) *Climate Change 2007: Climate Change Impacts, Adaptation and Vulnerability*. Cambridge: Cambridge University Press, pp. 811–841.

Yohe, G. W., N. G. Andronova and M. E. Schlesinger (2004) "To Hedge or Not against an Uncertain Climate Future", *Science* 306, pp. 416–417.

Yohe, G. W., M. E. Schlesinger and N. G. Andronova (2006) "Reducing the Risk of a Collapse of the Atlantic Thermohaline Circulation", *Integrated Assessment* 6, pp. 57–73.

Zickfeld, K. and T. Bruckner (2003) "Reducing the Risk of Abrupt Climate Change: Emissions Corridors Preserving the Atlantic Thermohaline Circulation", *Integrated Assessment* 4, pp. 106–115.

5-2

Risk assessment approach for seismic hazard mitigation and its application to adaptation to global climate change

Susumu Iai

5-2-1 Introduction

Despite the huge efforts to mitigate climate change, global environmental change has to be expected. In addition to mitigation, adaptive measures have to be taken if the rate of environmental change is relatively slow. Risk management measures must be mobilized if the rate of the environmental change is very fast.

In order to form a strategy for adaptation and risk management, variation and uncertainty in the environmental index, such as temperature or rain or snowfall, have to be evaluated. The variation and uncertainty are usually hidden when one discusses the global average temperature or global average of an economic index.

This chapter first introduces the discussions of the risk assessment approach established in seismic hazard mitigation. This performance-based approach has emerged from the experience of seismic damage during the 1995 Kobe earthquake in Japan (see Plate 5.2.1). In this approach, the fragility of a system, such as buildings and urban infrastructure, is evaluated together with the seismic hazard to the site where the system is constructed. Given the probability of a specified intensity of earthquake motion, the probability of the failure of the system under the specified earthquake motion is multiplied to give a combined probability of failure of the system. Integrated over the entire probability, the total probability of failure over the design period is computed. Given a financial index, such as cost for repair and financial loss due to the failure of a given sys-

Plate 5.2.1 Seismic damage to a highway bridge during the 1995 Kobe earthquake, Japan

tem, expected financial loss is computed by multiplying the total probability of failure. Introduction of a discount rate and other generalization is also possible. Given the initial cost for strengthening the system to reduce its fragility, total cost is evaluated by summing up the initial cost and the expected loss. This life-cycle cost approach is central in the modern approach to seismic hazard mitigation. If the consequence of failure is significant, the principle of minimum life-cycle cost recommends a strategy with larger initial cost (investment) as an overall optimized solution when we face the problems of uncertainties in terms of both the fragility of the system and the hazard due to earthquakes.

The chapter then moves on to discuss the possibility of applying this approach established for seismic hazard mitigation to the adaptation and risk management required in preparing ourselves for the various potential risks associated with global climate change, such as storm-induced flood, sea-level rise and loss of natural environment.

5-2-2 Performance objectives

The principles in the performance-based approach applied for urban structures may be summarized by following the guidelines presented in International Standard ISO23469 (Iai, 2005). In this approach, the objectives and functions of urban structures are defined in accordance with broad categories of use such as commercial, public and emergency.

Depending on the functions required during and after an earthquake, performance objectives for seismic design of structures are specified on the following basis:

- serviceability during and after an earthquake: minor impact to social and industrial activities, the structures may experience acceptable residual displacement, with function unimpaired and operations maintained or economically recoverable after temporary disruption
- safety during and after an earthquake: human casualties and damage to property are minimized, critical service facilities, including those vital to civil protection, are maintained and the structures do not collapse.

The performance objectives also reflect the possible consequences of failure. For each performance objective, a reference earthquake motion is specified as follows:

- serviceability during or after an earthquake: ground motions that have a reasonable probability of occurrence during the design working life
- safety during or after an earthquake: ground motions associated with rare events that may involve very strong ground shaking at the site.

Although these descriptions are very general, they constitute the essential principles of emerging methodologies for performance-based evaluation and design of urban structures.

5-2-3 Evaluation of serviceability through life-cycle cost

While safety should be a primary performance objective for ordinary buildings, serviceability and economy become higher-priority issues for port structures. For these structures, a methodology based on the principle of minimum life-cycle cost may be ideal (e.g. Sawada, 2003). This methodology is emerging, and will eventually be adopted as practice in the coming decade.

Life-cycle cost is a summation of initial construction cost and expected loss due to earthquake-induced damage. Probability of occurrence of earthquake ground motion (i.e. ground motions with all or varying return periods) is considered for evaluating the expected loss due to earthquake-induced damage. The life-cycle cost also includes intended maintenance cost and cost of demolishing or decommissioning when the working life of the structure ends.

When evaluating serviceability through life-cycle cost, failure of a port structure is defined by a state that does not satisfy the prescribed limits

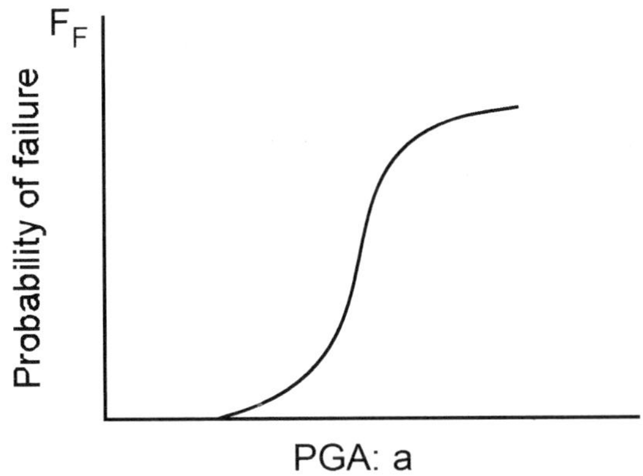

Figure 5.2.1 Schematic figure of a fragility curve

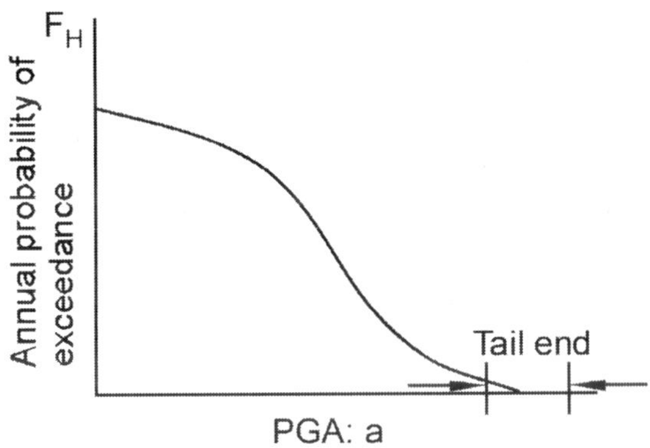

Figure 5.2.2 Schematic figure of a seismic hazard curve

typically defined by acceptable displacement, deformation or stress. If a peak ground motion input to the bottom boundary of soil structure systems is used as a primary index of earthquake ground motions, probability of failure $F_F(a)$ at peak ground motion a is computed considering uncertainty in geotechnical and structural conditions. A curve described by a function $F_F(a)$ is called a fragility curve (Figure 5.2.1). The probability of occurrence of earthquake ground motions is typically defined by a slope (or differentiation) of a function $F_H(a)$ that gives annual probability of exceeding a peak ground acceleration of a. A curve described by a function $F_H(a)$ is called a seismic hazard curve (Figure 5.2.2).

Given the fragility and seismic hazard curves for a port structure, annual probability of failure of structure P_1 is computed as follows:

$$P_1 = \int_0^{\infty} \left(-\frac{dF_{\mathrm{H}}(a)}{da} \right) F_{\mathrm{F}}(a)\, da \qquad \text{Equation 5.2.1}$$

If a design working life is T years, probability of failure of the port structure over the design working life is given by:

$$P_T = 1 - (1 - P_1)^T \qquad \text{Equation 5.2.2}$$

If loss due to earthquake-induced damage associated with the prescribed limit state is designated by c_{D}, expected loss over the design working life of a port structures C_{D} is given by:

$$C_{\mathrm{D}} = P_T c_{\mathrm{D}} \qquad \text{Equation 5.2.3}$$

Thus the life-cycle cost C_{LC} is given by adding initial construction cost C_{I}, maintenance cost C_{M} and demolishment cost C_{END} as:

$$C_{\mathrm{LC}} = C_{\mathrm{I}} + C_{\mathrm{D}} + C_{\mathrm{M}} + C_{\mathrm{END}} \qquad \text{Equation 5.2.4}$$

This is generalized further by introducing more than one serviceability limit state. Given the fragility curve defined for the ith limit state as $F_{\mathrm{F}i}(a)$ (Figure 5.2.3), Equations 5.2.1–5.2.4 are generalized as follows:

$$P_{1i} = \int_0^{\infty} \left(-\frac{dF_{\mathrm{H}}(a)}{da} \right) F_{\mathrm{F}i}(a)\, da \qquad \text{Equation 5.2.5}$$

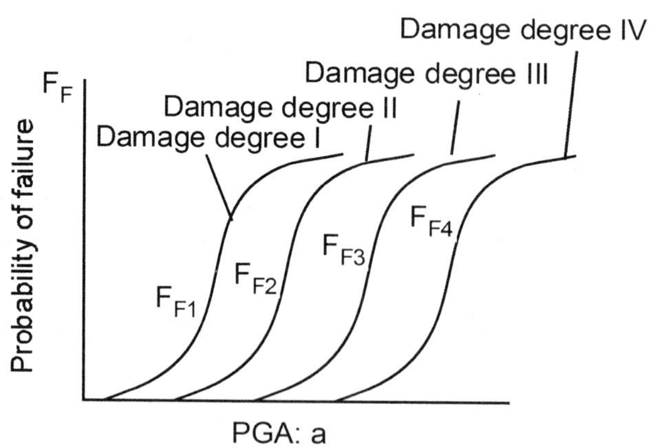

Figure 5.2.3 Schematic figure of a group of fragility curves for multiple limit states

$$P_{Ti} = 1 - (1 - P_{1i})^{T} \qquad \text{Equation 5.2.6}$$

$$C_{Di} = P_{Ti} c_{Di} \qquad \text{Equation 5.2.7}$$

$$C_{LC} = C_{I} + \sum_{i} C_{Di} + C_{M} + C_{END} \qquad \text{Equation 5.2.8}$$

As demonstrated for liquefaction hazard evaluation by Kramer, Mayfield and Anderson (2006), the probability evaluated by Equations 5.2.1 and 5.2.2 is a consistent index of hazard, and the conventional approach based on the return period prescribed in design provisions and codes can be either too conservative or unconservative, depending on the site. Expected loss evaluated by Equation 5.2.3 is an index that reflects the consequence of failure. Life-cycle cost evaluated by Equation 5.2.4 is an index that properly reflects the trade-off between initial cost and expected loss. The design option that gives the minimum life-cycle cost is the optimum in terms of overall economy, as shown in Figure 5.2.4. Thus the optimum design has a certain probability of failure, given by Equation 5.2.2. This probability is not prescribed by an authority (such as 10 per cent over 50 years), but rather determined as a result of the minimum life-cycle cost procedure. The probability of failure can be large if a consequence of failure in meeting the performance criteria, as measured by seismic loss c_D, is minor. The probability can be small, however, if a

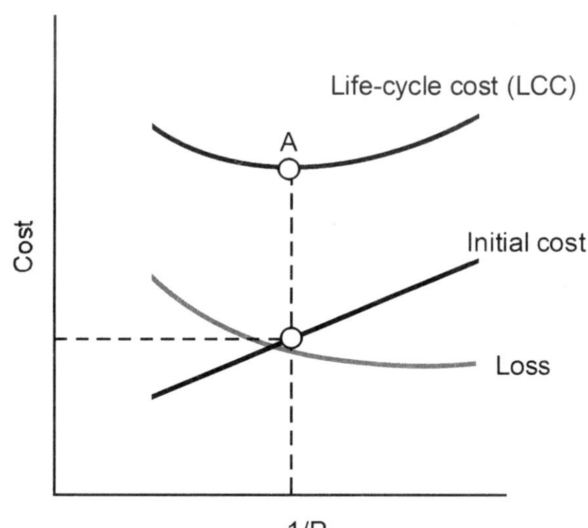

Figure 5.2.4 Principle of minimum life-cycle cost

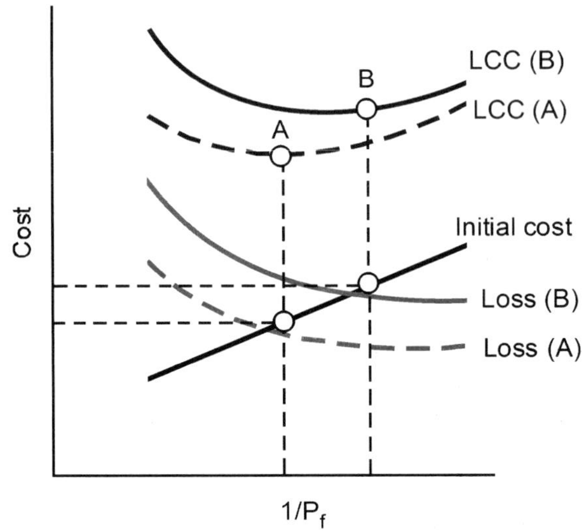

Figure 5.2.5 Effect of the consequence of failure on the minimum life-cycle cost

consequence of failure, as measured by c_D, is significant (Figure 5.2.5). Thus the minimum life-cycle cost procedure reflects the possible consequences of failure, and thereby satisfies the principles in performance objectives in the ISO guidelines described above.

5-2-4 Adaptation to global climate change

The risk assessment approach for seismic hazard mitigation reviewed here is readily applicable to form a reasonable strategy in adaptation to global climate change. The first step to achieve this application is to generalize the concepts of urban structures facing seismic risk in terms of a generalized system subject to an input that poses a certain risk (Figure 5.2.6).

In adaptation to global climate change, the input to the system can be an event in weather, including extremely hot or extremely cold events. The system can be a natural environment or a regional human society. Just as in risk assessment for seismic hazard mitigation, the input to the system has uncertainty, as represented by the hazard curve, posing a risk to the system. The system also has uncertainty as represented by the fragility curve. Evaluating the total risk to the system following the methodology of the life-cycle cost approach forms the basis for establishing a best strategy in adaptation to global climate change.

As shown in Figure 5.2.4, the strategy with larger initial cost (investment) will decrease the risks and consequently the expected loss due to

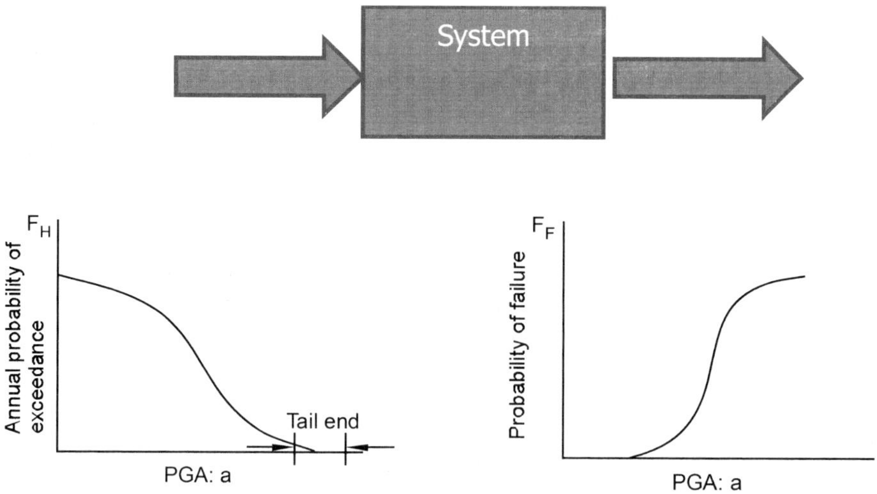

Figure 5.2.6 Hazard and fragility associated with uncertainties in input and response of an idealized system for adaptation to global climate change

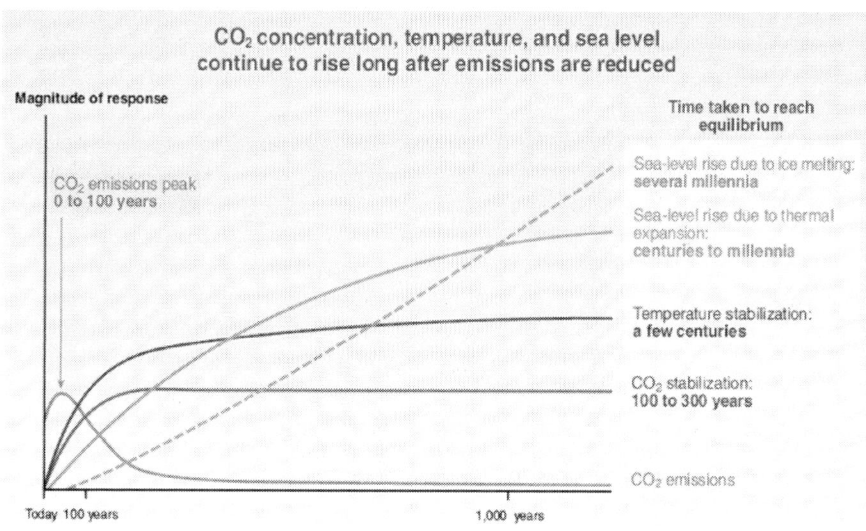

Figure 5.2.7 Various indexes of global climate change

global climate change. The best strategy is chosen when the life-cycle cost becomes the minimum. As shown in Figure 5.2.5, if the consequence of the failure is significant, then the strategy with larger initial cost (investment) becomes the best strategy.

When climate change is discussed, it is commonly explained in terms of global average temperature and similar indexes (Figure 5.2.7). This type of result does not show extremely hot weather, heavy rain, drought, cold weather, cold summers, storms, typhoons or high tides, all of which are key factors governing the critical threshold limit of the system facing global climate change.

Uncertainties associated with the average climate change can be explained through Figure 5.2.8. When the average temperature rises associated with global climate change, extreme hot days increase and cold days decrease, as shown in the left in the figure. This is the pattern of change most people implicitly expect when they hear the term “global warming”. Actually, this can be wrong. Even if there is no change in the average, there is a case that the variation becomes larger (middle in Figure 5.2.8). In this case, both extreme hot days and extreme cold days increase. Both the average and the variation can increase (right in Figure 5.2.8). In this case, extreme hot days increase but extreme cold days can also persist. Unexpected heavy snowfalls despite the average temperature rise can be categorized in this pattern. Although there is no definite consensus among experts on which pattern of these three should be expected in future, the importance of differentiating these patterns with respect to the variation may be understood from these figures.

Once these uncertainties associated with input to the system are idealized in terms of a hazard curve, the best strategy of adaptation can be established based on the minimum life-cycle cost principle described earlier.

Adaptation is associated with a case when the rate of change is relatively slow. Disaster mitigation may be required when the rate of change is too fast to adapt, or when people are too slow to act on global climate change.

Further generalization in forming the best strategy following the principle of minimum life-cycle cost may be applied when a double system is considered (Figure 5.2.9). In this figure, system A is associated with the adaptation strategy described earlier. System B is an idealized industrial and economic system that causes global climate change by emitting greenhouse gases. Investment to reduce the emission rate can be implemented in system B. Combining the assessment of the effects in systems A and B can give the best combination strategy that integrates mitigation and adaptation.

5-2-5 Conclusions

An overview is given on an emerging methodology for seismic evaluation and design of urban structures based on life-cycle cost.

For ordinary urban structures where primary objectives and functions are for commercial use, serviceability and economy become high-priority

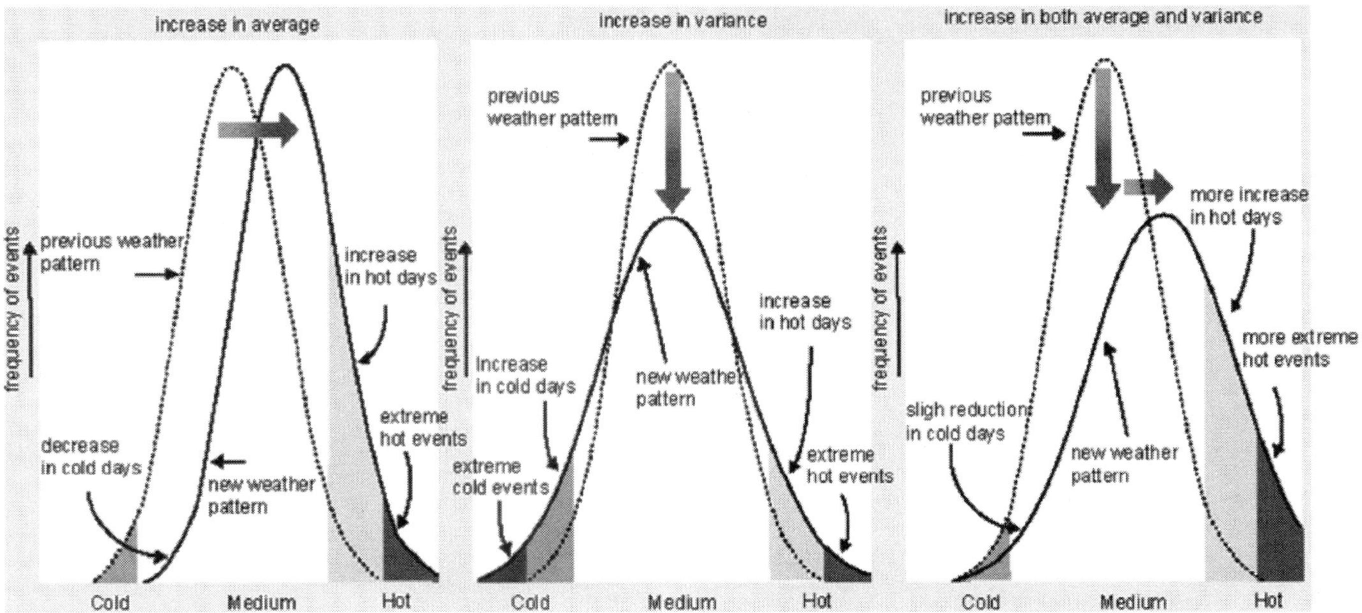

Figure 5.2.8 Uncertainties in the weather associated with global climate change

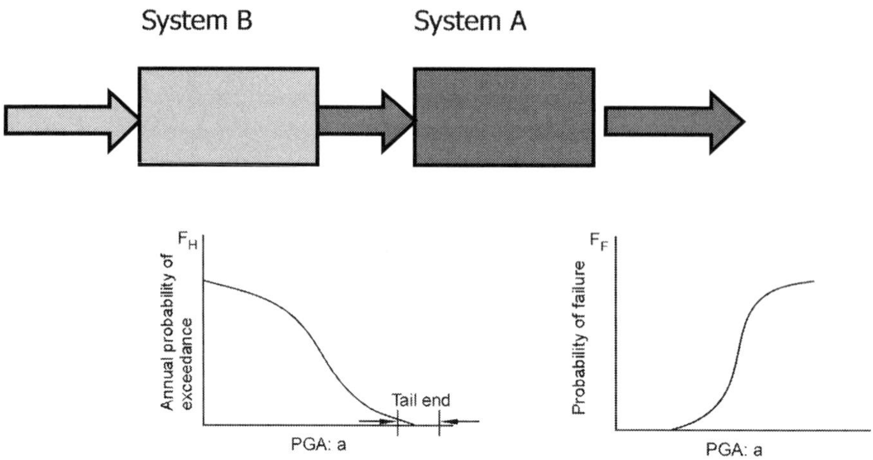

Figure 5.2.9 Double system approach in adaptation to global climate change

issues and a methodology based on life-cycle cost has potential advantages over conventional seismic design. In this methodology, failure is defined as the state where a structure does not meet the limits or acceptable damage level. Probability of failure over design working life is computed based on fragility curve(s) and a seismic hazard curve. The fragility curve(s) reflects uncertainty in geotechnical and structural conditions. The seismic hazard curve allows consideration of ground motions with all (or varying) return periods. Performance is evaluated in terms of expected loss due to earthquake-induced damage that reflects the consequence of failure. Life-cycle cost properly represents the trade-off between the initial construction cost and the expected loss. The design option that gives the minimum life-cycle cost is optimum in terms of overall economy.

This risk assessment approach for seismic hazard mitigation is readily applicable to form a reasonable strategy in adaptation to global climate change. The first step is to generalize the concepts of urban structures facing seismic risk in terms of a generalized system subject to an input that poses a certain risk. In adaptation to global climate change, the input to the system can be an event in weather, including extremely hot or cold events. The system can be a natural environment or a regional human society. Just as in risk assessment for seismic hazard mitigation, the input to the system has uncertainty, as represented by the hazard curve, posing a risk to the system. The system also has uncertainty represented by the fragility curve. To evaluate the total risk to the system following the methodology of the life-cycle cost approach forms a basis for establishing a best strategy in adaptation to global climate change.

This methodology has another potential (double system) approach to indicate the best balance (for investment) between mitigation measures and adaptation measures to global climate change.

REFERENCES

Iai, S. (2005) "International Standard (ISO) on Seismic Actions for Designing Geotechnical Works – An Overview", *Soil Dynamics and Earthquake Engineering* 25, pp. 605–615.

Kramer, S. L., R. T. Mayfield and D. G. Anderson (2006) "Performance-based Liquefaction Hazard Evaluation: Implications for Codes and Standards", paper presented at Eighth US National Conference on Earthquake Engineering, San Francisco, 18–22 April.

Sawada, S. (2003) "A New Look at Level 1 Earthquake Motions for Performance-based Design of Civil Engineering Structures", Japan Society of Civil Engineers; available at www.jsce.or.jp/committee/eec2/taishin/index.html.

5-3

Risk management of climate change and stochastic calculus

Jiro Akahori

The eighth Ritsumeikan international conference on stochastic processes and applications to mathematical finance was held in Kyoto in March 2008, organized under the joint auspices of the Department of Mathematical Sciences, Research Center for Finance and Research Center for Sustainability Science of Ritsumeikan University, Japanese Association of Financial Engineering and Econometrics and Center for Financial Engineering at Columbia University. The Ritsumeikan conference series is designed for those interested in the applications of stochastic calculus – the theory of stochastic processes and stochastic analysis – to mathematical finance. The conferences have been recognized as one of the most important meetings in Japan by researchers in this field, both in and outside Japan.

The main part of the conference was contributed talks on recent developments of mathematical finance, but there was also a special session on environmental finance on climate change, which is rapidly becoming an extremely important field in economics, finance and applied mathematics.

This chapter gives a short overview of this wide and growing field from a perspective of stochastic calculus. To achieve this, we can start by introducing the content of the special session: each contributed talk was basically a survey on different areas, and together they covered most of the important perspectives.

There were three speakers. First, Professor Takanobu Kosugi from Ritsumeikan University gave a survey on integrated assessment models (IAMs) of climate change. Second, Professor Yuji Yamada of Tsukuba

Plate 5.3.1 Ritsumeikan conference (March 2008)

University presented his results on pricing of weather derivatives (Yamada, 2008) together with a review of recent progress in the area. Finally, Professor Luca Taschini from the University of Zurich gave a talk on microeconomic models of emission trading markets, based on Chesney and Taschini (2008). These three lectures cover different areas of environmental finance on climate change, and a detailed description of their presentations gives a clear picture of what environmental finance is and how it is going to be developed.

One can find on the internet a basic idea of what environmental finance is; for example, according to Wikipedia, "the field of environmental finance, part of both environmental economics and the conservation movement, exploits various financial instruments (most notably land trusts) to protect biodiversity".

Given such a definition, I stress its "risk management" aspects. In the management of marketable risks, many tools from financial engineering are available. If one asks if/how the risk of climate change is divided into marketable risk and its complement, it can be a microeconomic question. The size of the risk could be studied in a macroeconomic framework such as optimal economic growth models or dynamic stochastic general equilibrium models.

The lectures in the special session are related to these three perspectives respectively. The IAM which Kosugi discussed deals with the question of how much risk we have in the future and how much risk we can reduce, using a generalized optimal growth model in a macroeconomic framework. The pricing of weather derivatives that Yamada studied is of course a problem of financial engineering, while the perspective of Taschini is much more microeconomic, since he works on modelling of price formation in an emission market.

These three approaches to environmental risk management have different perspectives, but in recent work some researchers, including the lecturers in the session, have something in common in methodology: they all use techniques from stochastic calculus. Beyond the intensive use of stochastic calculus in mathematical finance and financial engineering, there are growing demands for its use in both microeconomics and macroeconomics, especially in a field where risk (management) is essential, which no doubt includes environmental economics.

This chapter gives a brief survey of these three aspects of environmental finance in line with the talks given at Ritsumeikan, focusing on the role played by stochastic calculus in each approach. I suggest that there is a growing need to construct a model which "integrates" macroeconomic and microeconomic views with mathematical finance, or more specifically integrates IAMs, price formation models and derivative pricing in the emissions market.

The chapter discusses financial engineering in environmental finance, starting from a brief review of the role played by stochastic calculus in financial engineering. Next it considers the price theory of emissions, following Taschini (2010). Finally, I give a survey of IAMs, following Kosugi (2010), together with an illustration of our ongoing research (Akahori et al., 2010).

5-3-1 Financial engineering in environmental finance

Stochastic calculus in financial engineering

Let us start with discussing the role of stochastic calculus in financial engineering. Stochastic calculus applied to financial engineering is usually referred to as, or included in, mathematical finance. It is mainly founded on the basis of the no-arbitrage principle, which is far weaker and thus more robust than the utility maximization principle of (neoclassical) (micro)economics. With a complete market assumption and the no-arbitrage principle, a fair price of a derivative such as an option, bond and so on is obtained by calculating the expectation of the payoff under so-called risk-neutral measures. The well-known Black-Scholes formula (Black and Scholes, 1973) is a prototype of the framework.

The Ito formula, another chain rule that is central in stochastic calculus, has been proved to be very useful in financial engineering. It is very easy to handle, and this might be a reason why the use of stochastic calculus is now so widespread.

Nowadays not only "Ito's formula" but also many technical terms from stochastic calculus, such as martingales, Levy processes, Malliavin calculus and so on, are commonly used in the financial industry. To understand such technical words, higher mathematics (at least master's level) is required. In fact, since the 1980s many people with strong mathematical backgrounds have been working in banks in New York, London, Tokyo, etc. They are known as quantitative analysts, or quants. There have many fruitful interactions between quants, the practitioners, and academicians in universities. In Japan, the Japanese Association of Financial Engineering and Econometrics was founded in 1993 and has been one of the most active platforms for such interactions.

After the Lehman shock in 2008, however, there were criticisms that quants, or even financial mathematics (the phrase largely means stochastic calculus applied to mathematical finance), are to blame for the financial crisis. For example, Rocard (2008), the ex-prime minister of France, claimed that mathematicians had unknowingly committed a "crime against humanity" by letting their students become quants, and in the United Kingdom Lord Turner, the chair of the FSA, appeared to blame "misplaced reliance on sophisticated maths" for the crisis (Turner, 2009).

Such criticisms were, of course, far from acceptable to (financial) mathematicians. For example, Steven Shreve, a leading financial mathematician, pointed out that the quants had basically been kept away from decision-making in the banking industry (Shreve, 2008). Marc Yor, one of the greatest probabilists of our time, wrote a response to Rocard (Yor, 2008) claiming that stochastic calculus could be used for a deeper understanding of randomness, but not for gambling. Sir David Wallace, chair of the Council for Mathematical Sciences, wrote to Lord Turner to explain why mathematics is part of the solution to the banking crisis, and not part of the problem.

I myself share those opinions from the side of mathematics. To solve the financial problems, however, viewpoints from economics are necessary, as a matter of course. Financial engineering so far is founded on the basis of complete market assumptions like Gaussian, liquid and so on, many of which turned out to be naïve under the circumstances of the financial crisis. Very recently there has been intensive research activity by quants/financial mathematicians where they extend the traditional frameworks to match the real market situations. Microeconomic approaches like optimizations in incomplete markets are widely used, while macroeconomic points of view are comparatively less common in spite of their importance.

Financial engineering in emissions trading

For environmental finance, the same can be applied; mere applications of techniques from classical mathematical finance could be too naïve, especially when it comes to a less liquid market like emissions.

It has been recognized by quants/researchers that when they price derivatives in a real market like commodities, energy, real estate and so on, the standard argument of replicating a portfolio becomes meaningless due to the scarcity and illiquidity of the underlying asset (the "good" traded in the market). "Securitization" (creation of a secondary market) was a solution to this problem. They thought the risks could be sparsely spread out if there was enough space (independence), but there was not. Anyway, once a liquid secondary market comes into existence, the original market becomes stable, at least theoretically (if producers and consumers are risk averse, for example). Therefore, finding a way to create a secondary market would be important, and in doing this it is essential to establish how to price a derivative.

In Yamada's presentation he considered the pricing-hedging problem of a derivative on wind power, which is a kind of energy derivative. Since there is no liquid market in wind power, he proposed a new hedging scheme using virtual futures written on wind speed. This kind of approach is standard in pricing of derivatives on illiquid underlying assets; instead of using the asset itself, they rely on some other security which is strongly correlated to the underlying asset.

In the derivative pricing of emission markets, however, things are not that easy. Very few empirical data on the price process of the emissions are available, and so we cannot say which is "strongly correlated". Further, even if we have enough empirical data in the future, we need to be careful using these, because they are largely dependent on environmental policies, macroeconomic factors and the rules of the market.

To overcome this difficulty, one needs to construct a pricing model in which some mechanism of price formation is taken into account. Maeda (2004) and Kijima, Maeda and Nishide (2008) did pioneering work, and the model Taschini presented in the Ritsumeikan conference, based on Chesney and Taschini (2008), is also along this line. These studies are new in that they use microeconomics to model the price process; by contrast, in classical mathematical finance the price process of the underlying asset is basically exogenously given.

5-3-2 Microeconomics in environmental finance

Stochastic calculus in microeconomics

Before going into details, I briefly review the role of stochastic calculus in microeconomics.

Optimization under constraints is one of the principles in microeconomics. The question here is, do we need stochastic optimizations in microeconomics? With i.i.d. noise (white noise) as observation errors, some probability theory is required, but advanced stochastic calculus is only necessary when one considers a secondary market equals a financial market; in finance, one considers essentially an intertemporal optimization problem, and therefore modelling with stochastic processes and calculus on them, namely stochastic calculus, is indispensable. Here the optimization becomes a problem of stochastic control.

As mentioned, in incomplete market settings some optimization arguments are commonly used. Therefore, at least in respect of methodology, mathematical finance and financial microeconomics have much in common. But I dare say that the overlaps should be much more in environmental finance.

Price theory of emissions

Economically speaking, we should start by asking if emission trading is the best way to reduce greenhouse gas (GHG) under a given constraint. Subsidies and taxes could be alternatives. This "microeconomic" problem has been attacked by policy-makers and environmental economists for decades. According to the excellent survey of the issue by Taschini (2010), there is growing consensus that "marketable permits" are the best way.

At the same time, it is pointed out that the superiority of the marketable permits solution is heavily dependent on the degree of imperfection of the market. The pre-existing regulatory environment and concentration in both permit and output markets can impede the proper functioning of a permit system.

According to Taschini (ibid.), the main factors which affect the effectiveness of the permits market are its regulations, and to find a better system we need detailed studies on price formation under a given regulatory market. For example, we need to know how banking and borrowing opportunities or strategic trading interactions affect effectiveness. We may take into account the presence of asymmetric information in the emissions market; we may also ask if a secondary market can promote effectiveness.

These issues undoubtedly require advanced techniques from stochastic calculus and share perspectives with some problems in mathematical finance. Chesney and Taschini (2008) did pioneering work in this respect, and there will be more and more studies on these matters using higher financial mathematics.

5-3-3 Risk management of climate change from macroeconomic points of view

Integrated assessment models

In this microeconomic framework, a question about how much GHGs should be reduced is postulated. To attack the problem, macroeconomic points of view are required. This area has been one of the major fields of environmental economics for decades.

Most assessment models of climate change are based on an economic growth model originating from Ramsey (1928), with some modifications to take the effects of climate change into account. This kind of model is termed an integrated assessment model. There have been numerous variants of IAMs, and each was studied in detail.

In recent years the importance of studying stochastic versions of IAMs has been gradually recognized, as is pointed out in Kosugi's (2010) well-organized survey. In earlier days most studies on the standard economic growth model were devoted to obtaining qualitative results, while in recent progress quantitative models are much more appreciated. This growing demand forces one to consider using stochastic models to deal with parameter uncertainty. Model uncertainty could be another reason, and the randomness arising from both nature and markets should also be taken into account. There are still other causes; see Kosugi (ibid.).

For risk management of such uncertainties and randomness in economic growth under climate change, Manne and Richels (1992) claimed that "global warming insurance" might be useful.

Stochastic calculus in integrated assessment models

Many IAMs are constructed on the basis of an economic growth model with a Cobb-Douglass production function, by modifying the technical coefficient to be dependent on climate change. This parallels the real business cycle model by Kydland and Prescott (1982), or the recent dynamic stochastic general equilibrium (DSGE) models which are said to have "micro-foundation" (c.f. Kremer et al., 2006).

Though DSGE models are called stochastic, in their standard form stochastic calculus plays no role since they are discrete-time models. In contrast, in the study of optimal economic growth models, the use of continuous-time models is common, and recently the use of stochastic calculus became popular. This is the case also with the study of IAMs.

In ongoing research (Akahori et al., 2010), we construct a continuous-time version of the DICE model (see e.g. Nordhaus, 1994) which can be solved explicitly. In the process we make full use of stochastic calculus. One of the advantages of the explicit solution is that it facilitates sensitivity analysis of parameters; without an explicit solution, the computational cost of sensitivity analysis becomes a serious problem.

There is another reason why the continuous-time framework is desirable. In my view, to have a quantitative model it is necessary to take into account the feedback effects among macroeconomic factors, the emissions market and its secondary market. To construct such a hyper-integrated assessment model, we need to work on a continuous-time framework. This is for future study.

5-3-4 Concluding remarks

To summarize, I claim the following.

- In derivative pricing in an emission market, a detailed microeconomic study of price formation would be required.
- In the study of price formation, points of view from mathematical finance, including derivative pricing, are very important.
- In the microeconomic study of emission markets, the quantity by which to reduce GHGs should be given, but this is endogenous in IAMs.
- An IAM can be improved by integrating microeconomic models of the emission market and its secondary market.

Thus an (hyper-)integrated model of macroeconomics and microeconomics together with derivative pricing techniques will be the next-generation models in environmental finance (Figure 5.3.1). In this new integrated framework, stochastic calculus will play a central role.

Acknowledgements

I thank Professors T. Kosugi, L. Taschini and T. Sawa for kind assistance in writing this chapter.

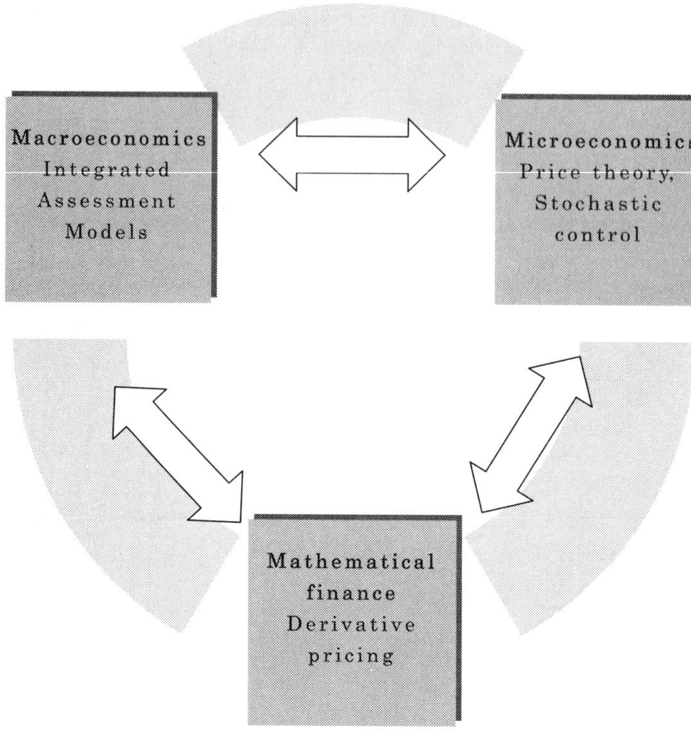

Figure 5.3.1 Trinity in environmental finance

REFERENCES

Akahori, Jiro, Takanobu Kosugi, Takafumi Kumazaki and Ken-ichi Oi (2010) "On a Stochastic Extension of Integrated Models for Climate Changes", in *Proceedings of 41st ISCIE International Symposium on Stochastic Systems Theory and Its Application*. Kyoto: ISCIE, pp. 229–264.

Black, F. and M. Scholes (1973) "The Pricing of Options and Corporate Liabilities", *Journal of Political Economy* 81(3), pp. 637–654.

Chesney, M. and L. Taschini (2008) "The Endogenous Price Dynamics of Emission Allowances and an Application to CO_2 Option Pricing", Swiss Banking Institute, University of Zurich.

Kijima, M., A. Maeda and K. Nishide (2008) "Equilibrium Pricing of Contingent Claims in Tradable Permit Markets", Faculty of Economics, Yokohama National University.

Kosugi, T. (2010) "Assessments of 'Greenhouse Insurance': A Methodological Review", *Asia-Pacific Financial Markets* 17(4), pp. 345–363.

Kremer, J., G. Lombardo, L. von Thadden and T. Werner (2006) "Dynamic Stochastic General Equilibrium Models as a Tool for Policy Analysis", *CESifo Economic Studies* 52(4), pp. 640–665.

Kydland, F. and E. C. Prescott (1982) "Time to Build and Aggregate Fluctuations", *Econometrica* 50(6), pp. 1345–1370.

Maeda, A. (2004) "Impact of Banking and Forward Contracts on Tradable Permit Markets", *Environmental Economics and Policy Studies* 6, pp. 81–102.

Manne, A. S. and R. Richels (1992) *Buying the Greenhouse Insurance: The Economic Costs of CO_2 Emission Limits.* Cambridge, MA: MIT Press.

Nordhaus, W. D. (1994) *Managing the Global Commons: The Economics of Climate Change*. Cambridge, MA: MIT Press.

Ramsey, F. P. (1928) "A Mathematical Theory of Saving", *Economic Journal* 38, pp. 543–545.

Rocard, M. (2008) "La crise sonne le glas de l'ultralibéralisme", *Le Monde*, 2 November (in French).

Shreve, S. (2008) "Don't Blame the Quants", *Forbes*, 7 October; available at www.forbes.com/2008/10/07/securities-quants-models-oped-cx_ss_1008shreve.html.

Taschini, L. (2010) "Environmental Economics and Modeling Marketable Permits: A Survey", *Asia-Pacific Financial Markets* 17(4), pp. 325–343.

Turner, A. (2009) "A Regulatory Response to the Global Banking Crisis", FSA Report, March, Financial Services Authority, London.

Yamada, Y. (2008) "Furyoku Yosoku Gosa ni Motoduku Furyoku Derivative no Saitekika Sekkei", *Japanese Association of Financial Engineering and Econometrics Journal* 7, pp. 152–181 (in Japanese).

Yor, M. (2008) "Ebauche de reponse a M. Michel Rocard", *Gazette des Mathematiciens* 119, pp. 75–76 (in French).

6

Policy recommendations towards global sustainability

6-1

Policy recommendations towards a low-carbon society in 2050

Takamitsu Sawa

6-1-1 Introduction

The interest in climate change tended to wane in the aftermath of the Kyoto conference. During that period, Japan's greenhouse gas emissions actually continued to rise and did not drop at all. In 2007, on the eve of the Kyoto Protocol's first commitment period, Japan's emissions had increased 9 per cent over its level in 1990, which serves as the benchmark for reductions. However, from 2007 on, interest in climate change suddenly grew. This chapter considers various aspects of this shift and their background. It also examines the potential for achieving the goals of the "Abe Initiative", which proposed "cutting global emissions by half from the current level by 2050", and offers the author's personal views on the steps needed to achieve that goal, such as innovative technological development, creation of an international funding mechanism and restructuring of the socio-economic system.

6-1-2 The climate change debate up to 2006

Potential for the development of revolutionary technologies

Even after the Kyoto conference, there was still a lack of consensus among experts on the necessity of reducing carbon dioxide (CO_2) and other greenhouse gases (GHGs: methane, nitrous oxide, two classes of fluorocarbons – perfluorocarbon and hydrofluorocarbon – and sulphur hexafluoride). In the United States there were quite a few Republican scientists and economists who believed that there was not sufficient scientific knowledge on the subject and it was therefore "unnecessary".

More specifically, there was a debate as to whether "early actions" were needed or whether "delayed actions" would suffice. Needless to say, the Kyoto Protocol sided with the "early actions" line of argument. When the administration of US President George W. Bush announced in March 2001 that the United States would reject the Kyoto Protocol, it took the view that "delayed actions" would suffice. Those who argued for "delayed actions" focused on the common theory that "the threshold for atmospheric CO_2 concentration is 550 ppm". The basis for this theory was not necessarily solid; it was a number that was chosen by roughly doubling the normal CO_2 concentration prior to the Industrial Revolution, which was 280 ppm. Given that there have been frequent occurrences of unusual weather since the start of the twenty-first century, one has to question the idea that there is some threshold that, once crossed, will result in disaster. In other words, even someone like me, who is a layman when it comes to meteorology, realizes that as the density of CO_2 in the atmosphere has increased, the frequency and strength of abnormal weather have steadily risen, and the temperature has been steadily rising as well.

Shortly after announcing that the United States would reject the Kyoto Protocol, President Bush stated that it had "fatal flaws". I would surmise he was referring to the following. Because the Kyoto Protocol takes a short-term perspective (it obligates industrialized nations to reduce the volume of their emissions over a five-year period that straddles 2010), it hinders the development of revolutionary technologies that could contribute to stopping global warming, and thus inevitably has a negative impact on mid- to long-term efforts to combat warming.

There are a number of examples of this type of large-scale technology: carbon capture and storage, which separates and collects the CO_2 in the smoke emitted by thermal power plants and sequesters it in underground aquifers; solar power generation in space, where rockets would carry large-scale solar panels to a space station and the panels would be connected by robots to create a generator which could produce more than 1 million kilowatts to be converted into microwaves and relayed to Earth; development of lithium-ion batteries that recharge quickly and have a high capacity, which would improve the performance of electric cars; lower-cost fuel cells; and technology to produce large quantities of hydrogen at a low cost.

Restructuring the socio-economic system

In order to provide incentives for reducing CO_2 emissions, and for the development of revolutionary technologies, it is essential that an environmental (carbon) tax, an emissions trading scheme and other economic measures are introduced. The environment tax was adopted in the early 1990s by Holland, Denmark and three of the Nordic countries, by Germany and the United Kingdom in the late 1990s and by France and Italy after the turn of the century. The EU Emissions Trading Scheme (ETS) was adopted in 2005, and is gradually shifting from a quota system to an auction system.

In February 2003 the city of London decided to impose a congestion charge of £5 on all cars – regardless of type – that entered the downtown area on weekdays between 7 am and 6.30 pm. However, emergency vehicles, buses (capacity of nine or more passengers), taxis and motorcycles were all exempt from the charge, and electric and natural gas automobiles could become exempt simply by paying a £10 annual registration fee. Also, residents within the "charging zones" were given a 90 per cent discount. Three months after the congestion charge was introduced, the London transportation authority measured its impact. The result was striking: compared to the same month the previous year, the number of vehicles entering the downtown area had dropped by 16 per cent. While some people transferred from car to public transport for their commute, many people began to carpool (for example, four neighbours share a ride to work in a single car), splitting the cost of gasoline and the congestion charge with their fellow passengers.

Automobile taxes can be generally classified as acquisition taxes and holding taxes. At present, at least in Japan, automobile taxes become revenue for a special road account and are earmarked for use in the repair and expansion of roads. Roads exist for the purpose of being driven on by automobiles. Thus it has been thought that, according to the benefit principle, automobile taxes must be earmarked as a source of funding for roads.

What would happen, however, if the automobile tax were changed to a tax that was completely proportional to fuel efficiency? Since electric cars and fuel-cell vehicles do not emit CO_2 during operation, the acquisition and holding taxes would be zero, while other vehicles would be taxed in inverse proportion to the vehicle's fuel mileage (km/L) based on the 10–15 mode fuel efficiency test. As of March 2009 the most fuel-efficient car is the Toyota Prius at 35.5 km/L, whereas the Toyota Century's mileage, by contrast, is 7.8 km/L. If a fuel-efficiency-based tax model were adopted, the holding tax on the Century would be 4.6 times higher than that on the Prius. In March 2009 the holding tax on the Prius was ¥34,500 per year, while the tax on the Century was ¥88,000. However, from April 2009 the tax on cars designated as fuel-efficient vehicles was significantly reduced. One cannot help but think that selecting specific car models and only reducing taxes on those models is a very Japanese method of administration. I am not alone in thinking that a much better system would be to tie the tax rate to fuel efficiency, so that switching to a car that is even slightly more fuel efficient would bring at least some benefit.

Rejection of economic methods

There is a fair amount of opposition in Japan – primarily from the business community – to an environmental tax, emissions trading and other economic methods. They give the following points as their rationale for why economic measures are not desirable.

- An environmental tax or emissions trading would slow the growth rate of gross domestic product (GDP). That is because the adoption of such economic measures would not only increase the price of gasoline and electric power, but would also raise the price of other consumer goods to one degree or another, and as a result it would put pressure on households and reduce consumer spending.
- Even if you adopt an environmental tax that raises the prices of fossil fuels, gasoline and electricity, there is little price elasticity of demand for energy, so the impact in terms of reducing CO_2 emissions would be negligible. In other words, an environmental tax would have little impact on reducing the consumption of fossil fuels.
- The emissions trading scheme (quota system) is inefficient. The so-called grandfathering method allots emissions to each company based on their past record, so companies that have not made an effort to date to cut emissions (and therefore have a low marginal cost of reduction) are allotted a relatively high emissions level, while those that have already made an effort (and have a high marginal cost of reduction) are assigned a relatively low emissions allotment. As a result, the emissions trading system is inefficient and unfair.
- Companies work to reduce CO_2 emissions through voluntary efforts that reflect their own environmental ethics, so there is no need for the government to intervene.

Let us try to refute these negative arguments against economic measures.

If the government were to lock up environmental tax revenues in a safe and leave them, or if it used the funds to reduce the budget deficit, then the adoption of an environmental tax would certainly lead to a slowing of economic growth. In essence, the environmental tax would transfer a portion of household income to the government, so it is difficult to avoid a drop in real personal consumption. However, if the government uses the environmental tax revenues wisely, then the tax should have a neutral impact on economic growth. For example, according to the principle of revenue neutrality, if personal income tax were decreased by an amount that corresponded exactly to the carbon tax revenues, then disposable income (personal income minus income taxes) would increase. Since personal consumption is a function of disposable income, consumption would therefore rise as well. So will consumer spending rise or decrease if an environmental tax is introduced? My answer to that is, "You won't know unless you try." Nonetheless, the absolute value that would result from these offsetting effects would undoubtedly be small. There are also other methods that can be applied, such as preferential tax treatment for eco-goods, or the eco-points system that allots tax revenues to the original source. In other words, as long as the tax revenues are used properly, the macroeconomic impact of the environmental tax will be neutral.

However, if you look at the microeconomic impact, the story is not so simple. The environmental tax will separate companies into winners and losers. Automobile manufacturers which are taking the lead in developing eco-cars, electronics makers which are leading in the development of energy-efficient air conditioners and solar panel manufacturers are all clearly winners. On the other hand, industries that use large amounts of energy in their manufacturing processes will be losers. The government must develop measures to compensate for the losses of these industries. For example, one idea is to make the fossil fuels that are used as raw fuel by energy-intensive industries tax-exempt. Another idea is that when exporting items such as iron and steel, the environmental tax would be repaid at the border; when those same items are imported, a tax would be charged, again based on the carbon units reported.

Certainly, just because the price of gasoline rises as a result of an environmental tax, people will not immediately decrease the distances they drive to any measurable degree. In that sense, the price elasticity of demand for gasoline and electricity is low in the short term. However, there is a high probability that the next time people go to buy a new car or air conditioner, they will factor the rise in gas and electric prices into their decision and choose a fuel-efficient car or an energy-conserving air conditioner. Accordingly, the environmental tax is undoubtedly significant in reducing CO_2 emissions over the medium term (three to six years). In addition, if consumer demand rises for fuel-efficient vehicles and energy-efficient air conditioners, then manufacturers will work on developing technology in response to that demand. If we take into account the long-term (10-year) effects, it is certainly no exaggeration to say that an environmental tax will have a striking impact on cutting CO_2 emissions.

If you go entirely with the auction method (as opposed to the quota system) for emissions trading, then it becomes an efficient system. Under auction-based emissions trading, when companies produce CO_2 through their own manufacturing processes, they must buy emissions rights from the government that are equal to the actual amount of CO_2 emitted. The price of the emissions is determined through auction; companies that have opportunities to reduce their emissions at a marginal cost that is lower than the price set at auction can voluntarily make those cuts at their own expense and participate in the auction after they have exhausted these opportunities. Accordingly, once the total emissions limits are set in advance for an applicable group of companies, the environmental (carbon) tax rate for keeping the total emissions within that limit would be left to the auction market to decide. Assuming that companies are rational, then an environmental tax that is decided in this way would be efficient in the sense that it would achieve the objective with minimal cost.

Most of the emission reduction targets indicated by the industry groups under the Nippon Keidanren umbrella are calculated per unit of production (i.e. the CO_2 emissions entailed in producing one unit), and are therefore at odds with the Kyoto Protocol, which uses total emissions as the basis for reductions.

Mitigation and adaptation approaches to climate change

In the past, researchers focused solely on the mitigation of climate change (CO_2 reduction), but over the last few years attention to adapting to climate change has been increasing. This is due to the fact that in recent years we have experienced abnormal weather of a type previously unthinkable, and that weather has brought with it the more frequent occurrence of large-scale disasters (see a list of examples in Chapter 2-3).

Because it is clear that the devastation and famine that accompany abnormal weather generally have the largest impact on poor developing nations, it was decided in 2005, at COP11, to establish the international Adaptation Fund. A system has been created whereby 2 per cent of the certified emissions reduction (CER) carbon credits that industrialized nations acquire through the clean development mechanism are provided to the Adaptation Fund. The fund then exchanges the CERs for cash through the EU ETS, and the money is either transferred or loaned to developing countries as adaptation funds.

Strategies must be devised to adapt not only to the direct impact of climate change – e.g. rising temperatures, rising sea levels and storm and flood damage – but also to the damage related to its indirect impact – i.e. on the water cycle, food supply production, health and other areas.

6-1-3 What happened in 2007, the "year of climate change"?

An Inconvenient Truth *and the IPCC Fourth Assessment Report*

For climate change, 2007 was a year to remember. It marked the tenth anniversary of the adoption of the Kyoto Protocol, the twentieth anniversary of the publication of *Our Common Future* (the report of the UN Brundtland Commission, which used the term "sustainable development" as a keyword and sounded the alarm on global environmental issues – particularly on global warming) and the fifteenth anniversary of the UN Framework Convention on Climate Change (UNFCC) agreed at the UN Conference on Environment and Development.

January of that year saw large audiences turn out for a newly released film, *An Inconvenient Truth*, which featured then Vice-President Al Gore giving a speech with slides and reflecting on his own past. Under the Bush administration, America had rejected the Kyoto Protocol and it was assumed at the time that Americans were not interested in climate change. However, the tremendous reception that the Gore movie received even within America provided ample evidence that there was a large gap between the thinking of the American people and the stance of the Bush administration. In fact, when former president Bill Clinton attended COP11, held in 2005 in Montreal, Canada, at the invitation of the mayor of Montreal, he stated in his speech that global warming is already occurring, and that not only would measures to stop it not be harmful to the economy, but that the use of solar, wind and other renewable energy sources would actually create employment. He wrapped up his speech by stressing, "It is the Bush administration that is opposing to the Kyoto Protocol, not the American people." It is clear that President Obama's thinking on this issue is similar to that of Clinton.

From late January to late April 2007 the IPCC released its Fourth Assessment Report, which consists of reports from three working groups. The report indicated that it is very likely (over 90 per cent certainty) that there is a causal relationship between GHG and climate change. Thanks to the IPCC report, the number of people who, as mentioned earlier, denied the need for "early action" based on "inadequate scientific knowledge" quickly dwindled.

The Abe Initiative

On 24 May 2007, at a symposium on "The Future of Asia", then Prime Minister Shinzo Abe presented a keynote speech, "Invitation to Cool Earth 50", in which he proposed a long-term goal of cutting global GHG emissions by half by 2050. In order to reach that goal, he stressed the need for "developing innovative technologies" and "building a low-carbon society" based on those technologies. This was the first positive statement made by a Japanese prime minister in the 10 years since the Kyoto Protocol was adopted, and it had an impact at many levels. In addition, the prime minister proposed three basic principles for creating a concrete framework for addressing global warming beyond 2013.

- The framework must include the participation of all major emitters (the United States, China, India), and it must go beyond the Kyoto Protocol and aim at reducing global emissions.
- The framework must be flexible and diverse, taking into consideration the circumstances of each country.
- The framework must seek compatibility between environmental protection and economic growth by utilizing technology for energy conservation, etc.

Finally, Abe stressed the need to create a "funding mechanism" to support developing countries, and called for a national campaign to reduce GHG emissions with the motto of "one person, one day, one kilogram". Japan's per capita GHG emissions are 2 tonnes per year if you limit it to the categories of households and non-commercial vehicles. "One person, one day, one kilogram" implies "one person, one year, 365 kilograms", which would be a reduction of 82 per cent. This reduction target was quite ambitious at a time when the increase in household CO_2 emissions was becoming an issue.

Abe's call to cut global GHG emissions in half was based on the concept of balancing the amount of CO_2 absorbed by plants, oceans, etc. and the amount emitted by man-made activities in such a way that from 2050 on there would be a gradual reduction in the atmospheric GHG concentration.

Is it possible to cut global GHG emissions in half by 2050?

Is it at all possible to achieve the target of "cutting global emissions in half by 2050"? The current jump in the price of oil has also brought a jump in the prices of such petroleum products as gasoline and diesel, which are the necessary fuels to run internal-combustion engines. This should prompt a move away from the internal-combustion engine for automobiles, airplanes and ships. Automobiles will probably run on electricity, planes on fuel cells, non-seagoing ships and fishing ships on electricity and seagoing ships on fuel cells, solar electricity and sails that have IT controls attached. Whether one likes it or not, the inevitable steep rise in oil prices will dramatically reduce CO_2 emissions in the transport sector.

According to the documentation for Mitsubishi Motor's first electric car, the i-MiEV, there is something to be seen in terms of the impact on reducing CO_2 emissions. The key points of the documentation are as follows: it recharges in seven hours (200 V) and can be driven for 160 km; maximum speed is 130 km per hour; and it can go 10 km on 1 kWh. Although it depends on the configuration of the electrical source, in Japan's case the CO_2 emitted by the source of electricity to produce 1 kWh is roughly 450 g. When one litre of gasoline is burned, it produces 2,300 g of CO_2. For a 10 km/L gasoline-engine automobile to drive 10 km, the cost of fuel is ¥120/L (as of August 2009). On the other hand, in the case of an electric car, overnight charging costs ¥7/kWh, so the fuel for an electric car is extraordinarily much cheaper and can cut CO_2 emissions by 80 per cent. The problem with electric cars at present is that the ¥200,000/kWh price of lithium-ion batteries is much too high (for example, if the battery capacity is 16 kWh like that of the i-MiEV, the battery price would be ¥3,200,000), and this is preventing the wider acceptance of electric cars. Decreasing the time needed to recharge the vehicle would also help in popularizing the cars.

If we completely eliminate the emissions from coal-fired thermal power plants by using what is often pointed to as a prime example of advanced technology, namely CCS (carbon capture and storage), we could reduce global emissions by 30 per cent. There are three issues with CCS. First, there is no guarantee that the aquifers in which to sequester CO_2 necessarily exist near thermal power stations. Also, even if there is an aquifer in close proximity, in a place as crowded as Japan the span between the power station and the aquifer will be packed with houses and buildings, so it would inevitably require a detour. Second, to separate and capture the CO_2 from the smoke and sequester that in the ground would require a fair amount of energy. The normal conversion efficiency of a coal-fired thermal power plant is more than 40 per cent. If, for example, you use half the power generated for CCS, the conversion efficiency falls to about 20 per cent, and the rationale for even having a coal-fired thermal power plant would be called into question. Third, in an earthquake-prone country like Japan, the possibility that an earthquake could cause the sequestered CO_2 to be released into the atmosphere is high.

It is estimated that by spreading Japanese manufacturers' energy-conserving technologies worldwide, we could cut emissions by 20 per cent. Looking only at Japan, because the country's population in 2050 will have shrunk to 95 million (by moderate estimates), just by sustaining the current per capita emissions rate, a roughly 25 per cent decrease in emissions is possible.

At the end of 2007 Al Gore and the IPCC were jointly awarded the Nobel Peace Prize. The fact that they popularized the term "climate security" was perhaps the basis for the granting of this award.

6-1-4 Developments from 2008 to early 2009

A lengthening of the time horizon

The publication of the 2007 IPCC assessment report may have been an original motivation, but the announcement of the Abe Initiative, stating the need to "cut current levels of global GHG emissions by half by 2050", was in reality the impetus for rephrasing climate change mitigation as "building a low-carbon society" and adopting a longer time horizon. For that purpose, a roadmap for a technological revolution by 2050 was drawn up. Since it was determined that a 60–80 per cent reduction would be needed from industrialized nations in order to halve total global emissions, on 24 July 2008 the administration of Yasuo Fukuda passed a cabinet resolution to cut Japan's GHG emissions by 60–80 per cent from the 2005 levels. In any case, the shift to a longer time horizon in the debate over how to mitigate climate change really became conspicuous from the start of 2008.

By taking a longer-term perspective, the development of revolutionary technologies to produce groundbreaking cuts in CO_2 emissions can be factored into the calculations. We can also anticipate that there will be major progress made towards restructuring the socio-economic system. Through the construction of an international funding mechanism, developing countries that have significant marginal reduction costs can take advantage of relatively inexpensive opportunities to reduce their emissions, and thus total global emissions can be greatly reduced.

Let us say a few words about the specific ideas for the funding mechanism. There are two possibilities. The first commitment period of the Kyoto Protocol ends in 2012. An agreement is expected to be reached at COP15, to be held in December 2009 in Copenhagen, on a post-2012 international framework, but the gap between the views of industrialized nations and emerging nations (particularly China and India) remains vast. Shielding themselves behind the "common but differentiated responsibilities" aphorism included in the UNFCCC, emerging nations are stubbornly refusing to accept obligations under the post-2012 protocol.

My personal view of the participation of emerging nations is as follows. We should conduct a business-as-usual estimate of those nations' GHG emissions. We should then obligate emerging nations to cut their emissions by a certain percentage based on that estimate. Figuratively speaking, we would have the emerging nations wear a relatively loose cap. By taking on this type of commitment, for example, Japanese investment in China would become joint initiatives and the two countries would decide through bilateral negotiations how much emissions volume China would transfer to Japan as compensation for the investment. If, for argument's sake, China did not make that commitment, Japanese investment in China would have to be handled under the clean development mechanism (CDM), and getting the approval of the CDM board requires a great deal of time and money. By taking on this commitment, then, emerging countries could attract large-scale investment and technology transfers from developed nations. The fact that investments from advanced nations could be received in the form of joint initiatives should work as an incentive for emerging nations to make a commitment.

If emerging nations do not agree to participate in the new protocol, it would force industrialized nations to take on reduction commitments that could not possibly be achieved through domestic measures alone. At the same time, the approval criteria for the CDM are loosened. It would be best to create a mechanism in this way to provide funding from advanced countries to emerging and developing nations.

Green New Deal

Looking ahead to 2050, the biggest issue is how the structure of the power supply should be changed. Power sources that do not produce CO_2 emissions include nuclear power, thermal power with CCS and renewable energy generation. President Obama is extremely enthusiastic about the use of renewable energy (solar, wind, biomass, geothermal, etc.). He has called for \$150 billion in investment over the next 10 years to cut CO_2 emissions and rebuild the US economy by increasing the relative proportion of renewable energy in the power supply. Through the spread of renewable energy, it is estimated that 5 million jobs ("green-collar workers") will be created.

In his January 2009 inaugural speech Obama warned that "the ways we use energy strengthen our adversaries and threaten our planet" and stated, "We will harness the sun and the winds and the soil to fuel our cars and run our factories." On 24 January 2009, in his weekly online address, President Obama said:

> To accelerate the creation of a clean energy economy, we will double our capacity to generate alternative sources of energy like wind, solar, and biofuels over the next three years. We'll begin to build a new electricity grid that lays down more than 3,000 miles of transmission lines to convey this new energy from coast to coast. We'll save taxpayers \$2 billion a year by making 75 per cent of federal buildings more energy efficient, and save the average working family \$350 on their energy bills by weatherizing 2.5 million homes.

In Germany, solar and wind-generated power is rapidly expanding at the output base thanks to the introduction of a "feed-in tariff" (a fixed-price transaction) system. At present, 46 countries and prefectures/counties have introduced feed-in tariffs. In Japan as well, a Japanese-style feed-in tariff is to be introduced from next fiscal year. However, the adjective "Japanese-style" indicates a number of differences: in contrast to Germany setting the purchase price for renewable energy at three times the market price, it is only double in Japan; while Germany buys all generated power, Japan buys only the excess power that is left over by a household; and whereas Germany covers all renewable energy, Japan limits it to solar power – and only solar power generated by households.

6-1-5 Conclusion

This chapter has focused on the direction in which the vector of change surrounding the climate change debate has headed over the past three years, and has closely examined the feasibility of achieving the objective of "halving global emissions by 2050". The development of revolutionary technologies, the restructuring of the socio-economic system and initiatives to involve the emerging nations in the process – these are the three keys to success. A change in conditions in the form of a rapid jump in crude-oil prices would contribute greatly to reaching the target. It has become hackneyed to talk about the "coexistence of the environment and the economy", and the idea that environmental protection inhibits economic growth and, conversely, reckless economic growth pollutes and destroys the environment. Today, the situation has changed. Measures for building a low-carbon society, or in other words measures for reaching the above objective, will provide a springboard for future economic growth.

6-2

A Green New Deal as an integration of policies towards sustainable society

Kazuo Matsushita

6-2-1 Introduction

The world is now facing a financial crisis, starting with the bankruptcy of Lehman Brothers investment bank in the United States in 2008 and the economic crisis which followed. In the meantime, there is no sign of any halt in the progressive worsening of the global environment, the most representative issue being climate change, a serious threat to the future sustainability of the human race. The gap between the financial economy, which moves the world temporarily in search of short-term profits, and the actual economy, which is constrained by the natural capital that is the environment, has produced a threefold crisis in the environment, economy and energy. According to this mode of thinking, the present global financial crisis clearly reveals the necessity to construct a sustainable economy within the constraints of the global environment. This crisis has provided an opportunity which cannot be missed.

As made evident in the 2007 Fourth Assessment Report of the IPCC (Intergovernmental Panel on Climate Change), global climate change is progressing at increasing speed. If global greenhouse gas emissions are not at least halved compared to 1990 levels by 2050, serious damage to the social economy is predicted (IPCC, 2007).

Our present society, both global and local, is calling for a transition to an economic system that is sustainable, in which the ecosystem can be maintained and which is socially fair. This type of economic system is called a "sustainable low-carbon society" for the purposes of this chapter.

A transition to a sustainable low-carbon society implies a conversion from the present fossil-fuel-centred energy system and technologies of production and consumption. Mere conservation and efficiency must be exceeded to achieve more humanly rich production and lifestyles. To support and promote these, there must be a creative process which carves out technologies and social systems through continuous innovation. What is called for is a combination of consistent financial spending, wise government that can promote structural reform and industrial spirit that can recognize environmental constraints, make challenges aimed at high environmental targets and develop innovations towards a low-carbon society.

Facing both the financial economic crisis and the environmental crisis, the New Deal implemented by US President Roosevelt during the Great Depression has been recalled, and countries have begun advocating a "Green New Deal" which makes selective investments in the areas of environment and energy aimed at stimulating the economy and creating new employment. Within the global call for a transition to a low-carbon society, an opportunity has arisen. The issues are what the Green New Deal will aim for, what system of policy is required to attain its fundamental intentions and in what manner can these be made into reality.

The Japanese economy, which is highly dependent on exports, has taken a particularly hard hit from the global recession originating in the United States. Faced with such difficulties, Japan must focus not only on temporary economic stimulation policy, but also look towards the future to induce economic structures to be lower carbon. It must achieve a drastic reduction in greenhouse gases while maintaining the level of economic welfare. In order to do so, environmental policy and economic policy cannot be pursued as separate; rather, the development of a package of consistent environmental and economic policies is required, which integrates both to form a sustainable society.

Based on awareness of these issues, this chapter will deliberate the contents of efforts around the world based on Green New Deal policy, in particular focused on the environmental and energy policy of US President Obama. Based on this deliberation, the present state of efforts and issues faced in Japan will be discussed.

6-2-2 The nature of the Green New Deal

So, what is a "Green New Deal"? The first to propose one was the UK-based Green New Deal Group (2008). Its report proposed an experiment to rebuild the world economy through mainly large-scale investments in clean energy in order to address the three issues of the financial crisis, global warming and the energy crisis. Based on this report, currently debated Green New Deals are generally thought of as economic policies addressing the world financial crisis that not only contain employment and industrial measures based on large-scale public investment in environment and energy-related areas, but are policy packages aimed at integrating solutions to global warming and the energy crisis.

At COP14 (fourteenth Conference of the Parties to the UN Framework Convention on Climate Change) held in December 2008, UN Secretary-General Ban Ki-moon called for a "global Green New Deal", stating in his address:

> we face two crises: climate change and the global economy. But these crises present us with a great opportunity – an opportunity to address both crises simultaneously ... An investment that fights climate change, creates millions of green jobs and spurs green growth ...[1]

The UN Environment Programme (UNEP, 2009) proposed the Green Economy Initiative to create employment strategically through green investment (investment in renewable energies, clean and efficient technologies, sustainable cities, etc.) of 1 per cent of global GDP (US$750 billion). US President Obama pledged that his administration would make large-scale investments in clean energy, proposing a "Green New Deal" policy to create new green jobs.

EU countries are also attempting to expand environmental investments in stimulation of the economy and employment measures. Germany already has over 250,000 people employed in the renewable energy sector (a 55 per cent increase from 2004), a figure which is expected to rise to exceed employment in automobile-related industries (approximately 900,000 persons) by 2020. The United Kingdom plans to construct 7,000 wind power facilities and increase employment by 160,000 persons by 2020 via an investment of £100 billion. France has placed creation of employment in the environmental field in its law, and plans to create employment for 500,000 persons in the future. The European Union decided in November 2008 to spend €30 billion to support renewable energies and green cars for the next generation. Further, in a cohesion policy announced in March 2009, spending of €105 billion in green economics and €48 billion in climate change policy was agreed.

In Asia as well, Korean President Lee Myung-bak has brought forward a Green New Deal as one of four key policies, investing approximately 50 trillion won (¥3.35 trillion) over four years in solar and battery technologies and creating 960,000 jobs in an effort to overcome the economic crisis. In China there are plans for public investment over the next two years of 4 trillion yuan (¥60 trillion) in measures linking railways, electricity grids, environment, housing construction and employment in an attempt to address the crisis. Of this budget, 350 billion yuan (¥5.3 trillion) is headed for environment and energy conservation fields.

In Japan the Cabinet Office and Ministry of Economy, Trade and Industry (2009) have taken a central role, announcing on 17 April 2009 the Strategy to Reclaim the Future, in which national funds of ¥1.6 trillion for a low-carbon revolution and ¥2.2 trillion total project funds are appropriated. Moreover, Minister of Environment Tetsuo Saito has announced a plan of his own, entitled "Green Economics and Societal Revolution" (Ministry of Environment, 2009).

Regarding the relationship between the economy and global warming, the most representative of climate change issues, *The Economics of Climate Change* (Stern, 2006) published by the UK government in October 2006 is a well-known work. This review of climate change and the economy was entrusted to former senior vice-president and chief economist of the World Bank, Lord Nicholas Stern, by then Prime Minister Blair and Chancellor of the Exchequer Brown. The review states that if the present state of affairs remains as is, global warming will progress, causing a loss of 20 per cent of global GDP and creating 200 million refugees. It predicts economic damages on the scale of the First and Second World Wars, and a direct effect on the foundations of life, such as drinking water, food, health and environment. On the other hand, if calculated measures using about 1 per cent of GDP are put towards finding early solutions, effectiveness can be increased, making the cost of measures drastically less than the cost of not taking any measures. The report particularly stresses the extreme importance of the types of investments, infrastructure and systems to be created over the next 10–20 years: a system of active policy guidance is necessary, calculating backwards from climate stabilization targets through the pricing of CO_2.

The Stern Review asserts that "the benefits of doing more clearly outweigh the costs. Delay would entail more climate change and eventually higher costs of tackling the problem" (ibid.: 306). The Green New Deal is significant in the fact that it would create green industry and jobs for the future through investment in environmental measures, and reveal the path to a future "sustainable low-carbon society". Incidentally, the necessary cost of measures to address global warming stated in the Stern Review (about 1 per cent of GDP) is in agreement with the amount of green investment (also 1 per cent of global GDP) proposed in UNEP's Green Economy Initiative.

6-2-3 Environmental policy integration aimed at a sustainable society

Green New Deal policy, which has been gaining attention of late, integrates environmental policy, energy policy, economy policy and so on, namely "policy integration". Policy integration involves deliberate unification of differing policy goals and methods from the early stages of policy development. It removes inconsistencies between policies, creates common mutual benefits and is expected to bring about mutual strengthening effects (Collier, 1995).

Environmental policy integration (EPI) involves integrating environmental targets and concerns into the policy-making and planning process of other policy areas (e.g. energy, transportation, agriculture, etc.), and is key to the realization of sustainable development. Comparatively, traditional environmental policy has treated environmental issues as independent, and has been prone to consist of end-of-pipe treatments after problems have already arisen.

The European Environment Agency (2005: 13) defines EPI in practice to be:

> a continual process to ensure environmental issues are taken into account in all policy phases, from the very beginning of the policy process. Importantly, EPI needs to lead to overall improvements in policy, policy implementation and policy outcomes. Environment will not necessarily come out on top in every policy that is adopted and implemented, but the overall trend should certainly be in the direction of sustainable development.

This chapter will examine the Green New Deal from the EPI perspective described above. The Green New Deal has two aspects. It is a short-term economic stimulation policy, and at the same time a long-term structural reform policy aimed at a low-carbon society. The appropriate combination of both is an issue.

6-2-4 President Obama's environment and energy policy

President Obama did not specifically use the words "Green New Deal" in public commitments during his election. However, an administration pledge released during the presidential race, called "New Energy for America" (Obama and Biden, 2008), strongly reflects the ideals of the Green New Deal concept in the nurturing of new green employment and industrial growth through strategic large-scale investments in the environment.

The content of the pledge is strategic investment of US$150 billion over the coming 10 years in clean energy and other fields to create jobs for 5 million people. Automobile fuel-efficiency standards are to be lowered by 4 per cent every year, while 1 million plug-in hybrid cars are to be running at 150 miles/gallon by 2015. The proportion of electricity from renewable energy sources is to be raised to 10 per cent by 2012 and 25 per cent by 2025. Through doing so, the level of dependence on oil from the Middle East and Central and South America is to be lessened, aiming to strengthen energy security.

The pledge also calls for housing insulation improvement assistance for low-income groups (insulation improvement for 1 million households every year over 10 years), and the building of a "smart" electric power grid that collects electricity generated by small-scale and distributed sources using renewable energy.

Climate change policy includes targets to reduce US greenhouse gas emissions to 1990 levels by 2020, and to 80 per cent below 1990 levels by 2050. Introduction of a cap-and-trade (total emission controls and trading) method of trading emissions is proposed which would implement distribution of emissions credits based 100 per cent on auctions. By so doing, the government would gain a revenue source through distribution of emissions credits. The revenue source of Obama's version of the Green New Deal would be a portion of the income from distribution by auction of emissions credits collected from greenhouse-gas-emitting industries. This implies that income earned by the government through selling CO_2 emissions credits would be invested in expansion of renewable energies, etc.

The Obama administration's aims

One outstanding characteristic of the Obama administration's energy and environment policy is that it is a consistent public policy system (package) which strives for closely connected integration of employment measures, promising new industry development measures and community development measures. Several implications can be interpreted from this policy system.

First, the fact that the Obama administration will take the lead in tackling the global concern of climate change is an attempt to restore US leadership in world society and strengthen the competitiveness of the US economy. In an Obama presidential administration public pledge, it was declared that the United States would again participate actively in negotiations under the umbrella of the UN Framework Convention on Climate Change and become a leader in climate change countermeasures. Furthermore, on 26 January 2009, immediately following inauguration,

President Obama signed a presidential order, which had been vetoed by former president Bush, to strengthen automobile exhaust regulations. This action was interpreted as a display of the new president's determination regarding environmental measures. Likewise, through strategic investment in the shift to a low-carbon society, the administration aims to strengthen US industry, increase employment, start up new industry and regenerate the US economy.

Secondly, the policy implies that the administration takes climate change science seriously, as represented in IPCC reports. This stance can also be inferred in the setting of an 80 per cent greenhouse gas emissions reduction target by 2050, based on the demands of scientific information. Further, a presidential assistant post in charge of climate change and energy policy was newly established in the presidential support staff, to which former administrator of the Environmental Protection Agency Carol Browner was appointed. Nobel Prize winner in physics Steven Chu, who is devoted to the development of alternative energy, was appointed as secretary of energy, creating a powerful line-up called the "dream team" by those in the environment field.

Thirdly, the policy system indicates the stance on further structural reforms in energy and environmental policy while boldly cutting into vested interests and ensuring social equity and economic efficiency. As stated previously, New Deal policy is generally understood to be the deployment of public projects accompanied by input of large-scale fiscal resources. However, President Obama's proposal for a domestic emissions trading system does not distribute emission credits to vested interests based on past emissions records, but bases distribution 100 per cent on auctions, calling for cost burdens that depend on CO_2 emissions. A portion of income earned from this distribution is to be the revenue source of the Green New Deal, and will also be shared with low-income groups.

Fourthly, the policy offers an educational training programme for young former soldiers and high-school dropouts, allowing them to participate in the new renewable energy economy. Through their participation, the policy attempts to promote weatherization of housing in low-income communities. Currently in the United States there are 800,000 young former military personnel who have returned from Iraq and Afghanistan; it is expected that an early withdrawal from Iraq will further increase this number. Additionally, many young people have missed opportunities for career training through dropping out of high school or delinquency, which is becoming a societal problem. First they can be involved in improving insulation and energy conservation in low-income housing, and stepping up from there can participate in concrete programmes prepared around the country to get them involved in the high-level renewable energy economy. This is an example of comprehensive and concrete policy integration which aims to accomplish simultaneously unemployment measures and career training, development of new industry, revitalizing communities, etc.

Of course, implementation of these policies will be considerably swayed by the present extremely harsh economic and fiscal state of affairs. Further, difficult coordination with the industrial world and Congress awaits. In particular, strong opposition is predicted from energy and automobile sectors that will actually be affected economically by the auction emissions trading system, which would make industries buy emission credits at a cost according to CO_2 emission levels. There are fears that within the legislation process this policy will face rough going in deliberation in Congress. The merits of the Obama administration, which started off with popularity and strong powers of persuasion among the people, will be tested.

Reasons behind the potential for a US policy shift

Accompanying the change in presidents in the United States, policy related to climate change is thought to be undergoing a great change. There are reasons for this.

The United States holds a presidential election once every four years, and various types and kinds of think-tanks compete to present a regime's concepts. Immediately following the start of the second term of the Bush administration (2005), the Democratic Party started up a think-tank named the Center for American Progress (CAP) for the purpose of rebuilding the party, with John Podesta, the last chief of staff of the Clinton administration, at its centre. A sizeable portion of this think-tank's "Green Recovery" (Center for American Progress, 2008) concept was adopted by President Obama. Podesta acted as co-chair of the Obama administration's transition team, and many members of CAP were involved in the new administration. In this manner, carefully prepared and consistent policy was formed, with the presidential election as just one event.

Moreover, due to the presidential system, it is actually easier for government to maintain consistency. In Japan there is often opposition evident between the Ministry of Economy, Trade and Industry and the Ministry of Environment surrounding energy and climate policy. However, as previously stated, the new US administration established a presidential assistant post in charge of climate change and energy policy and is trying to guarantee integration of climate protection and energy policy through maintenance of government structure. Further, appointing Steven Chu as secretary of energy lays out a set-up in which the entire Department of Energy will be dedicated to development of new energies.

6-2-5 Trends in Germany

Germany has been strategically investing in the environment field based on "ecological modernization theory" since the early 1990s. It has adopted policy aimed at technology innovation, economic growth and creation of jobs. Accordingly, the present-day Green New Deal concept can be seen as a continuation of this policy.

Based on these ideas, Germany was the first in the world to adopt a renewable energy feed-in tariff system (FiT), which led to an explosion in adoption of wind and solar power. The origin of the system was a power supply law enacted in 1991 which required power companies to purchase electricity generated from wind power facilities (electricity purchase compensation system), leading to the massive spread of wind power generation. In 2000 the Renewable Energy Law was enacted (revised in 2004), continuing the requirement for purchase by electrical utilities and setting compensation at a fixed rate for a 20-year period (adoption of a genuine FiT system).

In 1998, the start of the coalition government of the Social Democratic Party and the Green Party (the red-green coalition) led to the adoption of ecological tax reform based on coalition pledges.[2] Further, in April 2002 the National Strategy for Sustainable Development was adopted, which acts as a compass for environmental policy integration. In 2002 the authority for renewable energy was transferred from the Ministry of Economics to the Ministry for the Environment, further clarifying that the environment ministry was responsible for climate change policy.

In the present grand coalition government of the Christian Democratic Union and the Social Democratic Party (formed in November 2005), Chancellor Merkel's support for climate change policy and sustainable development is clear. Germany has shouldered the burden of taking leadership in climate change policy in the European Union, setting greenhouse gas reduction targets based on 1990 levels at 60 per cent by 2050 and 40 per cent by 2020.

6-2-6 Trends in the United Kingdom

As stated previously, in the era of Prime Minister Blair and Chancellor of the Exchequer Brown, the United Kingdom requested Nicholas Stern to conduct a review of "the economics of climate change". This review revealed that economic damages will become immense if appropriate measures to address climate change are not implemented at an early stage (Stern, 2006).

As a country, the United Kingdom has set targets to reduce greenhouse gas emissions by over 80 per cent by 2050 and CO_2 emissions by 26 per cent by 2020. A long-term reduction plan has been specified, and the Climate Change Act and Energy Act were passed (November 2008) to secure these targets, which are legally binding and specified in the Climate Change Act. Further, based on the Climate Change Act, a carbon budget (carbon reduction plan) for the first three five-year periods (15 years) was released in April 2009, setting reduction targets for greenhouse gases to at least 34 per cent compared to 1990 levels in the period up to 2022. These numerical targets are expected to be raised further if an agreement is reached on a post-2013 global framework at COP15 to be held in December 2009.

In October 2008 the Department of Energy and Climate Change was newly established, with Edward Miliband chosen as its first secretary of state.

Meanwhile, the Confederation of British Industry (CBI, comparable to the Japan Business Federation) released its "Climate Change Report" in November 2007 (Confederation of British Industry, 2007). In this report, the CBI indicated its opinion that the UK's 2050 target is achievable if efforts are made at an early stage, and that such efforts aimed at a low-carbon society provide business opportunities to the industrial world.

6-2-7 Collapse of Japan's environmental-advanced-nation illusion

What follows is an overview of Japan's current state of affairs. When discussing Japan's international contributions to global environmental problems, epithets such as "environmentally advanced nation", "energy conservation superpower" and "Japanese environmental technology reigns in the world" have been used. However, there is doubt that Japan can really be called an environmentally advanced nation.

According to the World Bank (2007), which evaluated the global warming measures of world countries, Japan's countermeasures came in at 62 out of 70 countries, the lowest rank of all developed nations and a shocking result.[3] This research analysed CO_2 emissions for the 10 years between 1994 and 2004, and related factors. According to the report, even though growth of Japan's economy and population was low, growth in CO_2 emissions was high. Background factors included an increase in thermal power from coal, one of the most CO_2-emitting fossil fuels, the extremely late introduction of renewable energies and the fact that emissions from offices and homes increased considerably, reflecting changes in information technology and lifestyles. This evidence reflects Japan's half-hearted global warming policy of late.

Furthermore, Japan has fallen behind in the area of renewable energy diffusion. For example, for many years Japan was number one in the world for cumulative quantity and yearly installation numbers of solar power generators. For simple yearly installation quantity, Japan was surpassed by Germany in 2004, and by 2007 had fallen to one-fifth the numbers of Germany and half of Spain. Japanese statistics for cumulative quantity were surpassed by Germany in 2005 (3.86 million kW), and ranked second (1.92 million kW). In manufacturing quantity, Japan accounted for 50 per cent of world production in 2004, but current share trails the European Union (29 per cent) at 24.6 per cent, followed by China at 22 per cent, Taiwan at 10 per cent and the United States at 7.1 per cent.

In the field of wind power generation, at the end of 2006 the global total facility capacity was approximately 74 GW (74.22 million kW), an increase of 25 per cent from 2005. Country statistics show Germany (20 GW) accounting for approximately 28 per cent of the total, followed by Spain (12 GW), the United States (11 GW) and India (6 GW). It is estimated that totals will double the 2006 statistics in 2010, with new introductions of 150–160 GW (World Wind Energy Association, 2009). The total number of Japanese domestic wind power generators (with output of 10 kW or above) stood at approximately 1,400 as of March 2007, with total facility capacity limited to 1.68 million kW. Further, compared to the previous year, introduction fell by half in 2007.

In the background, the fact that Germany, Spain and other countries have adopted fixed-rate purchase systems (such as the feed-in tariff), which ensure that electric utilities will purchase renewable energy at a favourable price over a long term, has strongly supported the above statistics. At the national level, Germany first adopted the FiT system in 1990, with the selling price of energy legally set, guaranteeing the purchasing price for operators of alternative energy sources over a fixed term (20 years, etc.). This price is periodically re-evaluated according to changes in diffusion volume and production costs, and deliberately successively decreased. However, re-evaluation does not influence the portion of renewable energy already adopted, thus the low investment risk for operators is assured.

In Japan, the Act on Special Measures concerning New Energy Use by Electric Utilities (RPS Act) has been adopted. RPS stands for Renewables Portfolio Standard, the law being a system for requiring electric companies to adopt renewable energy at a fixed ratio. However, the required (target) amount is set extremely low, at 1.35 per cent of total electricity volume by 2010 and 1.63 per cent by 2014, a factor which hinders introduction. This method has had some effect at the early stages of introduction; however, according to actual results in different countries to date, various demerits have been pointed out, including the high risk to power generating enterprises and low effectiveness in reduction of actual power generation costs.

These problems have been pointed out for a long time. On 24 February 2009 the Ministry of Economy, Trade and Industry revealed a system of purchasing surplus solar power, finally taking the first step in an actual fixed-rate system. According to this system, it is estimated that the recovery period for initial investment costs in solar power generation facilities will be reduced to 10-plus years from the 20-plus years of the past. However, this system is limited to support for solar power (moreover, to household surplus power only), and is not applicable to industrial-use solar power, wind power, biomass, geothermal or other renewable sources of energy. Further, many non-economic-related barriers remain, such as system-related issues. For the popularization of renewable energies, not only technological development and investment in facilities but also system reform for promotion of diffusion are important. In any case, from the standpoint of forming a future low-carbon society, open dialogue between the entirety of government and the people is required.

Japan's lagging progress towards a low-carbon society

Japan's climate change measures have until now focused on voluntary actions of businesses and public appeals, without any fundamental change in policy. For many years Japan has postponed adoption of environmental tax or emissions trading systems, which would provide incentives for continued reduction of greenhouse gases and technological development. However, in the preparations for the G8 summit in Toyako in 2008 an indication was shown that policy would be changed, given in a speech by then Prime Minister Fukuda entitled "Vision for Global Warming Measures" (Fukuda, 2008) and the subsequent Action Plan for a Low-carbon Society (Ministry of Environment, 2008). Called the Fukuda Vision, the speech was the first time Japan clearly stated its long-term targets to reduce CO_2 by 60–80 per cent compared to current conditions by 2050. Compared to previous government policy, this statement was a clear step forward.

The Action Plan for a Low-carbon Society sets forth a concrete path towards the shift to a low-carbon society for Japan, and was passed at a cabinet meeting. It clearly presents measures on:

- innovative technological development and diffusion of existing technology (substantial expansion of adoption of solar power generation, etc.)

- a device for moving the entire country towards a low-carbon society (economic methods such as emissions trading)
- support for citizen activities in localities (such as low-carbon model cities, community-building, campaigns to change business styles and lifestyles, etc.).

However, many issues remain, including the fact that the preparation process for this action plan was not transparent and mid-term emissions reduction targets are not indicated. Furthermore, concrete steps and creation of social mechanisms for building a low-carbon society are not specified, and too much focus is put on individual technologies and measures.

Based on this action plan, "trial implementation of emissions trading in the domestic integrated market" began in October 2008. However, many problems have been found in the domestic integrated market trial currently being implemented. In particular, regulation of total emissions (emissions caps) is not set, targets are a mix of basic units and total amounts, and participation by businesses is voluntary. Thus there is fear that formation of a fair price is difficult. In any case, this mechanism as it stands will in no way be accepted by the international carbon market.

At present, the emissions trading system that originated in the European Union is expanding as links are made with similar systems around the world, with movements towards policy shifts in Australia and the United States. Considering these circumstances, if Japan does not quickly accumulate some experience in new economic rules for the switch to a low-carbon society, in which emissions trading is central, it will be left behind in rule-making in the global economy. Japan is now the only major developed nation to not have a plan for introducing an emissions trading system with legal binding power and regulations on total emissions. At the current pace of trial implementation, full-scale adoption will not come for several years (likely after 2012). This is much too late.

Further, environmental tax reform was postponed in 2009. Environmental tax can be fairly imposed on a wide range of areas and businesses, and is a mechanism which induces emission-curbing behaviour in line with economic rationality by all kinds of bodies. In particular, it can be applied to sectors and individuals with small emission amounts, making it an extremely suitable method for gradually changing the daily lifestyles of citizens.

In addition to environmental tax, thorough review from the standpoint of sustainability of the nation's entire tax system (which dictates the shape of the nation) is an extremely important issue. Beginning with shifting the tax revenues earmarked for roads to general revenue, greening the whole tax system is central to this. However, in the government's budget proposal for fiscal year 2009, despite being the largest-scale budget in history, the shift of tax revenues from roads to general revenue and environmental tax reform were both postponed. Subsidies were provided for localities, of which 80 per cent are used for roads.

6-2-8 Japan's Green New Deal

On 17 April 2009 a Japanese version of a Green New Deal was proposed, mainly compiled by the Cabinet Office and Ministry of Economy, Trade and Industry. It included a clause on a "low-carbon revolution" with a national expenditure of ¥1.6 trillion, and ¥2.2 trillion in total project funds (of these, a considerable portion was budgeted in the second revised budget for fiscal year 2009). An outline of this plan is as follows.

- *Solar power generation and plan to lead the world in energy conservation:* raise the ratio of renewable energy in energy consumption to 20 per cent by 2020 (10 per cent in 2005); increase solar power generation by 20 times its current state by 2020; system of purchasing surplus electric power from solar power generation; energy conservation analysis and repair of public buildings (54,000 locations); and promotion of repurchasing of green home electronics (eco-points system).
- *World's fastest popularization of eco-cars:* promotion of repurchasing eco-cars and using them for public vehicles.
- *Low-carbon transport and urban revolution:* superconducting magnetically levitated vehicles, highway transportation system and environmental model cities.
- *Natural resources superpower realization plan:* product recycling system for rare metals, etc. (urban mine development).

Evaluating Japan's New Deal

It is important to consider how Japan's version of a Green New Deal, outlined in the "Strategy to Reclaim the Future" (Cabinet Office and Ministry of Economy, Trade and Industry, 2009), can be evaluated. Promotion of repurchasing of eco-cars, energy-conserving home electronics (refrigerators, televisions, air conditioners) and energy-conserving homes (and the solar power generators housed in them) will certainly bring about a short-term effect to stimulate the economy and provide relief to related industries worried about depressed market demand. However, as a whole, the plan is a limited menu of miscellaneous environmental measures that form part of a short-term economic stimulation policy. It cannot be seen as a clear vision for working towards a low-carbon society of the future. Further, it is extremely deficient from the standpoint of policy and system reform. In fact, it does not apply a long-term perspective to combine or coordinate the tax system, finance or incentive systems to bring about a low-carbon-economy-based society.

For example, the eco-points system to promote the repurchase of energy-conserving home electronics awards more eco-points the larger (higher ranking) the electronic device. In other words, the system dictates that the greater the CO_2 emissions, the greater the purchasing subsidy paid by the government. Normally, it is preferable to add to the price in some manner in relation to the amount of environmental burden, regardless of the type of product. Further, inconsistent policy that conflicts with the formation of a low-carbon society has also been adopted, such as drastic reductions in highway charges.

As there is a limit to the financial resources of government, and taking into consideration the present financial deficit situation, it is essential that these limited resources are used effectively. Social systems must be changed to promote a structural shift to a sustainable economy from a mid- to a long-term perspective. For this reason, a system which is not overly dependent on inducement by government subsidies is ideal. Towards this goal, ecological tax reform is necessary. A shift from a "goods" tax, which levies social insurance fees and tax based on the fruits of labour, to a "bads" tax, which levies tax based on environmental load, such as CO_2 and waste, is required. Further, Japan must give consideration to a low-carbon economy shift and securing revenue sources through reforms to the social system itself. Methods include immediate adoption of a fixed-rate purchasing system for renewable energy (FiT) and domestic emissions trading.

6-2-9 Required: A policy package and policy assessment index

The Green New Deal proposes that through strategic investment in the environment, new green employment and industrial growth can be nurtured, and energy security and community development can be endeavoured. The Green New Deal is the construction of a public policy system (policy package) that consistently promotes these goals. It is through implementation of such policy and projects that a sustainable economy, both environmentally and socially, is forecast. Package content builds the foundations of sustainability through public investment and policy to nurture new green industry, which is highly effective in employment and contributes to CO_2 reduction. One presupposition is the promotion of a low-carbon society shift via the pricing of CO_2. Further, there are several issues that require immediate efforts, including public transportation equipment, insulation and earthquake-proofing of buildings, expansion of renewable energies, maintenance of forests through thinning-method logging, biomass use and so on.

When public investments such as these are planned, application of a public investment policy assessment index is necessary, based on the perspective of level of contribution to sustainable development (Yoshida et al., 2009: 29–31). Such an index must give consideration to the scale of employment opportunities created, effectiveness in CO_2 reduction, influence on biodiversity and ripple effect on local industry.

In the process of creatively pursuing lifestyles and working styles which are less of a burden on the environment and also richer for humanity, the successive birth of yet-to-exist new industries (environmental future industries) is anticipated. A plan for strategic investment in the environment and an integrated policy package that contributes to current issues faced by Japan are ideal. These issues include regional disparity, decline of marginal settlements, agricultural regeneration, maintenance and restoration of natural woods and lands, regeneration of cities and so on.

What is certainly required at present is a consistent package that integrates environmental policy and economic policy to form a sustainable society, plus a clever government that promotes consistent financial spending and structural reform, combined with an entrepreneurial spirit to face challenges in high environmental targets that recognize environmental constraints and introduce innovations towards a low-carbon society.

Notes

1. See http://unfccc.int/files/meetings/cop_14/statements/application/pdf/cop_14_statement_ban_ki-moon.pdf.
2. Tax reform consisted of the raising of environmental tax to promote reduction in environmental burdens, and using this tax revenue to supplement pension finances in order to reduce the amount of pension payments, thereby simultaneously achieving promotion of employment through the lowering of hiring costs. The Schröder administration, which began in 1998 with a coalition with the Greens, adopted a German version of ecological tax reform in 1999, and for the years 2000–2003 raised energy tax rates annually while lowering pension payment rates each year.
3. A summary and evaluation of this report are given in Kawaguchi (2008).

REFERENCES

Cabinet Office and Ministry of Economy, Trade and Industry (2009) "Mirai Kaitaku Senryaku (Strategy to Reclaim the Future)", 17 April, Cabinet Office and METI, Tokyo (in Japanese).

Center for American Progress (2008) "Green Recovery"; available at www.americanprogress.org/issues/2008/09/pdf/green_recovery.pdf.

Collier, Ute (1995) *Energy and Environment in the European Union: The Challenge of Integration*, Avebury Studies in Green Research. Aldershot: Avebury.

Confederation of British Industry (2007) "Climate Change: Everyone's Business", Report from CBI Task Force on Climate Change, November, London.

European Environment Agency (2005) "Environmental Policy Integration in Europe", Technical Report No. 2/2005, EEA, Copenhagen.

Fukuda, Yasuo (2008) "Vision for Global Warming Measures", Prime Minister's Office, Tokyo; available at www.kantei.go.jp/jp/fukudaspeech/2008/06/09speech.html (in Japanese).

Green New Deal Group (2008) "A Green New Deal", July, New Economic Foundation, London.

IPCC (2007) *Climate Change 2007*, IPCC Fourth Assessment Report. Cambridge: Cambridge University Press.

Kawaguchi, Mariko (2008) "Nihon wa Kankyo Senshinkoku ka" ("Is Japan an Environmentally Advanced Nation?)", 20 March, Daiwa Institute of Research, Tokyo (in Japanese).

Ministry of Environment (2008) "Teitanso Shakai-zukuri Kodo Keikaku (Action Plan for a Low-carbon Society)", July, MOE, Tokyo (in Japanese).

——— (2009) "Midori no Keizai to Shakai no Kakumei (Green Economics and Societal Revolution)", 20 April, MOE, Tokyo (in Japanese).

Obama, B. and J. Biden (2008) "New Energy for America"; available at www.barackobama.com/pdf/factsheet_energy_speech_080308.pdf.

Stern, Nicholas (2006) *The Economics of Climate Change*; available at www.hm-treasury.gov.uk/stern_review_report.htm.

UNEP (2009) "Global Green New Deal: Policy Brief", March; available at www.unep.org/greeneconomy/.

World Bank (2007) "Growth and CO_2 Emissions: How Do Different Countries Fare?", October, Environment Department, World Bank, Washington, DC.

World Wind Energy Association (2009) *World Wind Energy Report 2008*. Bonn: WWEA.

Yoshida, Fumikazu, Tetsunari Iida, Nobutaka Tsutsui and Yu Tanaka (2009) *Nihonban Gurin Kakumei de Keizai Koyo wo Tatenaosu* (*Rebuilding the Economy and Employment: The Japanese Green Revolution*). Tokyo: Yosensha (in Japanese).

6-3

Climate security and its implications for integrating paradigms of development and security

Seiichiro Hasui

6-3-1 Introduction

This chapter focuses on climate security. This unfamiliar combination of words refers to the idea that climate change is a problem or threat to security. The accumulated reports of the Intergovernmental Panel on Climate Change (IPCC, 1995, 2001, 2007) stress that climate change is largely the result of human activities. The main thread of this discussion is that climate change not only poses threats to the entire human race but also causes political instabilities throughout the world that, in the end, could lead to wars.

This concept is not only a new way of looking at something, but is becoming a keyword when integrating policies in the search for a new world order in Europe and the United States. This chapter explains the concept and makes some policy recommendations for Japanese foreign diplomacy regarding UN reforms.

6-3-2 What is security?

Before discussing what climate security is, it is necessary to explore the controversial concept of "security" itself.

Together with development, the concept of security is the most important paradigm in international relations, the content of which has been the subject of continuing and intense dispute for more than 20 years.

Even now, there is no widely agreed and established definition. Many subjective elements affect security; because of this subjectivity, what a group of people use to define or ensure their safety is dictated by the consciousness of that group themselves with regards to the situation they find themselves in. While already having the most powerful army in the world, after the so-called 9/11 terrorist attacks we saw rapidly increased military spending by the US government under the rubric of a war against terror. Despite the sacrifice of many human lives, the American people were supportive towards their government's military intervention. Strict safety checks, bordering on anxiety, at airports are now characteristic of American airlines. These behaviours reflect the fact that the American people do not feel secure even though the United States has the world's most powerful military forces. Further, our recognition of security problems is also related to subjectivity. This is called securitization (Buzan, Waever and de Wilde, 1998: 23–26; Waever, 1995: 57–75): phenomena that previously have not been considered a threat to security are reconsidered and reframed as threats, one after another, and become subject to countermeasures. Climate security is an example of securitization. Changes in purposes and measures of security policies are inevitable following securitization. Naturally, there are areas where those defending the traditional concept of security and those who advocate new concepts cannot understand each other amid the rise of rapidly changing security paradigms.

The etymology of the term "security" came from the Latin word *securitas*, which means "without care". Also, the term "sure" (meaning certain or assured) came from the changed word *securitas*. From this, the word security was used until recently with a particular nuance; one that can be conveyed in Japanese as *daijobu* (being "all right") (Tsuchiyama, 2004: 77).

However, security, this greatest common denominator, is officially considered in current international politics to mean "a certain subject protects its value through some means from a threat". Normally, when discussed in international relations, security refers to national security and the measures for this taken in many policies. Values that a nation-state should protect include its territory, sovereignty and people (their lives and assets). The nation-state protects these values from invasion and infringement by other countries through military force and foreign diplomacy. The nation-state establishes and executes policies to this end.

In other words, security is "to protect the values that groups of people (especially nation states) acquired from being robbed (or from the threat of being robbed)" (ibid.: 82). The points in this definition are important. Security presumes that there are acquired values that should be protected. This suggests that security is a concept developed for the purpose of protecting the benefits acquired through economic development, thus to protect these benefits from being damaged by climate change, climate security studies are on the rise.

6-3-3 Climate security

Climate security is a term that has triggered intense debates in international society in recent years. One such was the remarks of then UK Foreign Secretary Beckett in the series of dialogues that started at the Gleneagles summit of 2005 and the UN General Assembly of 22 September 2006 (UN General Assembly, 2006: 20). At the ministerial dialogue conducted at Monterey, Mexico, on 2–4 October 2006, Foreign Secretary Beckett emphasized an approach which started public discussion in Japan (Ministry of Environment, 2007a). This particular concept has been the subject of reports from various countries since 2007.

Arguments over climate security theories are extremely complicated at present, with the meaning of "climate security" changing subtly depending on who uses it. These meanings can be broadly classified into four categories.

- Security of climate.
- Security problems caused by climate change.
- Security through climate change policy.
- Security for climate protection.

The first, security of climate, means protecting the atmospheric composition from changing in order to mitigate climate change. This is because of predicted decreases in food production and increases in natural calamities brought about by the significant changes that global warming causes in the natural environment. And the existence of the human race depends on the environment. This use is mainly employed by environmentalists hoping to promote various policies to prevent climate change. By attaching the "security" label, these advocates aim to marshal social focus, raise the level of priority among policies and acquire resources such as funding.

Proponents of the second category, security problems arising from climate change, stress that environmental changes and degradations resulting from climate change destabilize not only the lives of people living in and dependent on an ecosystem, but even the economy and politics of nation-states. They raise the concern that, in the end, such instability leads to civil wars and other forms of armed conflict. Examples of this kind of investigation are seen mainly in Canada and the United States, represented by the research conducted by Homer-Dixon (Homer-Dixon and Blitt, 1998; Homer-Dixon, 1999). Kanie (2007: 215) calls this way of thinking "military climate security".

The third category, security through climate change, is an idea much discussed in the European Union at present. It suggests that to address climate change, a new world order and a new international body based on that order should be formed, and that this is linked to the security of nations and the whole world. This approach, which Kanie (ibid.) calls "structural climate security", continues to appear in mainstream climate security studies. The arguments discussed in this chapter come entirely from this viewpoint.

The fourth category, security policies for climate protection, incorporates viewpoints revolving around the large-scale environmental destruction brought about by wars and preparation for wars (SIPRI, 1979; Westing, 1990; Fukuchi, 1996; Miyagi et al., 2002; Bertell, 2000). It holds that ensuring better international security is connected to protecting the environment, a view often held by pacifists. On the other side the military, such as the US forces, use this idea to advocate the transformation of the military into an environmentally friendly body (Durant, 2007). When designing weapons with superior capabilities, no consideration has been given to the environment; accordingly, emission of greenhouse gases from the military became very high, making it one of the most inefficient sectors (Ishii, 2008). Moreover, in line with the previous discussion, adding climate issues to the criticisms of the military can decrease support for the use of military force. They need to respond to these criticisms, and they have good reason to do so, as they can expect some improvement of weapon capabilities by getting better mileage from planes, vehicles and ships.

The four categories described above are mutually related. This shows that the current debate on climate security does not admit simplistic understanding; it requires caution in its handling.

From the form of these arguments, it is possible to consider climate security as an idea derived from the concept of "environmental security" into which researchers introduced new security concepts. That is, even if the words "climate" and "environment" are interchanged, practically the same arguments will be formed. Hence the question is, how have environment and security been discussed so far?

6-3-4 Environment and security – History of the debate

Academic research

Falk's 1971 book *This Endangered Planet* launched the academic dispute relating to environmental problems with security in 1971 (Barnett, 2003: 8). Although Falk did not use the expression, he described environmental security as follows.

> The territoriality of political units induces a certain tendency toward the defense of homeland, especially given conditions of scarcity and of inequality. That is, under world conditions of insufficient resources to satisfy total demand there is a natural tendency for those with less to seek a larger share. This tendency induces those with a larger share to organize their defenses against those with less and to use their superiority to obtain still more. The rich get richer, the powerful grow more so. But inequality in the face of insufficiency often induces a guilty conscience together with fear, and a policy of repression. Those who suffer from inequality, depending on their degree of deprivation, their level of awareness, and their belief system, are potential sources of revolutionary action. (Falk, 1971: 59)

Falk suggests the possibility that the depletion of resources could cause antagonism and violence. This kind of notion is characteristic of later thoughts on environmental security.

In 1972 the publication of the Club of Rome's *The Limits to Growth* (Meadows et al., 1972) and the UN Conference on the Human Environment (Stockholm conference) heightened global environmental consciousness. In the midst of this, research aimed at redefining security from the viewpoint of the relationship between environment and security was undertaken. Representative of this are studies by Brown (1977), Ullman (1983) and Mathews (1989), each under the same title: "Redefining Security". This research shows a common pattern of thinking: "environmental destruction–socio-economic impact–violent conflict". For example, Brown stated this thought as follows:

> The military threat to national security is only one of many that governments must now address. The numerous new threats derive directly or indirectly from the rapidly changing relationship between humanity and the earth's natural systems and resources. The unfolding stresses in this relationship initially manifest themselves as ecological stresses and resource scarcities. Later they translate into economic stresses – inflation, unemployment, capital scarcity, and monetary instability. Ultimately, these economic stresses convert into social unrest and political instability. (Brown, 1977: 37)

Further, while keeping a distance from so-called "resource wars" thinking which argues about non-renewable resources including oil and minerals, they have a common point of view that focuses on conflict about renewable resources which we call "environment". These studies stressed that the environment should be the subject of research as a cause for conflict, in the same way as politics. After 1989 the phrase "environmental security" rapidly became widespread. Since the studies indicated that environmental problems become causes of violence and conflict, the affinity between the traditional security view and this research was high; hence it had a strong influence during the Clinton administration, especially in the latter half of the 1990s, as evidenced by the creation of the position of deputy under-secretary of defense for environmental security in the US Department of Defense.

Much attention was given to the model developed by Thomas Homer-Dixon (1999), who was very influential in the security and foreign policies of Canada and the United States. As shown in Figure 6.3.1, his model follows the thoughts of the three papers mentioned above. However, it was the most advanced theoretical model.

At present, recognition of the causal relationship between climate change and armed conflict is growing very strong. Gleditsch, one of the most representative researchers in this field, and Buhan and Theisen presented a similar but more complicated model than Homer-Dixon (Buhan, Gleditsch and Theisen, 2008) (Figure 6.3.2).

This kind of discussion linking environment and security faced many criticisms: using inappropriate military measures to resolve environmental problems makes resolution difficult; further, militarization of environmental problems will be brought about (Deudney, 1991: 24). Gleditsch (1998) made a detailed analysis of the criticisms (Table 6.3.1). Despite these serious criticisms, the concept of environmental security has survived and grown into the concept of climate security.

Environmental politics

Environmental politics is international politics which manages environmental problems. The contention over the causal relationship between environmental problems and security started mainly in the late 1980s. The first impetus was the report of the World Commission on Environment and Development (WCED, or Brundtland Commission), *Our Common Future*. Section 11, entitled "Peace, Security, Development and Environment", followed the flow of thought "environmental destruction–socio-economic impact–violent conflict" and argued:

> Environmental stress is seldom the only cause of major conflicts within or among nations. Nevertheless, they can arise from the marginalization of sectors of the population and from ensuing violence. This occurs when political processes are unable to handle the effects of environmental stress resulting, for example, from erosion and desertification. Environmental stress can thus be an important part of the web of causality associated with any conflict and can in some cases be catalytic. (World Commission on Environment and Development, 1987: 291)

Although this report is considered important in that it brought out the concept of sustainable development, at the same time it is very significant

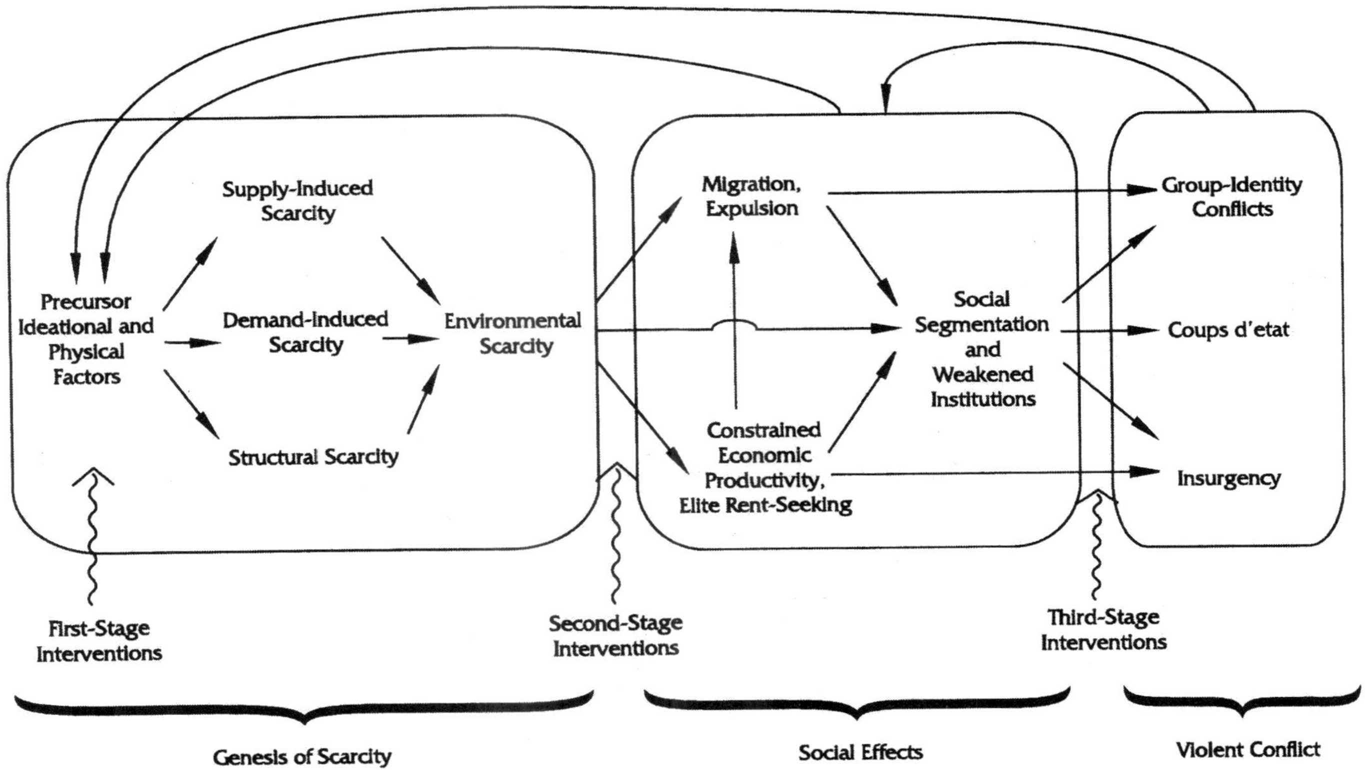

Figure 6.3.1 Homer-Dixon's core model of the causal links between environmental scarcity and violence
Source: Homer-Dixon (1999: 134)

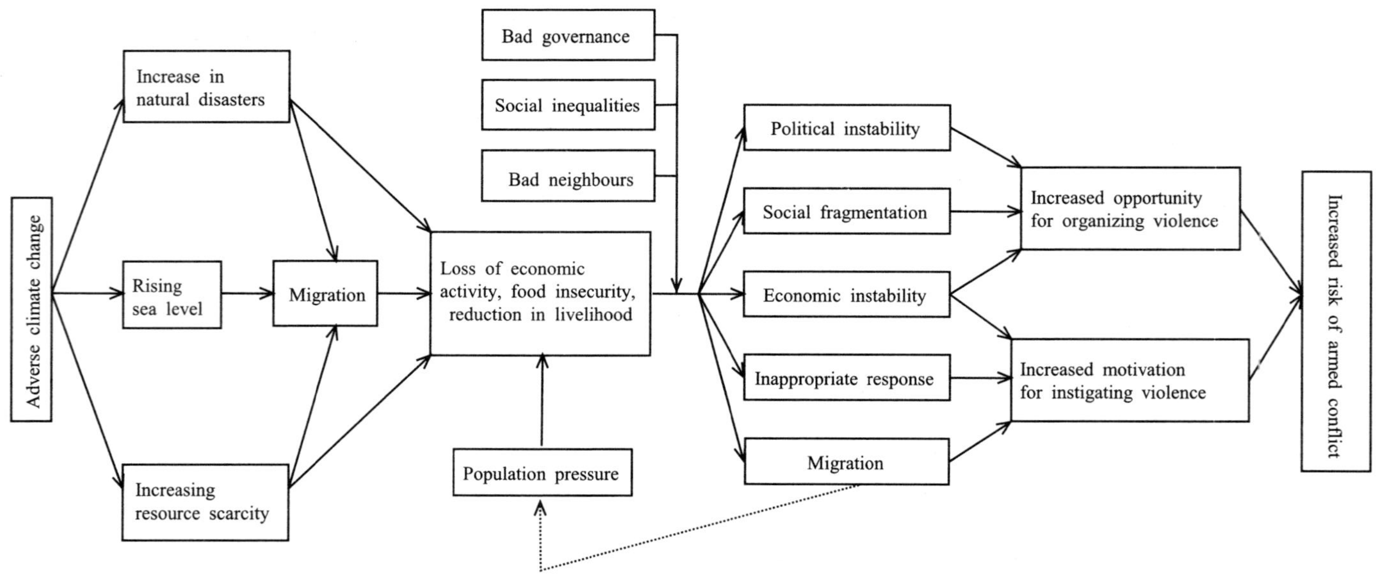

Figure 6.3.2 Possible pathways to conflict
Source: Buhan, Gleditsch and Theisen (2008: 14)

Table 6.3.1 Critique of environment and conflict studies

- There is a lack of clarity over what is meant by "environmental conflict"
- Researchers engage in definitional and polemical exercises rather than analysis
- Important variables are neglected, notably political and economic factors which have a strong influence on conflict and mediate the influence of resource and environmental factors
- Some models become so large and complex that they are virtually untestable
- Cases are selected on values of the dependent variable
- The causality of the relationship is reversed
- Postulated events in the future are cited as empirical evidence
- Studies fail to distinguish between foreign and domestic conflict
- Confusion reigns about the appropriate level of analysis

Source: Gleditsch (1998: 381).

in being the first to identify the relationship between environment and security at the level of environmental politics. It also suggests a recognition which includes the concept of climate security: "Environmental threats to security are now beginning to emerge on a global scale. The most worrisome of these stem from the possible consequences of global warming caused by the atmospheric build-up of carbon dioxide and other gases" (ibid.: 294).

With this report, 1988 became a crucial turning point (Yonemoto, 1994: 51). In the Toronto summit of the same year, agriculture and trade were the focus of attention, with the environment occupying an inconspicuous place at the bottom of the economic declaration agenda. The tail end of item 33 of this declaration made a passive reference to the Toronto conference: "We welcome the Conference on the Changing Atmosphere to be held in Toronto next week" (Toronto Economic Summit, 1988: 33). This conference on "The Changing Atmosphere: Implications for Global Security" was the first time that climate change and security were connected at the level of environmental politics. Yonemoto (1994: 48) judged it was important, as the first debate on global warming came to a clear understanding not only among scientists but in a conference also attended by bureaucrats, legislators, industrialists and even environmental NGOs. The declaration from the conference emphasized:

> Humanity is conducting an unintended, uncontrolled, globally pervasive experiment whose ultimate consequences could be second only to a global nuclear war. The Earth's atmosphere is being changed at an unprecedented rate by pollutants resulting from human activities, inefficient and wasteful fossil fuel use and the effects of rapid population growth in many regions. These changes represent a major threat to international security and are already having harmful consequences over many parts of the globe ... The best predictions available indicate potentially severe economic and social dislocation for present and

> future generations, which will worsen international tensions and increase risk of conflicts among and within nations. (WMO, 1989: 292)

Following the Toronto conference, at the UN General Assembly on 27 September of the same year, Eduard Shevardnadze, then minister of foreign affairs of the Union of Soviet Socialist Republics, defined the environment, nuclear and space threats as being on the same level, and the increasing urgency of these threats as a second front. Here, the environment was considered a threat to security on the same plane as military threats, including nuclear threat. He stated:

> For the first time we have seen clearly that, in the absence of any global control, man's so-called peaceful constructive activity is turning into global aggression against the very foundation of life on earth.
>
> For the first time we have understood clearly that we had guessed: that the traditional view of national and universal security, based primarily on military means of defense, is now totally obsolete and must be urgently revised.
>
> Faced with the threat of environmental catastrophe, the dividing lines of the bipolar ideological world are receding. The biosphere recognizes no division into blocs, alliances or systems. All share the same climatic system and no one is in a position to build his own isolated and independent line of environmental defense. (UN General Assembly, 1988a: 76)

Shevardnadze stressed that environmental destruction itself poses threats to the human race, and that we should change a sense of security biased towards the military. He also called for the need to institutionalize an "international regime of environmental security" (ibid.: 77).

In a form reminiscent of this speech, Mikhail Gorbachev, then general secretary of the Union of Soviet Socialist Republics, at the UN General Assembly of the same year gave a speech on "détente". He made many pronouncements regarding the importance of reducing the threat to the global environment and arms reduction, and proposed the establishment of a centre for emergency environmental assistance within the UN framework (UN General Assembly (1988b: 19).

These two speeches were the first examples where a head of state stressed that the environment was a security problem and the traditional military national security up to that point was inappropriate and obsolete.

From this year on, recognition of global environmental problems such as climate change as threats to security was publicly emphasized in the international political arena. Naturally, prevailing conditions in the then Soviet Union, such as *perestroika* being at an impasse and an economy saddled with a monstrous military budget, lie behind these discourses on détente. Both leaders, while expounding on environmental problems, were positively silent on the Chernobyl nuclear power plant accident of the previous year. After these UN sessions, however, the environmental problems caused by non-sustainable development were addressed within both academic research and environmental politics as realistic threats to security, indicating that these speeches were crucial turning points in how the concept of environmental security is thought about.

6-3-5 Climate change as a threat to security

The capacity to inflict harm

If we recognize climate change as a threat to our security, how would it be? To become a threat to security from the perspective of current academic research and environmental politics, several conditions must be met: there must be damage arising from it; it must be a social or anthropogenic phenomenon; and it must result from highly intentional actions.

First, what might be the extent of damage from climate change? The IPCC (2007) Fourth Assessment Report summarizes this in part (Table 6.3.2). Looking at the table, one can see that great harm will occur in relation to water and food production in the developing countries where a lot of conflict occurs at present. It is clear from current academic research that, although not directly linked with violent conflicts, these stresses can cause conflicts to expand or intensify, and thus make their resolution more difficult. This is why researchers in the United States consider climate change as a threat multiplier (CNA Corporation, 2007: 44).

Further, damages have started to be observed by AOSIS (Alliance of Small Island States) countries, including coastal erosion caused by rising seawater level, seawater inundation which decreases food production and freshwater availability and makes life impossible for the people, and submersion of territorial domain under water (Jimbo, 2004).

These are the phenomena that traditional security perceptions fail to foresee. "Who owns the territory?" was the important issue in traditional security studies. "Losing territory" implies that the territory was taken by someone, but there is still the possibility of taking it back. However, territory vanishing due to climate change implies the impossibility of taking it back. This is a serious consequence that cannot be addressed by traditional security studies and measures (diplomacy and military means).

Table 6.3.2 Impacts of climate change (excerpts)

Africa	• By 2020 75–250 million of people are projected to be exposed to increased water stress due to climate change (WGII 9.4, SPM) • By 2020, in some countries, yields from rain-fed agriculture could be reduced by up to 50 per cent. Agricultural production, including access to food, in many African countries is projected to be severely compromised. This would further adversely affect food security and exacerbate malnutrition (WGII 9.4, SPM) • Towards the end of the twenty-first century, projected sea-level rise will affect low-lying coastal areas with large populations. The cost of adaptation could amount to at least 5–10 per cent of GDP (WGII 9.4, SPM) • By 2080 an increase of 5–8 per cent of arid and semi-arid land in Africa is projected under a range of climate scenarios (high confidence) (WGII Box TS.6, 9.4.4)
Asia	• By the 2050s freshwater availability in Central, South, East and Southeast Asia, particularly in large river basins, is projected to decrease (WGII 10.4, SPM) • Coastal areas, especially heavily populated megadelta regions in South, East and Southeast Asia, will be at greatest risk due to increased flooding from the sea and, in some megadeltas, flooding from the rivers (WGII 10.4, SPM) • Climate change is projected to compound the pressures on natural resources and the environment associated with rapid urbanization, industrialization and economic development (WGII 10.4, SPM) • Endemic morbidity and mortality due to diarrhoeal disease primarily associated with floods and droughts are expected to rise in East, South and Southeast Asia due to projected changes in the hydrological cycle (WGII 10.4, SPM)
Latin America	• By mid-century, increases in temperature and associated decreases in soil water are projected to lead to gradual replacement of tropical forest by savanna in eastern Amazonia. Semi-arid vegetation will tend to be replaced by arid-land vegetation (WGII 13.4, SPM) • There is a risk of significant biodiversity loss through species extinction in many areas of tropical Latin America (WGII 13.4, SPM) • Productivity of some important crops is projected to decrease and livestock productivity to decline, with adverse consequences for food security. In temperate zones, soybean yields are projected to increase. Overall, the number of people at risk of hunger is projected to increase (medium confidence) (WGII 13.4, Box TS.6) • Changes in precipitation patterns and the disappearance of glaciers are projected to affect water availability for human consumption, agriculture and energy generation significantly (WGII 13.4, SPM)

Table 6.3.2 (cont.)

Small islands	• Sea-level rise is expected to exacerbate inundation, storm surge, erosion and other coastal hazards, thus threatening vital infrastructure, settlements and facilities that support the livelihood of island communities (WGII 16.4, SPM) • Deterioration in coastal conditions, for example through erosion of beaches and coral bleaching, is expected to affect local resources (WGII 16.4, SPM) • By mid-century, climate change is expected to reduce water resources in many small islands, e.g. in the Caribbean and Pacific, to the point where they become insufficient to meet demand during low rainfall periods (WGII 16.4, SPM) • With higher temperatures, increased invasion by non-native species is expected to occur, particularly on mid- and high-latitude islands (WGII 16.4, SPM)

Source: IPCC (2007: 50–52).

Anthropogenic aspect

Second, as discussed in political science, a threat should be social or anthropogenic. Whether climate changes are anthropogenic or natural phenomena has become a constant object of debate. The IPCC, in its Second Assessment Report, indicated "Global mean surface temperature has increased by between about 0.3 and 0.6°C since the late 19th century, a change that is unlikely to be entirely natural in origin. The balance of evidence ... suggests a discernible human influence on global climate" (IPCC, 1995: 5). The IPCC has come to emphasize the anthropogenic aspect of climate change.

In its Fourth Assessment Report, the scientific validity of which has been rated higher, the IPCC stresses strongly that "Most of the observed increase in global average temperatures since the mid-20th century is very likely due to the observed increase in anthropogenic GHG concentrations" (IPCC, 2007: 39). As the report states, this is a big advance from the Third Assessment Report's conclusion that "There is new and stronger evidence that most of the warming observed over the last 50 years is attributable to human activities" (IPCC, 2001: 5). In other words, the possibility that the current warming is an anthropogenic phenomenon which was socially induced is very high indeed.

Intentional aspect

The third condition is that the threats must be highly intentional. Before the IPCC reports, as depicted in Figure 6.3.3, seen from the viewpoint of

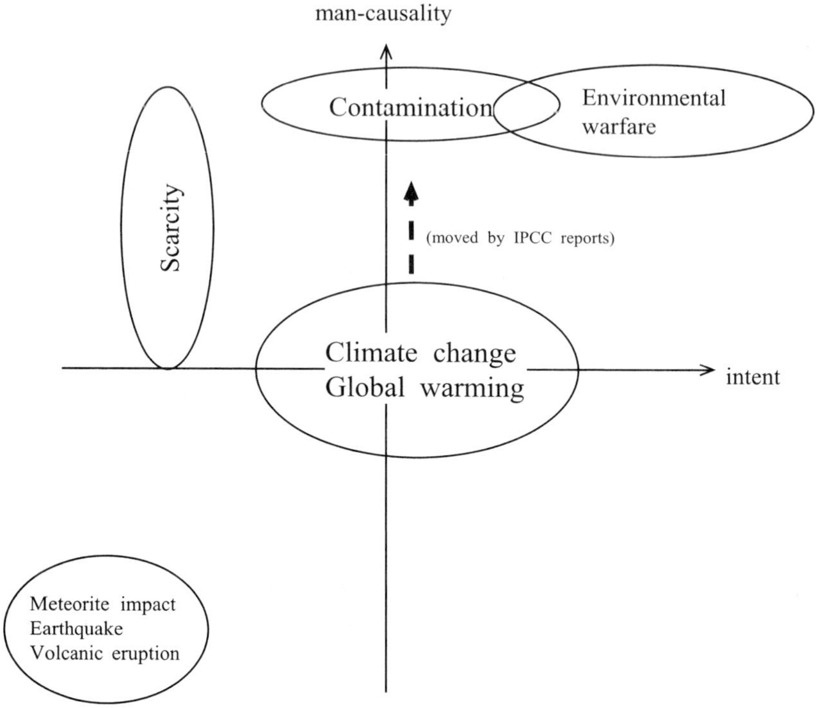

Figure 6.3.3 Intent and human causality in climate change and other phenomena

intent, in the emission of GHGs that cause climate change the degree of anthropogenic and intentional aspects was moderate and lacked sufficient attributes. Compared to environmental warfare using some environmental destruction as a kind of weapon, it was difficult to insist that these are clear threats to security.

However, publication of the IPCC Fourth Assessment Report has made us understand that climate change is an anthropogenic phenomenon and is a problem caused by a pollution-like substance. This is an important change in arguments on liability for climate change.

This reveals the coexistence of criminal intent liability and absence of direct criminal intent stemming from the legal theory of wilful negligence. Although wilful negligence does not mean direct intention to cause harm, it does imply a psychological state of tolerating harm to happen or awareness of a high probability of it happening. As a result, wilful negligence receives a penalty similar to an act of criminal intent to inflict harm.

Applying this principle to the problem of climate change, we find an interesting situation. Emissions of GHGs can be considered to be tantamount to intentional climate change. Because the scientific understanding of the relationship between climate change and GHG emission advanced, and that understanding is widely recognized as a result of worldwide public discussion, emitters cannot deny a clear connection between their emitting activities and criminal intent liability. From this legal aspect, emitting activities become almost synonymous with environmental warfare, since they intentionally cause the same anthropogenic environmental damage.

Anthropogenic environmental destruction used in environmental warfare is considered a clear threat to security even in a traditional sense. It is difficult to imagine any objection to this point. The IPCC Fourth Assessment Report clarified that GHG emissions have effects close to an act of war using the environment. Hence, it is now clear that we have to consider climate change as a threat to our security and an academic subject of international relations.

6-3-6 Current status of theories on climate security

How is the concept of climate security with this discourse history being disputed at present? What follows is a comparison of the current situation in Japan, the United States and European countries.

Japan

In Japan, discussions on climate security at the policy level started in February 2007, during meetings of the International Climate Change Strategy Global Environment Committee, Central Environment Council (Ministry of Environment, 2007a). The committee specified that the need for the concept had been recognized inside Japan after October 2006, when climate security was raised on several different occasions. The speech of UK Foreign Secretary Margaret Beckett at the Gleneagles dialogue held in October 2006 was a starting point, followed by many speeches along the same line by UN Secretary-General Kofi Annan, the Ugandan representative and Japan's Minister of Environment Masatoshi Wakabayashi.

However, despite knowing its potential importance, Japanese policymakers lacked an idea of how to use this concept of climate security strategically. Even the United States (which was then passive in negotiations on global warming) had started an evaluation led by then Secretary of State Condoleezza Rice in the National Security Council by that time (ibid.). This fact made the committee impatient; one official expressed this by saying, "Honestly, please, speed up your deliberation!" (ibid.) To respond to international circumstances, the possibility of policy implementation of the climate security concept was discussed three times in the committee, resulting in the preparation of the "Report on Climate Security" in May 2007 (Ministry of Environment, 2007e). The gist of the report is as follows.

- Despite the fact that there is only small progress in the negotiations on the UN Framework Convention on Climate Change, the concept of climate security is becoming widespread in the major countries and the United Nations.
- Progress in scientific understanding of the rapidly changing climate is obvious.
- The evolution of the concept of security can now include climate change as a threat.
- The notion of Japan's comprehensive security subsumes climate security.
- Unified global cooperative action to protect the climate as an international public good is indispensable.
- Using the concept of climate security, raising the level of priority assigned to policies and increasing the pressure to have reduction programmes and obligations involving developed countries and major gas-emitting countries can be achieved.
- To promote the policy of climate security, measures called for include cooperation with other countries, contribution to human security, breakthrough in the current deadlocked negotiations, promotion of the shift to "economic growth with a low-carbon society" in developing countries, prompt and appropriate adaptation measures for fragile developing countries and so on.
- Adopting the philosophy of Japanese "comprehensive security" in facing up to climate change problems.

The report recommends the positioning of the concept of climate security in national and international societies, and its effective use. However, the report did not go as far as specific positioning and methods of use; it only proposed foreign diplomacy focused on the Hokkaido Toyako summit, "Climate as Global Public Goods". Among the four categories of climate security discourse noted earlier, this climate security notion recognized the second and third categories, but could not realize them at that time. After this report, although references were made to climate security within the Ministry of Environment in discussions during press conferences and within the Global Environment Committee, climate security was not spelled out in a form similar to the US Climate Security Act of 2007 (US Congress, 2007) or the US American Clean Energy and Security Act of 2009 (US Congress, 2009a). The sole reference that could be considered as a policy was a statement that "global warming is a security problem that shakes the foundation of the survival of the human race" in the preamble to a proposed Basic Law Promoting the Creation of a Low Carbon Society submitted by the Liberal Democratic Party in July 2009 (not enacted yet at the beginning of 2010).

Why is it so difficult for climate security theories to become a major political issue in Japan? From the standpoint of academic research, one reason is the difference in attitude towards environmental security studies between Japan on one side and the United States and European countries on the other. As described above, the relationship between climate change and security has been researched and disputed in the context of environmental security studies since the 1980s. In the United States and Europe, research papers and books have been published continuously since the start of this century. However, with regards to research on the topic inside Japan, many scholars held a cautious position (Yamada, 1999; Ohta, 2002; Ochiai, 2001). Because of this, research as a whole has not been pursued actively. Even now, academic research in the Japanese social sciences on climate change and security has not made much progress.

The United States

It is not certain exactly when evaluation of the concept of climate security at the government level in the United States started. Under the Bush Jr administration, the United States took a passive stance *vis-à-vis* the global warming negotiations initiative of the EU countries. The accompanying discussions linking climate change and security were anaemic compared to those in the European countries.

However, the United States started to move in the year 2006. The CNA Corporation, a think-tank for military affairs, gathered retired generals in 2006 to start investigative research and published a report (CNA Corporation, 2007). Further, in his State of the Union address in January 2007, President Bush mentioned climate change as a serious problem for the first time. Surveying several reports, it is fair to say that policy-level discussion of climate security started in earnest in the United States in March 2007 (Busby, 2007: 1).

The question "how does climate change affect the national security of the United States?" came to the front of discussions in the United States under the Bush administration. Let us examine that question using two early representative reports.

The first is the CNA report, *National Security and the Threat of Climate Change* (CNA Corporation, 2007), which can be summarized under three themes.

- What conditions are climate changes likely to produce around the world that would represent security risks to the United States?

- What are the ways in which these conditions may affect America's national security interests?
- What actions should the nation take to address the national security consequences of climate change?

The report came up with the following conclusions with regards to these questions.

- Projected climate change poses a serious threat to America's national security.
- Climate change acts as a threat multiplier for instability in some of the most volatile regions of the world.
- Projected climate change will add to tensions even in stable regions of the world.
- Climate change, national security and energy dependence are a related set of global challenges.

The characteristics of these conclusions are that climate change threatens US national security in two ways. First, climate changes could cause an increase in natural disasters within the country; and second, they could cause worsening conditions in unstable regions outside the country. These claims are common to the reports of other military think-tanks; for example, the same analyses were put forward at the Global Climate Change: National Security Implications conference held in March 2007 by the US Army War College Strategic Studies Institute and Triangle Institute for Security Studies (Pumphrey, 2008).

The CNA report (CNA Corporation, 2007) offers five policy proposals.

- The national security consequences of climate change should be fully integrated into national security and national defence strategies.
- The United States should commit to a stronger national and international role to help stabilize climate change at levels that will avoid significant disruption to global security and stability.
- The United States should commit to global partnerships that help less-developed nations build the capacity and resilience to manage climate impacts better.
- The Department of Defense should enhance its operational capability by accelerating the adoption of improved business processes and innovative technologies that result in improved US combat power through energy efficiency.
- The Department of Defense should conduct an assessment of the impact on US military installations worldwide of rising sea levels, extreme weather events and other projected climate change impacts over the next 30–40 years.

Second is the special report on *Climate Change and National Security* written by Joshua Busby (2007) and published by the Council on Foreign Relations, which produces the well-known foreign diplomacy journal *For-*

eign Affairs. It summarizes interviews with experts and NGOs in the various fields involved in climate security studies conducted up to November 2007, and was one of the most comprehensive outlooks at that time.

The report highlighted that Hurricane Katrina in 2005 "gave Americans a visual image of what climate change – which scientists predict will exacerbate the severity and number of extreme weather events – might mean for the future" (ibid.: 1). With regard to the impact of climate change on national security, citing the 2006 National Security Strategy, the author says the domestic impact is that damages from epidemics and natural disasters, similar to the effects of weapons of mass destruction, would "swiftly kill or endanger large numbers of people and cause such large-scale disruption that local public health, law enforcement, and emergency response units would not be able to contain the threat" (ibid.: 5). In addition, sea-level rise will place 50 per cent of the American people living within 50 miles of the shore in precarious circumstances (ibid.).

Further, the author insisted there would be more direct impacts on military forces. Facilities such as air and naval bases are vulnerable to storms and other natural disasters; for example, he pointed out that in 1992 Hurricane Andrew caused great damage to Homestead air base in Miami, which led to its closure (ibid.: 6). American military bases outside the United States are also subject to the effects of climate change.

The author calls attention to the destabilization of international relations. For example, the thawing of the glaciers of the Arctic Circle offers advantageous marine transport in opening up northern sea routes and shortening navigation, but there is the possibility of international conflicts, even with Canada for example, arising over sea routes and the surrounding resources. Moreover, the effects on Indonesia, China and other environmentally vulnerable countries could impair US security (ibid.: 7–10).

The report recommends "no-regrets" policies with regard to these threats, insisting more importance should be given to adaptation rather than mitigation measures, such as promotion of research on the structural vulnerabilities of the United States and the creation of international regimes in countries where forests are being cut down, as in China, India and Indonesia (ibid.: 11–21).

Finally, to realize these recommendations, the author stresses the importance of institutional reforms. He emphasizes that several agencies and positions related to climate, environment and security which were abolished under the Bush administration, especially those under the Department of Defense, the National Security Council and special advisers for the president, should be brought back. With regard to policy integration, the author says: "The next president can ensure the issue gets the priority it deserves by integrating climate security concerns centrally into its National Security Strategy" (ibid.: 22–25). As will be explained, this is being realized under the Obama administration.

These two reports from American think-tanks under the Bush administration share one common point about the concept of climate security: climate changes are viewed as problems affecting the capability to protect national attributes (territory, sovereignty and people), and especially sovereignty; that is, the ability to protect one's own interests by oneself. Regarding the scale of disasters, and taking climate change as a premise, both reports warn that American military operational capability will be weakened. Busby (ibid.) relates this problem to the Bush administration's National Security Strategy, which recognizes: "Environmental destruction, whether caused by human behavior or cataclysmic mega-disasters such as floods, hurricanes, earthquakes, or tsunamis. Problems of this scope may overwhelm the capacity of local authorities to respond, and may even overtax national militaries, requiring a larger international response" (Bush, 2006: 47).

How does the Obama administration try to address this crisis? It is steadily preparing various policies on energy and climate security (Table 6.3.3). An important aspect is that in the American revival of reinvestment for the purpose of coping with the recent unprecedented financial crisis, more than $60 billion has been thrown at green energy and similar projects.

In June 2009 this plan was endorsed by science when the US Global Change Research Program produced *Global Climate Change Impacts in the United States* (Karl, Melillo and Peterson, 2009). The book admits human-induced aspects of global warming, warming over the United States, increasing heavy rain, decreasing snow and early thawing which changes flow rates of river systems, and increasing rates of sea-level rise. It calculated that each of these will reach a level wherein the social and personal impacts will be significant, indicative of a strong sense of crisis. For example, the number of people predicted to die due to heatwaves in Chicago even in the low-emission scenario will double by 2055 compared to 1975 (about 400 persons per year); in the high-emission scenario this number will quadruple (about 800 people per year) (ibid.: 90). The book agrees with adaptation measures and the Green New Deal, which stresses the importance of mitigating climate change through green energy. Needless to say, the Obama administration is pushing forward these policies.

Shortly after this, on 26 June 2009, the American Clean Energy and Security Act (ACES) passed the House of Representatives by a vote of 219 to 212. This comprehensive Act aims to integrate policies for climate change inside and outside the United States. If this bill is passed in Senate it will have major implications for the US concept of climate security, because it contains clear indications in the section concerning

Table 6.3.3 Key elements of the Obama energy and climate security plan

Goals	Objectives	Initiatives
Speeches		
• An end to the "tyranny of oil" • A "revolution" in energy efficiency • Diversified energy supplies	• Improving the electric grid • Increasing civilian nuclear energy to supply low-carbon energy • Making the Department of Energy a leader in renewable energy innovation • Advancing clean coal technologies • Creating and using reliable, consistent climate information	• Foster innovation through science and engineering fellowships, with R&D funding and by commercializing clean energy technologies • Develop biodiesels from organic waste and non-food crops, battery and other energy storage advances, smart electricity-saving tools for buildings and cheaper solar photovoltaic systems • Launch a National Climate Service in collaboration with several federal agencies
FY2010 budget		
• National energy security • Climate security • More American jobs that cannot be outsourced • A 25 per cent reduction in the federal government's energy bill by 2013	• Developing new electricity transmission and use technologies • Building research networks within the Department of Energy, across the government, throughout the nation and around the globe • Increasing the use of public transport • Create a national emissions cap-and-trade system	• Dedicate $15 million annually towards renewable energy research starting in 2012 • Establish a National Infrastructure Bank • Weatherize 1 million homes per year, and fund housing and urban development programmes to spur a new market for retrofitting and building more efficient new housing • Provide $1 billion annually in grants for high-speed rail

Table 6.3.3 (cont.)

Goals	Objectives	Initiatives
American Recovery and Reinvestment Act, 2009		
• A lower-carbon US economy • Economic recovery and job creation • Improved transportation and infrastructure	• Creating or saving more than 3.5 million jobs over the next two years • Reviving the renewable energy industry and providing the capital over the next three years to double domestic renewable energy capacity	• Protect critical infrastructure via $700 million allocated to NASA, the National Labs, State Department and Department of Homeland Security • Invest in high-risk, high-return research grants through the National Science Foundation • Invest in smart grids, efficiency and conservation technologies and related programmes

Source: Parthemore (2009: 8).

international adaptation programmes for climate change. Congress finds the following:

> (1) Global climate change is a potentially significant national and global security threat multiplier and is likely to exacerbate competition and conflict over agricultural, vegetative, marine, and water resources and to result in increased displacement of people, poverty, and hunger within developing countries …
>
> (6) The consequences of global climate change, including increases in poverty and destabilization of economies and societies, are likely to pose long-term challenges to the national security, foreign policy, and economic interests of the United States.
>
> (7) It is in the national security, foreign policy, and economic interests of the United States to recognize, plan for, and mitigate the international strategic, social, political, cultural, environmental, health, and economic effects of climate change and to assist developing countries to increase their resilience to those effects. (H.R. 2454.EH, Sec. 491)

If this Act is established, it will represent the first opportunity for the United States to institutionalize climate security at national policy level. Moreover, as a major doctrine of the Obama administration, it is likely to have a significant impact on the formation of the international order in the future. Even if the Act is not passed for the moment, as a symbolic document expressing the Obama government's stance on climate change, it is likely to occupy a significant position alongside the Climate Security Act of 2007.

However, because of its comprehensiveness, and also due to strong resistance from members concerned over falling US international competitiveness stemming from the financial crisis, deliberation of the Act ran into serious challenges in the Senate. Apart from ACES, climate bills passed one after another in the Senate: the Senate Energy and Natural Resources Committee passed the American Clean Energy Leadership Act 2009 (US Congress, 2009b) on 17 June, and the Senate Environment and Public Works Committee passed the Clean Energy Jobs and American Power Act 2009 (US Congress, 2009c) on 5 November. These bills address some parts of ACES.

On one hand, this means a sort of incremental approach to the goals of ACES; on the other, this may reduce the significance of and support for the comprehensive ACES Act itself. Certainly, a part of ACES is reducing GHG emissions. But there is big difference in purpose between ACES and the bills passed in the Senate. ACES has an aspiration to integrate climate, energy and development policies and diplomacy in the name of "security": a kind of paradigm shift in policy-making in US politics. Other bills pursue only energy efficiency, benefit, competitiveness, cap-and-trade systems and so on, and do not bring a paradigm shift in policy-making in the United States.

To push forward ACES, policy-making is also accelerating in the private sector. The Center for a New American Security (CNAS), which is said to be deeply connected to the Obama administration (Lozada, 2009), has released many reports since its formation up to the present day from its Energy Security and Climate Change project (e.g. Campbell, 2008). Although the CNAS is only a think-tank, the impact these recommendations have had upon the Obama government cannot be ignored. Past CNAS chair Michele A. Flournoy has already become US under-secretary of defense for policy, and many others in its executive-level personnel were given positions which have major impact on security policy. For example, on 30 June 2009 the CNAS announced its CEO and co-founder Kurt M. Campbell would serve as assistant secretary of state for East Asian and Pacific affairs. Furthermore, on 21 July CNAS Vice-President for Natural Security Sharon E. Burke gave testimony at a public hearing in the Senate alongside retired generals in regard to climate change and security. On 1 February 2010 CNAS President John Nagl was named to the independent panel to review the Department of Defense's 2010 Quadrennial Defense Review.

After the inauguration of the Obama administration, the field of security has become increasingly proactive. The report from a conference on energy and climate security held in Washington on 29 April 2009 analysed the Obama government's strategy as decreasing reliance on foreign oil and reducing greenhouse gases by investing in green employment and reducing energy demand (Parthemore, 2009: 5). It also recommends drafting an integrated national strategy and creating a plan to serve as a model for the low-carbon economy of the future, as well as a scorecard system for evaluating policy.

The CNAS also established a new Natural Security project in June 2009. CNAS Vice-President Sharon Burke (2009: 12) stated that "Consumption of natural resources, especially energy, non-fuel minerals, water, and land, can affect geopolitics and the stability of nations. At the same time, the consequences of high consumption rates of these resources, such as climate change and biodiversity loss, can also create geostrategic pressure, instability, and disasters." As a result, climate change poses a broad threat, from economic growth through to social stability, and can trigger humanitarian crises (ibid.: 18). Burke also warns that loss of biodiversity may trigger stress over natural resources, related to 40 per cent of world conflicts (ibid.: 19).

Burke defines natural security as follows: "Natural security ultimately means sufficient, reliable, affordable, and sustainable supplies of natural resources for the modern global economy" (ibid.: 9). The report recommends supervision and rectification from the natural security perspective that various government agencies currently lack, as well as the incorporation of natural security perspectives into US strategies such as the existing National Security Strategy (ibid.: 20).

The concept of natural security further expands the framework of climate security and presents quite a comprehensive security perspective, going so far as to include reductions in consumption of both renewable and non-renewable resources. In other words, in the future the Obama administration will turn towards integrating security/defence policies and economic/energy policies along the axis of the keywords of climate security or natural security.

In conclusion, characteristics of US climate security policy are to recognize climate change as a crisis of its sovereignty, and to integrate national and foreign policy along the axis of climate change in the name of security.

Europe

The term "climate security" was originally used politically by Britain when Margaret Beckett was foreign secretary in the Blair government.

Since then, the term has been used with great frequency on the UK side. At COP12 in November 2006, Foreign Secretary Beckett, the Japanese minister of the environment and others spoke on the topic of climate change as a security threat. UN Secretary-General Kofi Annan stated that "Climate change is not just an environmental issue, as too many people still believe. It is an all-encompassing threat" (UN Secretary-General, 2006). Since the COP12 conference, awareness of climate change as a security issue has rapidly expanded in international society.

On 17 April 2007, under an initiative by Foreign Secretary Beckett, who was chair of the UN Security Council, the Security Council for the first time raised the issue of climate change as a threat to international peace and security. This meeting was set as an open debate, so in addition to the permanent members, 40 other states also joined the discussion. EU members, Japan and several small island states agreed with Britain's line of argument; but the United States kept its passive stance, and the states from G77+China felt that this kind of agenda should not come under the authority of the Security Council but should rather be conducted in the UN General Assembly or the UN Economic and Social Council, stating that this was a procedural problem. This clearly reflected the opposed opinions within the Security Council.

The opposition has continued. After this meeting, a draft resolution on "Security and climate change" was submitted to the General Assembly by states mostly from the Commonwealth of Nations (the British Commonwealth) and small island states in September 2008. This proposal invited the UN Security Council to consider the threat posed by climate change to international peace and security (UN General Assembly, 2008a). However, when this resolution passed unanimously in June 2009, it was expressed in a weaker form reflecting the concerns of the developing nations group, merely inviting "the relevant organs of the United Nations, as appropriate and within their respective mandates, to intensify their efforts in considering and addressing climate change, including its possible security implications" (UN General Assembly, 2009).

The German Advisory Council on Climate Change completed a very significant report, "World in Transition: Climate Change as a Security Risk", in 2007 (WBGU, 2008). Germany at the time held the presidency of the European Parliament and together with Britain was at the leading edge of the Security Council climate security debate mentioned above. This comprehensive document, over 250 pages in length, classified the typical origins of conflict caused by climate change in four types (Figure 6.3.4): degradation of freshwater resources, decline in food production, storms and floods, and migrations. By combining these types in specific regions of the world, the report analysed the formation of "hotspots" (ibid.: 163).

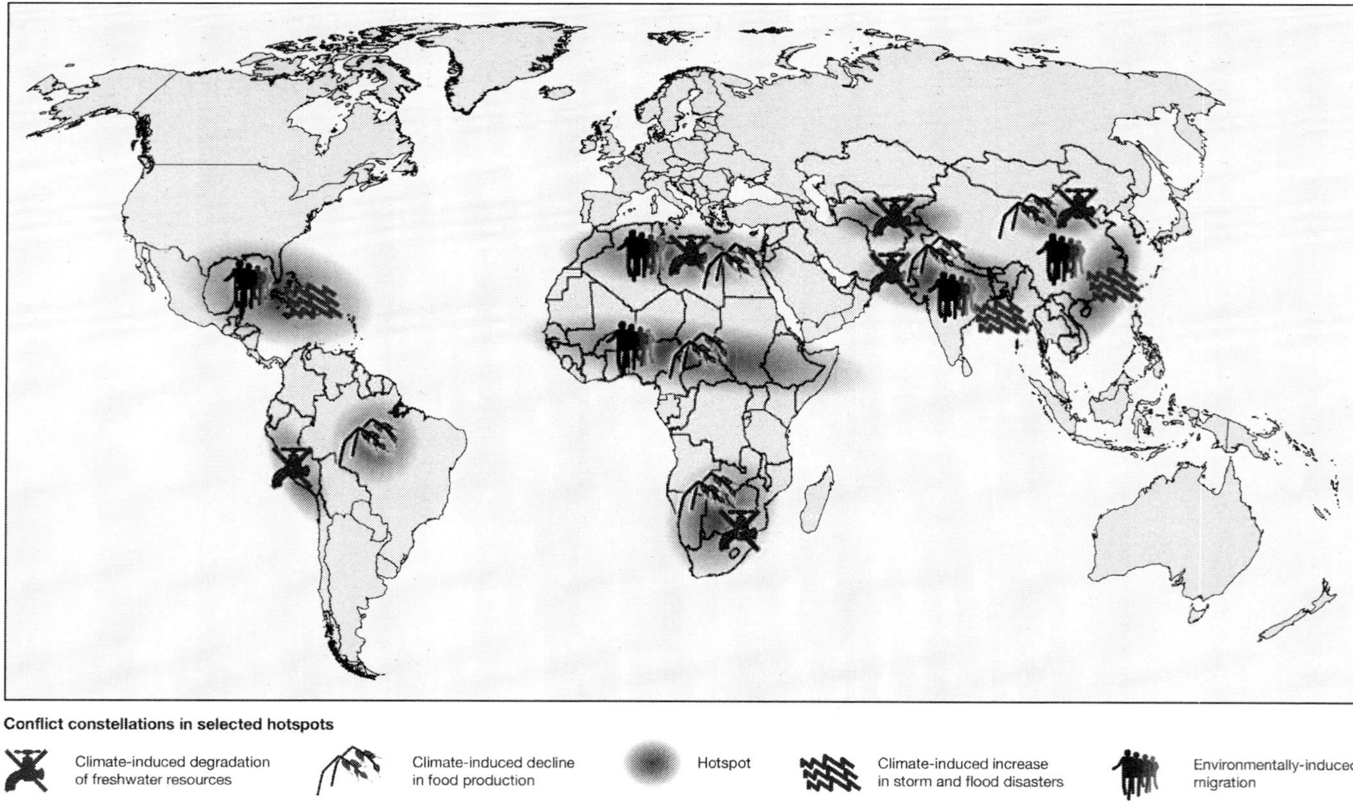

Figure 6.3.4 Conflict constellations in selected hotspots
Source: WBGU (2008: 163)

According to the WBGU, finding international policy settings that correspond to these hotspots will be difficult after the fall in US power following the rise of China and India. The world order is shifting from a unipolar to a multipolar system, and so far this shift has not occurred peacefully. Of course, this does not directly imply any violent confrontation among the great powers, but it does absorb precious time and resources for climate policy (ibid.: 54).

As a result, if mitigation measures fail, six threats to international security will arise.

- Possible increase in the number of destabilized states as a result of climate change.
- Risks for global economic development.
- Risks of growing distributional conflicts between the main drivers of climate change and those most affected.
- Climate change undermines human rights: calling emitters to account.
- Climate change triggers and intensifies migration.
- Climate change overstretches classic security policy (ibid.: 169–175).

Given this analysis, the WBGU makes several policy recommendations (Table 6.3.4). These represent a comprehensive scenario that assumes shifts in the international balance of power and, in the light of responses to climate change, constructs a world order that involves developing countries and creates strategies for adaptation and mitigation.

A characteristic of these recommendations from Europe, compared to arguments in the United States, is that rather than the integration of domestic policy, reorganization of the concept of climate security is positioned as a key concept of formation of a new world order. As Norichika Kanie (2007: 219) accurately indicated: "Current international leadership struggle surrounding climate change policies should be viewed as the politics about formation of an international order on climate security." For exactly this reason, these extremely outward-looking recommendations from European countries are remarkable.

This tendency was also evident at the European Council meeting of March 2008. The secretary-general and the high representative for the EU Common Foreign and Security Policy, Javier Solana, submitted a joint report with the European Commission on "Climate Change and International Security" (EU Commission, 2008) to the European Council. The report states that while climate change represents a key element of future international relations, "If recognised, it can even become a positive driver for improving and reforming global governance" (ibid.: 11). It expects the UN Security Council, the G8 and the UN specialized bodies to focus their attention on the security risks related to climate change (ibid.). It also calls for cooperation with third countries, giving more attention to the impact of climate change on security (ibid.). The European

Table 6.3.4 Overview of the nine WBGU initiatives for the mitigation of destabilization and conflict risks associated with climate change

Relevant policy area	Initiatives	
Fostering a cooperative setting for a multipolar world		
Foreign policy	Initiative 1 – Shaping global political change	Constructively managing the emergence of China and India as global powers alongside the United States; need for a strong European foreign policy; possible option to convene a world conference on geopolitical change; recognizing climate change as a common threat to humankind
Foreign, environmental and development policy	Initiative 2 – Reforming the United Nations	Gearing the present UN system more strongly towards prevention and a coordinated approach; reflecting on the role and tasks of the UN Security Council; strengthening UN capacities in the field of environmental policy; establishing a Council on Global Development and Environment
Climate policy as security policy I: Preventing conflict by avoiding dangerous climate change		
Environmental and foreign policy	Initiative 3 – Ambitiously pursuing international climate policy	Stipulating the 2°C guardrail as an international standard; further developing the Kyoto Protocol; adopting ambitious reduction targets for industrialized countries (including the United States) and integrating the newly industrializing and developing countries; conserving natural carbon stocks
Environmental, energy, economic and research policy	Initiative 4 – Transforming energy systems in the European Union	Strengthening the European Union's leading role; improving and implementing the energy policy for Europe; triggering an efficiency revolution; expanding renewables
Environmental, development, research and economic policy	Initiative 5 – Developing mitigation strategies through partnerships	Establishing climate protection as a cross-cutting theme in development cooperation; agreeing decarbonization partnerships with newly industrializing countries (especially China and India); agreeing an innovation pact within the framework of G8+5

Table 6.3.4 (cont.)

Relevant policy area	Initiatives	
Climate policy as security policy II: Preventing conflict by implementing adaptation strategies		
Development and research policy	Initiative 6 – Supporting adaptation strategies for developing countries	Industrialized countries must assist developing countries in adaptation to and mitigation of climate impacts; prioritize devising specific strategies for developing regions particularly at risk (e.g. Africa); mitigating water crises; gearing the agricultural sector to climate change; strengthening disaster prevention
Security and development policy	Initiative 7 – Stabilizing fragile and weak states that are additionally threatened by climate change	Stabilization of weak and fragile states to be taken into account to a greater extent in the German action plan on "Civilian Crisis Prevention, Conflict Resolution and Post-conflict Peacebuilding"; supporting and implementing the OECD's working principles; expanding the "whole-of-government" approach to encompass the environmental dimension; boosting the civil society potential of weak states in international forums and networks
Foreign, domestic and development policy	Initiative 8 – Managing migration through cooperation and further developing international law	Developing comprehensive international strategies for migration; integrating migration policy into development cooperation; including environmentally induced migration in international cooperation; enshrining the protection of environmental migrants in international law; permitting no weakening of the existing protection regime; adopting measures supplementary to the existing refugee regime
Development and research policy	Initiative 9 – Expanding global information and early warning systems	Actively supporting the development of a comprehensive global early warning system to provide information about all types of natural hazard, epidemics, technological risks, regional climate change and impacts, and environmental problems; improving the implementation of early warning information at national and local levels

Source: WBGU (2008: 193).

Council Presidency Conclusions echoed these calls (Council of the European Union, 2008).

6-3-7 Implications of climate security

Integrating development and security

The current status of climate security studies, as outlined in the discussion thus far, involves the US approach of integration of policy and the European approach of construction of a new world order, with Japan comparatively lagging behind. If we consider this situation, the implications posed by the concept of climate security become obvious.

Firstly, there are efforts to explicate further and firmly establish the organic links between the two paradigms of development and security, as principally undertaken by the United States through its policy integration.

Actually, this effort has a long history. The relationship of the two paradigms commenced in the 1940s. In international politics directly after the Second World War, US leaders were already mindful of the cause-and-effect relationship between development and security (Gaddis, 1987: 41). They were aware of the dangers of poverty caused by delayed development in Europe, which might give momentum to domestic communist forces and possibly see governments overturned. President Truman (1956: 113), quoting Assistant Secretary of State Dean Acheson regarding the Marshall Plan, stated: "He stressed the interrelation of food and freedom. 'The war,' he said, 'will not be over until the people of the world can again feed and clothe themselves and face the future with some degree of confidence.' "

In the post–Cold War world, too, it is generally believed that security must be achieved in order to drive development forward – for example, the World Bank called civil war "development in reverse" (Collier et al., 2003: 13–32).

Moreover, development is necessary for the sake of security: higher levels of security require a capable military force equipped with high-tech and high-priced armaments. According to the Stockholm International Peace Research Institute, global defence expenditure in 2008 was US$1.226 trillion (SIPRI, 2009: 180). The World Bank also states that an average of 2.8 per cent of GDP goes to military expenditure in developing countries in times of peace, and this reaches an average of 5 per cent in times of war (Collier et al., 2003: 20). In order to enable reductions in the burden of this expense, wealthy economies must be established and sustained through development.

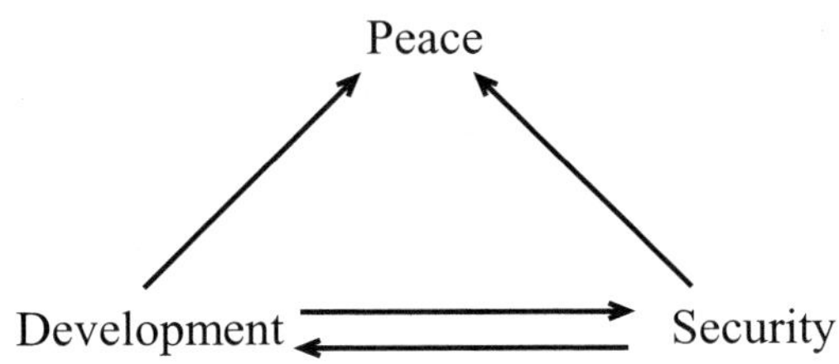

Figure 6.3.5 Triangular relationship of peace, development and security

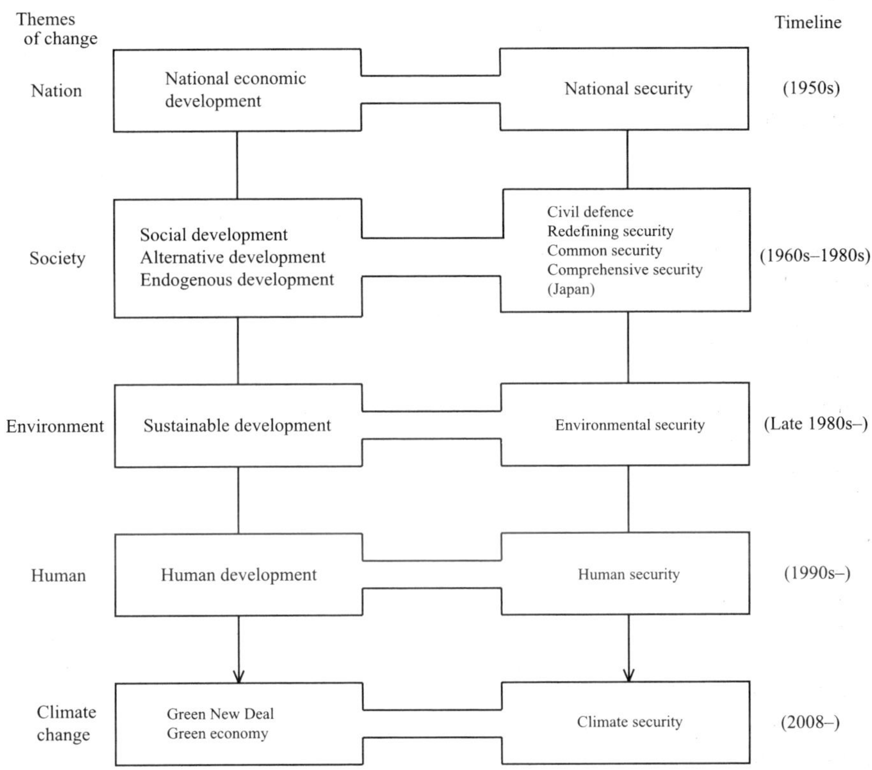

Figure 6.3.6 History of integration of development and security policies

Thus, we have come to believe that peace in the post-war world is supported by development and security, with both depending on each other's success (Figure 6.3.5). This triangular paradigm, in which development and security form a single set, was affected by the changing social themes of each era, which in turn drove corresponding changes, as indicated in Figure 6.3.6.

In the 1950s these themes were state-related: post-war recovery, independence from colonialism, nation building, modernization of national economy, etc. From the 1960s to the 1980s the focus was on society and community, and reconsideration of existing state-centric concepts was emphasized. Many researchers criticized the effects of traditional economic development and replaced it by social development (endogenous development). Critics of military security put emphasis on redefining security and introduced concepts of common or comprehensive security. The environment first gained serious political attention during the 1970s, and became firmly established by the late 1980s. The WCED tried to integrate two paradigms in the concepts of sustainable development and environmental security, both of which focused on the environment. In the 1990s the UNDP (UN Development Programme) focused on humanity, and implemented the concepts of human development and human security to try to integrate both at international policy level.

Thus, integration of both paradigms has proceeded as history develops. Compared to the traditional economic development and national security theories of the 1950s, human development and human security in the 1990s have been further integrated. According to past co-chair of the Commission on Human Security Amartya Sen (2003), these concepts are supposed to be used in combination.

The Obama administration has heavily emphasized this aspect of integration, but this movement is natural, given the principal theme of climate change in contemporary international society. In this twenty-first century, development and security will be integrated once more along the axis of climate change. This is because climate change, as stated in the IPCC reports and indicated by UN Secretary-General Kofi Annan at COP12, has the dimensions of an "all-encompassing threat". Whether in developed or developing countries, human life to a lesser or greater extent is reliant on the natural environment. Hence, climate change means an essential and fundamental change in environmental conditions of whole peoples. Thus it stands to reason that climate change represents a threat to all aspects of human life. But the current mosaic of reaction to climate-induced threats consists of the necessarily limited responses by existing bureaucratic organizations. Such responses immediately run into inconsistencies. One such example is Japan's stated emphasis on reduction of greenhouse gases, which is inconsistent with its ceaseless construction of coal-fired power plants combined with nuclear power plants to ensure a stable electricity supply.

Accordingly, in order to respond to climate change, various existing and newly established policies must be integrated with a unified sense of values and then implemented. At this time, one desirable key concept is to involve the interests of a great many people comprehensively and directly. The concept of climate security contains the conditions required for this.

The Obama administration's proposed ACES Act and the economic policy plan known as the Green New Deal do not only present climate change as a threat to both domestic and international security; they also represent an attempt at a comprehensive solution in the name of security that extends as far as international competitiveness and employment problems. As explained earlier, there are two arguments currently under way in the United States in response to climate change: one looks for a new style of economic development under the Green New Deal; the other is reform of the military. In both, "climate security" is the key phrase. This means that arguments for the broad integration of the paradigms of development and security in the United States are almost completed.

The new world order

One further implication of climate security is the formation of the world order as intended by European nations.

European arguments regarding climate security are characterized by seeking to prioritize a framework of cooperation among countries. Europe urged Russia's participation in order to effectuate the Kyoto Protocol. No matter which European nation's climate security discourse one chooses to examine, they all share a significant emphasis on multilateral frameworks, including the United Nations.

As I stressed previously, then UK Foreign Secretary Beckett's speech at the UN General Assembly in September 2006 represented the starting point for this line of argument. At the UN Security Council open debate in April 2007, various European countries such as Germany voiced their agreement with the UK argument (UN Security Council, 2007). Following these discussions, many Commonwealth nations and small island states submitted a draft resolution to the UN General Assembly in September 2008 (UN General Assembly, 2008a), which was later joined in October by the European nations (UN General Assembly, 2008b).

The recommendations of Germany's WBGU are also typical of the movements afoot to construct a world order aligned along the notions of climate security. As Table 6.3.4 shows, its Initiative 2 involves reforming the United Nations. Amidst all these recommendations, the calls for the establishment of the Council on Global Development and Environment are extremely interesting.

Recalling the line of argument on climate security that the United Kingdom introduced into the UN Security Council and General Assembly, we can see that any proposals to reform the Security Council to include climate change within its authority will not be easy without the agreement of China and the United States, since they possess veto power.

But what is needed here is the kind of legal coercive authority that the UN Security Council possesses over those who violate the UN Charter. One idea is the establishment, instead of the Economic and Social Council, of a high-level executive council that would exist alongside the Security Council with an equal authority. The WBGU outlined this idea in a 2005 policy document:

> WBGU considers that the only way to overcome the much-lamented lack of coherence in the international system and improve the enforceability of sustainability goals is to establish a new lead agency in the UN system. The Economic and Social Council (ECOSOC) cannot fulfil this role due to its focus on socio-economic issues and its lack of real authority. WBGU therefore recommends that it be replaced by a Council on Global Development and Environment, which should be established on the same hierarchical level as the Security Council. Environment and development issues are key to the future of humankind. They should therefore be given the same high priority as security issues in the UN system. (WBGU, 2005: 15)

This is a fairly radical proposal for UN reform. Actually, such a large-scale reform would involve amendment of the Charter, requiring a two-thirds vote by the General Assembly as well as a unanimous vote by the permanent Security Council member states. The WBGU (2008: 197) suggests that gaining the agreement of the United States and China seems unlikely in the near future, making this reform difficult to achieve; for this reason, it sets it as a long-term objective. On the other hand, as a more pragmatic measure, the report suggests the tactic of strengthening the legally coercive powers of the High-level Panel on System-wide Coherence in the fields of development, humanitarian aid and the environment (ibid.: 197–198).

Just from examining these recommendations and related issues, it is evident that formation of a new world order will not be an easy task. However, if the United States and Europe succeed in involving China and India, there is a good chance that prospects will take a turn for the better. Negotiations between the United States, European countries and the G77+China countries (such as China and India) will be a central theme of COP15 and succeeding conferences.

6-3-8 Policy recommendations: Necessity of paradigm integration and participating in a new world order

The idea of climate security revolves around arguments that are still very much under way. This causes intense controversies. In the field of environmental politics, while new concepts such as natural security are emerging, on the other hand scepticism regarding climate change and resistance from old economic interests are still strong. The Obama administration's ACES Act passed in the House of Representatives by only a tiny margin: 219 votes for and 212 votes against, with three abstaining. The Act faces strong resistance in the Senate. In Japan, regular parliamentary sessions in 2009 saw the submitting of two bills which touched upon the notion of climate security: the Liberal Democratic Party's "Basic Law to Promote Creation of a Low-carbon Society" and the Democratic Party's "Basic Proposal on Measures against Global Warming". Neither had been discussed in the National Diet by the beginning of 2010.

In the academic research field, too, environmental security theories, including climate security, have continually encountered deep-seated criticisms, with a history as long as the argument itself. These criticisms are not necessarily heard only from proponents of traditional concepts of military security, but have also come from pacifists concerned over increased opportunities for the use of military force. Of course, when the concepts of development and security are linked, some concerns do remain regarding the justification of use of military force to solve developmental problems, and the increased possibility its use.

There have been arguments regarding these possibilities even within comprehensive security theory in Japan. The report on comprehensive security published by the policy research group led by then Prime Minister Masayoshi Ohira is one example. It states that "the means to ensure military security do not end with military ones, but rather extend to comprehensive ones. In the same way, the means to ensure non-military security are not limited to non-military ones, but also extend to comprehensive ones" (Cabinet Secretariat, 1980: 26–27).

If we look at contemporary US policies and consider developments such as the CNAS argument for natural security, the policy integration with which the United States is presently moving forward may come to be seen in the future as legitimization for wars waged for natural resources.

While still fraught with this kind of criticism and concern, the United States and various European countries are already integrating the development and security paradigms along the concept of climate security. Japanese foreign policy cannot afford to ignore the fact that in this process of policy integration, a new world order is emerging. In considering this situation, what sort of options does Japan have within the international politics surrounding this key issue? Looking at Japan's current circumstances, one cannot see many options.

Firstly, with regard to the concept of climate security, for which policy certainly needs to be established, the arguments and reports of the Ministry of Environment clearly indicate that climate change has a major negative impact on Japanese territory (for example, Okinotorishima Island and its exclusive economic zone) and on the lives and assets of citizens (Ministry of Environment, 2007e: 14). However, by using the term "climate security", this report attempts to raise the level of priority of environmental foreign policy, and seeks principally for advantage in international negotiations with the European Union and the United States (or with developing countries), with the objective of thereby improving Japan's foreign policy capacities. This approach is undeniably important. But the report did not undertake adequate discussion; for example, as in Europe, how to use the concept of climate security with a view to forming a new world order, or how to use this within the framework of multilateral negotiations. It also did not take into account arguments over how to integrate various domestic policies, as in the US approach. Regardless, one committee member did make the following extremely apposite remarks:

> The point is not to be swept away by arguments over national defense by military means, but to ensure greater active participation of corporations, civil society, and even general consumers against climate change-induced threats to economic, social, environmental, and cultural values (which require protection). At the same time, if Japan becomes more familiar with using the concept of climate security to discuss the sorts of comprehensive measures that are required and the sorts of systems of international cooperation that should be formed to address this global-scale problem, then this concept will be effective in resolving fundamental problems both for Japan and for the world. (Ministry of Environment, 2007c: 2)

This lack of arguments and policies continues at the present moment. Several years after the publication of the report (Ministry of Environment, 2007e), few things have changed in Japanese policy-making. This lag is perhaps the greatest problem that Japan faces in regard to climate security politics. In the fields of foreign policy, understanding of the concept of climate security and its implications is not moving forward; accordingly, the significance of this term has not been fully appreciated. In fact, since this report was released, the term "climate security" has fallen into relative disuse. As described previously, it can be observed that in Japanese academic circles arguments linking the environment with security issues are often viewed quite negatively.

Consequently, Japanese political and academic fields do not share the discourses that serve as academic or intellectual grounds for the comparatively easy acceptance of the concept of "climate security" in Europe and the United States. Additionally, neither the word nor the concept of "security" has much currency among the Japanese. After great loss of life in the Second World War, many Japanese kept their distance from understanding concepts of security. As a result, their typical reaction is negative, because many citizens associate "security" with military affairs.

However, other factors worsened this problematic situation. The "ambitious" proposal to reduce GHGs by 15 per cent compared to 2005 levels launched by the Aso administration on 10 June 2009 was greeted with disappointment internationally, with UN Secretary-General Ban Ki-moon calling for Japan to be "a little bit more ambitious" (*Asahi Shinbun*, 2009). This illustrates deep-seated domestic scepticism over climate change and the influence of old-style economic interests. There is other evidence of this scepticism. In full-page advertisements placed in newspapers on 17 March 2009, the Japan Business Federation (Keidanren) warned against large reduction rates, as this policy would place a greater economic burden on Japanese households. Realizing policy integration is still influenced by such opponents. They also exist in the international arena to prevent the construction of a new world order of climate security. One committee official from the Ministry of Environment pointed out: "In the field of international negotiations, impacts of climate change are not the threats. Countermeasures for climate change are the threats. As a consequence, avoidance behaviors to evade such measures come to be their national interest" (Ministry of Environment, 2007b).

However, as Kanie (2007: 220) indicated, "being trapped in domestic affairs, if Japan loses a chance in participation in the formation of international order aligned along an axis of climate security in the future, it could be a great loss of 'national interest' ". This apprehension has clearly become a reality. Different from the COP14 conference, held at the end of the Bush administration and of which great results were not expected, COP15 held in Copenhagen in December 2009 aimed to "seal a deal", in the words of UN Secretary-General Ban Ki-moon. The first Climate Change Summit was held at UN headquarters in September 2009 to serve as a preparatory meeting for COP15; incidentally, this timing coincided with a Japanese change of administration. The new Hatoyama administration declared a target of 25 per cent GHG reduction below 1990 levels by 2020. However, it is doubtful that Japan will be able to prepare an independent and integrated policy cluster relating to climate change by the time of COP16 or even COP17. In 2010 the Democratic Party is preparing to submit a climate bill to the National Diet; this will face serious resistance, just as ACES did in the United States.

As a policy recommendation, in COP16 and succeeding conferences, unreserved support for a proposal for UN reform (like the WBGU proposal) submitted by Germany or EU countries would represent one of Japan's best remaining options.

Although establishing a new Council on Global Development and Environment is not very likely in the immediate future, strengthening the role of the UN Environment Programme has been suggested as one way to lay the groundwork for such a body. The WBGU (2008: 196–197) placed particular emphasis on the necessity of financial support to ensure stable activities in the medium term. It also emphasized the need for financial support in strengthening the High-level Panel on System-wide Coherence in the fields of development, humanitarian aid and the environment, as mentioned previously (ibid.). Japan can play an active role within this strategy. There was once speculation in the UNDP about the establishment of an Economic Security Council, in addition to ECOSOC (Haq, 1995: 186–199). There are also receptive bodies within the United Nations that may be open to accepting the WBGU recommendations.

We have to consider the situation if Japan's participation is delayed in this world order which is rapidly being formed by Europe through the United Nations to include China and/or India. Consequently, Japan's commitment to moving forward actively with these recommendations represents the securing of extremely important national interests.

If the establishment of the new Council on Global Development and Environment is achieved, and if Japan performs well in support of this process, Japan will not be left in the passive position of being a major emitting country, but will rather be participating as an active supporter of the new world order and a significant permanent council member. This council would possess the same legal coercive power as the UN Security Council, although it would be separated from that body and would likely have no authority over use of military forces.

The council would enable Japan to contribute to the United Nations in a fashion commensurate with its national capabilities, given the Japanese constitutional limits on the use of military forces. This should also gain wider understanding and support from Japanese citizens. It is the best option for our national interest, because Japan's long-cherished wish for a permanent position on the existing Security Council now seems hopeless. For this reason, the climate security discourse arguing that "air pollution from large-scale greenhouse gas emissions damages global commons, which in turn threatens international peace and security" must be shared to a certain extent among UN member states.

In working towards this major objective, domestic policy must first be integrated, either along a climate security or a broader environmental security axis, as the United States has almost done. Despite the fact that domestic research and policy discussions on this kind of security have been infrequent (compared to Europe and the United States) ever since the emphasis on comprehensive security of the Ohira administration, a certain accumulation of knowledge relating to climate security has been achieved in Japan (for example, see House of Councillors, 1992). Using these resources, and given cooperative relations between various relevant political and economic organs under strong political leadership, it should be possible to organize a coherent policy cluster that includes existing policy. Europe and the United States have already created some momentum in this direction. The next few years will be crucial in determining whether or not Japan is able to jump on board in time.

There are also issues of academic research that need to be resolved. The discussion relating to climate security does not entail a paradigm shift, but rather a process of integration of the two paradigms of development and security along an environmental axis that includes climate change. More research projects that transcend existing academic barriers are absolutely essential. The WCED successfully made sustainability an international political issue by integrating four values in international relations: development, security, environment and peace. The problem today is how to integrate these values again. The WCED gave some hints: integrating the development argued in the field of development economics with the security argued in the field of international relations along the axis of either climate change or broader environmental issues and pursuing peace. However, what kind of peace do we pursue by such integration? What sort of world order do we have to build for this purpose? These are the most significant global-scale issues that our future holds. The answer may be that we have to shift from peace by environmentally disastrous development and security to the environmental peace which the WCED once suggested.

REFERENCES

Asahi Shinbun (2009) "Kangaete mimasenka. Watashitachi minna no futangaku (Think About Our Burden)", *Asahi Shimbun*, 29 June (morning edn), p. 11.

Barnett, Jon (2003) "Security and Climate Change", *Global Environmental Change* 13, pp. 7–17.

Bertell, Rosalie (2000) *Planet Earth: The Latest Weapon of War*. London: Women's Press.

Brown, Lester (1977) "Redefining National Security", Worldwatch Paper No. 14, Worldwatch Institute, Washington, DC.

Buhan, Halvard, Nils Petter Gleditsch and Ole Magnus Theisen (2008) "Implications of Climate Change for Armed Conflict", paper presented at World Bank Workshop on Social Dimensions of Climate Change, Washington, DC, 5–6 March.

Burke, Sharon (2009) *Natural Security*. Washington, DC: Center for New American Security.

Busby, Joshua W. (2007) *Climate Change and National Security: An Agenda for Action*. New York: Council on Foreign Relations.

Bush, George W. (2006) "The National Security Strategy of the United States of America"; available at http://georgewbush-whitehouse.archives.gov/nsc/nss/2006/.

Buzan, Barry, Ole Waever and Jaap de Wilde (1998) *Security: A New Framework for Analysis*. Boulder, CO: Lynne Rienner.

Cabinet Secretariat (ed.) (1980) *Sougou Anzenhoshou Senryaku* (*Strategy for Comprehensive Security*). Tokyo: National Printing Bureau.

Campbell, Kurt M. (2008) "National Security and Climate Change in Perspective", in Kurt M. Campbell (ed.) *Climatic Cataclysm: The Foreign Policy and National Security Implications of Climate Change*. Washington, DC: Brookings Institution Press.

CNA Corporation (2007) *National Security and the Threat of Climate Change*. Alexandria, VA: CNA Corporation.

Collier, Paul, V. L. Elliott, Håvard Hegre, Anke Hoeffler, Marta Reynal-Querol and Nicholas Sambanis (2003) *Breaking the Conflict Trap: Civil War and Development Policy*. Washington, DC: World Bank.

Council of the European Union (2008) "Presidency Conclusions of the Brussels European Council", 7652/1/08 REV 1, Brussels, 20 May; available at www.consilium.europa.eu/uedocs/cms_Data/docs/pressdata/en/ec/99410.pdf.

Deudney, Daniel (1991) "Environment and Security: Muddled Thinking", *Bulletin of Atomic Scientists*, April, pp. 23–28.

Durant, Robert F. (2007) *The Greening of the US Military: Environmental Policy, National Security, and Organizational Change*. Washington, DC: Georgetown University Press.

EU Commission (2008) "Climate Change and International Security", 7249/08, 3 March; available at http://register.consilium.europa.eu/pdf/en/08/st07/st07249.en08.pdf.

Falk, Richard A. (1971) *This Endangered Planet: Prospects and Proposals for Human Survival*. New York: Random House.

Fukuchi, Hiroaki (1996) *Kichi to Kankyohakai* (*Military Bases and Environmental Degradation*). Tokyo: Doujidaisya.

Gaddis, John Lewis (1987) *The Long Peace: Inquiries into the History of the Cold War*. New York: Oxford University Press.

Gleditsch, Nils Petter (1998) "Armed Conflict and the Environment: A Critique of the Literature", *Journal of Peace Research* 35(3), pp. 381–400.

Haq, Mahbub ul (1995) *Reflections on Human Development*. New York: Oxford University Press.

Homer-Dixon, Thomas (1999) *Environment, Scarcity, and Violence*. Princeton, NJ: Princeton University Press.

Homer-Dixon, Thomas and Jessica Blitt (1998) *Ecoviolence: Links among Environment, Population and Security*. Lanham, MD: Rowman & Littlefield.

House of Councillors (1992) *90 Nendai Nihon no Yakuwari: Kankyo to Anzenhosyo no Arikata* (*Japan's Role for the 1990s: Environment and Security*). Tokyo: Sangiin Gaiko Sougouanzenhosyo ni Kansuru Chousakai.

IPCC (1995) *IPCC Second Assessment: Climate Change 1995. A Report of the Intergovernmental Panel on Climate Change*. Geneva: IPCC.

——— (2001) "Climate Change 2001: Synthesis Report"; available at www.grida.no/publications/other/ipcc_tar/.

——— (2007) "Climate Change 2007: Synthesis Report"; available at www.ipcc.ch/publications_and_data/publications_ipcc_fourth_assessment_report_synthesis_report.htm.

Ishii, Toru (2008) "'Kiko-anpo' Aitsugi Gironnni ('Climate Security': Continuous Debate)", *Asahi Shinbun* (morning edn), 6 December, p. 19.

Jimbo, Tetsuo (2004) *Tsubaru: Chikyu Ondanka ni Shizumu Kuni* (*Tuvalu: A Country Sinking in the Global Warming*). Tokyo: Shunjusha.

Kanie, Norichika (2007) "Kikoanzenhosyou wo Meguru Kokusaichitsujo Keisei he: Haiporithikusuka suru Kankyoseiji no Sinso (Towards Formation of Climate Security: Truth of High-politicizing Environmental Politics)", *Gendai Shiso* (*Review of Contemporary Thought*), October, pp. 210–221.

Karl, Thomas R., Jerry M. Melillo and Thomas C. Peterson (eds) (2009) *Global Climate Change Impacts in the United States*. Cambridge: Cambridge University Press.

Lozada, Carlos (2009) "The 'It' Think Tank", *Washington Post*, 7 June, p. B4.

Mathews, Jessica (1989) "Redefining Security", *Foreign Affairs* 68(2), pp. 162–177.

Meadows, Donella H., Dennis L. Meadows, Jørgen Randers and William W. Behrens III (1972) *The Limits to Growth: A Report for the Club of Rome's Project on the Predicament of Mankind*. New York: New American Library.

Ministry of Environment (2007a) "International Climate Change Strategy Global Environment Committee, Central Environment Council, Record of 15th Meeting"; available at www.env.go.jp/council/06earth/y064-15a.html.

——— (2007b) "International Climate Change Strategy Global Environment Committee, Central Environment Council, Record of 16th Meeting"; available at www.env.go.jp/council/06earth/y064-16a.html.

——— (2007c) "Supplemental 2-3: Opinions for Discussion of 'Climate Security'"; available at www.env.go.jp/council/06earth/y064-16/mat02_3.pdf.

——— (2007d) "International Climate Change Strategy Global Environment Committee, Central Environment Council, Record of 17th Meeting"; available at www.env.go.jp/council/06earth/y064-17a.html.

——— (2007e) "Report on Climate Security"; available at www.env.go.jp/en/earth/cc/CS.pdf.

Miyagi, Yasuhiro, Shigekazu Mezaki, Shinnichi Hanawa, Masayuki Onishi and Etsuko Urashima (2002) *Jugon no Umi to Okinawa: Kichi no Sima ga Toitsudukeru Mono* (*Sea of Dugong and Okinawa: Question from Islands of Military Base*). Tokyo: Koubunken.

Ochiai, Kotaro (2001) "Kankyoanzenhosyo – Kakusan Suru Gainen (Environmental Security – Diffusion of Concept)", in Tatsuo Akaneya and Kotaro Ochiai (eds) *Atarashii Anzenhosyouron no Shiza* (*Perspectives on New Security Studies*). Tokyo: Akishobo, pp. 150–182.

Ohta, Hiroshi (2002) "Kankyomondai wo Meguru Kikikanri to Yobo (Crisis Management and Prevention for Environmental Problems)", in Hiroshi Kimura (ed.) *Kokusaikikigaku* (*International Crisis Studies*). Kyoto: Sekaisisosha, pp. 324–345.

Parthemore, Christine (2009) *The Obama Plan for Energy and Climate Security*. Washington, DC: Center for New American Security.

Pumphrey, Carolyn (ed.) (2008) *Global Climate Change: National Security Implications*. Carlisle, PA: Strategic Studies Institute.

Sen, Amartya (2003) "Box 1.3 Development, Rights and Human Security", in Commission on Human Security (ed.) *Human Security Now*. Washington, DC: Communications Development, pp. 8–9.

SIPRI (1979) *Ecological Consequences of the Second Indochina War*. Stockholm: Stockholm International Peace Research Institute/Almqvist & Wiksell.

——— (2009) *SIPRI Yearbook: World Armaments and Disarmament*. Stockholm: Almqvist & Wiksell.

Toronto Economic Summit (1988) "Toronto Economic Summit Economic Declaration", 21 June; available at www.g8.utoronto.ca/summit/1988toronto/communique.html.

Truman, Harry S. (1956) *Memoirs by Harry S. Truman: Years of Trial and Hope*. New York: Doubleday.

Tsuchiyama, Jitsuo (2004) *Anzenhosyo no Kokusaiseijigaku* (*International Politics on Security*). Tokyo: Yuhikaku.

Ullman, Richard H. (1983) "Redefining Security", *International Security* 8(1), pp. 129–153.

UN General Assembly (1988a) "Provisional Verbatim Record of the Sixth Meeting", A/43/PV.6, New York, 27 September; available at http://documents-dds-ny.un.org/doc/UNDOC/PRO/N88/641/58/pdf/N8864158.pdf?OpenElement.

——— (1988b) "Provisional Verbatim Record of the Seventy-second Meeting", A/43/PV.72, New York, 7 December; available at http://documents-dds-ny.un.org/doc/UNDOC/PRO/N88/645/59/pdf/N8864559.pdf?OpenElement.

——— (2006) "Sixty-first Session Sixteenth Plenary Meeting", A/61/PV16, New York, 22 September; available at http://daccess-dds-ny.un.org/doc/UNDOC/GEN/N06/533/17/PDF/N0653317.pdf?OpenElement.

——— (2008a) "Security and Climate Change", Resolution A/62/L.50, 10 September; available at http://daccess-dds-ny.un.org/doc/UNDOC/LTD/N08/502/84/PDF/N0850284.pdf?OpenElement.

——— (2008b) "Security and Climate Change", Resolution A/63/L.8*, 27 October; available at http://daccess-dds-ny.un.org/doc/UNDOC/LTD/N08/571/82/PDF/N0857182.pdf?OpenElement.

——— (2009) "Climate Change and Its Possible Security Implications", Resolution A/RES/63/281, 11 June; available at http://daccess-dds-ny.un.org/doc/UNDOC/GEN/N08/487/65/PDF/N0848765.pdf?OpenElement.

UN Secretary-General (2006) "Citing 'Frightening Lack of Leadership' on Climate Change", Press Release SG/SM/10739 ENV/DEV/904, New York, 15 November; available at www.un.org/News/Press/docs/2006/sgsm10739.doc.htm.

UN Security Council (2007) "5663rd Meeting", S/PV.5663, New York, 17 April; available at http://daccess-dds-ny.un.org/doc/UNDOC/PRO/N07/309/08/PDF/N0730908.pdf?OpenElement.

US Congress (2007) "America's Climate Security Act of 2007", S.2191, 18 October; available at http://frwebgate.access.gpo.gov/cgi-bin/getdoc.cgi?dbname=110_cong_bills&docid=f:s2191is.txt.pdf.

——— (2009a) "American Clean Energy and Security Act of 2009", H.R. 2454, 15 May; available at http://frwebgate.access.gpo.gov/cgi-bin/getdoc.cgi?dbname=111_cong_bills&docid=f:h2454ih.txt.pdf.

——— (2009b) "American Clean Energy Leadership Act 2009", S.1462, 16 July; available at http://frwebgate.access.gpo.gov/cgi-bin/getdoc.cgi?dbname=111_cong_bills&docid=f:s1462pcs.txt.pdf.

——— (2009c) "Clean Energy Jobs and American Power Act", S.1733, 30 September; available at http://frwebgate.access.gpo.gov/cgi-bin/getdoc.cgi?dbname=111_cong_bills&docid=f:s1733is.txt.pdf.

Waever, Ole (1995) "Securitization and Desecuritization", in Ronnie D. Lipschutz (ed.) *On Security*. New York: Columbia University Press.

WBGU (2005) "Policy Paper 4: Development Needs Environmental Protection: Recommendations for the Millennium+5 Summit", German Advisory Council on Global Change; available at www.wbgu.de/wbgu_pp2005_engl.pdf.

——— (2008) "World in Transition: Climate Change as a Security Risk", German Advisory Council on Global Change; available at www.wbgu.de/wbgu_jg2007_engl.pdf.

Westing, Arthur H. (1990) *Environmental Hazards of War: Releasing Dangerous Forces in an Industrialized World*. London: Sage Publications.

WMO (1988) *The Changing Atmosphere: Implications for Global Security*, Conference Proceedings, Toronto, 27–30 June. Geneva: World Meteorological Organization.

World Commission on Environment and Development (1987) *Our Common Future*. Oxford and New York: Oxford University Press.

Yamada, Takahiro (1999) "Kankyoanzenhosyo to Kokusaitouchi (Environmental Security and International Governance)", in Msatsugu Naya and Isami Takeda (eds) *Sinnanzenhosyoron no Kouzu* (*Construct of New Security Studies*). Tokyo: Keiso Shobo, pp. 115–148.

Yonemoto, Shohei (1994) *Chikyukankyomondai toha Nanika* (*What Are the Global Environmental Problems?*). Tokyo: Iwanami Syoten.

Index

"n" refers to notes